Lecture Notes in Computer Science   9357

Commenced Publication in 1973
Founding and Former Series Editors:
Gerhard Goos, Juris Hartmanis, and Jan van Leeuwen

More information about this series at http://www.springer.com/series/7409

Ismail Khalil · Erich Neuhold
A Min Tjoa · Li Da Xu · Ilsun You (Eds.)

Information and Communication Technology

Third IFIP TC 5/8 International Conference, ICT-EurAsia 2015
and 9th IFIP WG 8.9 Working Conference, CONFENIS 2015
Held as Part of WCC 2015
Daejeon, Korea, October 4–7, 2015
Proceedings

 Springer

Editors

Ismail Khalil
Institute of Telecooperation
Johannes Kepler University Linz
Linz
Austria

Erich Neuhold
Department of Computer Science
University of Vienna
Vienna
Austria

A Min Tjoa
Institute of Software Technology
Vienna University of Technology
Vienna
Austria

Li Da Xu
Information Technology and Decision
  Sciences
Old Dominion University
Norfolk, VA
USA

Ilsun You
Soon Chun Hyang University
Asan
South Korea

ISSN 0302-9743   ISSN 1611-3349 (electronic)
Lecture Notes in Computer Science
ISBN 978-3-319-24314-6   ISBN 978-3-319-24315-3   (eBook)
DOI 10.1007/978-3-319-24315-3

Library of Congress Control Number: 2015948857

LNCS Sublibrary: SL3 – Information Systems and Applications, incl. Internet/Web, and HCI

Springer Cham Heidelberg New York Dordrecht London

Printed on acid-free paper

Springer International Publishing AG Switzerland is part of Springer Science+Business Media
(www.springer.com)

Preface

It was a great honor that this year's ICT-EurAsia 2015 and CONFENIS 2015 were held in conjunction with the 23rd IFIP World Computer Congress (WCC 2015), the flagship event of the International Federation for Information Processing (IFIP).

The Information & Communication Technology-EurAsia Conference (ICT-EUR-ASIA 2015) is thought of as an international platform for researchers and practitioners to present their latest research findings and innovations. The conference is especially focused on the very vivid and agile development of ICT-research in the last decade with a special focus on European and Asian developments.

The 2015 Asian Conference on Availability, Reliability, and Security (AsiaARES 2015) was held as a Special Track Conference within ICT-EURASIA 2015 and aimed specifically to improve the flow of IT-security research results to and from the Asian region. The ultimate goal is to establish a community and a meeting point for security researchers and to make travel shorter and the venues more easily accessible for researchers from Asia. Moreover, AsiaARES emphasizes the interplay between foundations and practical issues of security in emerging areas and is devoted to the critical examination and research challenges of the various aspects of secure and dependable computing and the definition of a future road map.

The 2015 edition of the International Conference on Research and Practical Issues of Enterprise Information Systems (CONFENIS 2015) was mainly focused on aspects of big data, text mining, visualization, and impacts of enterprise information systems (EIS). CONFENIS 2015 at WCC provided an international forum for the IFIP community to discuss the latest research findings in the area of EIS. The conference specifically aimed at facilitating the exchange of ideas and advances on all aspects and developments of EIS with the broader ICT-audience present at IFIP WCC 2015.

Both ICT-EurAsia 2015 and CONFENIS 2015 received high-quality submissions from all over the world. After a rigorous peer-reviewing process by the Program Committees a total of 35 papers were accepted for presentation. We believe that the selected papers will trigger further ICT-related research and improvements.

Finally, we would like to give our special thanks to all authors for their valuable contributions as well as to the Program Committee members for their valuable advice. At the same time, we would like to acknowledge the great support of the WCC-2015 conference organization team as well as that of the ICT-EurAsia 2015 and CONFENIS 2015 organization team, in particular Ms. Niina Maarit Novak for her timely help, organization, and contribution which made this edition of the conference proceedings possible.

October 2015

Ismail Khalil
Erich Neuhold
A Min Tjoa
Li Da Xu
Ilsun You

Organization

Information & Communication Technology – EurAsia Conference 2015, ICT-EurAsia 2015

General Chairpersons

Erich Neuhold   Chairman of IFIP Technical Committee on Information Technology Application

Chairpersons

Wichian Chutimaskul	King Mongkut's University of Technology Thonburi, Thailand
Isao Echizen	National Institute of Informatics, Japan
A Min Tjoa	Vienna University of Technology, Austria
Ilsun You	Soon Chun Hyang University, South Korea (Availiability, Reliability and Security Track)
Forrest Lin	Chinese Institute of Electronics, China

Program Committee

Ladjel Bellatreche	Laboratoire d'Informatique Scientifique et Industrielle, France
Alfredo Cuzzocrea	University of Calabria, Italy
Khabib Mustofa	Universitas Gadjah Mada, Indonesia
Amin Anjomshoaa	Vienna University of Technology, Austria
Masatoshi Arikawa	University of Tokyo, Japan
Hoang Huu Hanh	University of Hue, Vietnam
Josef Küng	University of Linz, Austria
Ismail Khalil	Int. Org. for Information Integration and Web-based App. & Services
Made Sudiana Mahendra	Udayana University, Indonesia
Günther Pernul	University of Regensburg, Germany
Maria Raffai	University of Györ, Hungary
Hamideh Afsarmanesh	University of Amsterdam, Netherlands
Gerhard Budin	University of Vienna, Austria
Somchai Chatvichienchai	University of Nagasaki, Japan
Key Sun Choi	KAIST, South Korea
Tetsuya Furukawa	University of Kyushu, Japan
Zainal Hasibuan	University of Indonesia, Indonesia

Christian Huemer	Vienna University of Technology, Austria
Dieter Kranzlmüller	Ludwig-Maximilians-Universität München, Germany
Lenka Lhotska	Czech Technical University, Czech Republic
Luis M. Camarinha Matos	Universidade Nova de Lisboa, Portugal
Bernardo Nugroho Yahya	Hankuk University of Foreign Studies, South Korea
Dimitris Karagiannis	University of Vienna, Austria
Geert Poels	Ghent University, Belgium
Josaphat Tetuko Sri Sumantyo	Chiba University, Japan
Nguyen Tuan	University of Information Technology, Vietnam
Bundit Thipakorn	King Mongkut's University of Technology Thonburi, Thailand
Valeria De Antonellis	University of Brescia, Italy
Phayung Meesad	King Mongkut's University of Technology North Bangkok, Thailand
Nguyen Xuan Hoai	Hanoi University, Vietnam
Huynh Quyet Thang	Hanoi University of Science and Technology, Vietnam
Mauridhi Hery Purnomo	Institut Teknologi Sepuluh Nopember (ITS), Indonesia
Arif Djunaidy	Institut Teknologi Sepuluh Nopember (ITS), Indonesia
Mikhail Lavrentyev	Novosibirsk State University, Russia
Robert P. Biuk-Aghai	University of Macau, China
Chandrashekhar Meshram	RTM Nagpur University, India

The 2015 Asian Conference on Availability, Reliability, and Security, AsiaARES 2015

Program Committee Chairperson

Ilsun You	Soon Chun Hyang University, South Korea

Program Committee

Kensuke Baba	Kyushu University, Japan
Jakub Breier	NTU, Singapore
Aniello Castiglione	Università degli Studi di Salerno, Italy
Mala Chelliah	National Institute of Technology, India
Hsing-Chung Chen	Asia University, Taiwan
Xiaofeng Chen	Xidian University, China
Tianhan Gao	Northeastern University, China
Adela Georgescu	University of Bucharest, Romania
Nan Guo	Northeastern University, China
Shinsaku Kiyomoto	KDDI R&D Laboratories Inc., Japan
Igor Kotenko	SPIRAS, Russia
Fang-Yie Leu	Tunghai University, Taiwan

Kazuhiro Minami	Institute of Statistical Mathematics, Japan
Masakatsu Nishigaki	Shizuoka University, Japan
Marek R. Ogiela	AGH University of Sci. and Tech., Poland
Francesco Palmieri	Università degli Studi di Salerno, Italy
Kouichi Sakurai	Kyushu University, Japan
Kunwar Singh	National Institute of Technology, India
Masakazu Soshi	Hiroshima City University, Japan
Shiuh-Jeng Wang	Central Police University, Taiwan
Shuichiroh Yamamoto	Nagoya University, Japan
Akihiro Yamamura	Akita University, Japan
Siuming Yiu	The Univeristy of Hong Kong, Hong Kong
Qin Xin	University of the Faroe Islands, Denmark
Baokang Zhao	National University of Defense Technology, China

International Conference on Research and Practical Issues of Enterprise Information Systems – CONFENIS 2015

General Chairperson

| Ismail Khalil | University of Linz, Austria |

Chairperson

| Lida Xu | Old Dominion University, USA |

Program Committee

Rogério Atem de Carvalho	Instituto Federal Fluminense, Brazil
Hanh Huu Hoang	Hue University, Vietnam
A Min Tjoa	Vienna University of Technology, Austria
Sohail S. Chaudhry	Villanova University, USA
Amin Anjomshoaa	MIT - Massachusetts Institute of Technology, USA
Ota Novotny	Prague University of Economics, Czech Republic
Charles Møller	Aalborg University, Denmark
Josef Basl	Prague University of Economics, Czech Republic
Petr Doucek	Prague University of Economics, Czech Republic
Klara Antlova	Technical University Liberec, Czech Republic
Michel Avital	Copenhagen Business School, Denmark
Jan Claes	Ghent University, Belgium
Geert Poels	Ghent University, Belgium
George Feuerlicht	University of Economics Prague, Czech Republic
Frederik Gailly	Ghent University, Belgium
Bee Hua Goh	National University of Singapore, Singapore
Jingzhi Guo	University of Macau, China

Björn Johansson	Lund University, Sweden
Rob Kusters	Eindhoven University of Technology, The Netherlands
Satish Krishnan	Indian Institute of Management (Kozhikode), India
Mehran Misaghi	UNISOCIESC, Brazil
Young Moon	Syracuse University, USA
Maria Raffai	Szechenyi University, Hungary
Muthu Ramachandran	Leeds Metropolitan University, UK
Flavia Santoro	UNIRIO, Brazil
Petr Sodomka	Brno University of Technology, Czech Republic
Frantisek Sudzina	Aalborg University, Denmark
Per Svejvig	Aarhus University, Denmark
Chris Zhang	University of Saskatchewan, Canada
Shang-Ming Zhou	Swansea University, UK
Hongxun Jiang	Renmin University of China, China
Subodh Kesharwani	Indira Gandhi National Open University, India
Lu Liu	Beijing University of Aeronautics and Astronautics, China
Victor Romanov	Russian Plekhanov Academy of Economics, Russia
Zhaohao Sun	Papua New Guinea University of Technology, Papua New Guinea

Organizational Coordination Chairperson (ICT-EurAsia, AsiaARES 2015, CONFENIS 2015)

Niina Maarit Novak	Vienna University of Technology, Austria

Contents

Data Management and Information Advertising

Applied Modeling and Simulation

Network Security

Dependable Systems and Applications

Multimedia Security

Cryptography

Big Data and Text Mining

Social Impact of EIS and Visualization

Networks and System Architecture

Reducing Keepalive Traffic in Software-Defined Mobile Networks with Port Control Protocol

Kamil Burda, Martin Nagy[✉], and Ivan Kotuliak

Faculty of Informatics and Information Technologies, Slovak University
of Technology in Bratislava, Ilkovičova 2, 842 16 Bratislava, Slovakia
{xburdakamil,martinko.nagy}@gmail.com, ivan.kotuliak@stuba.sk

Abstract. User applications, such as VoIP, have problems traversing
NAT gateways or firewalls. To mitigate these problems, applications
send keepalive messages through the gateways. The interval of sending
keepalives is often unnecessarily short, which increases the network load,
especially in mobile networks. Port Control Protocol (PCP) allows the
applications to traverse the gateways and to optimize the interval. This
paper describes the deployment of PCP in software-defined networks
(SDN) and proposes a method to measure keepalive traffic reduction
in mobile networks using PCP. The proposed solution extends the battery life of mobile devices and reduces the traffic overhead in WCDMA
networks.

Keywords: Middleboxes · Keepalives · Port Control Protocol · Mobile
networks · Software-defined networking

1 Introduction

User applications that require long-term connections, such as Voice over IP
(VoIP), Instant Messaging or online gaming, may have problems establishing
connections if hosts running the applications are located behind network address
translation (NAT) gateways or firewalls, hereinafter referred to as *middleboxes*.

For each connection, a middlebox contains a mapping entry that is manually
configured or dynamically created when the connection is being established.
In case of NAT gateways, the mapping entry usually consists of the following
fields: internal IP address, external IP address, internal port, external port and
mapping lifetime.

If a connection is idle for longer than the corresponding mapping lifetime,
the middlebox blocks the connection without notifying the communicating hosts.
To keep the connection alive, the application sends keepalive messages (such
as empty TCP or UDP datagrams) toward the destination host. Because the
application does not know the exact connection timeout, keepalives are sent
in very short intervals, which increases the network load. The unnecessarily
high amount of the keepalive traffic reduces battery lifetime on mobile devices,
especially those connected to mobile networks, where each message sent imposes
additional overhead in the form of signaling traffic.

© IFIP International Federation for Information Processing 2015
I. Khalil et al. (Eds.): ICT-EurAsia 2015 and CONFENIS 2015, LNCS 9357, pp. 3–12, 2015.
DOI: 10.1007/978-3-319-24315-3_1

This paper proposes a network architecture to deploy the Port Control Protocol (PCP) in the core of software-defined mobile networks and a method to measure the keepalive traffic reduction with PCP in WCDMA networks.

The rest of this paper is structured as follows. Section 2 briefly reviews existing NAT traversal and keepalive reduction methods. Section 3 describes the basics of the PCP protocol and the advantages of the deployment of PCP in SDN networks. Section 4 describes the architecture of the core network and its components. Section 5 describes the method to measure the battery life extension of mobile devices and signaling traffic reduction in WCDMA networks [1,8]. The final section provides concluding remarks and challenges for future work.

2   Related Work

Protocols such as Session Traversal Utilities for NAT (STUN) [2], Traversal Using Relays around NAT (TURN) [3] or Interactive Connectivity Establishment (ICE) [4] can resolve NAT traversal issues for user applications. Additional methods for proper NAT traversal are defined for IPSec ESP [5] and mobile IP [6].

A method proposed in [7] aims to reduce the keepalive traffic in mobile IPv4 networks and in IPSec communication by replacing UDP keepalives with the so-called TCP wake-up messages, given the considerably greater mapping lifetime for TCP connections on NAT and firewall devices from popular vendors [8]. The results of the experiments conducted suggest that the keepalive traffic reduction is significant in 2G (GSM) and 3G (WCDMA, HSDPA) networks, but not in IEEE 802.11 Wireless LAN [7].

3   Port Control Protocol

PCP [9] allows IPv4 and IPv6 hosts to determine or explicitly request network address mapping, port mapping and mapping timeout (also called *mapping lifetime*) directly from middleboxes. From this information, a host behind a middlebox can establish communication with a host in an external network or in another internal network behind another middlebox and can optimize the interval of sending keepalives. PCP does not replace the function of proxy or rendezvous servers to establish connections between hosts in different internal networks. PCP requires that hosts run a PCP client and middleboxes run a PCP server [9].

Based on the existing research [7], the reduction of the keepalive traffic in mobile networks can be considerable. PCP introduces a more universal approach that allows to optimize keepalive traffic for multiple transport protocols (any protocol with 16-bit port numbers) and other upper-layer protocols, such as ICMP or IPSec ESP [9].

PCP may be vulnerable to security attacks such as denial of service or mapping theft [9]. The security of PCP is currently under discussion [10]. An RFC draft specifies an authentication mechanism to control access to middleboxes [11].

3.1   Port Control Protocol in Software-Defined Networks

Software-defined networking (SDN) [12–14,19] is a novel approach to managing computer networks which separates the control and data planes of network devices to controllers and forwarders, respectively, and achieves greater network flexibility by allowing to program the network behavior. Existing networks are expected to migrate to SDN given the aforementioned advantages.

With SDN, a PCP server can run on a controller, thereby reducing the processing overhead on middleboxes, increasing vendor compatibility and avoiding the need to upgrade the middleboxes to support PCP server functionality. If multiple middleboxes are placed in an SDN network, mapping lifetime can be determined from the controller instead of every middlebox separately. There is an ongoing effort to support advanced firewall functionality in SDN networks by introducing new PCP message types [15].

4   Network Architecture

This section describes the architecture of the SDN-based mobile core network, which incorporates PCP to reduce the signaling traffic. The essential components of the architecture are shown in Fig. 1. For the implementation, OpenFlow [14,16] is used as the communication protocol between the controller and the forwarders.

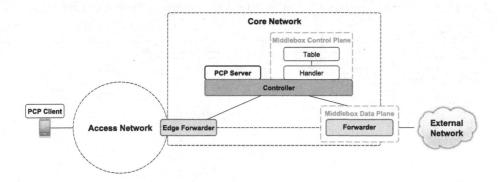

Fig. 1. Architecture of the proposed network.

An end host running a user application with a PCP client is located behind an existing access network (such as UTRAN in case of 3G networks). The access network connects to the core network via the edge forwarder. The edge forwarder forwards PCP requests to the controller, PCP responses from the controller back to the PCP client and other traffic further through the core network.

In the proposed architecture, the control and the data plane of a middlebox are decoupled. The middlebox data plane resides on another forwarder, placed between the core and the external network (the Internet). The middlebox data plane executes the rules installed by the control plane, such as overwriting IP addresses and transport protocol ports in packets in case of NAT.

The controller runs the middlebox control plane, which is responsible for maintaining mappings stored in a table. The handler accepts requests from the PCP server to create or remove a mapping and instructs the controller to add or remove the corresponding rules on the forwarder.

The PCP server running on the controller receives PCP requests, instructs the middlebox control plane to create a mapping for the client and sends PCP responses back to the client once the middlebox control plane successfully creates a mapping. The PCP server address is assumed to be the address of the default gateway, so PCP clients must use this address to communicate with the PCP server. Dynamic PCP server discovery options [9,17,18] are currently not considered.

In order to verify the proper traversal of packets behind middleboxes and the keepalive traffic reduction, a custom, simple NAT gateway is implemented in the network that supports only IPv4 addresses and TCP and UDP as the upper-layer protocols. A custom firewall, IPv6 or other upper-layer protocols are not implemented in the network, as the verification and evaluation method of the proposed solution is identical and would not affect the results.

The control plane of the NAT is responsible for creating NAT table entries from the configured pool of external IP addresses and ports. Each NAT table entry contains the following items: internal IP address, internal port, external address, external port, upper-layer protocol and mapping lifetime. The NAT data plane is represented as a set of flow tables and entries shown in Fig. 2.

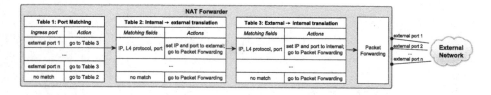

Fig. 2. Flow entries in the NAT forwarder.

The design does not address the security of PCP. The authentication mechanism specified in [11] could be used to control the access to the controller running the PCP server.

5 Evaluation

This section describes a method to measure the battery life extension and signaling traffic reduction based on the values of keepalive intervals to prove the feasibility of the deployment of PCP in WCDMA networks. The method is based on the measurements performed by Haverinen et al. [8] and Signals Research Group, LLC [1], both performed in WCDMA networks.

5.1 Requirements

No other network data, except keepalives, are sent over the network. This is done to isolate the useful network traffic that is usually unpredictable in practice, which would distort the results.

CELL_PCH and CELL_FACH Radio Resource Control (RRC) states are assumed to be enabled in the WCDMA network. When sending a keepalive, the mobile device uses the following RRC state transition: CELL_FACH → CELL_PCH → CELL_FACH → CELL_PCH → ...

The WCDMA inactivity timers are assigned the values used in the first measurement in [8]. In particular, the T2 inactivity timer (causing transition from CELL_FACH to CELL_PCH) is set to 2 s. Keepalives must be sent one at a time, until the mobile device re-enters the lower RRC state (with lower power consumption).

To quantify the battery life saving and signaling traffic reduction, reference values must be defined. For example, suppose that an application currently uses a keepalive interval of 20 s (such as IPSec ESP [5]). If the keepalive interval is increased, the mobile device consumes that much less battery charge compared to the original (reference) keepalive interval. Likewise, the network and the device generate fewer signaling messages.

5.2 Battery Power Saving

Battery Consumption Figures. The first experiment in [8] consisted of sending one keepalive at a time. In the experiment, the inactivity timers and the RRC state transitions were identical to those specified in the Sect. 5.1. The results showed that the average current in the CELL_FACH state is 120 mA (disregarding the negligible variance of the current due to the actual data transmission), and the cost of a single keepalive in the 3G WCDMA network ranged from 0.15 to 0.6 mAh.

Method. Let T be the time period over which the measurement is performed. Over time period T, n_{ref} keepalives are sent given the original (reference) keepalive interval t_{ref} (i.e. the user application originally used the interval t_{ref}). Likewise, n keepalives are sent given the new keepalive interval t_{new}. The number of keepalives sent can be computed as $n = T/t$, where $1/t$ is the number of keepalives sent per second.

The amount of battery consumption saved (in mAh) can be determined as follows:

$$reduction\,(t_{new}) = k_{ref} - k = (n_{ref} - n) \cdot cost = cost \cdot T \cdot \left(\frac{1}{t_{ref}} - \frac{1}{t_{new}} \right) \quad (1)$$

where $k = n \cdot cost$ is the total cost of keepalives over time T.

In order to determine the battery power saving given the desired and reference keepalive intervals (t_{new} and t_{ref}, respectively), the battery capacity C of the mobile device (in mAh) must be known. The relative amount of battery life consumed by sending keepalives can be determined as k/C.

By increasing the keepalive interval to t_{new}, the amount of the battery life saved, given the battery capacity C, can be determined as follows:

$$battery\ power\ saved = \frac{k_{ref}}{C} - \frac{k_{new}}{C} = \frac{reduction\,(t_{new})}{C} \tag{2}$$

From the Eq. (2), one can conclude that, by using a higher keepalive interval t_{new}, such percentage of battery consumption was saved over time T.

From the end-user perspective, an alternative measure may better indicate the power consumption reduction: how much longer the battery will last before recharging it. Suppose that the cost of a single keepalive ($cost$) and the average current while sending a single keepalive ($\bar{I}_{keepalive}$) are known. The total time of the battery life saved can then be computed as follows:

$$battery\ life\ saved = (n_{ref} - n) \cdot \frac{cost}{\bar{I}_{keepalive}} = \frac{reduction\,(t_{new})}{\bar{I}_{keepalive}} \tag{3}$$

Results. Figure 3 shows the battery power saving with increasing keepalive interval, given the time period, cost of a single keepalive, battery capacity and the reference keepalive interval of 20, 40, 80 and 120 s, respectively.

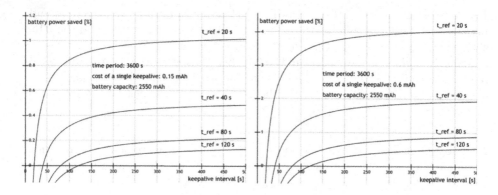

Fig. 3. Battery power saving based on keepalive intervals relative to reference values.

The percentage of the battery power saving increases significantly when the keepalive interval is increased by the first few tens of seconds from the reference interval. Above 400–600 s, the difference in the increase starts to be negligible.

Table 1 shows the percentage of the battery power saving for the chosen representative values of battery capacity, reference values and the keepalive interval of 400 s.

If the application running on a smartphone with battery capacity of 2550 mAh (Samsung Galaxy S6) originally used the keepalive interval of 20 s, 1–4 %

Table 1. Battery power saved for a mobile device connected a WCDMA network given battery capacity and the following reference values: $t_{ref} = 20$ s, $t_{new} = 400$ s, $T = 3600$ s, $cost : 0.15 - 0.6$ mAh.

Battery capacity [mAh]	Battery power saved [%]
300 (Samsung Gear S smart watch)	8.5–34.2
2550 (Samsung Galaxy S6 phone)	1–4
7340 (iPad Air 2 tablet)	0.35–1.4

of the battery life can be saved over 3600 s for the cost ranging from 0.15 to 0.6 mAh. For the reference interval of 40 s, the battery power saving is halved. The battery power saving proves to be significant for devices with relatively low battery capacity, such as smart watches (provided that they support WCDMA), and less significant for devices with higher battery capacity, such as tablets.

If the battery lifetime saving is considered, approx. 13–52 min of battery life can be saved for the keepalive cost ranging from 0.15 to 0.6 mAh, the average current of 120 mA (CELL_FACH state) [8], the reference keepalive interval of 20 s and the new keepalive interval of 400s.

5.3   Signaling Traffic Reduction

Signaling Traffic Figures. In [1], several measurements were performed in two 3G WCDMA networks, observing the number of signaling messages generated in the networks and the battery power consumption in mobile devices. In one of the measurements, the mobile devices sent keepalive messages to the network. In the observed networks, the mobile devices entered the CELL_DCH state when sending a keepalive. According to the results, sending one keepalive causes 40–50 signaling messages to be exchanged between a mobile device and the network (referred to as "observed" messages), and estimated 20 signaling messages generated in the network not captured on the mobile device (referred to as "unobserved" messages).

Method. Let s be the number of signaling messages sent per a single keepalive. The total number of signaling messages sent over time T given keepalive interval t_{new} is $S = n \cdot s$. The reduction of signaling messages in the network with increased keepalive interval can then be computed as:

$$reduction\,(t) = S_{ref} - S = (n_{ref} - n) \cdot s = \left(\frac{1}{t_{ref}} - \frac{1}{t_{new}} \right) \cdot s \cdot T \qquad (4)$$

Results. As seen in Fig. 4, the reduction of the number of signaling messages grows rapidly up to the keepalive interval of approx. 400 s. The growth of the reduction starts to be negligible from approx. 1800 s, which can be considered an acceptable keepalive interval for WCDMA networks. Table 2 quantifies the results for reference keepalive intervals of 20 and 120 s.

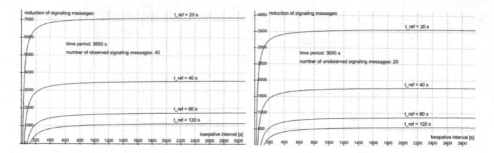

Fig. 4. Number of signaling messages reduced based on keepalive intervals and reference values.

Table 2. Number of signaling messages reduced given the following reference values: $t_{new} = 1800$ s, $T = 3600$ s.

Number of signaling messages per keepalive	Reference keepalive interval [s]	Number of signaling messages reduced	Reference keepalive interval [s]	Number of signaling messages reduced
40 (observed)	20	7120	120	1120
50 (observed)	20	8900	120	1400
20 (observed)	20	3560	120	560

It should be noted that the reduction of the number of signaling messages was computed for one mobile device running a single application. Considering that hundreds of thousands of mobile devices are connected to a network, each running one or more always-on applications, the decrease in the network load on elements in the network core may prove to be significant.

5.4 Determining PCP Mapping Lifetime

From the perspective of a mobile device and its battery life, the keepalive interval of 400–600 s is suitable for most applications. When considering the amount of signaling traffic generated in a mobile network, the keepalive interval of approx. 1800 s is sufficient to greatly reduce the signaling traffic.

For mappings created by PCP requests with the MAP opcode (i.e. user applications function as servers), user applications must send PCP MAP requests at the interval of at least 1/2 of the mapping lifetime [9]. In order to sustain the interval of 1800 s, the mapping lifetime for PCP MAP mappings should be doubled, i.e. set to 3600 s. Beside PCP MAP requests, applications may still have to send keepalives to the destination host to maintain the end-to-end connectivity. In order to keep the number of RRC state transitions to a minimum, applications should send PCP MAP requests to the PCP server and keepalives to the destination host at the same time.

For mappings created by PCP PEER requests, and given the relatively high keepalive interval of 1800 s suitable for WCDMA networks, it may be sufficient for the application to send the keepalives 7/8 of the mapping lifetime. Therefore, the mapping lifetime for PCP PEER mappings could be approx. 2100 s.

6   Conclusions

This paper described the architecture for the deployment of the Port Control Protocol in software-defined networks. Using the SDN approach, this architecture separates the control and the data plane of middleboxes and allows to run the PCP server outside the middleboxes according to SDN principles. This improves vendor device compatibility and avoids the processing overhead imposed by running the PCP server.

With PCP deployed in the network, mobile devices connected to mobile networks can reduce the amount of keepalive traffic sent, which results in extended battery life of mobile devices. Additionally, the network throughput is increased due to signaling traffic reduction in access networks. The keepalive interval of approx. 1800 s proves to be suitable for most applications in WCDMA networks. The battery power saving by using higher keepalive intervals is more significant in devices with relatively small battery capacity, such as smartphones and smart watches. Given the recommended keepalive interval, PCP server should assign mapping lifetime of at least 3600 s for PCP MAP mappings and 2100 s for PCP PEER mappings.

Acknowledgments. This work is a result of the Research and Development Operational Program for the projects Support of Center of Excellence for Smart Technologies, Systems and Services, ITMS 26240120005 and for the projects Support of Center of Excellence for Smart Technologies, Systems and Services II, ITMS 26240120029, co-funded by ERDF. This project was also partially supported by the Tatra banka Foundation under the contract No. 2012et011.

References

1. Signals Research Group, LLC: Smartphones and a 3G Network, reducing the impact of smartphone-generated signaling traffic while increasing the battery life of the phone through the use of network optimization techniques, May 2010
2. Wing, D., et al.: Session Traversal Utilities for NAT (STUN). RFC 5389, October 2008
3. Matthews, P., et al.: Traversal Using Relays around NAT (TURN): Relay Extensions to Session Traversal Utilities for NAT (STUN). RFC 5766, April 2010
4. Rosenberg, J.: Interactive Connectivity Establishment (ICE): A Methodology for Network Address Translator (NAT) Traversal for Offer/Answer Protocols. RFC 5245, April 2010
5. Huttunen, A., et al.: UDP Encapsulation of IPsec ESP Packets. RFC 3948, January 2005

6. Levkowetz, H., Vaarala, S.: Mobile IP Traversal of Network Address Translation (NAT) Devices. RFC 3519, April 2003
7. Eronen, P.: TCP Wake-Up: Reducing Keep-Alive Traffic in Mobile IPv4 and IPsec NAT Traversal. Nokia Research Center (2008)
8. Haverinen, H., et al.: Energy consumption of always-on applications in WCDMA networks. In: 2007 IEEE 65th Vehicular Technology Conference, VTC2007-Spring, pp. 964–968, April 2007
9. Boucadair, M., et al.: Port Control Protocol (PCP). RFC 6887, April 2013
10. Wing, D.: Port control protocol. The Internet Protocol Journal 14(4)
11. Reddy, T., et al.: Port Control Protocol (PCP) Authentication Mechanism. Internet-Draft draft-ietf-pcp-authentication-07, December 2014
12. Open Networking Foundation: Software-Defined Networking: The New Norm for Networks. https://www.opennetworking.org/images/stories/downloads/sdn-resour ces/white-papers/wp-sdn-newnorm.pdf. [Online; Accessed 30th November 2014]
13. Nadeau, T.D., Gray, K.: SDN: Software Defined Networks. O'Reilly Media, Sebastopol (2013)
14. Nagy, M., Kotuliak, I.: Utilizing openflow, SDN and NFV in GPRS core network. In: Leung, V.C.M., Chen, M., Wan, J., Zhang, Y. (eds.) TridentCom 2014. LNICST, vol. 137, pp. 184–193. Springer, Heidelberg (2014)
15. Reddy, T., et al.: PCP Firewall Control in Managed Networks. Internet-Draft draft-reddy-pcp-sdn-firewall-00, December 2014
16. Open Networking Foundation: OpenFlow Switch Specification, version 1.3.0. https://www.opennetworking.org/images/stories/downloads/sdn-resources/ onf-specifications/openflow/openflow-spec-v1.3.0.pdf. [Online; Accessed 5th December 2014]
17. Boucadair, M., et al.: DHCP Options for the Port Control Protocol (PCP). RFC 7291 (2014)
18. Penno, R., et al.: PCP Anycast Address. Internet-Draft draft-ietf-pcp-anycast-02, August 2014
19. Skalný, J. et al.: Application of software defined networking (SDN) in GPRS network. In: IIT SRC 2014: Student Research Conference in Informatics and Information Technologies, pages 553–558, Bratislava. Nakladatełstvo STU, April 2014

A SDN Based Method of TCP Connection Handover

Andrej Binder[(✉)], Tomas Boros, and Ivan Kotuliak

Faculty of Informatics and Information Technologies,
Slovak University of Technology in Bratislava, Ilkovičova 2,
842 16 Bratislava, Slovakia
andrej@binder.sk, tomas.boros92@gmail.com,
ivan.kotuliak@stuba.sk

Abstract. Today, TCP is the go-to protocol for building resilient communication channels on the Internet. Without much overstatement, it can be said that it runs the majority of communication on the planet. Its success only highlights the fact that it also has some drawbacks, of which one of the oldest ones is the inability to hand over running connections between participating hosts. This paper introduces a method that relies on the advantages of Software Defined Networks to overcome this limitation.

Keywords: Software Defined Networks · Network protocols · Transmission control protocol · Telecommunications

1 Introduction

TCP handover is the act of handing over the role of one of the two communicating endpoints to a third endpoint that was initially not a part of the communication.

The reasons for this can be for example:

- Load-balancing
- Traffic path optimization
- A transparent redirection mechanism
- Switchover of network interfaces

The common solution for this problem was to terminate the running connection and re-initiate the connection with a new host. This is a common practice on the interned today [5, 13].

The problems with this approach are:

- Latency caused by additional TCP handshake
- Needs to be implemented on application layer
- Non-transparent
- TCP-windows are reset resulting in sub-optimal performance

One area where this problem is especially apparent is the area of Content Delivery Networks. Most CDN architectures leverage a redirect mechanism to initiate connection between a client and the most appropriate server to serve specific content.

I. Khalil et al. (Eds.): ICT-EurAsia 2015 and CONFENIS 2015, LNCS 9357, pp. 13–19, 2015.
DOI: 10.1007/978-3-319-24315-3_2

Introducing delays in this step results in noticeably slower content playback startups that are even more apparent in the case of CDN Federations where multiple redirects often take place before the client can connect to the server [3, 6, 7, 8].

Our method to address this issue is to make use of Software Defined Network technology. This technology makes it possible to enhance the network with the functionality that not only allows TCP handovers but also makes them controllable by the SDN controller itself [9, 15].

2 Software Defined Networks

The main disadvantage of traditional network technologies is lack of flexibility in implementing new features. Because of requirements related to standardization, testing and the drawbacks of deploying new code in a fully proprietary environment, new features usually take years to be agreed upon. Even then they often face limited success because of the difficulties and risks related to changing something in an environment that was essentially designed to serve a very specific purpose. One example of such technology is multicast that has existed for decades but did not succeed in being globally distributed because of the reasons listed above [1, 10–12, 14].

Software Defined Networks (SDN) present a radically different approach to designing networks that is built from ground up to make implementation of new features and services as easy as possible. It achieves this by splitting the data plane (responsible for forwarding traffic) and the control plane (responsible for higher level decision-making and configuration of the data plane) into two separate entities. Furthermore it also changes the logical placement of these entities. In traditional networks both the control plane and the data plane was confined within a single networking device, making development of complex control plane to control plane communication protocols necessary. In SDNs the data plane stays distributed but the control plane is removed from the physical device and placed into a centralized node responsible for managing all the data planes in the network. This centralized control plane is called a Controller in SDN terminology [2, 9].

The SDN Controller is a fully software-based element that does not have the burden of having to communicate every single decision to any of its peers. This means that new features can be quickly added to the controller and they will be instantly available throughout the whole network that is under its control. The resources available in the data plane under its controls are the Controller's only limiting factor. It does not have to follow a specific protocol that dictates exactly how these resources should be used [4].

3 TCP Handover Method in SDN Networks

Our approach to addressing TCP handover relies on the following features of Software Defined Networks:

- The ability to intercept specific packets and redirect them for processing in the control plane

- The ability to modify the data plane in such a way that it rewrites the destination IP address of a packet according to a rule defined by the control plane
- The fact that a SDN network is limited to a single autonomous system (administered by a single organization), in which the occurrence of triangular routing is not considered a problem as long as its fully controlled

In addition to these requirements at least one of the following features must also be available:

- The ability to synchronize (increment or decrement according to a rule) TCP SEQ and ACK numbers in the data plane
- The ability to synchronize (increment or decrement according to a rule) TCP SEQ and ACK numbers in the host device
- The ability to be able to predict the SEQ number that would be chosen by a host for a new incoming connection (described later)

The initial use case that this method was designed for was the implementation of a transparent redirect mechanism for use in Content Delivery Networks so we will use this environment to describe the method's operating principle. We will later describe how to use the method in any other scenario.

When a client initializes a new TCP connection to a server, it sends a TCP segment encapsulated in IPv4 or IPv6 packet to a destination address that identifies the service to be accessed. In the first TCP segment the client sets the SYN flag, chooses a initial sequence number (SEQ), sets the ACK number to 0, sets the window size and optionally sends some OPTION parameters. The server on the receiving side goes to the SYN_RCVD state and sends back his TCP packet and parameters to the client. Sets the SYN and the ACK flag, choses a sequence number and sets the ACK number to sequence number + 1 of the client. Using this he acknowledges the client to send the next TCP window. The server chooses a window size too and sets some optional parameters in OPTION fields. The client then sends back an ACK message to acknowledge the parameters of the server. At this moment the session goes to ESTABLISHED state. Now the client may request the data (for example in a HTTP GET message).

This happens normally in networks but lets say that the IP address that the client was communicating with was not an IP address directly attached to a specific server but an IP address defined in the network as and address used to identify a specific service. Any TCP packets sent to this IP, that are meant to initiate a TCP connection with a server, will not be delivered directly to a server but redirected to a SDN Controller for further processing instead. The controller would then keep on acting on behalf on the server up to the point when it can decide which actual server would be best to deliver the service. In the context of CDN networks this means up until the point when the Controller is aware of the HTTP URI that the client intends to access. It would then modify the data plane to rewrite the destination IP address of all future packets from the client to the IP address of the chosen server.

This would work perfectly in an UDP-based scenario where packets are considered as separate atomic elements. In TCP environment all communication is treaded in the context of sessions that are kept consistent by communicating the sequence numbers of packets in each transmission and acknowledging them on the other side. The problem with this approach in context with our method is that we cannot control the initial SEQ number that the client choses or the SEQ number that the final server would chose. This means that, without addressing this issue, the communication would not work because even if the source and destination addresses of the packets were correct, the TCP session would not work because both sides would not be able to agree on which sequence number should follow.

The full method is depicted in the following sequence diagram:

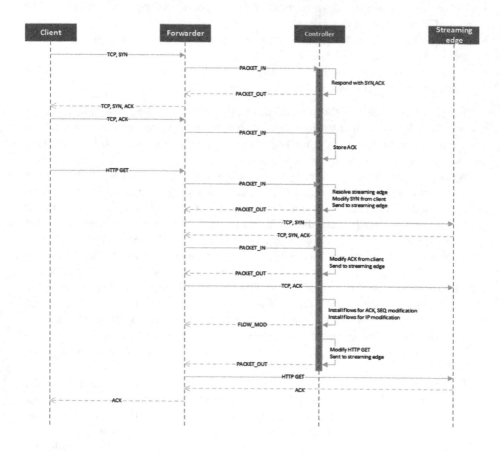

There are two basic ways to address this:

- Be able to synchronize the SEQ and ACK numbers by incrementing or decrementing them in the data plane
- Be able to predict the SEQ number that the server will chose so that the connection from the controller can be started with a SEQ number that would be in sync with the SEQ number that the server would chose right from the start

The first approach has the only disadvantage that the SDN data plane (also called SDN Forwarder) closest to the server would need to have the capability to increment and decrement the SYN and ACK numbers according to a chosen rule. The fact is that while rewriting of destination IP address is a standard SDN data plane function that is available in basically all SDN Forwarders, the functions of incrementing or decrementing of SYN and ACK numbers are not standard functions. This means that most hardware data plane elements would not be able to perform the operation.

This can be easily addressed in environments where we have the server under control. We simply place a small SDN Forwarder in the operating system of the server and link it to the controller. This small forwarder would be a data plane element only capable of doing the operation of synchronizing the SYN/ACK numbers, an operation that is very easy to implement in the all-software environment of a server.

The following figure depicts this scenario:

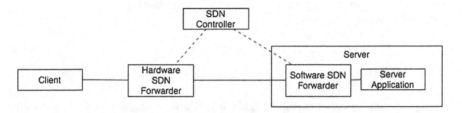

The second approach requires the modification of the TCP stack on the server. The SEQ number the TCP stack choses would not be chosen randomly as it is usually done, but it will be chosen according to a hash of the incoming SYN packet. This means that when a SYN packet is sent to such server, the sender has the ability to calculate and predict the initial SEQ number that the server will chose. In order to maintain security, a shared secret (shared between the controller and the server) can also be added to the SYN packet in order to make it harder for a third party to step into the communication.

4   Implementation and Testing

To prove that the approach is fully functional, we have implemented a prototype and tested it with real clients and servers in the environment of CDN networks.

We have created a new version of the Ofsoftswitch13 SDN Forwarder with the additional TCP SEQ and ACK synchronization functions. We did this by adding a new action based on to the SET_FIELD action defined by the OpenFlow 1.3 standard. We called these actions SET_TCP_ACK and SET_TCP_SEQ in order to be able to modify the ACK and SEQ numbers respectively.

For example if we install an action with SET_TCP_SEQ with argument 1000, incoming TCP connection which matches the matching rule will have its Sequence number incremented by 1000 on the outgoing interface. The same thing will happen for the ACK number. Using correctly these actions we will be able to synchronize the TCP sequence and acknowledge numbers for the two separate TCP connections.

In addition to the modified SDN Forwarder we also needed our own SDN Controller that we could easily modify. In the end we chose the Ryu SDN controller. It is an open-source SDN controller that is freely available, well documented and easy to modify. This controller also fully supports the OpenFlow 1.3 protocol which allowed us to re-use most of the needed functionality. The controller was also modified to be able to track the state of the session in order to get more visibility into what is happening in the network.

These two components allowed us to fully test our method. The testing also shower that in addition to proving that the method actually works, it also has the following benefits:

- Faster session establishment and shorter interruption in comparison with application-level redirect methods
- No need for extra DNS queries
- No need to implement application-level redirect mechanisms
- Fully transparent to the client

5   Conclusion

We designed, implemented and thoroughly tested a new method of TCP connection handover in the environment of SDN networks.

We have created a prototype SDN Forwarder and a prototype SDN Controller that we used to prove the functionality of the method.

Our tests using these prototypes proved that we can achieve faster handover times as compared to traditional application-level redirect methods that require a complete re-establishment of TCP sessions. Furthermore this was all done in a manner that is fully transparent to the client and requires no modification of the server application.

In the end the method proves that SDN technology is a great platform for implementing interesting new functions into the network environment.

Acknowledgements. This work is a result of the Research and Development Operational Program for the projects Support of Center of Excellence for Smart Technologies, Systems and Services, ITMS 26240120005 and for the projects Support of Center of Excellence for Smart Technologies, Systems and Services II, ITMS 26240120029, co-funded by ERDF.

The authors would like to thank Oskar van Deventer and his team at the Dutch Organization for Applied Scientific Research (TNO) for their invaluable help.

References

1. Feamster, N., Rexford, J., Zegura, E.: The road to SDN: an intellectual history of programmable networks, December 2013
2. OPEN NETWORKING FOUNDATION.: OpenFlow Switch Specification: Version 1.3.0 Implemented (Wire Protocol 0x04) (2012)
3. Niven-Jenkins B., Le Faucheur F., Bitar N.: Content Distribution Network Interconnection (CDNI) Problem Statement

4. TEAM, RYU PROJECT. RYU: SDN Framework (Online). Ryu book. http://osrg.github.io/ryu-book/en/Ryubook.pdf
5. Network Working Group. RFC: 2616 - Hypertext Transfer Protocol – HTTP/1.1
6. van der Ziel, S.: CDN interoperability reality check
7. ETSI TS 182 032 CDN Interconnection Architecture
8. Bertrand, G., Le Faucheur, F., Peterson, L.: Content Distribution Network Interconnection (CDNI) Experiments, Internet Engineering Task Force, draft-bertrand-cdni-experiments, 02 February 2012. http://tools.ietf.org/id/draft-bertrand-cdni-experiments-02.txt
9. Kim, M.-K., Kim, H.-J., Chang, D., Kwon, T.: CDNI Request Routing with SDN, Internet Engineering Task Force, draft-shin-cdni-request- routing-sdn-00, July 2012. http://tools.ietf.org/id/draft-shin-cdni-request-routing-sdn-00.txt
10. Kokku, R., Rajamony, R., Alvisi, L., Vin, H.: Half-Pipe Anchoring: An Efficient Mechanism for TCP Connection Handoff
11. Bonaventure, O., Handley, M., Raiciu, C.: An Overview of Multipath TCP
12. Beda, E., Ventura, N.: Socketless TCP - an end to end handover solution (2014)
13. IETF RFC 793.: Transmission control protocol, September 1981. http://www.ietf.org/rfc/rfc793.txt
14. Kozemčák, A., Kováčik, T.: Different network traffic measurement techniques - possibilities and results. In: Proceedings ELMAR-2012: 54th Symposium ELMAR-2012, pp. 93–96. Society Electronics in Marine, Zadar, 12–14 September 2012. ISBN: 978-953-7044-13-8
15. Halagan, T., Kováčik, T.: Modification of TCP SYN flood (DoS) attack detection algorithm. In: Numerical Modelling and Simulation : International Interdisciplinary PhD Workshop IIPhDW, Tatranske Matliare, Slovak republic, 20–22 May 2014. 1. vyd. Warsaw : Elektrotechnical institute, 2014, [4] s. ISBN: 978-83-61956-29-7

IP Data Delivery in HBB-Next Network Architecture

Roman Bronis[✉], Ivan Kotuliak, Tomas Kovacik, Peter Truchly, and Andrej Binder

Faculty of Informatics and Information Technologies, Institute of Computer Systems and Networks, Slovak University of Technology in Bratislava, Ilkovicova 2, 84216 Bratislava, Slovakia
{roman.bronis,ivan.kotuliak,tomas.kovacik,
peter.truchly,andrej.binder}@stuba.sk
http://fiit.stuba.sk

Abstract. Digital television enables IP data delivery using various protocols. Hybrid television HbbTV enhances digital television with applications delivery. HBB-Next is an architecture which enhances HbbTV with additional features. However it does not specify IP data delivery despite it has access to both broadcast and broadband channel. This paper proposes architecture and protocols for IP data delivery in HBB-Next. To achieve this goal we designed new node (Application Data Handler - ADH) in HBB-Next architecture and new communication protocols (Application Data Handler Control Protocol - ADHCP, and Hybrid Encapsulation Protocol - HEP) for data transmission. We created Stochastic Petri Net (SPN) model of designed protocols and implemented them in ns2 network simulator to verify our solution. Results of SPN model simulation and ns2 network simulation are discussed and HEP protocol is compared to existing encapsulation protocols used in DVB systems.

Keywords: IP data encapsulation · HBB-Next · DVB · SPN · ns2 · Application Data Handler (ADH) · Hybrid Encapsulation Protocol (HEP)

1 Introduction

Evolution from digital television to hybrid television started with Multimedia Home Platform (MHP) [1]. It was later surpassed by hybrid television standard - Hybrid Broadcast Broadband Television (HbbTV) [2]. HbbTV applications are CE-HTML based and can take advantage of broadband return channel. HbbTV applications can be interactive and mostly serve for TV providers as enhanced EPG (Electronic Program Guide) applications (archive, informations about movies and shows, trailers etc.). HbbTV applications can not only serve as TV information portals, but can be also used in other areas such as in e-learning [3].

© IFIP International Federation for Information Processing 2015
I. Khalil et al. (Eds.): ICT-EurAsia 2015 and CONFENIS 2015, LNCS 9357, pp. 20–29, 2015.
DOI: 10.1007/978-3-319-24315-3_3

To enhance HbbTV application capabilities, HBB-Next platform was designed [4]. It provides additional features as user recognition (by face or voice etc.), content recommendation and user management. As in HbbTV, HBB-Next terminals are connected to broadband Internet which is used for application data or media streams delivery. In HBB-Next, service provider has access to broadcast channel, but it is used only for media streaming.

HBB-Next platform does not specify IP data delivery. Protocols for IP data delivery in digital television could be used, but they were not designed to utilize both broadcast and broadband channel. In this paper we propose enhancement to HBB-Next architecture and we design protocols to deliver IP data from applications to terminals using both broadcast and broadband channel. We compare it to similar solutions and describe its advantages.

This paper is organized as follows: the second section describes protocols used for IP data delivery in DVB systems and current state of next generation of hybrid television. The third section proposes Application Data Handler (ADH) node and ADH-Control Protocol (ADHCP). In fourth section Hybrid Encapsulation Protocol (HEP) and HEP Hash Table (HHT) protocols are described. The fifth section describes Stochastic Petri Net (SPN) model of designed communication, its properties and results of simulations. The sixth section describes implementation of designed protocols in ns2 network simulator and results of simulations. The seventh section concludes this paper.

2 IP Data Delivery in DVB and in HBB-Next

In this section we describe current state of IP data delivery in DVB systems and current state of HBB-Next architecture.

2.1 IP Data Delivery in DVB

Multi-Protocol Encapsulation (MPE) protocol was designed for IP data delivery in first generation DVB systems (DVB-S/C/T) [5]. It is the most used protocol to receive IP data over broadcast channel in areas without connection or with limited broadband connection. MPE can work in two modes. In padding mode, MPE frame's unused data are filled with invalid data. In packing mode, MPE frame's unused data are filled with next packet. Padding mode is available to all devices with MPE support, however MPE packing mode is optional. Packing mode is more effective but is not supported by all end-devices.

Unidirectional Lightweight Encapsulation (ULE) protocol was designed as lightweight alternative to MPE protocol [6]. It has reduced header (header size: MPE - 16 B, ULE - 4 B) and is using packing mode by default.

For second generation DVB systems (DVB-S2 etc.), new protocol for IP data delivery can be used [7]. Generic Stream Encapsulation (GSE) protocol is the most effective in DVB-S2 systems, but it is not compatible with first generation of DVB systems. Despite GSE's highest efficiency, MPE is still used in many cases. During transition to DVB-S2, providers stayed with MPE protocol because it had wider support in consumers' end-devices and was still used by DVB-S systems.

2.2   HBB-Next

HBB-Next is platform of next-generation hybrid television. It was designed to provide additional features to hybrid television. HBB-Next architecture consists of three main layers: application provider, service provider and terminal (Fig. 1).

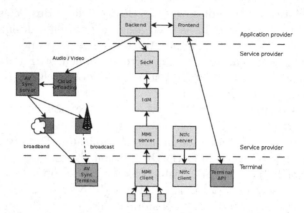

Fig. 1. HBB-Next architecture (high-level view)

Application provider layer represents application, its data and frontend. Applications can be HbbTV compatible and can take advantage of features of Service provider layer.

Service provider is HBB-Next core architecture provider. Service provider layer consist of multiple nodes. It is designed to provide advanced features such as user recognition (Multi-modal Interface)[8], content recommendation, enhanced identity management (IdM) and security management (SecM), and audio and video synchronisation and delivery (CloudOffloading and AV Sync nodes).

Terminal is end-point device which is able to receive transmission on broadcast channel and is also connected to broadband channel. Broadband channel's bandwidth is not specified but HBB-Next terminal is considered to have enough bandwidth for face recognition data and multimedia streaming reception.

Applications in HBB-Next can send data to terminal by broadband channel. Broadcast channel is solely used for audio and video data delivery. However, this channel could be used for delivery of other application data as well. To provide this feature HBB-Next architecture need to be enhanced.

HBB-Next does not specify IP data delivery in its core. Standard DVB encapsulation protocols (MPE, ULE, GSE) could be used for IP data delivery in HBB-Next only by bypassing its core. HBB-Next platform could take advantage of its core and its connection to broadcast and broadband channels to transfer IP data from applications to terminals.

3   Application Data Handler (ADH) and ADH-Control Protocol (ADHCP)

HBB-Next architecture is not suitable for delivery of application data through broadcast channel. Only node which is connected to both broadband and broadcast channel is AV Sync node. For applications to be able to deliver IP data we created a new node - Application Data Handler (ADH) in service layer (Fig. 2).

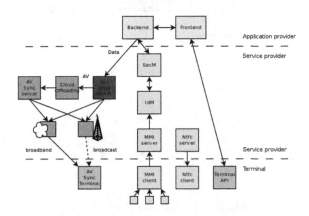

Fig. 2. HBB-Next architecture with ADH node

ADH node is used to receive application data and send them through appropriate broadcast or broadband channel according to applications' needs.

Data are sent from application to ADH node using ADHCP protocol (Fig. 3). This protocol was designed to allow application data encapsulation (data field, <1435 B), link type selection (link type field) and addressing (address type and address fields). Hash field in ADHCP headers is used as checksum for encapsulated data. ADHCP communication is based on request and reply messages and they use two different header formats. Application is requesting data transfer from ADH ((1) in Fig. 3). ADHCP request header consist of link type, address type, address (optional), data (encapsulated data) and hash value (of encapsulated data). ADH node response in case of failure with response ADHCP message ((2) in Fig. 3). ADHCP response header consists of hash value of message which was not delivered correctly and response code. Response code is:

- 00 - refused: in case of ADH refuse to transmit data over selected link,
- 11 - retransmission request: in case any of terminals failed to receive data and they are no longer in ADH cache,
- 01 and 10 - reserved.

In Fig. 3 part A there is ADHCP messages exchange when there is insufficient bandwidth on broadcast channel (ADH refuses to send data). Part B shows correct data transmission with ADHCP to ADH. In part C ADHCP messages exchange in case of transmission failure on broadcast channel is shown.

HBB-Next's Application layer is considered to be connected with Service provider layer with sufficient bandwidth. ADHCP is encapsulated in TCP/IP to achieve reliable transmission.

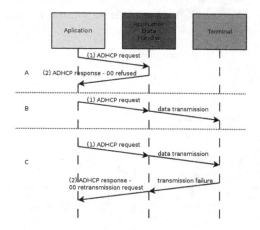

Fig. 3. ADHCP messages flow

4   Hybrid Encapsulation Protocol (HEP) and HEP Hash Table (HHT) Protocol

To transmit data from ADH to terminal, new lightweight protocol was designed. Hybrid Encapsulation Protocol (HEP) can be used either in DVB broadcast channels encapsulated in MPEG-TS or in broadband channel over TCP/IP. Broadcast channels are not reliable medium. To check correct reception of received data, HASH values are sent from ADH to terminal using HEP Hash-Table - HHT ((1) in Fig. 4). HHT consist of list of items. One item consist of fields (size of field in brackets):

- hash value (256 b) - hash value of data received from application,
- link type (4 b) - expected link to receive HEP frame,
- reception time (32 b) - expected time of HEP frame reception, in Unix time format, and
- sequence number (20 b) - position in terminals reception stack.

One or multiple items may be send in one HHT message. HHT is sent to selected terminal by broadband channel using TCP/IP and it consists only from items addressed to selected terminal.

After HHT communication, HEP message is sent to terminal ((2) in Fig. 4). HEP message consists of encapsulated data sent from ADH (originally from application). For HEP messages received from broadcast channel terminal counts Hash value and check if the message was received correctly. Counted value is compared to one terminal received in HHT. If received correctly, counted Hash value will match to one from terminals HHT list. In case of transmission error, counted Hash value will not match any of items in HHT list. Terminal periodically checks reception time and requests frames ((3) in Fig. 4) which were not delivered within reception time in terminals HHT. Requesting HEP message consist of number of requested frames with their hash values following. After ADH receives HEP request, it can either resend data (if still cached) or request application for retransmission with ADHCP response ((4) in Fig. 4).

HEP encapsulation was designed to be more efficient then previously used protocols. ULE protocol was designed to reduce MPE's header to achieve higher efficiency [9,10]. GSE protocol is even more efficient, but it is used only in second generation DVB channels [11]. HEP's encapsulation over broadcast channel is more efficient as MPE, ULE or GSE because it has no header. It is using HHT protocol instead which is solely transmitted over broadband channel and therefore saves broadcast channel bandwidth.

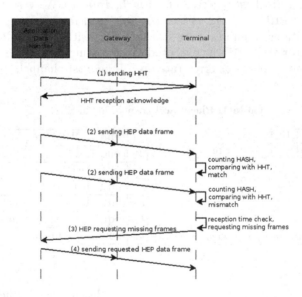

Fig. 4. HHT and HEP communication

5   Petri Net Model of Communication

Petri Nets consist of places, transitions, arcs and tokens. Places are connected to transitions by arcs. Firing a transition (t_1 - Fig. 5) can move token between connected places (from p_0) in a direction of an arc (to p_1). Stochastic Petri Nets enable transitions to be fired with given probability or rate.

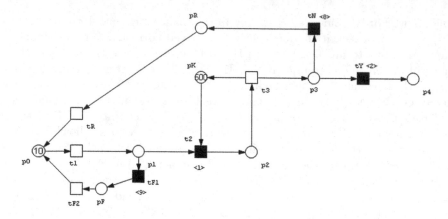

Fig. 5. Communication model using Petri Nets

To verify properties of designed protocols, we created model of their communication using Stochastic Petri Nets (Fig. 5, Table 1). We verified its selected properties using PIPE tool [12]. Place p_K was used to simulate broadcast link capacity. Transitions t_Y and t_N were stochastic transition set to simulate broadcast channel error rate - t_Y was executed every 2 times, t_N was executed every 8 times what represents 20 % error rate on a broadcast channel.

Table 1. Places and transitions in SPN

p_0	ADHCP request sent	t_1	send ADHCP request
p_1	ADHCP request received	t_2	send HHT
p_2	HHT received	t_3	send HEP frame
p_3	HEP received	t_Y	data check - correct
p_4	correct data	t_N	data check - incorrect
p_F	full channel	t_R	request for retransmission
p_K	link capacity	t_F	denial of transmissin
p_R	incorrect data, retransmision		

Results showed that PN is not safe and can be dead-locked - which means that sent messages can be delivered and halt in terminal's last state p_4 - correct data reception. This is considered as correct protocol behavior, because it represents that data can be delivered to final destination (p_4 - correct data reception). There was no other dead-lock identified. We tested boundedness for places representing link capacity (p_K) and results showed that these places are bounded, therefore communication can not overload link capacity. Boundedness for whole model was also tested and results showed that the whole model is bounded.

Using Snoopy [13] we simulated SPN model sending 10 and 1000 messages (Fig. 6). Simulation results show correct reception of all messages - purple line

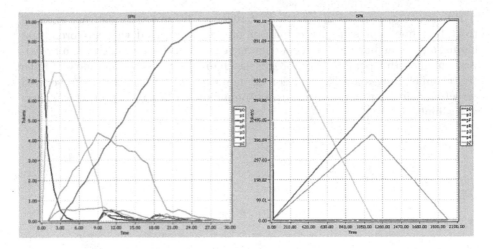

Fig. 6. SPN simulation - 10 messages, 1000 simulations

of p_4 place leads to sent messages count, and correct retransmission request in case of an error on broadcast channel - highlighted red line of p_R place.

6   Simulation in ns2

In order to simulate our protocols, we implemented their version using ns2 network simulator. Application (APP) was sending its messages using ADH node broadcasting to 100 terminals through DVB gateway (DVB_GW). We set terminals' error reception rate on broadcast channel to various percentages (0–99 %). Terminal Term_(0) had 0 % error rate reception, terminal Term_(1) had 1 % error rate reception, and so forth. Simulation scenario was set to requeste every erroneous message again over broadband channel through IP gateway - IP_GW (Fig. 7).

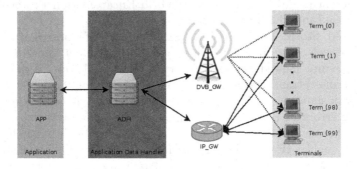

Fig. 7. Simulated topology

Results (Fig. 8) show dependence of received frames on broadcast channel error. Red line represent percentage of messages received through broadcast channel and green line represents percentage of messages received through broadband channel. Independently on broadcast channel error rate, summary of both line (channels) gives 100 % reception of messages on terminal. Results verified correct transmission and retransmission behaviour of designed protocols in network simulator.

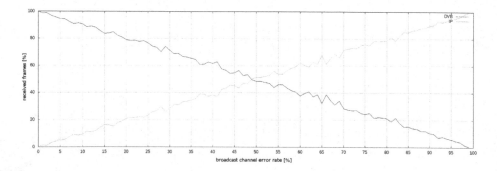

Fig. 8. Results of ns2 simulation

7   Conclusion

In this paper we proposed architecture and protocols for IP data delivery in DVB broadcast channels in next generation hybrid television - HBB-Next. We identified missing specification for IP data delivery in HBB-Next, which could take advantage of broadband channel.

We designed new node in HBB-Next architecture - Application Data Handler (ADH). ADH receives all application data and transmits them to terminals using either broadcast or broadband channels. In order to communicate with ADH we designed ADH-Control Protocol (ADHCP). For data delivery to terminals through different channels we designed Hybrid Encapsulation Protocol (HEP) and HEP Hash-Table (HHT) protocols.

We created Stochastic Petri Net (SPN) model of communication with designed protocols. We analysed properties of SPN model and simulated its behaviour. Results showed desired properties and simulations verified correct transmission and retransmission of messages. Later we implemented our protocols in network simulator and simulated communication with multiple terminals with different error rate on broadcast channel. Results showed correct data transmission over broadcast channel and retransmission over broadband channel.

Our work enables IP data delivery in HBB-Next from applications to terminals over HBB-Next service provider layer. Applications can not only serve as multimedia provider and HbbTV content provider, but with our changes they can also behave as IP data providers. Our HEP encapsulation has also reduced frames' header overhead on DVB broadcast channels. Instead it is using broadband channel to deliver HHT (header-like data).

Future work includes further comparison of SPN simulations with network simulations, testing of parallel transmission in various complex scenarios and implementation and testing on real hardware.

Acknowledgments. This work is a result of the Research and Development Operational Program for the projects Support of Center of Excellence for Smart Technologies, Systems and Services, ITMS 26240120005 and for the projects Support of Center of Excellence for Smart Technologies, Systems and Services II, ITMS 26240120029, co-funded by ERDF and was supported by the Slovak national research project VEGA 1/0708/13, KEGA 047STU-4/2013 and Slovak Research and Development Agency project APVV-0258-12.

References

1. ETSI TS 102 812: Digital Video Broadcasting (DVB); Multimedia Home Platform (MHP) Specification 1.1.3, ETSI, v1.3.1, May 2012
2. ETSI TS 102 796: Hybrid Broadcast Broadband TV, ETSI, v1.2.1, November 2012
3. Kovacik, T, Bronis, R., Kotuliak, I.: HBB platform for e-learning improvement. In: IEEE 10th International Conference on Emerging eLearning Technologies and Applications, ICETA 2012, November 2012, Stara Lesna, The High Tatras, Slovakia, pp. 207–211 (2012). ISBN: 978-1-4673-5122-5
4. Podhradsky, P.: Evolution trends in hybrid broadcast broadband TV. In: Proceedings of 55th International Symposium ELMAR-2013, September 2013, pp. 7–10 (2013). ISBN: 978-953-7044-14-5, ISSN: 1334–2630
5. ETSI EN 301 192: Digital Video Broadcasting (DVB); DVB specification for data broadcasting, ETSI, v1.4.2, April 2008
6. IETF RFC 4326: Unidirectional Lightweight Encapsulation (ULE) for Transmission of IP Datagrams over an MPEG-2 Transport Stream (TS), IETF, December 2005
7. ETSI TS 102 606: Digital Video Broadcasting (DVB) - Generic Stream Encapsulation (GSE) Protocol, ETSI, v1.1.1, October 2007
8. Kovacik, T., Bronis, R., Kotuliak, I.: Towards novel HBB application platform: experimental testbed. In: 2012 5th Joint IFIP Wireless and Mobile Networking Conference, Bratislava, Slovakia, 19–21 September 2012, pp. 133–137 (2012). ISBN: 978-1-4673-2994-1
9. Fairhurst, G., Matthews, A.: A comparison of IP transmission using MPE and a new lightweight encapsulation. In: IEEE Seminar on IP over Satellite - The Next Generation: MPLS, VPN and DRM Delivered Services, pp. 106–120 (2003)
10. Xilouris, G., et al.: Unidirectional lightweight encapsulation: performance evaluation and application perspectives. IEEE Trans. Broadcast. **52**(3), 374–380 (2006). ISSN: 0018–9316
11. Mayer, A., et al.: Analytical and experimental IP encapsulation efficiency comparison of GSE, MPE, and ULE over DVB-S2. In: International Workshop on Satellite and Space Communications, IWSSC 2007, pp. 114–118. IEEE, September 2007. ISBN: 978-1-4244-0938-9
12. PIPE: tool fol Petri Nets. http://sourceforge.net/projects/pipe2/
13. Snoopy2: tool for Petri Nets. http://www-dssz.informatik.tu-cottbus.de/DSSZ/Software/Snoopy

Syn Flood Attack Detection and Type Distinguishing Mechanism Based on Counting Bloom Filter

Tomáš Halagan, Tomáš Kováčik[✉], Peter Trúchly,
and Andrej Binder

Faculty of Informatics and Information Technologies,
Slovak University of Technology in Bratislava,
Ilkovičova 2, 842 16 Bratislava, Slovakia
{tomas.halagan, tomas.kovacik, peter.truchly,
andrej.binder}@stuba.sk

Abstract. Presented work focuses onto proposal, implementation and evaluation of the new method for detection and type identification of SYN flood (DoS) attacks. The method allows distinguishing type of detected SYN flood attacks – random, subnet or fixed. Based on Counting Bloom filter, the attack detection and identification algorithm is proposed, implemented and evaluated in KaTaLyzer network traffic monitoring tool. Proof of correctness of the approach for TCP SYN flood attack detection and type identification is provided – both in practical and theoretical manners. In practice, new module for KaTaLyzer is implemented and TCP attacks are detected, identified and network administrator is notified about them in real-time.

Keywords: DoS detection · DoS identification · Counting Bloom Filter · TCP · SYN · Flood attack · Network security

1 Introduction

Internet allows people to connect with each other in different ways. However, every new functionality, service, new way of communication, new invention designed for the benefit of humanity may pose a potentially exploitable threat which network and systems' administrators need to be aware of.

Computer network security and privacy has a lot of attention, it is currently of very high importance-various detection algorithms or protection mechanisms are implemented on various network layers, network devices and in operating systems (a good example is the widespread use of VPN networks [1] and aims to enhance security in mobile networks [12]). Despite of all mentioned facts, the very important issue remains in information about currently ongoing attack which administrators need to have as soon as possible to take an action. Development of new effective solutions to detect and provide such information is thus open case [3, 4].

Among the most common DoS attacks there are flooding attacks which exploit holes in used network protocols [5]. In our work we focus on proposal of modification

© IFIP International Federation for Information Processing 2015
I. Khalil et al. (Eds.): ICT-EurAsia 2015 and CONFENIS 2015, LNCS 9357, pp. 30–39, 2015.
DOI: 10.1007/978-3-319-24315-3_4

of SYN flood attack detection mechanism and its implementation into KaTaLyzer. KaTaLyzer is a network traffic monitoring tool developed at STUBA [6].

Based on existing Counting Bloom Filter (CBF) mechanism, our main contribution described in this paper is modification of method utilizing CBF for attack detection. With the aim of lower memory requirements we use modified CBF structure (one vector) for storing counters of half-open TCP connections [8]. Along the possibility to detect SYN flood attack, our method allows to distinguish the type of the attack. More information about DoS SYN flood attack can be found e.g. in [7, 9].

After detection of ongoing SYN flood attack, network administrator is notified. TCP SYN flood attacks can be distinguished into:

- Random – spoofed source IP address for each packet is generated randomly
- Subnet – spoofed source IP address is for each packet generated from specific subnet range
- Fixed– several chosen IP addresses are used.

Section 2 of this paper describes Bloom filter data structure for storing data and its modifications. In Sect. 3 description of CBF modification is presented while in Sect. 4 new S-Orthros algorithm is given. Section 5 with evaluation of proposed method is followed by discussion and paper conclusion.

2 Bloom Filter and Its Modification

In the early 70's of the 20th century, H. Burton Bloom [10] introduced new hash-coding methods, which have become the cradle of a new approach to storing data into a data structure, later called the Bloom filter. His efficient structure provides a way to reduce space required for storing data, at the cost of false-positive members. As described in [11], Bloom Filter data structure is widely used in today's internet, viruses, worms and network intruders which cause service damages with enormous economic impact. In our approach it will be modified and used for storing data about attacking IP addresses.

2.1 Bloom Filter Algorithm

Mathematics behind the Bloom Filter data structure is following:
consider a set of m elements, in our case a set of m IP addresses

$$IP = \{ip_1;\ ip_2;\ ip_3;\ \ldots ip_m\}$$

The set will be after application of Bloom filter described by vector V which is n bits long, it is initially set to n zeros:

$$V = (v_1,\ v_2, \ldots v_n) = (0, 0, \ldots 0)$$

Consider k independent hash functions which are used by the Bloom filter to generate k hash values from each element from the IP set

$$K_i = h_i\left(ip_j\right), 1 \leq i \leq k, 1 \leq j \leq m$$

The hash functions output values are integers $K_i \in \{1, \ldots, n\}$ and represent index in the vector V. If x-th hash function h_x, $1 \leq x \leq k$, applied to one member of set IP, $ip_j \in IP$, $1 \leq j \leq m$ results in value K_x, i.e. $K_x = h_x(ip_j)$, K-th bit of the V vector is set to 1

$$V = \left(v_1, v_2, \ldots v_k, \ldots v_n\right) = \left(v_1, v_2, \ldots 1, \ldots v_n\right)$$

For each element $ip_i \in IP$, $1 \leq i \leq k$, K-th bit of V vector is set to 1, while $K = h_i(ip_j)$, for each $1 \leq j \leq m$, $1 \leq i \leq k$. This way k hash functions applied to m members of IP set change k bits in vector V (true, if the K index is always different). If two or more hash functions result in the same index K, the bit in vector V is not changed more than once, it is set to 1 once.

To find out whether an IP address H was not a member of set IP, the hash functions are applied to it and appropriate bits in vector V are checked. If even one of these bits is set to 0, H was not a member of IP set. Due to overlapping possibility of setting bits by hash functions to 1, Bloom filter does not provide reverse information, i.e. whether the H was a member of IP set.

According to relations among the hash functions and overlapping of their results, bits in V vector can be set to 1 multiple times. However, only the first setting of the bit to 1 changes the value of the bit.

2.2   Counting Bloom Filter

Assume a situation in which the elements of IP set change periodically and thus they are being inserted to and deleted from the data structure. Inserting elements is a simple process which has been described above. However, during deletion of an element from Bloom Filter data structure, we need to set the corresponding bits to zero. It is possible that this operation will affect bits which were set to 1 by hash function also for different element of the IP set. In this situation the Bloom filter no longer provides correct representation of the elements of the IP set. This problem has been solved in [2] which outlined new data structure called Counting Bloom Filter (CBF). In this structure, bits in vector V are replaced by long integers which are used as counters and each hash function has its own vector of these counters. If we want to save a track of element ip_x in the data structure, each counter corresponding value of independent hash functions will be incremented. During deletion of an element appropriate counters are decremented.

2.3   Independent Hash Functions

Finding well designed set of hash functions is important for the correct storage and distribution of elements in the CBF data structure.Performance of the hash functions is also important. In a comparative study performed by Chen and Yeung in [13], there are independent hash functions designed which have low probability of collisions. 32-bit IP address is used as a key for the hash functions.

The hash functions are defined as follows:

$$h_i(IP) = (IP + IP \bmod p_i) \bmod n, 1 \leq i \leq k$$

where mod denotes the modulus operation, n is the row length of the hash table, and p_i is a prime number less than n.

Following table from work of Chen and Yeung shows comparison of the proposed hash function with other known hash functions [13] (Table 1).

In our work our examination resulted in setting variables of the above mentioned function as follows: n = 1024, k = 4

Table 1. Tested hash functions [13]

Hash function	Consumed time (s)	Number of collisions
Our function	0.187	0
Robert's 32-bit function	0.188	3838
Robert's 96-bit function	0.250	0
Cruth's function	0.031	977
Hybrid function	0.328	0

3   New Proposal of Modified CBF (MCBF)

The biggest disadvantages of CBF data structure compared to Bloom Filter are:

- more memory space is needed to store data: consider k independent hash functions which require one row (vector) of counters per function. In this case $k = r$, where r is number of needed rows of counters. Next, consider n as number of counters in a row. The complexity of the space needed for stored elements in the data structure CBF can be expressed as $n*r$.
- possible overflow of counters may pose a risk especially with increased savings of elements.

Simplification of the CBF data structure is one of our contributions in this paper. Compared to CBF, we propose to use only 1 vector of counters (as in BF) where independent hash functions increment values while saving an IP address from which half-open TCP connection is initiated (SYN packet is received). The counters are decremented when a connection is fully opened from the IP address (ACK is received) (Fig. 1).

As in our attack detection approach the data structure is cleared periodically after defined time interval (see following chapter), one vector of long integer counters is sufficient for storing IP addresses of half-open connections by incrementing and decrementing the counters. It is designed to fit the proposed solutions to detect SYN flood attack and these will be described in later section describing S-Orthros detection algorithm.

4 Detection Module S-Orthros

Our method for detecting SYN Flood attack uses MCBF data structure. Modification of the CBF data structure resulted into simplification and clarification of the solution and also the method itself. The intention is therefore the evaluation of the conditions and thus attack detection and evaluation in a given constant time interval.

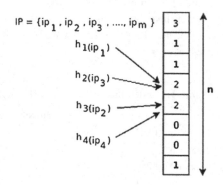

Fig. 1. Storing data in MBCF data structure using 4 hash functions and counters

4.1 S-Orthros in Nutshell

Consider the case where the detection algorithm cooperates with a measuring tool which is used to capture and analyse network traffic in real time. At the beginning, continuous process of capturing network traffic statistical data is started and runs as continuous process.

After a defined time interval (set by administrator, usually 1 min), process analysing captured network traffic data is started. In this process, also data important for S-Orthros detection algorithm are saved - source and destination IP addresses of SYN and ACK packets. These IP addresses are saved using chosen hash functions to the MCBF structure. It consists of two tables containing n long integer counters (2*1024*4B).

The first table is used to store source IP addresses, the second table stores destination IP addresses. During the analysis, the detection algorithm S-Orthros collects information about initiated connections (i.e. SYN packets) and confirmations of the connections (i.e. ACK packets). If the analysis detects a SYN packet, the MCBF data structures are incremented counters in both tables are incremented according to results of hash functions applied to IP addresses. In case of receipt of ACK confirming previous SYN packet, counters in data structures in both tables are decremented. If there is no flood attack, the TCP handshakes are correct (i.e. number of SYN and ACK packets are the same) and data structures remain empty.

In case of a flood attack, values in MCBF structure are rising fast. Threshold of acceptable half-open connections has been according to experiences (e.g. settings of CISCO routers [19] or different operating systems) set to 50. Attack detection process checks the number of half-open connections against the threshold and alerts administrator.

The data stored in the MCBF can be analysed and distribution of values can show type of SYN flood attack - fixed, random, subnet (see following chapter).

5 Evaluation

For theoretical evaluation of our type of attack-distinguishing approach, we implemented the algorithm in spreadsheet table processor Microsoft Excel. Regarding the practical method, we used generated SYN flood DoS attacks which were detected by our new SYN flood attack-detection module implemented in KaTaLyzer. Detected attacks have proven correctness and functionality of the implemented detection algorithm.

5.1 Theoretical Evaluation

Using MCBF we are able to simulate different variations of SYN flood attacks. We have simulated 3 types Random SYN flood, Subnet SYN flood, Fixed SYN flood.

To obtain input data for simulations in Excel, it is necessary to define (in case of Fixed attack) and generate (in case of Random and Subnet attacks) IP addresses from which the hash functions calculate their values. These values are stored in the MCBF data structure.

For our simulations, an IP address is represented by numeric representation of 32 bit number. For instance, well-known address 192.168.0.1 has been calculated as follows:

$$1 * 256^0 + 0 * 256^1 + 168 * 256^2 + 192 * 256^3 = 3232235521$$

For Random and Subnet SYN flood attacks we have generated 250 000 IP addresses in Excel (they represent number of half-open connections). We chose following ranges for particular attacks:

- Random – *RANDBETWEEN(1; 4294967295)* – covers whole range of IPs
- Subnet – *RANDBETWEEN(3232235776; 3232236031)* - covers IP addresses from 192.168.1.0 to 192.168.1.255

Both of these attacks can be distinguished thanks to the typical arrangement of IP addresses stored in the used data structure. This arrangement of IP addresses has been verified on sample of 250.000 IP addresses with proposed hash functions, which are for Excel defined as follows:

$$MOD((D1 + MOD(D1;307));1024),$$

where D1 represent cell containing IP address, 307 is prime number and 1024 is length of vector.

The results of simulations are shown below in Figs. 2 and 3. As we can observe, numbers of half-open connections in MCBF during simulated Random attack have equal distribution – small amounts of half-open connections are measured for each IP address. On the other hand, Fixed attack is typical with high numbers of half-open connections for specific IP addresses. For Subnet attack it is typical that chosen range of IP addresses have relatively high amount of half-open connections.

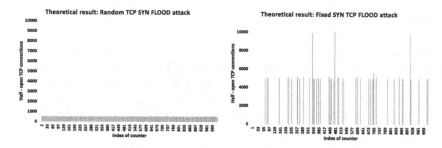

Fig. 2. Theoretical results - Random and Fixed TCP SYN Flood attacks

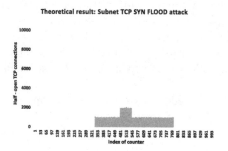

Fig. 3. Theoretical results - Subnet TCP SYN Flood attack

5.2   Practical Evaluation

There are number of tools for generating DoS attacks. Project Neptune is used to generate SYN Flood attack, it can continuously send TCP SYN packets at a rate 248 SYN packets per second [14]. For our purposes we tested hping3 tool [15] sending TCP SYN packets on port 443 to target host and sending TCP SYN packets with the ACK flag set to target host. We also used Letdown tool [16] and Ev1syn [17].

To verify the basic functionality of our proposed and into KaTaLyzer implemented detection method, a TCP SYN Flood attack has been executed using Ev1syn. As expected, S-Orthros module was able to correctly detect even weak SYN Flood attack (121 half-open connections).

Fixed Attack Identification. Fixed TCP SYN flood attack was generated from 4 IP addresses. They can be identified in the graph shown in Fig. 4 as 4 tipping points. S-Orthros module stored information about each IP address in the data structure of MCBF 4 times with 4 independent hash functions.

As expected, attack generated on real network had similar characteristics as the theoretical run of the attack – compare Figs. 2 and 4. Minor measured variations are caused by a variety of regular communications which were captured together with the attack on the server – monitored network is connected to regular network.

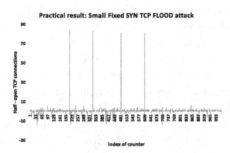

Fig. 4. Practical results – Fixed TCP SYN flood attack

Random Attack Identification. In the next step we evaluated detection of Random SYN Flood attack. The test also evaluated stability of the implemented module, as well as the stability of the measurement tool KaTaLyzer during high load. All tools used for attack generation randomly generated the source IP address for each packet, the destination IP address was the address of measuring server.

For more detailed comparison of theoretical and practical approaches we closely investigated theoretical and measured attacks (see Fig. 5). It is necessary to take into account that the algorithm used to generate random IP addresses in Excel and the algorithm used to generate random spoofed IP addresses implemented in the attack generator give us different but similar input data. Nonetheless, a way of storing data in the MCBF data structure should be retained and therefore the results from both graphs in Fig. 5 show uniformly stored data.

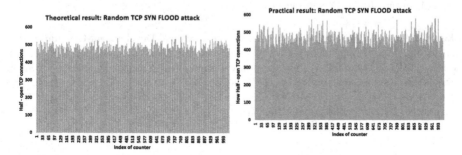

Fig. 5. Detailed Random TCP SYN flood attack - theoretical and practical results

6 Discussion

Security and protection against DoS attacks can be addressed at different levels. It is even possible to avoid such threats in operating system by simple firewall settings [18].

Nevertheless, we can still find unsecured systems and security holes through which the attack can be successfully performed. Network traffic measuring tool KaTaLyzer, which runs 24/7, allows not only to analyze and to save the network traffic statistical data. Thanks to the new implemented attack detection module it provides an additional level of network protection. Obtained results show us, that network administrator obtains almost immediate notification about ongoing SYN flood attack, thanks to which he can take the necessary steps to mitigate or eliminate the ongoing attack. The type of attack can be also distinguished.

Correctness, completeness and functionality of the proposed detection algorithms are confirmed by the results obtained by practical methods and theoretical methods described in this paper. Comparison of theoretical and practical results show similar statistical characteristics of generated attacks. We generated TCP SYN flood attack for several hours so that we not only verify the stability of the implemented module, but also the entire measuring tool KaTaLyzer in which the module was added.

7 Conclusion

We proposed fast and memory-effective method for SYN Flood DoS attack detection and type identification. It is based on modification of Counting Bloom Filter, multiple vectors of counters are replaced by one vector. Appropriate counter in the vector is incremented by new half-open TCP connection and decremented by successful TCP connection establishment. Large number of half-open TCP connections evokes SYN flood attack in progress. Without an attack, the counters remain empty.

Through modified Counting Bloom Filter, we are able to distinguish three main TCP SYN flood attacks (random, fixed, subnet) which may significantly help the network administrator to mitigate or avert the ongoing attack.

The new method has been implemented into new S-Orthros module for network monitoring tool KaTaLyzer. After detection and identification of SYN Flood DoS attack, the module informs network administrator.

Detection method has been verified by theoretical and practical methods for random, subnet and fixed SYN flood DoS attack.

Acknowledgement. This work is a result of the Research and Development Operational Program for the projects Support of Center of Excellence for Smart Technologies, Systems and Services, ITMS 26240120005 and for the projects Support of Center of Excellence for Smart Technologies, Systems and Services II, ITMS 26240120029, co-funded by ERDF. It is also a part of APVV-0258-12, VEGA 1/0708/13 and KEGA 047STU-4/2013. It is also part of Katalyzer project katalyzer.sk and initiative ngnlab.eu.

References

1. Kotuliak, I., Rybár, P., Trúchly, P.: Performance comparison of IPsec and TLS based VPN technologies. In: ICETA 2011: 9th IEEE International Conference on Emerging eLearning Technologies and Applications, October 27–28, 2011, Stará Lesná, The High Tatras, Slovakia, pp. 217–221. IEEE, Piscataway (2011). ISBN 978-1-4577-0050-7
2. Fan, L., et al.: Summary cache: A scalable wide-area web cache sharing protocol. IEEE/ACM Trans. Netw. **8**(3), 281–293 (2000)
3. Kambhampati, V. et al.: A taxonomy of capabilities based DDoS defense architectures. In: 9th IEEE/ACS International Conference on Computer Systems and Applications (AICCSA), pp. 157–164 (2011)
4. Rejimol Robinson, R.R, Thomas, C.: Evaluation of mitigation methods for distributed denial of service attacks. In: 7th IEEE Conference on Industrial Electronics and Applications (ICIEA), pp. 713–718 (2012)
5. Habib, A., Roy, D.: Steps to defend against DoS attacks. In: 12th International Conference on Computers and Information Technology, ICCIT 2009, pp. 614–619 (2009)
6. Network monitoring tool Katalyzer. http://www.katalyzer.sk/
7. CERT Advisory CA-1996-21 TCP SYN Flooding and IP Spoofing Attacks, September 1996. http://www.cert.org/advisories/CA-1996-21.html
8. IETF RFC 793.: Transmission control protocol, September 1981. http://www.ietf.org/rfc/rfc793.txt
9. CERT Advisory CA-1996-21 TCP SYN Flooding and IP Spoofing Attacks [CA-96.21] CERT, September 1996. http://www.cert.org/advisories/CA-1996-21.html
10. Bloom, Burton H.: Space/Time trade-offs in hash coding with allowable errors. Commun. ACM **13**(7), 422–426 (1970)
11. Tabataba, F.S., Hashemi, M.R.: Improving false positive in Bloom filter. In: 19th Iranian Conference on Electrical Engineering (ICEE), p. 1. IEEE (2011)
12. Nagy, M., Kotuliak, I.: Enhancing security in mobile data networks through end user and core network cooperation. In: MoMM 2013: The 11th International Conference on Advances in Mobile Computing and Multimedia, Vienna, Austria, pp. 253–259. ACM, New York (2013). ISBN: 978-1-4503-2106-8
13. Yeung, D., Chen, W.: Throttling spoofed syn flooding traffic at the source. Telecommunication Systems **33**(3), 47–65 (2006)
14. Cardinal, S.: Use offense to inform defense. Find flaws before the bad guys do. SANS Institute 2000 – 2012, 31 August 2014. http://pen-testing.sans.org/resources/papers/gcih/neptunec-birth-syn-flood-attacks-102303
15. Hping – Active Network Security Tool, 31 August 2014. http://www.hping.org/
16. Acri, E.: Complemento Howto (2011). http://complemento.sourceforge.net/howto/
17. Ev1Syn - A SYN Flood with Random Spoofed Source Address. http://gopherproxy.meulie.net/sdf.org/0/users/wisdomc0/code_c/ev1syn.c. Accessed 31 August 2014
18. Brouer, J.: Mitigate TCP SYN Flood Attacks with Red Hat Enterprise Linux 7 Beta, 11 April 2014. http://rhelblog.redhat.com/2014/04/11/mitigate-tcp-syn-flood-attacks-with-red-hat-enterprise-linux-7-beta/
19. Davis, P.T.: Securing and Controling CISCO Routers. CRC Press, Boca Raton (2002)

Integrating Mobile OpenFlow Based Network Architecture with Legacy Infrastructure

Martin Nagy[✉], Ivan Kotuliak, Jan Skalny, Martin Kalcok,
and Tibor Hirjak

Faculty of Informatics and Information Technologies,
Slovak University of Technology in Bratislava, Bratislava, Slovakia
{martinko.nagy,hirjak.tibor}@gmail.com,
ivan.kotuliak@stuba.sk, jan@skalny.sk

Abstract. UnifyCore is a concept of SDN centric, OpenFlow based and access agnostic network architecture, which changes the way networks are being built today. It is designed in a way, so present access technologies can be easily integrated in it. It provides set of architectural components and rules, which help to easily decouple components of the access technology and put their functionalities into UnifyCore building blocks. This simplifies the overall network architecture and allows the use of common transport core for all access technologies. First proof of concept built on UnifyCore is the GPRS network, which is a challenge for SDN, since it does not have split user and control plane transport. In this paper we introduce and explain features that allow fully SDN UnifyCore to be integrated with existing legacy network infrastructure (switches/routers).

Keywords: 3GPP networks · GPRS · SDN · Software defined networking · NFV · Network functions virtualization · OpenFlow · Signaling and user data separation · Wireless networks · Cellular networks · PCU-ng · PCUng · ePCU · vGSN · ReST · MAC tunneling · Ethernet tunneling · ICMP topology discovery · ARP APN search

1 Introduction

One of the drivers behind software defined networking (SDN) trend was the inflexibility of existing networking approaches and industry that limited the space for innovation. On the other hand, researchers also struggled with black box networking approaches and architectures, which limited the experimental capabilities of existing network equipment. Since then, SDN spread through wired networks and it is making its way, together with network functions virtualization (NFV), to the network operator world, where most of the industry struggles with network equipment, which is often hard to integrate with existing infrastructure that does not provide open interfaces, so complicated work arounds need to be done.

In UnifyCore architecture we are trying to address the heterogeneity and inflexibility of the network infrastructure, which causes complicated network management, control, new service deployment and orchestration. This is the case mainly with large

I. Khalil et al. (Eds.): ICT-EurAsia 2015 and CONFENIS 2015, LNCS 9357, pp. 40–49, 2015.
DOI: 10.1007/978-3-319-24315-3_5

network operators, who provide services over multiple technologies such as multiple wireless technologies (GPRS/UMTS/LTE), xDSL and optical at the same time. Customers naturally expect same look and feel of the service regardless of the technology being used. With standard networking approaches, this hard and often expensive to reach.

Our UnifyCore approach offers joint control by using open APIs on the central SDN controller and access network control elements (access managers). By using this approach, network operators can easily orchestrate and have better control of the network.

The paper is structured as follows. First two sections give an overview of the foundation of mobile networks and SDN. Next, state of the art in the area of mobile software defined networks is briefly introduced. Rest of the paper focuses on the UnifyCore architecture and its features. Last section concludes the paper.

2 Mobile Networks Basics

As general packet radio service (GPRS) was the first network technology we integrated into UnifyCore, we will first introduce some essential concepts of this network. In this paper we focus only on the packet switched part of the network, therefore we won't explain procedures and nodes of the circuit switched part of the network.

GPRS network consists of the radio access network (RAN) and the core network (CN). In RAN, base transceiver station (BTS) and base station controller (BSC) are located. BTS is a device which handles the radio interface. It is responsible for modulation/demodulation, error checking and correction and communicates with BSC on one side and mobile station (MS) on the other side. In BSC, all logic of the radio access network is located. Multiple BTSs are controller by a single BSC. BSC connects the RAN to the core network, more precisely to the serving GPRS support node (SGSN). This node is responsible for mobility management, session management, authentication and ciphering in the GPRS network. Further to the core network, SGSN connects to the gateway GPRS support node (GGSN). As the name implies, this node is a gateway from the mobile network to the external networks such as Internet or corporate intranet/VPN.

A basic call flow in mobile network includes two main procedures. Fist attach procedure is executed. During this procedure the mobile station is authenticated and gets connected to the network. At this point, mobile station does not have any IP connectivity. Circuit switched calls and SMSs are available (attach both to circuit switched and packet switched part of the network is assumed). In order to communicate for example with the Internet, second procedure called PDP context activation has to be executed. In this procedure, the mobile station specifies the service, which is requested by filling up the access point name information element (APN). If the procedure succeeds, the network assigns an IP address to the mobile station and transfer of the data across the network is possible.

Further details about GPRS and other mobile networks such as universal mobile telecommunications system (UMTS) and long term evolution (LTE) technologies can be found in respective 3GPP standards or books [1–3].

3 Software Defined Networking

As mentioned before, the key driver behind SDN was situation in network industry, that mainly used black boxes from different vendors, which provided only CLI or SNMP for management and integration, and there was no standard APIs providing full control over the network appliance. This situation made integration of network infrastructure of different vendors very difficult and expensive. Such integration complicated network automation and integration processes. It also led to a vendor lock-ins in some cases. From the research point of view, black boxes provide little to no space for experiments, so SDN was introduce to challenge these limitations.

SDN brings separation of user and control plane of the network appliance. By doing this, each plane can evolve separately and can be optimized for its needs. Moreover as these two functions formerly residing in the same box are split by SDN, need for a communication protocol or API between these two planes was evident. Most successful SDN approach is probably the OpenFlow protocol.

3.1 OpenFlow

OpenFlow, as the name induces, builds on the idea of network flows. A flow in the network is specified by n-tuple of protocol header fields. Different set of protocol headers and header fields are supported in each version of the protocol. OpenFlow network is composed of OpenFlow controller which communicates with OpenFlow switches or forwarders in other words.

Forwarder is composed by set of flow tables, where flow entries can be written and by which packets are processed. In each flow entry, selected protocol header fields – match fields are specified, and set of actions to be performed after match are associated with it. Flow entries are installed by the SDN controller at any time. When a packet is received by the OpenFlow forwarder, its header fields are compared against flow entries and in case of match actions and instruction are executed. This way, any new networking approach is dependent only at the logic in the controller, since the OpenFlow protocol and OpenFlow switch capabilities are standardized and at atomic level (network flow) [4].

There are many more SDN related approaches, both academic – I2RS [5], ForCES [6], PCEP [7] and vendor specific – OnePK [8], but these have little relevance to our work, moreover OpenFlow is the leader on the market and the academia.

4 Related Work

Most of the present work focusing on mobile SDN is addressing different kinds of mobile gateway nodes decomposition or network functions placement [9, 10]. Then there are approaches, which address network architectures in general and bring new use cases and functionalities, which are enabled by OpenFlow [11]. Some of telco vendors address mobile SDN with their specific approaches such OpenFlow's mobile counterpart MobileFlow [12] or extend standard OpenFlow protocol with mobile specific features [13]. Third part of the SDN mobile related research is the SDN based/controlled RAN [14, 15].

The vast majority of the papers focus on the same technology – LTE. However GPRS, on which the UnifyCore demo is based, is the dominant technology for the M2M services, thanks to its maturity and simple radio interface that enables low terminal price that is crucial for massive M2M deployment. Finally, GPRS is expected to continue to provide such services and an umbrella fallback network for next one or two decades.

5   UnifyCore – Novel Core Network Architecture

UnifyCore architecture was developed with backwards compatibility and SDN focus in mind. It is aimed to provide mobile services and features of packet core (GPRS/UMTS/LTE), but can be also used as a transport core platform for aggregation of traffic from different access technologies and provide umbrella control and automation platform.

In UnifyCore architecture, the access technology specific protocols are terminated as close to the border between access network and core network as possible. The idea behind this is to use a common transport core, which is not complicated by various access technologies. Different access technologies such as GPRS, UMTS and LTE or WiFi are controlled by dedicated control elements called access managers. These nodes understand the signaling protocols used by the access network and terminals and provide necessary operations such as mobility/session management and signaling. As we mentioned before, common transport core is independent of access technologies connected to it, thus is controlled by a logically separate element – SDN controller. Core control SDN controller and access managers communicate via ReSTful API.

Traffic in the different access networks is usually encapsulated to various access specific protocols, moreover some technologies combine control and user data in a single stream of messages (for example GPRS, as shown later in the evaluation part). For separation of user and control plane data, UnifyCore uses OpenFlow enabled border forwarders called adaptors. Some of the access network protocols are not compatible with present OpenFlow match rules, so we use OpenFlow extensions to support such protocols. These extensions have to be supported on both access managers and border forwarders (adaptors), however they do not have to be supported in core, as it is access agnostic and based just on Ethernet tunneling [16]. This further emphasized the aim for simple common core.

From the mobile networks architecture, UnifyCore borrows the APN concept. As mentioned in the second section, in 3GPP mobile network, the APN is associated with GGSN (P-GW in LTE) interface and signifies a service offered at that point. We use the concept of APN, but as we do not have a GGSN or P-GW in our architecture, our APNs may be located at any border forwarder Fig. 1.

Further details on the philosophy and architecture can be found in previous paper on the topic [16]. In this paper, we focus on the backwards compatibility enablers of the UnifyCore – mainly ICMP topology discovery and ARP APN search.

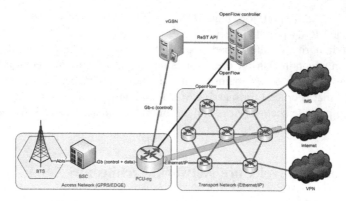

Fig. 1. High level UnifyCore architecture

5.1 ICMP Topology Discovery

In order to setup a MAC (Ethernet) tunnel, few procedures have to be executed. These procedures include ICMP topology discovery (executed when a new OpenFlow forwarder joins UnifyCore topology) and ARP discovery for localization of traffic egress and ingress points (APNs). For the topology discovery UnifyCore uses its own topology discovery method based on the ICMP protocol.

Process works in two phases. First phase includes bootstrap of OpenFlow enabled forwarders. When a forwarder joins UnifyCore controller, it is asked to clear its whole configuration. Next a new OpenFlow rule is installed to first flow table (Table 0 in our case). This rule forwards all ICMP echo requests with given destination IP to the controller. Together with this topology discovery flow rule, a rule for ARP discovery is installed as well (explained in separate section of the paper). If this new node is an adaptor type, extra rules are installed. These rules ensure adaptation of access network user traffic for core network and routing of control plane messages to the access network manager.

Second phase is the topology discovery itself and starts when controller constructs ICMP echo request with encoded source forwarder ID (datapath ID) and source port ID in the payload of ICMP message and injects them to all ports of newly joined forwarder. As these packets reach the adjacent forwarders (these forwarders joined network before), they are matched with the ICMP discovery rule and are forwarded back to the controller. Controller examines the message that has been just forwarded to it and extracts the source forwarder ID and source port from the OpenFlow header and originator forwarder ID and port from the ICMP payload. From this information, controller is able to construct a view of topology.

ICMP topology discovery method, same as MAC tunneling, is compatible with standard featureless L2 switches. If a L2 switch (or group of switches) connects two forwarders, incoming ICMP echo will be flooded to all ports of the switch and finally will reach some adjacent OpenFlow forwarder, which will send the ICMP echo to the controller. Controller will examine the content of the OpenFlow header and payload and update the topology accordingly. In this case, the L2 switch connecting two

OpenFlow forwarders is considered to be a direct link between the sending and receiving forwarder. However this L2 switch does not break the UnifyCore concept and capabilities in any way. If there are more interconnected switches between two forwarders, the ICMP echo may be received by the controller multiple times and multiple connections may be discovered (Fig. 2).

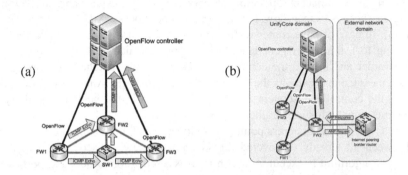

Fig. 2. ICMP topology discovery (a) and ARP search (b).

5.2 ARP Search – Ingress and Egress Point (APN) Discovery

As mentioned before, the APN represents the ingress and egress point of the UnifyCore domain.

At the very start, UnifyCore controller looks at its configuration file and finds all the APNs (ingress and egress points) it is serving. Each APN name from the configuration file gets resolved by the DNS lookups to an IP address. Next, when a forwarder joins the network, together with ICMP topology discovery ARP search process is executed at this forwarder.

The process has several phases. It starts with the deletion of the whole flow table configuration (as mentioned earlier). This first step is common for ARP search and ICMP topology discovery. Next, rules for ARP search are installed on this new forwarder (together with ICMP discovery rules as mentioned before). First flow rule installed is the redirection of all ARP replies to the controller. At this rule we match Ethernet type 806 and ARP operation 2. Action for this flow rule is to forward ARP replies to controller, where it could be further processed. It has to be noted, that from the definition, OpenFlow forwarders do not feature ARP logic, therefore ARP message processing has to be done in the controller (or non-standard OpenFlow extensions have to be used).

Next, the controller sends an ARP request from each port of the forwarder. For each APN in the database (from the configuration file) controller sends one ARP request per forwarder port (target IP address of the APN). Following this approach, we expect, that at the APN location (adjacent network domain) there is a non-SDN capable edge router, thus we use a standard "legacy" ARP procedure. If a SDN capable domain was behind the UnifyCore domain, we could have used some SDN inter-domain signaling. This approach further improves UnifyCore compatibility with existing legacy networks.

It has to be noted, that since ARP is a LAN protocol, the source IP address has to be from the same subnet, as is the APN. Moreover different APNs can have and normally they have different IP addresses from different subnets, therefore controller choses addresses from these domains.

When these ARP request are sent out through all ports of newly added forwarder, they are captured and processed by the adjacent forwarders or an edge router serving the APN. In case of adjacent OpenFlow forwarder nothing happens and no ARP reply is generated (because OpenFlow forwarders do not process ARP the way standard routers do). In case of edge router with given IP address (serving the APN controller was looking for), the router generates ARP response, which will be received by the given forwarder and sent to the controller (ARP reply rule matched). Controller processes the message and extracts the forwarder ID and port ID from OpenFlow header. This way, the controller discovers APNs, their location in the network topology and can construct tunnels for user traffic transport (Fig. 2).

When a new ingress or egress point (APN) location is found, controller starts tunnel setup between all already discovered APNs and this newly discovered one. First a shortest path algorithm is executed, which returns a set of forwarders and ports which should be used along the way from one APN to another. If an ingress point is an adaptor, first flow table is left for the traffic adaptation rules, which are set on a user basis. Rules in this table will strip off the access specific headers and forward packets to second table, which is the MAC tunnel table. Here the destination MAC address of the Ethernet frame is set and the frame itself is forwarded to tunnel by assigned interface. Next forwarders along the way perform very similar task. They match the destination MAC address and forward the frame to respective port (given by the OpenFlow rule). The very last forwarder in the way may change the destination MAC address to match the MAC address of the egress point (APN). This is the case only when more MAC tunnels are established to the same egress point (APN), for example for different QoS classes or tunnels from different source. In case of single tunnel towards this given APN, destination MAC address corresponds to the MAC address of the router in the adjacent domain.

In the opposite direction (downlink), border router serving given APN in the adjacent domain could search for MAC address of an IP address present in the access network. As mentioned before, forwarders do not have the capability to respond to ARP request, so this is forwarded to the controller by an OpenFlow rule. Controller responds with the MAC address of the tunnel belonging to given end device in the access network. After receiving the requested MAC address, the edge router sends packet to the edge forwarder. This forwarder examines the destination MAC address and forwards it to a given port, specified by the OpenFlow rule. Next forwarders in the way to the access network forward the Ethernet frame in a similar manner. The access edge forwarder (adaptor) finally appends the access specific protocol headers, and in case there are more tunnels towards this endpoint, sets the destination MAC address to the MAC address of the first network node in the access network.

It has to be noted, that uplink and downlink tunnels have different tunnel IDs (MAC addresses), and so traffic can be routed in an asymmetrical manner.

Presence of tunnels even before any need for data transfer further enhances the session setup time. In comparison with for example GPRS or UMTS, where the tunnels are created in a dynamic manner based on mobile station requests. Tunnel setup by exchange of signaling messages between SGSN and GGSN takes naturally more time, than proactive tunnel setup at UnifyCore start.

6 Evaluation

For our initial UnifyCore proof of concept, we chose a rather specific use case – GPRS over UnifyCore. As mentioned before, most of the mobile oriented SDN research papers deal with LTE or UMTS. However, both technologies share the split user plane and control plane approach, thus introduction of SDN to such system is rather trivial.

Our work focuses on GPRS, which is basically the oldest packet based 3GPP network. Despite its age, it is still being heavily used around the globe. Moreover development on this technology continues and for example release 13 GPRS/EDGE terminals and networks bring further enhancements for the M2M use cases [17]. This indicates that even now, GPRS is highly relevant network technology and integration of GPRS and SDN is an interesting topic.

We implemented the UnifyCore GPRS architecture in the following way. We removed SGSN and GGSN from the architecture and split their logic between SDN controller and GPRS access manager called vGSN (virtual GPRS Support Node). Session management (tunnel management) functions are centralized in the SDN controller and GPRS signaling (mobility management, signaling and authentication) is performed on the vGSN. This function split is following the UnifyCore concept introduced in one of previous paper [16]. In user plane we use a GPRS adaptor (GPRS enabled OpenFlow forwarder), which first splits GPRS message stream into user plane data and signaling messages. Next the signaling is sent to vGSN and user plane data is adapted to pure Ethernet (MAC tunneling). In the downlink direction, the GPRS adaptor encapsulates the pure Ethernet data into GPRS protocols and sends it to GPRS radio access network (Fig. 3). We named the GPRS adaptor ePCU or PCU-ng. This stands for enhanced PCU or PCU for next generation networks.

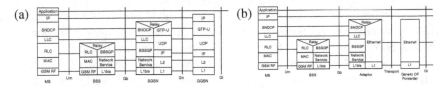

Fig. 3. GPRS protocol stacks (user plane) in standard 3GPP architecture [1] (a) and in UnifyCore based architecture (b).

For the evaluation, we implemented the whole solution over the open-source software. As a controller base, Ryu controller framework was used. In the controller, OpenFlow extensions were added, in order to enable controller to command the ePCU (GPRS protocol stack extensions). As a forwarder, ofsoftswitch13 was chosen. GPRS protocol stack extensions were implemented here as well. The GPRS access manager module is based on open-source code from a hacker community, which is focusing on security holes in mobile networks – osmocom. Snippets of source code of two projects – osmo-sgsn and openGGSN were combined in order to build our vGSN. In the GPRS access network sysmoBTS hardware was used. This base station is compatible with osmo-sgsn and compliant to standard 3GPP Gb interface signaling.

The setup was verified using off-the-shelf mobile phones of different types – from smart phones to feature phones. During tests, terminals were not aware of any changes in the core network, which was basically one of our most important goals and GPRS data transfer was functional in both directions.

7 Conclusion

The transformation from classical network architectures to SDN based is inevitable. However, very similar to IPv4 to IPv6 transition, for a certain time, classical networks and SDN networks will coexist. First in the form of SDN islands inside classical network sea, next the situation will be just the opposite. Finally, SDN will become the dominant networking technology.

For this transition period, UnifyCore features set of approaches such as ICMP discovery and ARP search, which enable it to integrate with standard router/switch based transport architecture. These methods not only allow UnifyCore to communicate with existing adjacent infrastructure, but also allow operators to protect past investments in the existing hardware with which is UnifyCore fully compatible.

Both ARP APN discovery and ICMP topology discovery mechanisms might seem redundant, but it has to be noted, that pure OpenFlow forwarders do not support standard features of switches or routers such as ARP message processing or Ethernet broadcast forwarding/flooding. Processing of such messages has to be set by the controller by OpenFlow match rules, actions and instructions.

From the 3GPP mobile network point of view, the UnifyCore easily integrates with standard 3GPP networks – end to end by Gb and Gi interfaces. Our prototype proves that even complicated Gb interface (without user data and signaling separation) is easy to integrate into UnifyCore with a flexible SDN approach.

At the time being we are starting with performance evaluation of the key features of the GPRS prototype. As mentioned before, functional validation was already done with real mobile phones, however such setup was unable to generate traffic load.

Performance of MAC tunneling implemented over user space forwarder application (ofsoftswitch13) is being evaluated using common iPerf2 and iPerf3 tools. For the GPRS related parts (signaling and user data separation, GPRS encapsulation/ decapsulation) we are not aware of any free open-source performance measurement tools. Therefore, commercial tools such as Spirent LandSlide [18] or Ixia EPC test [19] need to be used, or new tool for such evaluation has to be implemented from scratch.

Acknowledgments. This work is a result of the Research and Development Operational Program for the projects Support of Center of Excellence for Smart Technologies, Systems and Services, ITMS 26240120005 and for the projects Support of Center of Excellence for Smart Technologies, Systems and Services II, ITMS 26240120029, co-funded by ERDF.

References

1. 3GPP: 23.060 rel. 13.1.0 – General Packet Radio Service (GPRS); Service description; Stage 2 (2014)
2. 3GPP: 23.002 rel 13.1.0 – Network architecture (2014)
3. Ahtiainen, A., Kaaranen, H., Laitinen, L., Naghian, S., Niemi, V.: UMTS Networks: Architecture, Mobility And Services. Wiley, Chichester (2005). ISBN 0-470-01103-3
4. Open Networking Foundation: OpenFlow Switch Specification 1.4.0 (2013). https://www. opennetworking.org/images/stories/downloads/sdnresources/onf-specifications/openflow/ openflow-spec-v1.4.0.pdf
5. IETF: Interface to the Routing System (2015). http://datatracker.ietf.org/wg/i2rs/charter/
6. IETF: Forwarding and Control Element Separation workgroup (2015). https://datatracker. ietf.org/wg/forces/documents/
7. Le Roux, J., Vasseur, J.: RFC 5440 – path computation element communication protocol (2009)
8. Cisco: Cisco's One Platform Kit (onePK) (2015). http://www.cisco.com/c/en/us/products/ ios-nx-os-software/onepk.html
9. Basta, A., Kellererm, W., Hoffmann, M., Morper, J.H., Hoffmann, K.: Applying NFV and SDN to LTE mobile core gateways, the functions placement problem. In: Proceedings of the 4th workshop on all things cellular: operations, applications (2014)
10. Hampel, G.; Steiner, M., Bu, T.: Applying software-defined networking to the telecom domain. In: Computer Communications Workshops (INFOCOM WKSHPS) (2013)
11. Jin, X., Li, E.L., Vanbever, L., Rexford, J.: SoftCell: scalable and flexible cellular core network architecture. In: Proceedings of the Ninth ACM Conference on Emerging Networking Experiments and Technologies (2013)
12. Pentikousis, K., Yan, W., Weihua, H.: Mobileflow: toward software defined mobile networks. IEEE Commun. Mag. **51**(7), 44–53 (2013)
13. Kempf, J., Johansson, B., Pettersson, S., Luning, H., Nilsson, T.: Moving the mobile evolved packet core to the cloud. In: WiMob (2012)
14. Yang, M., Yong, L., Jin, D., Su, L., Ma, S., Zeng, L.: OpenRAN: a software-defined RAN architecture via virtualization. In: SIGCOMM Computer Communication (2013)
15. Gudipati, A., Perry, D., Li, E.L., Katti, S.: SoftRAN: software defined radio access network. In: Proceedings of the second ACM SIGCOMM Workshop on Hot topics in Software Defined Networking (HotSDN 2013) (2013)
16. Nagy, M., Kotuliak, I.: Utilizing OpenFlow, SDN and NFV in GPRS core network. In: Leung, V.C., Chen, M., Wan, J., Zhang, Y. (eds.) TridentCom 2014. LNICST, vol. 137, pp. 184–193. Springer, Heidelberg (2014)
17. Nokia: Nokia LTE M2M, Optimizing LTE for the Internet of Things (2014)
18. Spirent: Landslide (2015). http://www.spirent.com/Ethernet_Testing/Software/Landslide
19. Ixia: EPC test (2015). http://ixiacom.com/solutions/wireless/epc-test

Teaching and Education

Making Computer Science Education Relevant

Michael Weigend[(✉)]

Institut für Didaktik der Mathematik und der Informatik, University of Münster,
Fliednerstr. 21, 48149 Münster, Germany
michael.weigend@uni-muenster.de

Abstract. In addition to algorithm- or concept-oriented training of problem
solving by computer programming, introductory computer science classes may
contain programming projects on themes that are relevant for young people. The
motivation for theme-driven programmers is not to practice coding but to create
a digital artefact related to a domain they are interested in and they want to learn
about. Necessary programming concepts are learned on the way ("diving into
programming"). This contribution presents examples of theme-driven projects,
which are related to text mining and web cam image processing. The development and learning process is supported by metaphorical explanations of
programming concepts and algorithmic ideas, experiments with simple programming statements, stories and code fragments.

Keywords: Computer science education · Programming · Metaphor · Text
mining · Image processing · Internet computing · Python

1 Diving into Programming

Computer science (CS) education at schools is supposed to "introduce the fundamental
concepts of computer science" (CSTA, [1]) and foster computational thinking [2],
which includes abstraction, modeling, problem solving and creating algorithms using
formal language. In contrast to information technology (IT) education, computer science education is not just about using digital tools but about designing software [1].
Programming (the skill of writing a program to a given task) is considered as a new
literacy [3] and an important part of general education, since it is creative, constructive
and precise [4].

Programming is a problem solving activity and implies a transfer of knowledge to
new scenarios. Among other cognitive operations [5], transfer in problem solving
requires recognition (of an analogue problem or a well known general pattern),
abstraction (finding general structures by focusing the important aspects), mapping
(relating familiar concepts to a new scenario), flexibility (in applying a general pattern
on a special scenario) and embedment (combining elements to a whole program).
Developing programming skills means practicing knowledge transfer by writing programs and solving similar tasks again and again. Consider this programming task:

"Last rainy day. Develop a program for which the input is 365 integers indicating
the amount of rain in each day of the year; and the output is the (index of the) last rainy
day." [6].

© IFIP International Federation for Information Processing 2015
I. Khalil et al. (Eds.): ICT-EurAsia 2015 and CONFENIS 2015, LNCS 9357, pp. 53–63, 2015.
DOI: 10.1007/978-3-319-24315-3_6

The solution is a special variant of a general pattern, a "max computation", in which all elements of a sequence have to be compared to a given value and a variable eventually must be updated depending on the result of this comparison. Out of 95 Israeli 11-graders, 69 (73 %) were able to solve this task without any help after one year of Java programming. [6] assume, that the others (23 %) had difficulties in flexibility and failed to customize a general pattern to the specifics of a new situation. I mention this example just to illustrate that writing a program from scratch without external help is not easy and requires a lot of training and experience. It is a competence that is developed gradually in many exercises. Typical tasks for practicing contain short and precise descriptions of pre- and post-conditions, which make it possible to check the correctness of the solution. For each concept (algorithmic patterns, language constructs) there are many variants of tasks embedded in scenarios from different domains. Diversity is important (to practise transfer-related operations) but the domains can be chosen rather arbitrarily. For practising search algorithms it does not matter, what to search – the last rainy day in a sequence of weather documents or the last phone call from Anna in a collection of telephone call metadata.

Computer science topics listed in curricula represent the teachers' perspective: "To be well-educated citizens in a computing-intensive world and to be prepared for careers in the 21st century, our students must have a clear understanding of the principles and practices of computer science." (CSTA) But these "principles and practices" – as such – are not necessarily interesting for high school students. For example in Germany the requirements for final high school exams include topics like object oriented programming (classes, inheritance, polymorphism, UML) and finite state automata. Probably most 15 or 16 years old students, who have to decide whether or not they take CS classes, do not even understand what these terms mean.

According to the international ROSE study, most young people in Europe and other well developed countries have a positive attitude towards science and technology but they have a problem with school science. "Topics that are close to what is often found in science curricula and textbooks have low scores on the rating of interest" [7]. Science and technology topics are not interesting as such, but they can get fascinating for young people, when they are embedded in a real life context. There are massive differences between genders: Girls like to learn about body and health, boys are interested in violent and spectacular contexts (e.g. chemical explosives). Both genders are especially interested in unusual and mysterious things (most popular topic: The possibility of life outside earth).

The motive for learning programming is not necessarily intrinsic. Someone might be not interested in "the principles and practices of computer science" at all, but gets involved because she or he wants to create something exciting.

Protagonists of constructionism [8, 9] claim that developing digital artefacts is a very intense experience leading to deeper knowledge than just reading text books. Programming is a way to elaborate knowledge. Construct something interesting and learn on the way. This constructionist approach of "theme-driven programming" has some major implications:

- Diving into programming. When the learner starts a project she or he possibly has only little knowledge about programming and must learn a lot in a short time.

- Once-in-your-life-experience instead of repetition. Creating a digital artefact is a rich experience leading to a unique product. Richness implies that many things happen and many circumstances came together to make the project possible: Motivations that were satisfied through the project, an assignment, collaboration with other persons. In contrast to this unique experience, practicing programming implies repetition of similar activities.
- Priority of the artefact. The primary (subjective) goal of the learner is not to practise programming but to create an artefact. Anna has seen something cool and wants to make a similar thing. Opposed to the practicing approach the product has a higher value than the process of implementation.
- Limitation to basic designs. Programs developed in the classroom differ from professional programs. They are implemented as simple as possible.
- Using scaffolds. In contrast to the practicing approach the primary goal of a project is not to gain fluency (it will happen anyway). The project is the reason for going deeper into programming. Exploring new programming techniques requires "just in time" explanations that open the mind.
- Tinkering. Learning by doing requires the possibility to experiment. The learner modifies the code, runs the program and sees the effect.

Some programming languages/environments support "diving into programming". Python has a very "low threshold" which is easy to overcome by beginners. The line

```
print("Hello!")
```

is a valid Python program. In the interactive mode (Python shell) the user can experiment by writing individual statements which are interpreted and executed after having hit the ENTER-key. The result is displayed in the next line:

```
>>> len("Hello!")
6
```

Scratch is a visual programming environment which allows users to "build" scripts by moving block with the mouse on screen (https://scratch.mit.edu/). In this way syntax errors never happen. Children can rather easily create videos, games or animations.

2 How to Support Diving into Programming

A challenge for teachers and text book authors is to create program examples that are relevant (attractive) and easy to implement. A "dive-into" structure for text book units and classroom activities is this:

1. Present a relevant context. The context is an informatics-related theme or field that students consider to be interesting and important. The social aspects of technology are pointed out; its impact on everyday life and the environment are made aware. Since the interests of young people are diverse, the context should inspire to a variety of concrete projects. For

2. Explain relevant programming concepts and visualize those using metaphors. According to Lakoff [10] metaphors can serve as vehicles for comprehending new concepts. A structural metaphor is a mapping from one domain of knowledge (source) to another domain (target). A variable (target) is a container for data (source). Calling a function (target) is to delegate a job to a specialist (source). Metaphors help understanding new concepts from a target domain, if the source domain is familiar. Another facet of intuitive models is simplicity. Good metaphors represent intuitive models, Gestalt-like mental concepts, which people are very confident about. People use them when they try to understand, develop or explain programs. Programmers may use different metaphors for the same programming concept. For example, a function can be visualized by the metaphor of a factory, which takes data as input, processes them und outputs new data. A different metaphor is a tool changing the properties of an object, which keeps its identity during the process.

3. Give examples for individual statements (not context-related) for hands-on experimenting and elaborating. Novices need to experiment with new commands or functions. Often, just reading the language reference is not enough if you want to be really confident about the meaning.

4. Give a very simple prototype project ("starter project") that can be copied and tested. This can be the starting point for the development of an extended, more sophisticated program. A starter project is supposed to inspire students to do their own project in this field. Scratch users find starter projects for several topics on the Scratch website, a platform where Scratch users can publish their projects. Scratch cultivates "remixing", that is copying, changing and extending projects. For each project the remixes (successors) and preceding projects are documented. In this way ideas are reused but not stolen, since each contributor is mentioned in the history of a piece of software. A problem of remixing is that "blind copying" does not help understanding. Someone might take a program, change a small part and make it look different still not understanding the other parts.

A starter project can initiate a development process in the style of agile programming (Extreme Programming [11]). Students start with a very short program that implements a basic story. They test it and debug it until it works and until it is fully understood. This is the first iteration. Then they add a few lines of code to implement the next story. They develop the project in a couple of very quick iterations and learn on the way step by step. In that way – ideally – both programming competence and the program (the digital artefact) grow in parallel.

It is essential to step on not before the present iteration works fine and is fully understood. Debugging and testing is an essential part of the process. Beginners will fail to find errors if the program is too complex and contains concepts they do not understand. So the starter project must be really simple and is probably not attractive in itself. Its beauty lies in the fact that it is the first step on the way to something interesting.

3   Text Mining

Generally speaking, text mining means making profit out of text documents that are publicly available. The text is considered as a resource that can be exploited in order to produces additional value. Text mining can be considered as a threat, when someone searches for telephone numbers, names or e-mail addresses and misuses this information. But there are many useful applications like searching for rhymes or traffic information.

An important concept in text mining is regular expressions. Programming novices have to learn two things, (a) the general idea of pattern matching and (b) specific formal details of regular expressions (placeholders like the dot. or operators like + and *).

The general idea of pattern matching is used (in a naive way) in everyday live, when we identify things or find things and separate them from others. Metaphors for regular expressions are

- a sieve that separates certain objects from other objects
- a "grabbing-device" that can only interact with objects that have certain surface properties (lock-key concept) (Fig. 1)

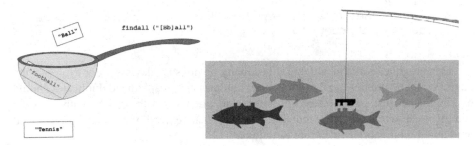

Fig. 1. Two different metaphors illustrating the concept of finding strings with regular expressions.

The formal details of regular expressions are best understood by reading the language reference and experimenting with individual statements. The function findall() from the Python module re takes a regular expression and a string as arguments and returns a list of all matching substrings. Here is a mini series of experiments illustrating how to find words that end with "eep":

```
>>> text= "Keep it. Reeperbahn is a street in Hamburg."
>>> findall("\w*eep", text)
['Keep', 'Reep']
>>> findall("\w*eep ", text)
['Keep ']
```

3.1 Mining Mark Twain - Using Literature for Finding Rhymes

In the Project Gutenberg you can find 50 000 free e-books, including the entire works of Mark Twain (http://www.gutenberg.org/ebooks/3200). Download the utf-8 text file (15.3 MB) and store it in your project folder. This book (with 5598 pages) can be used for finding rhymes. The following listing shows a starter program (Python). The call of findall() in line #1 returns a sequence of words that end with the giving ending (plus a space). Statement #2 transforms the list to a set (without duplicates) and prints it on screen.

```
from re import *
f = open("marktwain.txt", mode="r", encoding="utf-8")
book = f.read()
f.close()
ending = input('Ending: ')
while ending:
    wordlist = findall("\w*" + ending + " ", book)    #1
    print(set(wordlist))                               #2
    ending = input('Ending: ')
```

This is the output from an example run:

```
Ending: eep
{'sheep ', 'Weep ', 'Sheep ', 'deep ', 'asleep ', 'keep
', 'steep ', 'creep '. ...}
```

This program works nicely, but it has many obvious weaknesses. For example, the output could be prettier (no curly brackets, commas etc.), capitalized duplicates should be eliminated (just weep instead of Weep and weep), and the space-symbols at the end of each word could be cut off. Learners can extend the starter project and implement more stories in further iterations.

3.2 Mining Social Media

Small programs are not per se easy to understand just because they are small. Some statements may adopt advanced programming concepts that are difficult to understand. Let me discuss an example.

The Python module tweepy supports accessing twitter tweets. When someone submits a tweet, this event is documented in a json-string that is publicly available. This record contains the text of the tweet as well as information about the tweeter. If you want to create an application for processing tweets, you need to register your application on the twitter website. You get some keywords, which your program needs for authentication (consumer key, consumer secret, access token, access secret). The following program implements this story (1): Select all tweets about "gaming" and "smart city" from a live stream and store them in a text file.

It runs until it is stopped by a keyboard interrupt. Within a few hours one can collect thousands of tweets, which can be analyzed later.

```
from tweepy import OAuthHandler
from tweepy.streaming import StreamListener
from tweepy import Stream

f = open('my_tweets.txt', 'w')
class MyListener(StreamListener):                    #1
    def on_data(self, data):
        f.write(data)
        f.flush()
        return True

auth = OAuthHandler('consumer key   ', 'consumer secret   ')
auth.set_access_token('access token   ', 'access secret   ')
listener = MyListener()
stream = Stream(auth, listener)
stream.filter(track=['smart city', 'gaming'])        #2
```

This is an object oriented program. It contains several object instantiations and the definition of a derived class (#1). The programmer must override the method on_data(), which processes each tweet that is taken from the firehose. The parameter track defines a selection pattern. Twitter allows at most 1 % of all tweets in the Firehose to be selected. Obviously, rather advanced programming concepts are involved. How to explain this to a beginner, who is diving into this technology? (Fig. 2)

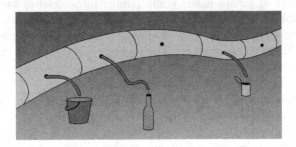

Fig. 2. Mining the Twitter Firehose

Figure 3 gives an intuitive model of the whole project. In Extreme programming this is called a "project metaphor". It is one holistic idea how to mine a Twitter live stream. In addition one can map elements of the image to formal constructs in the program text: The Stream-object is represented by a big pipe, the AuthHandler-object – resposible for access to the Firehose – is visualized by a red pipe, the file storing tweets, is a container (bottle, bucket or can) and so on.

The text file containing collected tweets can easily be analysed using the standard methods of string objects. Example (Python):

```
>>> text = "This is a tweet."
>>> text.count("is")
2
```

Further stories could include these: (2) Check the frequency of tweets about topics like "gaming" or "smart city". (3) Estimate the average age of persons tweeting about certain topics by analysing the language they use.

An approach to implement story 3 is searching for certain stylistic elements that are age-dependent. For example, young tweeters use more often the words "I", "me", "you", capitalized words like "LOL" or "HAHA" and they use more often alphabetic lengthening like "niiiice" instead of "nice". Tweets from older users on the other hand contain more hyperlinks and references to the family ("family", "son", "daughter") [12]. Table 1 shows the results of a "toy analysis" of tweets, which were collected during the same time slot (14 h on May 17th 2015).

Table 1. Results from a toy analysis of tweets containing CS-related phrases.

Phrase	Number of tweets	Average length (words)	"Old" stylistic elements	"Young" stylistic elements
Smart city	226	24.6	2.8 %	7.4 %
Internet of things	1718	27.9	4.4 %	11.2 %
Gaming	19928	26.4	3.6 %	11.6 %

4   Web Cam Analysis

Webcams make live at certain places really public. In contrast to surveillance cams which are accessible only by authorized persons, the images of public webcams can be observed and analysed by everyone. Running webcam-related programs implies interacting with the social environment. The input device is a public spot. This might provoke thinking about legal, political and ethical aspects of public webcams and digital technology (personal rights, security, and privacy).

Figure 3 shows screenshots from two different Python programs displaying and evaluating images public webcams.

The first application observes two areas (marked by white rectangles in the lower right quadrant of the image) and detects any motion at these spots by comparing the present picture with a photo taken a few seconds earlier. The application uses the marked areas for picking the answers of two teams in a quiz. Imagine questions with two response options (yes and no). Each team answers "yes" by moving on "it's spot". It selects the answer "no" by keeping the area free from any activity.

The second application observes a small rectangular area on a freeway, counts the number of motions in ten minutes, and estimates the density of the traffic [13].

Both programs consist of approx. 60 lines of code. A student – say Anna – could just copy such program from a text book. But if Anna is not familiar with the concepts included, this would not necessarily lead to comprehension. An alternative to copying letter by letter is *reconstruction*. Anna starts with a very simple nucleus, tests it until it is fully understood and then extends and changes it in iterations (similar as in Extreme Programming). This can be supported by the text book. Here is an example of a

Fig. 3. Screenshots from Python programs, showing and processing the live image of public webcams at the Friedensplatz in Dortmund, Germany (left hand side) and at a freeway junction at Frankfurt, Germany (right hand side).

program which could be the first reconstruction step in both projects. Story 1: Get an image from a webcam and show it on screen.

```
import io
from urllib.request import urlopen
from PIL import Image
URL = "http://.../friedensplatz/current.jpg"
f = urlopen(URL)
imgText = f.read()
f.close()
imageBin = io.BytesIO(imgText)
img = Image.open(imageBin)                              #1
img.show()
```

This linear program just demonstrates how to get an image from the internet on the display of the computer at home. The image data must be transformed in several steps. Finally (in line #1) a PIL.Image-Object has been created. Figure 4 illustrates the idea depicting physical images printed on different materials and in different types of frames. Different types of objects represent the same image. But they serve different purposes and are processed in different ways using different methods.

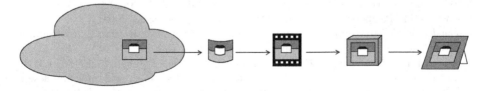

Fig. 4. A chain of format changes

Story 2: Draw something on the image, say a rectangle. This story is implemented by adding a few lines of code:

```
from PIL import ImageDraw
...
A = (305, 375, 325, 395)
...
draw = ImageDraw(img)                    #2
draw.rectangle(A, outline="white")       #3
```

These few lines of code demonstrate the idea of a PIL.ImageDraw-Object. In line #2 a new ImageDraw-object (named `draw`) is created and connected to a PIL.Image-object named `img`. When `draw` receives a message (like in #3) it changes the state of the connected image.

Further stories (which can be used in both projects) are: (3) Show the image in an application window and update it every *x* seconds. (4) Detect motion in two rectangular areas. (5) Show the results of the motion detection on a label below the photo.

At some point refactoring is necessary. This means to improve the technical quality of the program (without changing its functionality). The target program is a well readable well structured object oriented program. Students will take the given program as an inspiration and add their own ideas.

5   Conclusion

Making CS relevant for young people is a major challenge for teachers and text book authors. Digital technology is omnipresent in our lives. But this does not guarantee that young people are interested in taking CS classes at schools. Fundamental principles and practices of CS must be imbedded in contexts that inspire young people. We need interesting project ideas (stories) that can be implemented quickly in small programs and media (images) that explain the idea of program code very quickly.

References

1. Seehorn, D., Carey, S., Fuschetto, B., Lee, I., Moix, D., O'Grady-Cuniff, D., Verno, A.: CSTA K-12 Computer Science Standards (2011). http://csta.acm.org/Curriculum/sub/CurrFiles/CSTA_K-12_CSS.pdf
2. Wing, J.M.: Computational thinking. Commun. ACM **49**(3), 33–35 (2006)
3. Prensky, M.: Programming is the new literacy. Edutopia magazine (2008)
4. Gander, W.: Informatics and general education. In: Gülbahar, Y., Karataş, E. (eds.) ISSEP 2014. LNCS, vol. 8730, pp. 1–7. Springer, Heidelberg (2014)
5. Mayer, R.E., Wittrock, M.C.: Problem solving. Handb. Educ. Psychol. **2**, 287–303 (2006)
6. Ginat, D., Shifroni, E., Menashe, E.: Transfer, cognitive load, and program design difficulties. In: Kalaš, I., Mittermeir, R.T. (eds.) ISSEP 2011. LNCS, vol. 7013, pp. 165–176. Springer, Heidelberg (2011)
7. Sjøberg, S., Schreiner, C.: The ROSE Project: An Overview and Key Findings. University of Oslo, Oslo (2010)

8. Papert, S.: Mindstorms: Children, Computers, and Powerful Ideas. Basic Books Inc., New York (1980)
9. Resnick, M., Maloney, J., Monroy-Hernández, A., Rusk, N., Eastmond, E., Brennan, K., Kafai, Y.: Scratch: programming for all. Commun. ACM **52**(11), 60–67 (2009)
10. Lakoff, G., Núñez, R.: The metaphorical structure of mathematics: sketching out cognitive foundations for a mind-based mathematics. In: English, L. (ed.) Mathematical Reasoning: Analogies, Metaphors, and Images, pp. 21–89. Erlbaum, Hillsdale (1997)
11. Beck, K.: Extreme Programming Explained: Embrace Change. Addison-Wesley Professional, Reading (2000)
12. Nguyen, D., Gravel, R., Trieschnigg, D., Meder, T.: How Old Do You Think I Am? A study of language and age in Twitter. In: Proceedings of the Seventh International AAAI Conference on Weblogs and Social Media. AAAI Press (2013)
13. Weigend, M.: Raspberry Pi programmieren mit Python, 2nd edn. MITP (2015)

Analyzing Brain Waves for Activity Recognition of Learners

Hiromichi Abe, Kazuya Kinoshita, Kensuke Baba$^{(\boxtimes)}$, Shigeru Takano, and Kazuaki Murakami

Kyushu University, Fukuoka, Japan
{hiromichi.abe,baba}@soc.ait.kyushu-u.ac.jp

Abstract. Understanding the states of learners at a lecture is expected to be useful for improving the quality of the lecture. This paper is trying to recognize the activities of learners by their brain wave data for estimating the states. In analyses on brain wave data, generally, some particular bands such as α and β are considered as the features. The authors considered other bands of higher and lower frequencies to compensate for the coarseness of simple electroencephalographs. They conducted an experiment of recognizing two activities of five subjects with the brain wave data captured by a simple electroencephalograph. They applied support vector machine to 8-dimensional vectors which correspond to eight bands on the brain wave data. The results show that considering multiple bands yielded high accuracy compared with the usual features.

1 Introduction

Understanding the states or emotions of learners is useful for improving the quality of the lecture. Learners' states are usually observed visually by the lecturer at the time or estimated by exams conducted after the lecture as a degree of understanding. However, especially in massive or on-line lectures, it is difficult to know the state of each learner at the lecture. Detecting learners' states automatically and in real time is expected to innovate in the current style of learning.

The aim of our research is to detect the states of learners from several kinds of sensor data. On the assumption that some particular activities of a person correspond to the states, we try to recognize activities to understand the states of learners. Activity recognition has been widely explored using video data. Recently, a spread of depth sensors enabled us to analyze the subject in terms of 3-dimensional coordinates [4]. A camera with a depth sensor can recognize some motions, facial expressions, and eye movements with high accuracy. However, the target of our study is learners who are sitting with small moves, and hence we need another kind of sensor data in addition to image data for activity recognition with high accuracy.

We focused on brain waves, electroencephalography (EEG), captured by a simple electroencephalograph for activity recognition of learners as additional data to video data. Generally, it is said that EEG changes by the influence of

© IFIP International Federation for Information Processing 2015
I. Khalil et al. (Eds.): ICT-EurAsia 2015 and CONFENIS 2015, LNCS 9357, pp. 64–73, 2015.
DOI: 10.1007/978-3-319-24315-3_7

the emotion of the person. However, usual electroencephalographs have a lot of electrodes and are not suitable for use by learners in a lecture. Moreover, some expert systems are expensive and unsuitable for a large amount of use. Especially for massive lectures, electroencephalographs are required to be easy to use and cheap.

In this paper, we evaluated the validity of using multiple bands of brain wave data captured by a simple electroencephalograph for activity recognition of learners. In usual researches of activity or emotion recognition by EEG data, some particular bands, called α and β waves, are used as features for analysis. We considered other bands of higher and lower frequency in addition to the usual features, α and β waves and their combinations, to improve low accuracy of the activity recognition by simple electroencephalographs. In our experiment, the subjects performed two activities, calculation and meditation, with a simple electroencephalograph which can output a spectrum of brain waves with the 8 kinds of bands. Then, we applied support vector machine (SVM) [5] to the 8-dimensional vectors, and investigated the accuracy of the activity recognition by comparison with scalar data based on the values of one or two bands.

As a result, the accuracy of the activity recognition by the data of the 8 kinds of bands was high compared with considering one or two features. Additionally, we confirmed that the simple electroencephalograph has a possibility of use for the activity recognition of learners.

The rest of this paper is organized as follows. Section 2 surveys related work of activity recognition of learners with EEG data. Section 3 describes the activities, the collected brain wave data, and the data analysis in our experiments. Section 4 reports the results of the experiments. Section 5 shows considerations about the results and future directions of our study.

2   Related Work

Our study is considering EEG data of learners captured by a simple electroencephalograph for state recognition.

A viewpoint of this survey is EEG data of *learners*. Some studies indicated a possibility of state or emotion recognition of learners by analyzing their EEG data. Wan et al. [11] investigated the characteristics of EEG data of learners in a Web-based lecture. Chaouachi and Frasson [3] showed a relation between EEG data of learners and the response time to some questions. These studies were using electroencephalographs with many electrodes rather than simple one.

The other viewpoint is EEG data by a *simple electroencephalograph*. Electroencephalographs with a few (dry) electrodes are less accurate than expert one, but those are easy to use for learners. Ishino and Hagiwara [6] proposed a system which estimates the feeling of subjects by EEG data captured by a simple electroencephalograph with three electrodes. Vourvopoulos and Liarokapis [10] evaluated a usability of a commercial and simple electroencephalograph for brain-computer interfaces. These studies were not necessarily considering learners as the target.

The study by Yoshida et al. [13] is similar to ours in the sense of the two viewpoints. They considered the changes of EEG data to evaluate the states of learners who repeated simple calculations. Then, they reported that the ratio of α wave to β wave was related to the activity in their experiment. Some recent studies investigated more complex relations between emotional states and the range of brain waves rather than the discriminated one such as the relation between relaxation and α wave. For example, Wang et al. [12] classified EEG data into some categories based on emotional states by machine learning. In our experiment, we considered the difference between two kinds of activities and compared the other kinds of waves in EEG data systematically in addition to α and β waves and the combinations of the waves.

3   Methods

The purpose of this paper is to clarify whether considering multiple bands of brain wave is useful for activity recognition compared with usual features based on a single band or a scalar from a few bands. We collected brain wave data of persons with two activities, and tried to recognize the activities from the data with considering several kinds of features.

3.1   Collected Data

We collected brain wave data of five subjects with the two activities:

– Calculation of simple additions and
– Meditation with the eyes closed.

We used 10×10 matrixes with randomly chosen 20 single-digit numbers (Fig. 1) for the activity of calculation. We prepared a sufficient number of matrixes printed on papers, and the subjects tried to fill the matrixes as much as possible in each trial. The time for a single trial of an activity was 2 min, and the subjects repeated the two activities alternately 5 times for each with no interval. Therefore, the total time of the experiment for a subject was 20 min.

We used a simple electroencephalograph MindWave Mobile (Fig. 2) by NeuroSky[1] for collecting brain wave data. The simple electroencephalograph has only two electrodes and does not need any gel on the head of a subject for capturing potential differences. One of the electrodes is placed at front polar (the middle point of Fp1 and Fp2 in the international 10–20 system) and the other is placed at left earlobe (A1 in the international 10–20 system). The electroencephalograph (and an attached module) can output a spectrum of brain waves with the following 8 bands:

– δ: 0.5–2.75 Hz,
– θ: 3.5–6.75 Hz,

---

[1] NeuroSky, MindWave Mobile, http://mindwavemobile.neurosky.com/ (accessed in May 2015).

	2	3	7	9	4	1	8	5	0	6
5										
9										
6										
1										
3					7					
0										
7										
2										
4										
8										

Fig. 1. An example of the matrixes used for the activity of calculation. The subject fills each blank with the sum of the corresponding numbers.

Table 1. The numbers of the vectors for the five subjects and the two activities in the sample set.

	Calculation	Meditation	Total
Subject 1	602	605	1,207
Subject 2	602	625	1,227
Subject 3	602	609	1,211
Subject 4	604	622	1,226
Subject 5	601	628	1,229
Total	3,011	3,089	6,100

- Low-α: 7.5–9.75 Hz,
- High-α: 10–11.75 Hz,
- Low-β: 13–16.75 Hz,
- High-β: 18–29.75 Hz,
- Low-γ: 31–39.75 Hz, and
- Mid-γ: 41–49.75 Hz.

The sampling frequency was 512 Hz. The output rate of the spectrum was about 1 for a second. Therefore, we obtained about 6,000 ($= 60 \times 20 \times 5$) 8-dimensional vectors with the label for one of the two activities. Table 1 shows the numbers of the generated vectors for the five subjects and the two activities. We simultaneously took video data of the subject for adjusting the time of each trial to the labels.

3.2   Data Analysis

We tried to recognize the two activities from the collected data. First, we considered the following 19 kinds of scalars:

Fig. 2. The simple electroencephalograph MindWave Mobile used for collecting brain wave data. The picture was downloaded from http://mindwavemobile.neurosky.com/ in May 2015.

- Each element of the 8 bands,
- The sum of low-α and high-α,
- The sum of low-β and high-β, and
- The ratio of β to α for the 9 combinations of (low-α, high-α, and the sum) and (low-β, high-β, and the sum).

Next, we considered the 8-dimensional vectors by the 8 elements.

Additionally, we considered the simple moving averages of the collected data with ranges 10 and 20. The simple moving averages of a time series data v_t with a range n is the time series data

$$u_t = \frac{v_t + v_{t-1} + \cdots + v_{t-n+1}}{n}.$$

Then, we obtained two data sets S_{10} and S_{20} in addition to the collected data set S_1.

For the 20 cases, we applied SVM with a linear kernel to the three data sets. Concretely, we used the function ksvm in the package kernlab [8] for R^2 with the default values for the parameters. Then, we conducted 5-fold cross-validation [2], where the *accuracy* of an activity recognition is the ratio of the numbers of the vectors whose label was predicted correctly to the total number of the vectors. We set each test set in the cross-validation to correspond to a single trial of a subject, because vectors in the same trial tend to have similar values. The activity recognition was conducted for each subject separately, and the accuracy was calculated as the mean of the results for the 5 subjects.

---

[2] The R Project for Statistical Computing, http://www.r-project.org/ (accessed in May 2015).

Table 2. The accuracy of the activity recognition by SVM for the 20 kinds of features with the three data sets S_1, S_{10}, and S_{20}.

	S_1	S_{10}	S_{20}
8 bands	**79.1** (%)	**86.3** (%)	**86.3** (%)
δ	69.1	78.7	76.6
θ	64.7	78.3	79.0
Low-α (α_1)	55.3	64.7	66.3
High-α (α_2)	57.2	68.3	72.9
Low-β (β_1)	57.4	68.8	69.9
High-β (β_2)	61.4	71.4	73.2
Low-γ	69.6	81.2	80.0
Mid-γ	68.8	78.1	76.4
$\alpha_3 = \alpha_1 + \alpha_2$	54.2	62.0	64.1
$\beta_3 = \beta_1 + \beta_2$	60.6	71.6	72.0
β_1/α_1	50.4	51.0	50.4
β_2/α_1	51.9	57.4	55.2
β_3/α_1	51.5	53.7	53.8
β_1/α_2	57.5	67.8	70.1
β_2/α_2	59.6	70.4	72.1
β_3/α_2	59.7	71.0	72.6
β_1/α_3	56.8	65.5	67.0
β_2/α_3	59.8	71.1	70.5
β_3/α_3	59.6	70.7	70.6

4   Results

Table 2 shows the accuracy of the activity recognition for the 20 cases with the three data sets. The accuracy by considering the 8 bands was higher than other 19 cases for any data set, the accuracy was the highest (86.3 %) with S_{10} and S_{20}. The accuracy by low-γ was the highest in the 8 bands for the three data set. The accuracy by considering the ratio of β to α was not high in any combination even compared with each case of the 8 bands. The graphs for some cases showed 5 peaks which correspond to the change of the activities. Figure 3 is an example of the graph for the change of brain wave data over time. We can see from the graph that the data of low- and mid-γ divide the two activities.

5   Discussion

5.1   Major Conclusion

We found that the two activities could be recognized with high accuracy by considering multiple bands in brain wave data compared with usual features. At the

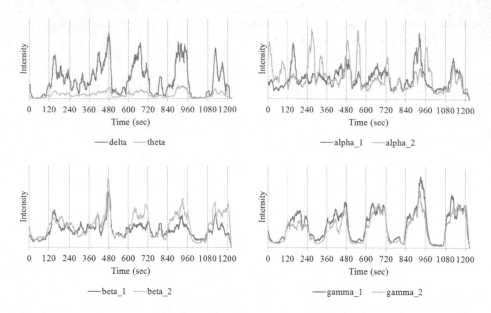

Fig. 3. The changes of the brain data over time, where the values are for the 8 bands with the simple moving average of the range 20 of a subject.

same time, we confirmed that brain wave data obtained by the simple electroencephalograph includes useful information for this kind of activity recognition.

5.2 Key Findings

The optimal length of the range of the simple moving average was 16. By Table 2, the accuracy was improved when we considered the average of the data for 10 or 20 s for any criterion. We additionally investigated the relation between the accuracy and the range of the simple moving average for the case of the 8 dimensional vectors. Figure 4 shows the accuracy against the range. The accuracy was the highest (86.9 %) when the range was 16. Considering the average of data for about 20 s seems to be suitable for the activity recognition, which corresponds to the same analysis on another kind of activity recognition with EEG by a simple electroencephalograph [1].

We experimentally conducted personal identification by the collected data. In the experiments, we observed differences of brain waves between the subjects. Table 3 shows the results of the personal identification. We applied SVM with a linear kernel and 5-folds cross-validation as the activity recognition. We could not earn high accuracy for the personal identification with the data. The accuracy by the data for the activity calculation (43.9 %) was better than meditation (28.8 %). The results indicate that we need other techniques to utilize the EEG data for personal identification.

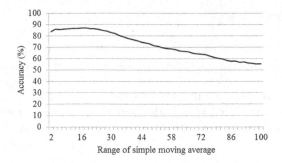

Fig. 4. The accuracy of the activity recognition against the range of the simple moving average with the 8 dimensional vectors.

Table 3. The confusion matrix of the personal identification with the five subjects by S_{20}.

Predicted\Actual	1	2	3	4	5	Precision (%)	F-measure (%)
Subject 1	83	106	42	27	84	24.3	29.1
Subject 2	66	79	2	50	26	35.4	35.1
Subject 3	14	18	70	30	14	47.9	37.5
Subject 4	22	11	113	90	7	37.0	38.3
Subject 5	42	13	0	30	96	53.0	47.1
Recall (%)	38.6	34.8	30.8	39.6	42.3	36.8	

5.3 Future Directions

The original goal of our research is to recognize the states of learners such as being concentrated or absentminded. In this paper we found that the collected brain wave data could divide the two activities, calculation and meditation, with a degree of accuracy, however there are some deviations between the activities and the states of the subjects. For example, we can consider the following noises: the brain wave data might have effects of (1) the move of the hands and (2) whether the eyes were closed. Therefore, our future work includes extra experiments with other activities such as

(1) Calculation without writing, or moving the hand and
(2) Meditation with the eyes opened, or opening and closing the eyes.

We are also planning to use EEG data for activity recognition with data collected by other sensors. Kamizono et al. [7] conducted a similar experiment of activity recognition of learners using video data with depth information. They considered four activities with great moves of the face (meditation, reading texts, looking away, and talking to another person). Moreover, it is possible to capture the heart rate of the subject from video data [9]. Therefore, we can expect improvement of the accuracy of activity recognition by combining these kinds of data with EEG data.

6   Conclusion

We evaluated the validity of using brain wave data with multiple bands for activity recognition of learners in a lecture. We conducted the experiments of activity recognition for two activities, calculation of simple additions and meditation with the eyes closed, with a simple electroencephalograph. We found that two activities could be recognized with high accuracy by considering multiple bands in the collected brain wave data compared with usual features. Additionally, we confirmed that brain wave data obtained by the simple electroencephalograph includes useful information for this kind of activity recognition.

Acknowledgment. This work was partially supported by a joint research with Panasonic Corporation from 2014 to 2015 and the Center of Innovation Program from Japan Science and Technology Agency, JST.

References

1. Abe, H., Baba, K., Takano, S., Murakami, K.: Towards activity recognition of learners by simple electroencephalographs. In: Proceedings of the International Conference on Information Systems and Design of Communication, ISDOC 2014, pp. 161–164. ACM, New York (2014)
2. Bishop, C.M.: Pattern Recognition and Machine Learning. Information Science and Statistics. Springe, New York (2006)
3. Chaouachi, M., Frasson, C.: Exploring the relationship between learner EEG mental engagement and affect. In: Aleven, V., Kay, J., Mostow, J. (eds.) ITS 2010, Part II. LNCS, vol. 6095, pp. 291–293. Springer, Heidelberg (2010)
4. Chen, L., Wei, H., Ferryman, J.: A survey of human motion analysis using depth imagery. Pattern Recogn. Lett. **34**(15), 1995–2006 (2013)
5. Hastie, T., Tibshirani, R., Friedman, J.: The Elements of Statistical Learning: Data Mining, Inference and Prediction, 2nd edn. Springer, New York (2008)
6. Ishino, K., Hagiwara, M.: A feeling estimation system using a simple electroencephalograph. In: 2003 IEEE International Conference on Systems, Man and Cybernetics, vol. 5, pp. 4204–4209, October 2003
7. Kamizono, T., Abe, H., Baba, K., Takano, S., Murakami, K.: Towards activity recognition of learners by kinect. In: 2014 IIAI 3rd International Conference on Advanced Applied Informatics (IIAIAAI), pp. 177–180, August 2014
8. Karatzoglou, A., Smola, A., Hornik, K., Zeileis, A.: Kernlab - an S4 package for kernel methods in R. J. Stat. Softw. **11**(9), 1–20 (2004)
9. Poh, M.-Z., McDuff, D.J., Picard, R.W.: Non-contact, automated cardiac pulse measurements using video imaging and blind source separation. Opt. Express **18**(10), 10762–10774 (2010)
10. Vourvopoulos, A., Liarokapis, F.: Evaluation of commercial brain-computer interfaces in real and virtual world environment: a pilot study. Comput. Electr. Eng. **40**(2), 714–729 (2014)
11. Wan, J., Hu, B., Li, X.: EEG: a way to explore learner's affect in pervasive learning systems. In: Bellavista, P., Chang, R.-S., Chao, H.-C., Lin, S.-F., Sloot, P.M.A. (eds.) GPC 2010. LNCS, vol. 6104, pp. 109–119. Springer, Heidelberg (2010)

12. Wang, X.-W., Nie, D., Lu, B.-L.: Emotional state classification from EEG data using machine learning approach. Neurocomputing **129**, 94–106 (2014)
13. Yoshida, K., Hirai, H., Sakamoto, Y., Miyaji, I.: Evaluation of the change of work using simple electroencephalography. Procedia Comput. Sci. **22**, 855–862 (2013). 17th International Conference in Knowledge Based and Intelligent Information and Engineering Systems - KES2013

Authentication and Profiling

A Multi-factor Biometric Based Remote Authentication Using Fuzzy Commitment and Non-invertible Transformation

Thi Ai Thao Nguyen[✉], Dinh Thanh Nguyen, and Tran Khanh Dang

Ho Chi Minh City University of Technology, VNU-HCM,
Ho Chi Minh City, Vietnam
{thaonguyen, dinhthanh, khanh}@cse.hcmut.edu.vn

Abstract. Biometric-based authentication system offers more undeniable benefits to users than traditional authentication system. However, biometric features seem to be very vulnerable - easily affected by different attacks, especially those happening over transmission network. In this work, we have proposed a novel multi-factor biometric based remote authentication protocol. This protocol is not only resistant against attacks on the network but also protects biometric templates stored in the server's database, thanks to the combination of fuzzy commitment and non-invertible transformation technologies. The notable feature of this work as compared to previous biometric based remote authentication protocols is its ability to defend insider attack. The server's administrator is incapable of utilizing information saved in the database by client to impersonate him/her and deceive the system. In addition, the performance of the system is maintained with the support of random orthonormal project, which reduces computational complexity while preserving its accuracy.

Keywords: Remote authentication · Biometric template protection · Biometric authentication · Fuzzy commitment · Orthonormal matrix

1 Introduction

In modern world, services for people's daily needs are being digitalized. E-commerce happens everywhere, in every aspect of life. As e-commerce is being used as widely as of today, an essential need for its long survival, beside quality, is security. The first security method to be mentioned is authentication. Traditional authentication method that most e-commerce providers are using is username/password. However, this method is revealing its natural setbacks. Password cannot identify legal user with an imposter who is able to access to user's password. Besides, the more complicated – more secured a password is, the harder it is for users to remember. That is to say, a "true" password is difficult for people to remember but easy for computer to figure out. Especially, with recent technology development, computer ability is being enhanced; meaning password cracking chance is rising too. For that reason, biometric based authentication method was born; with its advantages, this method is gradually replacing its predecessor. The first advantage to be mentioned is that biometric (such as face, voice, iris, fingerprint, palm-print, gait, signature,...) reflects a specific individual

© IFIP International Federation for Information Processing 2015
I. Khalil et al. (Eds.): ICT-EurAsia 2015 and CONFENIS 2015, LNCS 9357, pp. 77–88, 2015.
DOI: 10.1007/978-3-319-24315-3_8

which helps preventing multi-user usage from one account [1]. Moreover, using bio-metric method is more convenient for users since they do not have to remember or carry it with them.

However, advantages are accompanied with challenges. Usage of method related to biometric requires technology to eliminate interferences happening when the sensor process biometric features. Beside, concerns of security and privacy, especially in remote architecture, are also put on table. The fact that human has a limited number of biometric traits makes users cannot change their biometric over and over like password once it is compromised [2]. Moreover, some sensitive information could be revealed if biometric templates are stored in database server without strong security techniques. In this case, the user's privacy could be violated when the attackers can track their activities by means of cross-matching when a user employs the same biometrics across all applications. Therefore, all the authenticating servers should not be trustworthy to process a user's plaint biometric, and the level of trust of these servers should be discussed more. Last but not least, the network security is also the important compo-nent in biometric based remote authentication scheme. When the authentication process is carried out over an insecure network, anyone with their curiosity can approach the biometric information transmitted [3].

The goal of this study is to present an effective approach for preserving privacy in biometric based remote authentication system. Concretely, biometric template stored in database is protected against the leakage private information while preserving the revocability property. Besides preventing the outside attacks, proposed protocol is also resistant to the attacks from inside.

The remaining parts of this paper are organized as follows. In the Sect. 2, related works is briefly reviewed. We show what previous works have done and their limi-tations. From that point, we present our motivation to fill the gap. In Sect. 3, we introduce the preliminaries and notations used in the proposal. In the next section, our proposed protocol is described in detail. In the Sect. 5, the security analysis is presented to demonstrate for our proposal. Finally, the conclusion and future work are included in the Sect. 6.

2 Related Works

Over the years, there have been plenty of works which research on preserving privacy in biometric based authentication system. Biometric template protection is one of indispensable part to this research field. In [4], Jain et al. presented a detailed survey of various biometric template protection schemes and discussed their strengths and weaknesses in light of the security and accuracy dilemma. There are two approaches to deal with this issue, including feature transformation and biometric cryptosystem. The first approach identified as feature transform allows users to replace a compromised biometric template while reducing the amount of information revealed. However, some methods of the approach cannot achieve an acceptable performance; others are unre-alistic under assumptions from a practical view point [3]. The other approach tries to combine the biometrics and cryptography technique in order to take advantages of both. The schemes employing these methods aim at generating a key, which derived from the biometric tem-plate or bound with the biometric template, and some helper data. Both the biometric template and the key are then discarded, only the helper data is stored in the database for reproducing the biometric or the secret key later. Nevertheless, the biometric cryptosystem seem to lose the revocability property that requires the ability to revoke a compromised template and reissue a new one based on the same biometric data. On this account, some recent studies tend to integrate the advantages of both approaches to enhance only the security but also the performance of the system. The combination of secure sketch and ANN (Artificial Neural Network) was proposed in [5]. The fuzzy Vault was combined with Periodic Function-Based Transformation in [6], or with the non-invertible transformation to conduct a secure online authentication in [7]. The homomorphic cryptosystem was employed in fuzzy commitment scheme to achieve the blind authentication in [8]. In this paper, we try to integrate the ideal of fuzzy commitment and the non-invertible transformation to guarantee the security for user's biometric template.

In recent years, many biometric based remote authentication protocols have been proposed. However, most previous protocols only protect the client side and the transmission channel, neglecting the server side. In [9], the authors utilizes Biometric Encryption Key (BEK) to encrypt Private Key and safeguard Private Key. The BioPKI system proposed in the paper turned around the security of private key, and left the biometric feature out security aspect.

In 2010, Kai Xi et al. proposed a bio-cryptographic security protocol for remote authentication in mobile computing environment. In this protocol, fingerprint was used for verification, and the genuine points were protected by the fuzzy vault technique which inserts randomly a great number of chaff points into the set of genuine points. All elements in the newly created set were given index numbers. The server only stored the index numbers of all genuine points. The communication between client and server was protected a Public Key Infrastructure (PKI) scheme, Elliptic Curve Cryptography (ECC) which offered low computational powers with the same security strength as the RSA. However, the authors focused only on the security of the client side (mobile devices) and the transmission channel. The server was supposed to have higher security strength, so the authors did not care about the attacks on the server or even the attacks from the server. In addition, the authors argued that to prevent replay attack and brute force attack, a biometric-based session key was generated separately from the set of a genuine points; nonetheless, the server only had the list of index numbers of these points so it was unable to generate the key independently as described in [10].

In 2013, Hisham et al. presented another approach that combined steganography and biometric cryptosystem in order to obtain the secure mutual authentication and key exchange between client and server in remote architecture [11]. In this paper, the authors provided some references for proving that hiding biometric data in a cover image based on steganography technique can increase the security of transferring biometric data between unsecure networks [12]. Moreover, in order to protect biometric template stored in the authentication server while preserving the revocability property, the protocol employed the invertible transformation technique using random orthonormal matrices to project biometric feature vectors into other spaces while preserving the original distances. The new approach obtained not only the secure mutual authentication but also the immunity from replay and other remote attacks. However, the authors have not considered the ability that the authentication server itself stoles the data in its own database to impersonate its users in order to conduct the illegal transactions. This attack will be particularly dangerous in case that server is bank. The bank with its dark intention is totally free to impersonate its customers. It abused its privileges to login into customers' accounts, draw all money and leave no guilty evidence. Nonetheless, almost current researches only focus on biometric template protection or how to defend against the attack from outside; they have not spent enough concerns for the attacks from inside yet. More concretely speaking, the ability that the server accesses into the system on behalf of a user and carries out some criminal actions should be taken into account.

In addition, the scalability property needs to be discussed more in the remote authentication architecture. When the number of users and the number of servers is growing, the number of templates which belongs to a user is large, and each server has to remember every user's template. That design makes the system vulnerable and wastes our resources. To guarantee the scalability properties, Fengling et al. presented a biometric based remote authentication which employed the Kerberos protocol [13]. A biometric-Kerberos authentication protocol was suitable for e-commerce applications. The benefit of Kerberos is that expensive session-based user authentication can be separated from cheaper ticket-based resource access. However, the Achilles' heel of the proposed scheme is Key Distributed Center (KDC) – authentication server which is supposed to be trusted. Therefore, there were no techniques protecting the private information of client against the insider attacks.

The contribution of this work is that we propose the biometric-based remote authentication protocol which has the ability to prevent an authentication server from impersonating its clients. In addition, the proposal is resistant to the outside attacks from an insecure network by combining the orthonormal random project with the fuzzy commitment scheme. The mutual authentication and the key agreement are also guaranteed in this protocol.

3 Preliminaries and Notations

3.1 Fuzzy Commitment Scheme

Fuzzy commitment scheme as proposed in [14] belongs to the first class of biometric cryptosystem approach. It is the combination two popular techniques in the areas of Error Correcting Codes (ECC) and cryptography. To understand how fuzzy commitment scheme works, we have to learn about ECC. Formally speaking, ECC plays a central role in the fuzzy commitment scheme. An ECC contains a set of code-words $\mathcal{C} \subseteq \{0,1\}^n$ and a function to map a message to a code-word before it is transmitted along a noisy channel. Given the message space $\mathcal{M} = \{0,1\}^n$, we define the translation function (or encoding function) $g : \mathcal{M} \to \mathcal{C}$, and the decoding function $f : \{0,1\}^n \to \mathcal{M}$. Therefore, g is a map from $\mathcal{M}$ to $\mathcal{C}$; however, f is not the inverse map from $\mathcal{C}$ to $\mathcal{M}$ but a map from arbitrary n-bit strings to the nearest code-word in $\mathcal{C}$.

In fuzzy commitment scheme, a biometric data is treated as a corrupted code-word. During registration stage, a client provides biometric template B to server. Server

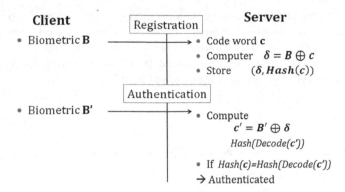

Fig. 1. Fuzzy commitment scheme.

randomly picks a code-word c then calculates $= B \oplus c$, and the hash version of code-word c. Next, server stores the pair of $(\delta, Hash(c))$ into the database. During authentication stage, a new biometric with noise B' is distributed to server by the client. From its side, server calculates $c' = B' \oplus \delta$, proceeds decoding c', then compares hash version of the result with $Hash(c)$ previously stored in the database. If the two are matched, client is authenticated. This process is demonstrated in Fig. 1.

3.2   Orthonormal Random Projection

Random Orthonormal Projection (ROP) is a technique that utilizes an orthonormal matrix to project a set of points into other space while preserving the distances between points. In the categorization of template protection schemes proposed by Jain [4], ROP belongs to the non-invertible transformation approach. It meets the revocability requirement by mapping a biometric feature into a secure domain through an ortho-normal matrix. The method to effectively deliver orthonormal matrix was introduced in [15]. It can be used to replace traditional method of Gram-Schmidt. Given the bio-metric feature vector x of size $2n$, orthonormal random matrix A of size $2n \times 2n$, random vector b of size $2n$, we have the transformation $y = Ax + b$.

The orthonormal matrix A of size $2n \times 2n$ owns a diagonal which is a set of n orthonormal matrix of size $n \times n$. The other entries of A are zeros. We present the example of matrix A in (1) where the values $\{\theta_1, \theta_2, \ldots, \theta_n\}$ are the random numbers in the range $[0 : 2\pi]$

$$A = \begin{bmatrix} \cos\theta_1 & \sin\theta_1 & 0 & 0 & & 0 & 0 \\ -\sin\theta_1 & \cos\theta_1 & 0 & 0 & & 0 & 0 \\ 0 & 0 & \cos\theta_2 & \sin\theta_2 & & 0 & 0 \\ 0 & 0 & -\sin\theta_2 & \cos\theta_2 & & 0 & 0 \\ 0 & 0 & 0 & 0 & & \cos\theta_n & \sin\theta_n \\ 0 & 0 & 0 & 0 & & -\sin\theta_n & \cos\theta_n \end{bmatrix} \quad (1)$$

By using this technique to produce the orthonormal matrix, there is no need for a complex process such as Gram-Schmidt. Beside its effectiveness in computational complexity, it can also improve the security while guaranteeing intra-class variation. When client is in doubt of his template getting exposed, he only needs to create another orthonormal matrix A to gain a new transformed template.

3.3 Notations

In the rest of the paper, we will use the following notations:

- B is a biometric feature vector of a client
- M is an orthonormal matrix that a client creates.
- B_{TC} is a transformed biometric stored in the database as a template.
- H(m) is the hash version of the message m.
- BL is a biometric lock of a client.
- P is a permutation
- Pu & Pr are respectively the public key and the private key of a cryptosystem.
- $E_{PuX}(m)$ is the encryption of the message m using the public key of X.
- K_A is the authentication key generated randomly by the client.
- $E_{kA}(m)$ is the symmetric encryption of the message m using the secret key K_A.
- S is the mobile serial number provided by the client.
- S_T is the mobile serial number of the client which is stored in the database.
- C is a client.
- S_1, S_2 are respectively the first server and the second server.

4   Proposal Protocol

4.1   Enrollment Phase

In the enrollment phase, the client employs a random number K_m stored on the his/her device to generate the random orthonormal matrix M (based on the technique described in Sect. 3.2). After being extracted, the feature vector B is combined with matrix M to produce the cancellable version B_{TC} of B which is sent to server S_1 after that. In addition, the client also needs to register a secret number PIN to server S_1. The hash version of PIN is then stored in the database by server S_1. Parallel to that process, the client has to send serial number of his/her mobile device to another server (server S_2). The act of dividing client's information into two different databases is meant to reduce workload for the server; more importantly it serves to limit the control of server over client's private information. The process is illustrated in Fig. 2.

4.2   Authentication Phase

In this phase, we apply the ideal of fuzzy commitment scheme to obtain the secure biometric based remote authentication. Instead of transmitting the plain biometric data

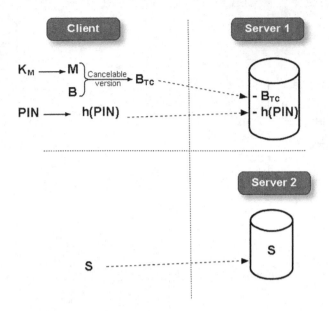

Fig. 2. Enrollment phase.

over the insecure network as the original scheme, client sends a biometric lock (*BL*) or a helper data to a server. At the server side, a biometric lock is combined with the component Y related to the client's biometric which is stored in database at the enrollment phase. The result of this combination is the authenticated key. The process is presented by the Fig. 3.

More details of the authentication phase are described in the Fig. 4. The authentication function is undertaken by the second server S_2. Meanwhile, the first server S_1 takes the responsibility for computing the encryption of the authentication key and then sends the result to S_2 to do the next steps.

In authentication phase, the client sends request to server S_1. This server creates a random number (Nonce – Number used ONCE) N_a, then sends it to the client. Note that all messages between the client and the server over transmission network are protected by asymmetric cryptosystem (PKI – Public Key Infrastructure). In the mean time, the client generates transformed biometric feature B_C from biometric feature B'

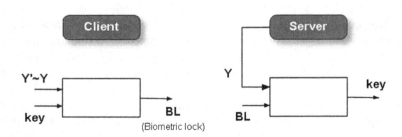

Fig. 3. The fuzzy commitment in the proposal authentication phase.

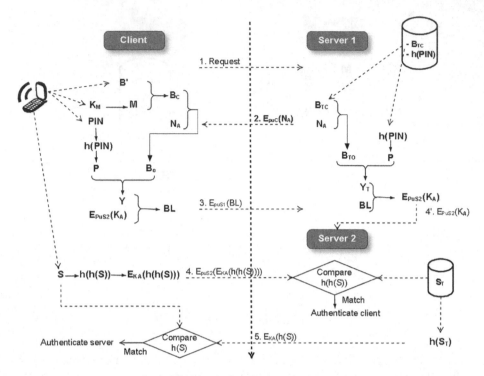

Fig. 4. Authentication phase.

which is extracted in this phase, and orthonormal matrix M from K_M. From the same client, biometric feature B in registration phase and B' in authentication phase cannot be identical due to noises. Calculated B_C combines with N_a to produce another version of transformed biometric – B_O. This step is done to ensure every time the client sends his/her request, a different version of B_O is created to avoid replay attack. This B_O's items are permuted through permutation P which is generated from the hash version of *PIN*. This operation results in Y. It is meant to improve security by eliminating the characters of each biometric feature, enabling random distribution of biometric feature's value. Following that, Y and the encryption of the authentication key K_A become inputs of the fuzzy commitment process to generate biometric lock BL (described in Fig. 3.). Client then sends BL to server S_1 for authentication purpose.

At server side, after generating the NONCE N_A, S_1 retrieves the B_{TC} and h(PIN) from the database. The one time version of biometric template B_{TO} is created from the combination between B_{TC} and N_A. Some parts of this process are similar to the process at client side. After B_{TO}, server generate Y_T by shuffling B_{TO} using P which is computed from h(PIN). Then, Y_T is used to unlock the BL to reproduce the encryption of authentication key K_A.

At step fourth, client retrieves the mobile serial number S, hashes it twice to have h($h(S)$), encrypts the result by the authentication key, and encrypts once more time by the public key of the server S_2 before sending to S_2. Together with this step, at the step

4', server S_1 sends the encryption of the authentication key using public key of server S_2 to S_2. S_2 uses its private key to obtain the authentication key K_A. Server S_2 uses its private key as well as the newly achieved K_A to decrypt the message from the client. If the decryption process is successful, it also means the biometric the client provided matches with the transformed biometric template stored in the database of server S_1. The result of this decryption is compared with the double hashed version of S_T stored in the database of S_2. If they are matched, the client is authenticated; otherwise, the authentication is failed.

For the mutual authentication purpose, the protocol is not stopped here. After successful authentication, server S_2 computes $h(S_T)$, then encrypts it with the authentication key K_A before sending the result back to the client. The client decrypts the message. If the decryption is successful, he/she can be sure that the authentication server also possesses the same key. The client carries out the comparison between the h (S) of client and the $h(S_T)$ of the server. If they are match, the server is authenticated. The client can feel secure about the authentication server which he/she communicated with. Once the mutual authentication is successfully accomplished, K_A is used to protect the communication between the client and the server.

5   Security Analysis

The protocol indicates that the authenticity of the client needs following factors:

- Client's biometric data
- The number used once N_A
- The token that holds the key K_M to generate the random orthonormal matrix
- The *PIN*
- The mobile serial number S.

The multi-factor authentication enhances security since the ability that an attacker steals client's authentication information to enter the system is reduced. In this section, we analyze in detail how the proposal protocol is robust against some main attacks.

5.1   Biometric Template Attack

The original biometric is protected by the non-invertible transformation function. Server keeps the transformed version, but it is impossible for server to infer the client's original biometric from this template. Using orthonormal matrix as a non-invertible function ensures the revocability of biometric template. In case the client is in doubt that his/her biometric template is compromised, he/she only needs to alter parameter K_M to produce new orthonormal matrix, then registers the new transformed biometric template to the server. This process is similar to that of changing password in traditional authentication system.

Another useful factor helps against biometric template attack is the permutation. A one-time version of the transformed biometric feature B_O is re-ordered by a permutation P. This operation is meant to improve security by eliminating the characters of each biometric feature, enabling random distribution of biometric feature's value. This, eventually, weakens the ability of attacker to infer the value of biometric feature.

5.2 Replay Attack

Replay attack happens when attackers reuse old information to impersonate either client or server with the aim to deceive the other side. This attack is prevented by using N_A and session key K_A which are used only once. The system only collapses once the attackers steal private key. In that case the attacker is able to obtain the 3rd message in authentication phase (see Fig. 4) to calculate BL. After that, the attacker reuses the BL to deceive server in a new session. The proposed protocol is immune from this type of attack as the BL generated every time the clients request contains new N_A produced by the server. In the event of attacker using old BL, the authentication process cannot calculate exact authentication key K_A.

More concretely speaking, in authentication phase, the transformed biometric features, BC at client side and BTC at server side, are combined with the same number NA by a simple addition operation. This action creates a one-time version of the transformed biometric feature; therefore, attacker cannot reuse the old transformed biometric feature to delude the server. Thanks to that, the security of the entire protocol is strengthened without scarifying the accuracy. The accuracy is maintained because addition operation does not modify intra-class variation of the biometric features, which results in unchanged distance between transformed biometric feature & its original. In other words, the error rate stabilizes while security is strengthened.

5.3 Man-in-the-Middle Attack

MITM (Man-in-the-middle) attack considers as an active eavesdropping, attackers make an independent connection and replays messages between client and server in order to impersonate one side to delude the other side. Concretely speaking, the communication in this case is controlled by attacker while client or server still believes that they are talking to each other over a private connection.

MITM attack happens when the attacker catches the messages between client and server then impersonates one side to communicate with the other side. In our proposed protocol, this type of attack cannot occur since the protocol presents mutual authentication requirement, not only does it requires the server to authenticate its right client but also enables the client to perform its own process to confirm requested server.

5.4 Insider Attack

This type of attack happens when the administrator of authentication server exploits client's data stored in the database to legalize his authentication process on behalf of the client. The proposed protocol is capable of reducing the risk from insider attack by splitting authentication server into two different servers. Each server has its own function and data. Server S_1 stores transformed biometric template and some supporting information to generate authentication key. Authentication function is carried out by server S_2. To perform this function, server S_2 has to receive authentication key calculated by server S_1 and authentication information provided by the client. Consequently, server S_2 can only store authentication information (client's mobile serial number) to proceed authenticating client (described in Sect. 4.2). At the same time, such information is used by client to reversibly authenticate server.

6 Conclusion

In this paper, we have presented an unsusceptible biometric based remote authentication protocol to most of sophisticated attacks over an open network. The proposed protocol combines client's biometric with the other authentication factors to achieve the high level of security. Thanks to the combination of fuzzy commitment and non-invertible transformation technologies as well as a mutual challenge/response, the protocol is resistant to some main attacks to biometric-based authentication system such as biometric template attack, replay attack, man-in-the-middle attack. The remarkable point of this work is that we solved the problem at the unsecure server. We reduce the ability that the administrator utilizes the client's authentication information saved in the database to impersonate him/her and cheat the system. By using the random orthonormal project instead of traditional orthonormal project, the computational complexity is reduced while the accuracy is remained.

Acknowledgements. This research is funded by Vietnam National University - Ho Chi Minh City (VNU-HCM) under grant number TNCS-2014-KHMT-06. We also want to show a great appreciation to each member of D-STAR Lab (www.dstar.edu.vn) for their enthusiastic supports and helpful advices during the time we have carried out this research.

References

1. Jain, A.K., Ross, A.: Multibiometric systems. Commun. ACM **47**(1), 34–40 (2004)
2. Rathgeb, C., Uhl, A.: A survey on biometric cryptosystems and cancelable biometrics. EURASIP J. Inf. Secur. **2011**(1), 1–25 (2011)
3. Upmanyu, M., et al.: Blind authentication: a secure crypto-biometric verification protocol. IEEE Trans. Inf. Forensics Secur. **5**(2), 255–268 (2010)
4. Jain, A.K., Nandakumar, K., Nagar, A.: Biometric template security. EURASIP J. Adv. Signal Process. **2008**, 1–17 (2008)
5. Huynh, V.Q.P., et al.: A combination of ANN and secure sketch for generating strong biometric key. J. Sci. Technol. Vietnamese Acad. Sci. Technol. **51**(4B), 30–39 (2013)
6. Le, T.T.B., Dang, T.K., Truong, Q.C., Nguyen, T.A.T.: Protecting biometric features by periodic function-based transformation and fuzzy vault. In: Hameurlain, A., Küng, J., Wagner, R., Thoai, N., Dang, T.K. (eds.) TLDKS XVI. LNCS, vol. 8960, pp. 57–70. Springer, Heidelberg (2015)
7. Lifang, W., Songlong, Y.: A face based fuzzy vault scheme for secure online authentication. In: Second International Symposium on Data, Privacy and E-Commerce (ISDPE) (2010)

8. Failla, P., Sutcu, Y., Barni, M.: eSketch: a privacy-preserving fuzzy commitment scheme for authentication using encrypted biometrics. In: Proceedings of the 12th ACM Workshop on Multimedia and Security, pp. 241–246. ACM, Roma (2010)
9. Nguyen, T.H.L., Nguyen, T.T.H.: An approach to protect private key using fingerprint biometric encryption key in BioPKI based security system. In: The 10th International Conference on Control, Automation, Robotics and Vision, ICARCV (2008)
10. Xi, K., et al.: A fingerprint based bio-cryptographic security protocol designed for client/server authentication in mobile computing environment. Secur. Commun. Netw. 4(5), 487–499 (2011)
11. Al-Assam, H., Rashid, R., Jassim, S.: Combining steganography and biometric cryptosystems for secure mutual authentication and key exchange. In: The 8th International Conference for Internet Technology and Secured Transactions (ICITST 2013) (2013)
12. Jain, A.K., Uludag, U.: Hiding biometric data. IEEE Trans. Pattern Anal. Mach. Intell. 25 (11), 1494–1498 (2003)
13. Fengling, H., Alkhathami, M., Van Schyndel, R.: Biometric-Kerberos authentication scheme for secure mobile computing services. In: The 6th International Congress on Image and Signal Processing (CISP 2013) (2013)
14. Juels, A. Wattenberg, M.: A fuzzy commitment scheme. In: Proceedings of the 6th ACM Conference on Computer and Communications Security, pp. 28–36. ACM, Kent Ridge Digital Labs, Singapore (1999)
15. Al-Assam, H., Sellahewa, H., Jassim, S.: A lightweight approach for biometric template protection. In: Proceedings of SPIE (2009)

Profiler for Smartphone Users Interests Using Modified Hierarchical Agglomerative Clustering Algorithm Based on Browsing History

Priagung Khusumanegara, Rischan Mafrur, and Deokjai Choi[✉]

Department of Electronics and Computer Engineering,
Chonnam National University, 77 Yongbong-Ro, Buk-Gu,
Gwangju, South Korea
{priagung.123,rischanlab}@gmail.com, dchoi@cnu.ac.kr

.

Abstract. Nowadays, smartphone has been a life style for many people in the world and it has become an indispensable part of their live. Smartphone provides many applications to support human activity which one of the applications is web browser applications. People spend much time on browsing activity for finding useful information that they are interested on it. It is not easy to find the particular pieces of information that they interested on it. In this paper, user-profiler is presented as way of providing smartphone users with their interest based on their browsing history. In this study, we propose a Modified Hierarchical Agglomerative Clustering algorithm that uses filtering category groups on a server-based application to aid provides smartphone user profile for interests-focused based on browsing history automatically. Based on experimental results, the proposed algorithm can measure degree of smartphone user interest based on browsing history of web browser applications, provides smartphone users interests profile and also outperforms the C4.5 algorithm in execution time on all memory utilization.

Keywords: Smartphone · User interests · Modified Hierarchical Agglomerative Clustering

1 Introduction

Today, many vendors such as Google and Yahoo store historical data in a users' browser to understand the type page that user is visiting. This information is used to show ads that might appeal to users based on their inferred interest categories. For example, if a user browses many sport-related websites displaying AdSense ads or watch sport-related videos on YouTube, it means Google and Yahoo may associate a sport interest category with their history and show the user sport-related ads. Information about user interests is useful both for users and service providers, user can easily find the information that they needed so they do not spend time to find it and in point of view service providers, they can also easily to provide advertisement and recommendation to the users who use their service. It is not easy to find the particular pieces of information that users interested on

© IFIP International Federation for Information Processing 2015
I. Khalil et al. (Eds.): ICT-EurAsia 2015 and CONFENIS 2015, LNCS 9357, pp. 89–96, 2015.
DOI: 10.1007/978-3-319-24315-3_9

it. In this paper, we implement a server-based application to provide smartphone user profile based on browsing history of web browser application. We propose a Modified Hierarchical Agglomerative Clustering algorithm that is inspired by Hierarchical Agglomerative Clustering algorithm. Our method can automatically provide smartphone user profile for interests-focused based on browsing history of web browser applications. First, we extract the useful information of historical web browser applications from smartphone users. Second, we use a distance function to calculate similarity distances between the extracted data. Third, we use Modified Hierarchical Agglomerative Clustering algorithm that use filtering category groups to provide smartphone user profile for interests-focused. The reminder of this paper is structured follows. The Sect. 2 describes the previous studies. The data extraction and user profiling algorithm is presented in Sect. 3. We then show the experimental results and evaluations of our work in Sect. 4. Finally, we conclude our findings and suggestions for future research in Sect. 5.

2 Related Work

In this section, we will review some existing works on web log data mining. Previous researchers have investigated how to generate user profile based on web server data logs using various data mining technique. Most of the approaches concerned on user classification (supervised) method and clustering (unsupervised) method based on useful information from web server data logs. In Jian's et al. work [1], classification (supervised) method is used to predict users' gender and age from web browsing behavior. Santra et al. [2] research about identification interested users using naïve Bayesian classification based on web log data and also comparison between decision tree algorithm C4.5 and Naïve Bayesian Classification algorithm for identifying interested user. JinHua Xu et al. [3] used KMeans algorithm for clustering web user based on web data logs. Xia Min-jie et al. [4] research using clustering technique based on web logs and users' browsing behavior to implement an ecommerce recommendation system. Neetu et al. [5] used classification technique to predict kid's behavior based on collected internet logs. Li et al. [6] focused on web log data processing to analyze and research the user's behavior. Shuqing et al. [7] provided novel algorithm to extract user's interest based on web log data and describes including long term interest and short term interest. Tsuyoshi et al. [8] described in his paper a method for clarifying user's interests based on an analysis of the site keyword graph. In this paper, we concern on how to provide smartphone user profile automatically using Modified Hierarchical Agglomerative Clustering Algorithm based on their historical logs of web browser applications in smartphone.

3 Data Extraction and User Profiling

In this section, we will describe about data extraction and each process to provide smartphone user profile for interest-focused based on browsing history of web browser applications.

3.1 Data Extraction

In this work, we use browsing history data of 30 smartphone users that is collected during one month. In this study, we develop an android application that can be used to collect browsing history from all browser applications and then we install that application on each user's smartphone. The structure of collected data from user's smartphone is shown in Table 1.

Table 1. The example of collected data

User ID	Visit time	URL
10	1399652396.55	http://www.kakao.com/fightingkorea
7	1399809440.79	http://cyber.kepco.co.kr/ckepco/
1	1400251354.06	http://asked.kr/ask.php?id=1927949
5	1399553574.34	http://m.winixcorp.com/
5	1399637818.62	http://www.dalkomm.com/

Based on the Table 1, each row of collected data represents the URLs that the user visits. Attributes of the data include user ID, visit time, and URL data. A URL (Uniform Resource Locator) is the unique address of documents and other resources on the World Wide Web. The first part of URL structure is called a protocol identifier which indicates what protocol that is used, and the second part is called a resource name which specifies the IP address or domain name where the resource is located. In our work, we extract collected data to derive a resource name part of URL structure which is useful information to analyze user interests and after that the Modified Hierarchical Agglomerative Clustering algorithm is assigned to provide smartphone user profile for interest-focused.

3.2 Modified Hierarchical Agglomerative Clustering Algorithm

In this study, we have Modified Hierarchical Agglomerative Clustering to aid in providing smartphone user profile for interest-focused. We use *Levenshtein* distance function to measure minimum distance between two extracted URL data. We use *Levenshtein* distance to measure minimum distance between two extracted URL data. *Levenshtein* distance between two extracted URL data url_1, url_2 is given by $dist_{url_1,url_2}(|url_1|,|url_2|)$, where,

$$dist_{url_1,url_2}(i,j) = \begin{cases} \max(i,j) & if \ \min(i,j) = 0, \\ \min \begin{cases} dist_{url_1,url_2}(i-1,j)+1 \\ dist_{url_1,url_2}(i,j-1)+1 \\ dist_{url_1,url_2}(i-1,j-1)+1_{(url_i \neq url_j)} \end{cases} & otherwise. \end{cases}$$

Where, $1_{(url_i \neq url_j)}$ is the indicator function equal to 0 when $url_i = url_j$ and equal to 1 otherwise.

The Modified Hierarchical Agglomerative Clustering algorithm that is implemented in our work is following below.

Algorithm. Modified Hierarchical Agglomerative Clustering

Input:

A set X of extracted URL data $\{URL_1, \dots, URL_n\}$

URL Filtering Categories $C_{4xn} = \begin{bmatrix} key_{1,1} & key_{1,2} & \cdots & key_{1,n} \\ key_{2,1} & key_{2,2} & \cdots & key_{2,n} \\ key_{3,1} & key_{3,2} & \cdots & key_{3,n} \\ key_{4,1} & key_{4,2} & \cdots & key_{4,1} \end{bmatrix}$

A Lavenshtein distance function $dist(c_1, c_2)$

output:

Degree of Interest, user interests

1: $C_{group_1} = []$

2: $C_{group_2} = []$

3: $C_{group_3} = []$

4: $C_{group_4} = []$

5: **for** $i = 1$ *to* n

6:    $c_i = \{URL_i\}$

7: *end for*

8: $C = \{c_1, \dots, k\}$

9: $l = n + 1$

10:   **While** $C.size > 1$ *do*

11:   $(c_{min1}, c_{min2}) = min.\,distance\,(c_i, c_j)$ *for all* c_i, c_j *in* C

12:   *Remove* c_{min1} *and* c_{min2} *from* C

13:   *Add* $\{c_{min1}, c_{min2}\}$ *to* C

14:   *If* $\{c_{min1}, c_{min2}\}$ *any* $[key_{1,n}]$, *where* $n = 1,2,..,n$:

15:       *Add* $\{c_{min1}, c_{min2}\}$ *to* C_{group_1}

16:   *elif* $\{c_{min1}, c_{min2}\}$ *any* $[key_{2,n}]$, *where* $n = 1,2,..,n$:

17:       *Add* $\{c_{min1}, c_{min2}\}$ *to* C_{group_2}

18:   *elif* $\{c_{min1}, c_{min2}\}$ *any* $[key_{3,n}]$, *where* $n = 1,2,..,n$:

19:       *Add* $\{c_{min1}, c_{min2}\}$ *to* C_{group_3}

20:   *elif* $\{c_{min1}, c_{min2}\}$ *any* $[key_{4,n}]$, *where* $n = 1,2,..,n$:

21:       *Add* $\{c_{min1}, c_{min2}\}$ *to* C_{group_4}

22:   $l = l + 1$

23: *end while*

24:   *Degree of Interest* $C_{group_1} = \dfrac{length.C_{group_1}}{\sum_{i=1}^{4} length.C_{group_i}}$

25:   *Degree of Interest* $C_{group_2} = \dfrac{length.C_{group_2}}{\sum_{i=1}^{4} length.C_{group_i}}$

26:   *Degree of Interest* $C_{group_3} = \dfrac{length.C_{group_3}}{\sum_{i=1}^{4} length.C_{group_i}}$

27:   *Degree of Interest* $C_{group_4} = \dfrac{length.C_{group_4}}{\sum_{i=1}^{4} length.C_{group_i}}$

28: set C_{group_i} which has max (*Degree of Interest*) *as user interests*

First is start by assigning each extracted URL data to a cluster, if we have n URLs, it means we have n clusters. Second, we compute the minimum distance between each cluster using Levenshtein distance function. Third, we find the closest (most similar) pair of clusters and merge them into a single cluster. Forth, we filter element of clusters using URL filtering categorizes. URL filtering categorizes will filter clusters based on keywords of users' interests. Fifth, we compute distances between the new cluster and each of the old clusters. We repeat steps 3, 4 and 5 until all extracted URL data has been clustered into a category of users' interests. After that we calculate interest degree for each category groups.

Table 2. URL filtering categories

Category group	Category type
Business	Business/Economy, Job Search/Careers, real estate, and shopping
Communications and search	Blog/Web Communication, social networks, email, and search engines/portals
General	Computer/Internet, education, news/media, and reference
Lifestyle	Entertainment, games, arts, humor, religion, restaurants/food, and travel

In our real work, we classify URL filtering categories into four main categories. The categories and their category type are shown on Table 2. Filtering categories consists of business category group, communications and search category group, general category group, and life style category group. The matrix C of size $4 \times n$ to represent filtering categories can denoted as

$$
C_{4xn} = \begin{bmatrix}
key_{1,1} & key_{1,2} & \dots & key_{1,n} \\
key_{2,1} & key_{2,2} & \dots & key_{2,n} \\
key_{3,1} & key_{3,2} & \dots & key_{3,n} \\
key_{4,1} & key_{4,2} & \dots & key_{4,n}
\end{bmatrix}
$$

Where rows represents category group of users' interests and columns represent keywords on each category group. We categorize the clustered results into category group based on keywords on matrix of filtering categories.

4 Experimental Results

In our study, we collected browsing history data of 30 smartphone users during one month continuously. Browsing history data was tested on log files stored by the server. We extracted collected data and then use proposed algorithm which is called by Modified Hierarchical Agglomerative Clustering to provide smartphone user profile for interests-focused. In our experiment, we compare the performance between our method and C4.5 algorithm.

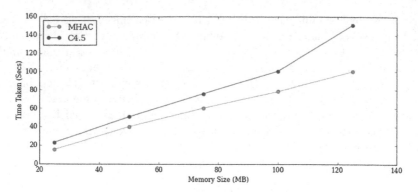

Fig. 1. Execution time comparison with C4.5 algorithm

Figure 1 presents the execution time results of Modified Hierarchical Agglomerative Clustering algorithm (MHAC) and C4.5 algorithm. Our method consistently outperforms the C4.5 algorithm on all memory utilization in execution time. The results of degree of smartphone users' interests for each category are shown on Fig. 2. Finally, the results of smartphone user profile for interests-focused based on the highest degree for each user is shown on Fig. 3.

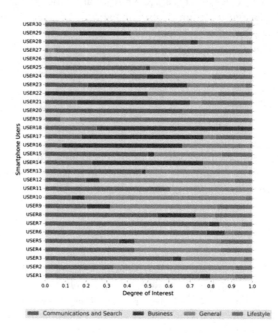

Fig. 2. Degree of smartphone user interests

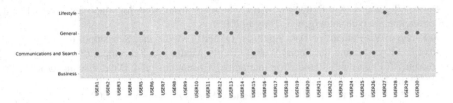

Fig. 3. Results of smartphone user profile for interests-focused

5   Conclusion and Future Work

In this paper, we have implemented a server-based application that can be used to provide user profile for interests-focused based on browsing history of web browser applications. In our approach, we propose a Modified Hierarchical Agglomerative Clustering to cluster extracted data which can automatically provide an interests profile of smartphone users. Based on experimental results, the proposed method can measure degree of users' interests based on browsing history of web browser applications, inferring particular pieces of information that they interested on it, and outperforms the C4.5 algorithm in execution time on all memory utilization. Because amount of data that will be processed is increased, so in the future we need to implement Map-Reduce algorithm on Modified Hierarchical Agglomerative Clustering to enhance performance of clustering algorithm.

Acknowledgements. This research was supported by Basic Science Research Program through the National Research Foundation of Korea (NRF) funded by the Ministry of Education (2012R1A1A2007014).

References

1. Hu, J., Zeng, H.-J., Li, H., Niu, C., Chen, Z.: Demographic prediction based on user's browsing behavior. In: International World Wide Web Conference, Beijing (2007)
2. Santra, A.K., Jayasudha, S.: Classification of web log data to identify interested users using Naïve Bayesian classification. IJCSI Int. J. Comput. Sci. Issues **IX**(1), 381–387 (2012)
3. Xu, J.H., Liu, H.: Web user clustering analysis based on KMans algorithm. In: International Conference on Infrmation, Networking and Automation (ICINA), HangZhou (2010)
4. Min-jie, X., Jin-ge, Z.: Research on personalized recommendation system for e-commerce based on web log mining and user browsing behaviors. In: International Conference on Computer Application and System Modeling, ZhengZhou (2010)
5. Anand, N.: Effective prediction of kid's behaviour based on internet use. Int. J. Inf. Comput. Technol. **IV**(2), 183–188 (2014)
6. Li, J.: Research of analysis of user behavior based on web log. In: International Conference on Computational and Information Sciences, Anshan (2013)
7. Wang, S., She, L., Liu, Z., Fu, Y.: Algorithm research on user interests extracting via web log data. In: International Conference on Web Information Systems and Mining, Chengdu (2009)

8. Murata, T., Saito, K.: Extracting users' interests from web log data. In: International Conference on Web Intelligence, Tokyo (2006)
9. McKinney, W.: Python for Data Analysis. O'Reilly Media Inc, Sebastopol (2012)
10. Russell, M.A.: Mining the Social Web. O'Reilly Media Inc, Sebastopol (2011)
11. Rossant, C.: Learning IPython for Interactive Computing and Data Visualization. Packt Publishing Ltd, Birmingham (2013)
12. Vaingast, S.: Beginning Python Visualization. Springer, New York (2009)

Data Management and Information
Advertising

Strength of Relationship Between Multi-labeled Data and Labels

Masahiro Kuzunishi[1](✉) and Tetsuya Furukawa[2]

[1] Faculty of Economics, Aichi Gakuin University, Meijyo 3-1-1,
Kita, Nagoya 462-8739, Japan
kuzunisi@dpc.agu.ac.jp
[2] Department of Economic Engineering, Kyushu University, Hakozaki 6-19-1,
Higashi, Fukuoka 812-8581, Japan
furukawa@econ.kyushu-u.ac.jp

Abstract. Collected data must be organized properly to utilize well and classification of data is one of the efficient methods. Individual data or an object is classified to categories and annotated with labels of those categories. Giving ranks to labels of objects in order to express how close objects are to the categories enables us to use objects more precisely. When target objects are identified by a set of labels $\mathcal{L}$, there are various strength of relationship between objects and $\mathcal{L}$. This paper proposes criteria for objects with two rank labels, primary and secondary labels, such as a label relates to $\mathcal{L}$, a primary label relates to $\mathcal{L}$, every primary label relates to $\mathcal{L}$, and every label relates to $\mathcal{L}$. The strongest criterion which an object satisfies is the level of the object to express the degree of the strength of relationship between the object and $\mathcal{L}$. The results for two rank objects are extended to k rank objects.

Keywords: Multi-labeled data · Ranks of labels · Levels of data · Criteria for the strength

1 Introduction

With increasing various kinds of data such as numerical data, texts, images, and movies, utilization of collected data is becoming more important [4,11,12]. Such data must be organized properly to utilize well and classification of data is one of the efficient methods [3,8]. Individual data is classified to a category by a certain attribute, for example, region or industry, and the data is annotated with the label of the category [1].

When data relates to multiple categories, the data is classified to those categories and annotated with the set of labels [9]. However, the strength of relationship between data and categories is different in general. Ranks of the labels which express how close the data is to categories enable us to use the data more precisely. Suppose that data are classified by business categories and annotated with sets of labels of the categories. If ranks are given to the labels of a data according to the financial figures (net revenues, net income, etc.) of the relating

© IFIP International Federation for Information Processing 2015
I. Khalil et al. (Eds.): ICT-EurAsia 2015 and CONFENIS 2015, LNCS 9357, pp. 99–108, 2015.
DOI: 10.1007/978-3-319-24315-3_10

business field, users can compare the data of automobile and finance as primary categories with the data of automobile as a primary category and finance as a secondary category.

Although ranks of labels give us richer information, target data identified by a set of labels are not clear because there are various strength of relationship between the data and the set of labels. Even if users need the data which relate to a set of labels more closely, there are cases that the strength can not be decided.

Example 1. For the strength of relationship between data and a set of labels $\mathcal{L}_1 = \{Transportation, Electronics\}$, it is not decided clearly whether the data on the company where automobile, mobile phone, and finance are primary relates to $\mathcal{L}_1$ more closely than the data on the company where only automobile is primary and mobile phone and finance are secondary. While the former data relates to $\mathcal{L}_1$ more closely if the primary categories related to $\mathcal{L}_1$ are evaluated before the unrelated category to $\mathcal{L}_1$, the latter data is closer to $\mathcal{L}_1$ if the primary categories after the unrelated category.

Criteria for the strength of relationship between data and a set of labels enable to evaluate the degree of the strength. The purpose of this paper is to propose such criteria by discussing the strength of relationship between data and a set of labels. This paper also refers to the strength of the criteria and introduces levels of data, which is decided by the strongest criterion that the data satisfies.

Ranks in classification of data have been studied in the field of information retrieval mainly. Those researches focus on the accuracy and the efficiency of automatic ranking of data [5,6]. After ranking, personal preferences of queries are measured and the ranks of data based on those numerical values are applied to the advanced information retrieval [10]. Many researches focus on ranking data known as *Top-k*, where significant data are selected by measuring the degree of relationship between data and a set of labels [2,7]. While their purpose is to evaluate data on a specific domain quantitatively to develop applications, the purpose of this paper is to build fundamental theories of multi-labeled data by evaluating data qualitatively.

This paper is organized as follows. Section 2 refers to the strength of relationship between data without ranks and a set of labels, and introduces criteria to decide the strength. In Sect. 3, criteria for data with ranks are discussed. Section 4 proposes the strength of the criteria and the levels of data to express the degree of the strength. The discussions of Sects. 3 and 4 are for two rank data, which are extended to k rank data in Sect. 5. Section 6 concludes the paper.

2   Strength of Relationship Between Objects and Labels

Individual data or an object is classified by a certain type of characteristic, which is called an attribute. For example, an object is classified to manufacturing, transportation, automobile, etc., where the attribute is industry. This paper assumes that an object is classified to the lowest category to which the object is related in a given classification hierarchy.

Let o be an object, L be a label, and $\boldsymbol{L} = \{L_1, L_2, \cdots, L_n\}$ be a set of labels. When o is classified to multiple categories, o is annotated with the set of labels of those categories, which is denoted by $L(o)$ and called a set label of o.

For labels L_1 and L_2, L_1 is lower than L_2 (L_2 is higher than L_1) if the category of L_1 is a lower concept of the category of L_2, and $L_1 \preceq L_2$ denotes that L_1 is lower than or equal to L_2. L_1 relates to L_2 if $L_1 \preceq L_2$ and a label L relates to a set of labels $\boldsymbol{L}$ if L relates to a label of $\boldsymbol{L}$. Label *Transportation* relates to label *Manufacturing* because *Transportation* $\preceq$ *Manufacturing*.

For sets of labels $\boldsymbol{L}$ and $\boldsymbol{L'}$, the set of the labels of $\boldsymbol{L}$ which relate to $\boldsymbol{L'}$ is described by $Rel_{\boldsymbol{L'}}(\boldsymbol{L}) = \{L \mid L \in \boldsymbol{L}, \exists L' \in \boldsymbol{L'}, L \preceq L'\}$. Let $\mathcal{L}$ be a set of labels to be used to identify target objects. If there is such a label in $L(o)$ that relates to $\mathcal{L}$ ($Rel_{\mathcal{L}}(L(o)) \neq \phi$), o relates to $\mathcal{L}$. Let $\overline{\mathcal{L}}$ be the set of objects relating to $\mathcal{L}$.

There are several kinds of objects in $\overline{\mathcal{L}}$ such as objects which relate to multiple labels of $\mathcal{L}$, objects which relate to other labels than $\mathcal{L}$, and so on.

Example 2. For a set of labels $\mathcal{L}_2 = \{Transportation\}$, $\overline{\mathcal{L}_2}$ includes object o_1 such that $L(o_1) = \{Automobile\}$, object o_2 such that $L(o_2) = \{Automobile, Motorcycle\}$ where multiple labels of $L(o_2)$ relate to $\mathcal{L}_2$, object o_3 such that $L(o_3) = \{Automobile, Finance\}$ where *Finance* does not relate to $\mathcal{L}_2$, etc.

There are various ways to decide the degree of how strong an object o relate to $\mathcal{L}$, and the number of labels relate to $\mathcal{L}$ may not be affected on the strength of relationship between o and $\mathcal{L}$. This paper focuses on the qualitativeness of relationship and does not mention the number of the labels which relate to $\mathcal{L}$.

There are several kinds of objects identified by $\mathcal{L}$, and the strength of relationship between objects and $\mathcal{L}$ is different in general. Criteria for the strength enable us to select proper objects according to their purposes.

For objects o_1 and o_2, $o_1 <_{\mathcal{L}} o_2$, $o_1 < o_2$ if $\mathcal{L}$ is obvious, denotes that o_2 relates to $\mathcal{L}$ more closely than o_1. A condition cnd is a criterion for strength of relationship between a set of labels and an object if o_2 satisfies cnd and o_1 does not for any objects o_1 and o_2 such that $o_1 <_{\mathcal{L}} o_2$.

3 Criteria for the Strength of Relationship

This section introduces ranks to express how close objects are to the categories. The more number of ranks give us the richer information and allow more precise analysis. This section discusses the cases where the number of ranks is two for simplicity. The discussions for two rank objects are extended to k rank objects in Sect. 5.

Let the ranks of labels of set labels be primary and secondary.

- Primary labels: If an object is classified to a category and relates to the category mainly, the label of the object is a primary label.
- Secondary labels: If an object is classified to a category and relates to the category but not mainly, the label of the object is a secondary label.

For an object o, let $P(o)$ and $S(o)$ be the set of the primary labels and the set of the secondary labels of $L(o)$, respectively.

Property 1. $L(o) = P(o) \cup S(o)$.

Property 2. $P(o) \cap S(o) = \phi$.

Property 3. $P(o) \neq \phi$.

The rest of this section discusses criteria for two rank objects. It is reasonable to think that an object o_1 relating to a set of labels $\mathcal{L}$ ($Rel_{\mathcal{L}}(L(o_1)) \neq \phi$) relates to $\mathcal{L}$ more closely than an object o_2 not relating to $\mathcal{L}$ ($Rel_{\mathcal{L}}(L(o_2)) = \phi$). Thus the condition whether a label of $L(o)$ relates to $\mathcal{L}$ is a criterion for the strength of relationship between o and $\mathcal{L}$.

cnd_{LE}: For a set of labels $\mathcal{L}$ and an object o, there exists a label of $L(o)$ which relates to $\mathcal{L}$, that is, $Rel_{\mathcal{L}}(L(o)) \neq \phi$.

Since it is acceptable to think that an object o_1 relating to a set of labels $\mathcal{L}$ mainly ($Rel_{\mathcal{L}}(P(o_1)) \neq \phi$) relates to $\mathcal{L}$ more closely than an object o_2 not relating to $\mathcal{L}$ mainly ($Rel_{\mathcal{L}}(P(o_2)) = \phi$), the condition whether a primary label of $L(o)$ of an object o relates to $\mathcal{L}$ is a criterion for the strength of relationship between o and $\mathcal{L}$.

cnd_{PE}: For a set of labels $\mathcal{L}$ and an object o, there exists a primary label of $L(o)$ which relates to $\mathcal{L}$, that is, $Rel_{\mathcal{L}}(P(o)) \neq \phi$.

There are cases that secondary labels of $L(o)$ affect the strength of relationship between o and $\mathcal{L}$. If $Rel_{\mathcal{L}}(P(o)) = \phi$, the strength by $S(o)$ is equivalent to cnd_{LE}. Suppose $Rel_{\mathcal{L}}(P(o)) \neq \phi$. For an object o_1 such that $Rel_{\mathcal{L}}(P(o_1)) \neq \phi$ and $Rel_{\mathcal{L}}(S(o_1)) \neq \phi$ and an object o_2 such that $Rel_{\mathcal{L}}(P(o_2)) \neq \phi$ and $Rel_{\mathcal{L}}(S(o_2)) = \phi$, both o_1 and o_2 do not relate to $\mathcal{L}$ more closely than the other.

Example 3. Suppose the labels of object o_1 and object o_4 are $P(o_1) = \{Automobile\}$, $S(o_1) = \phi$, $P(o_4) = \{Automobile\}$, and $S(o_4) = \{Mobile\ Phone\}$ for set of labels $\mathcal{L}_3 = \{Manufacturing\}$. Although *Mobile Phone* of $L(o_4)$ relating to $\mathcal{L}_3$ is a secondary label, it is not acceptable to think that o_1 relates to $\mathcal{L}_3$ more closely than o_4 because o_1 and o_4 have primary label *Automobile* for $\mathcal{L}_3$, namely, both of them relate to *Manufacturing* mainly.

For object o_4' such that $P(o_4') = \{Automobile, Mobile\ Phone\}$ and $S(o_4') = \phi$, it is not reasonable to think that o_4 relates to $\mathcal{L}_3$ more closely than o_4' because *Mobile Phone* of $L(o_4')$ is a primary label and *Mobile Phone* of $L(o_4)$ is a secondary label. Since the number of the labels which relate to $\mathcal{L}_3$ does not affect the strength, the strength of relationship between o_4' and $\mathcal{L}_3$ is the same as the strength of relationship between o_1 and $\mathcal{L}_3$.

For a set of labels $\mathcal{L}$ and objects o_1 and o_2, it can be regarded that o_1 relates to $\mathcal{L}$ more closely than o_2 if $L(o_1)$ does not include other labels than $\mathcal{L}$ and $L(o_2)$ includes such labels.

cnd_{LN}: For a set of labels $\mathcal{L}$ and an object o, there does not exist a label of $L(o)$ which does not relate to $\mathcal{L}$, that is, $Rel_{\mathcal{L}}(L(o)) = L(o)$.

It is also acceptable to think that an object o_1 relates to $\mathcal{L}$ more closely than an object o_2 if $P(o_1)$ does not include other labels than $\mathcal{L}$ while $P(o_2)$ includes other labels than $\mathcal{L}$.

cnd_{PN}: For a set of labels $\mathcal{L}$ and an object o, there does not exist a label of $P(o)$ which does not relate to $\mathcal{L}$, that is, $Rel_{\mathcal{L}}(P(o)) = P(o)$.

For the criteria for secondary labels of $L(o)$ which relate to other labels than $\mathcal{L}$, if there are labels of $P(o)$ which relate to other labels than $\mathcal{L}$, such labels of $S(o)$ do not affect the strength of relationship.

Example 4. Suppose object o_3 such that $P(o_3) = \{Automobile, Finance\}$ and $S(o_3) = \phi$ and object o_3' such that $P(o_3') = \{Automobile,\ Finance\}$ and $S(o_3') = \{Education\}$ are evaluated for $\mathcal{L}_3 = \{Manufacturing\}$. Although o_3' has secondary label *Education* which relates to other labels than *Manufacturing*, it is not acceptable to think that o_3' relates to $\mathcal{L}_3$ more closely o_3.

For object o_3'' such that $P(o_3'') = \{Automobile, Finance, Education\}$, it is not acceptable to think that o_3'' relates to $\mathcal{L}_3$ more closely than o_3' because o_3'' has primary label *Education*. Thus $o_3' < o_3''$ is not satisfied. The strength of relationship between o_3'' and $\mathcal{L}_3$ is the same as the strength of relationship between o_3 and $\mathcal{L}_3$ because both of them have primary labels relating to $\mathcal{L}_3$.

If there are no labels of $P(o)$ which relate to other labels than $\mathcal{L}$, the strength of relationship is decided by whether there exist labels of $S(o)$ which relate to other labels than $\mathcal{L}$. If there exist such labels in $S(o)$, it means that there exist labels of $L(o)$ which relate to other labels than $\mathcal{L}$, and this condition is equivalent to cnd_{LN}.

This section gave the criteria for the strength of relationship between o and $\mathcal{L}$. cnd_{LE} and cnd_{PE} are based on relationship between $L(o)$ and the labels of $\mathcal{L}$, and cnd_{LN} and cnd_{PN} are based on relationship between $L(o)$ and other labels than $\mathcal{L}$.

4   The Strength of the Criteria

This section discusses the strength of the criteria. When the strength of relationship between an object o_1 and a set of labels $\mathcal{L}$ is compared with the strength of relationship between an object o_2 and $\mathcal{L}$, a criterion cnd_2 is stronger than a criterion cnd_1 for $\mathcal{L}$ if the strength can be decided by whether an object satisfies cnd_2 rather than cnd_1. In other words, if $o_1 < o_2$ for o_1 and o_2 such that o_1 dose not satisfy cnd_2 and o_2 satisfies cnd_2 regardless of whether o_1 or o_2 satisfies cnd_1, cnd_2 is stronger than cnd_1 for $\mathcal{L}$. That's because the strength can be decided if o_1 does not satisfy cnd_2 while o_1 may be relate to $\mathcal{L}$ more closely than o_2 by cnd_1.

Definition 1. *For a set of labels $\mathcal{L}$ and criteria cnd_1 and cnd_2, cnd_2 is stronger than cnd_1 for $\mathcal{L}$ if $o_1 <_{\mathcal{L}} o_2$ for any objects o_1 and o_2 such that o_1 satisfies cnd_1 but not cnd_2 and o_2 satisfies cnd_2, denoted by $cnd_1 <_{\mathcal{L}} cnd_2$, or $cnd_1 < cnd_2$ if $\mathcal{L}$ is obvious.*

The set of the objects of $\overline{\mathcal{L}}$ which satisfy a criterion cnd is denoted by $\overline{\mathcal{L}}^{cnd}$ $(=\{o \mid o \in \overline{\mathcal{L}}, o$ satisfies $cnd\})$. The strength of criteria can be decided by the inclusion relation among the set of the objects which satisfy each of the criteria.

Lemma 1. *For a set of labels $\mathcal{L}$ and criteria cnd_1 and cnd_2, $cnd_1 < cnd_2$ if and only if $\overline{\mathcal{L}}^{cnd_2} \subseteq \overline{\mathcal{L}}^{cnd_1}$.*

Proof. For objects o_1 in $\overline{\mathcal{L}}^{cnd_1}$ and o_2 in $\overline{\mathcal{L}}^{cnd_2}$, if $o_1 \notin \overline{\mathcal{L}}^{cnd_2}$, $o_1 < o_2$ because cnd_2 is a criterion. Since o_1 satisfies cnd_1 but not cnd_2 and o_2 satisfies cnd_2, $cnd_1 < cnd_2$.

If $\overline{\mathcal{L}}^{cnd_2} \subseteq \overline{\mathcal{L}}^{cnd_1}$ is not satisfied, there exists such an object o_2 that $o_2 \in \overline{\mathcal{L}}^{cnd_2}$ and $o_2 \notin \overline{\mathcal{L}}^{cnd_1}$. o_2 satisfies cnd_2 but not cnd_1. On the other hand, $o_2 < o_1$ for such an object o_1 that $o_1 \in \overline{\mathcal{L}}^{cnd_1}$ and $o_1 \notin \overline{\mathcal{L}}^{cnd_2}$ because cnd_1 is a criterion. Although o_2 satisfies cnd_2 and o_1 satisfies cnd_1 but not cnd_2, $cnd_1 < cnd_2$ is not satisfied because $o_1 < o_2$ is not satisfied. Thus $\overline{\mathcal{L}}^{cnd_2} \subseteq \overline{\mathcal{L}}^{cnd_1}$ if $cnd_1 < cnd_2$.

If a criterion cnd_1 implies a criterion cnd_2 ($cnd_1 \Rightarrow cnd_2$), $\overline{\mathcal{L}}^{cnd_1} \subseteq \overline{\mathcal{L}}^{cnd_2}$ and vice versa. Thus the strength of cnd_1 and cnd_2 is decided by implication of cnd_1 and cnd_2 because Lemma 1 shows that the strength of cnd_1 and cnd_2 is decided by the inclusion relation of the objects satisfying cnd_1 and cnd_2.

Theorem 1. *For criteria cnd_1 and cnd_2, $cnd_1 < cnd_2$ is equivalent to $cnd_2 \Rightarrow cnd_1$.*

Proof. If $cnd_1 < cnd_2$, $\overline{\mathcal{L}}^{cnd_2} \subseteq \overline{\mathcal{L}}^{cnd_1}$ by Lemma 1. If $\overline{\mathcal{L}}^{cnd_2} \subseteq \overline{\mathcal{L}}^{cnd_1}$, $cnd_2 \Rightarrow cnd_1$ because objects satisfying cnd_2 also satisfy cnd_1. On the other hand, if $cnd_2 \Rightarrow cnd_1$, $\overline{\mathcal{L}}^{cnd_2} \subseteq \overline{\mathcal{L}}^{cnd_1}$. Lemma 1 shows that $cnd_1 < cnd_2$ if $\overline{\mathcal{L}}^{cnd_2} \subseteq \overline{\mathcal{L}}^{cnd_1}$.

If one criterion implies another criterion, those criteria are based on the same point of view, which means that the criteria can be used to evaluate the strength of relationship of objects and sets of labels consistently by Theorem 1. The rest of this section discusses implication of the criteria to decide the strength of the criteria.

If an object o satisfies cnd_{PE}, there exists a label of $P(o)$ relating to $\mathcal{L}$, which is a label of $L(o)$ and o satisfies cnd_{LE} too.

Lemma 2. *For cnd_{PE} and cnd_{LE}, $cnd_{PE} \Rightarrow cnd_{LE}$.*

Proof. For an object o which satisfies cnd_{PE}, since $Rel_{\mathcal{L}}(P(o)) \neq \phi$ by satisfying cnd_{PE} and $L(o) = P(o) \cup S(o)$ by Property 1, $P(o) \subseteq L(o)$. Thus $Rel_{\mathcal{L}}(L(o)) \neq \phi$, and o satisfies cnd_{PE}.

If o satisfies cnd_{LN}, there is no label of $L(o)$ which relates to other labels than $\mathcal{L}$. It means that there is no label of $P(o)$ which relates to other labels than $\mathcal{L}$ and o satisfies cnd_{PN} too.

Lemma 3. *For cnd_{LN} and cnd_{PN}, $cnd_{LN} \Rightarrow cnd_{PN}$.*

Proof. For an object o which satisfies cnd_{LN}, $Rel_{\mathcal{L}}(L(o)) = L(o)$, in other words, $L(o)$ does not include a label relating to other labels than $\mathcal{L}$. Since $L(o) = P(o) \cup S(o)$ by Property 1, $L(o)$ does not include labels which relate to other labels than $\mathcal{L}$, and $Rel_{\mathcal{L}}(P(o)) = P(o)$. Thus o satisfies cnd_{PN}.

If o satisfies cnd_{PN}, there is no label of $P(o)$ which relates to other labels than $\mathcal{L}$. Since there always exist labels of $P(o)$, there are labels of $P(o)$ which relate to $\mathcal{L}$ and o satisfies cnd_{PE} too.

Lemma 4. *For cnd_{PN} and cnd_{PE}, $cnd_{PN} \Rightarrow cnd_{PE}$.*

Proof. For an object o which satisfies cnd_{PN}, $Rel_{\mathcal{L}}(P(o)) = P(o)$, in other words, $P(o)$ does not include a label relating to other labels than $\mathcal{L}$. Since $P(o) \neq \phi$ by Property 3, there always exists a label of $P(o)$ which relates to $\mathcal{L}$, and $Rel_{\mathcal{L}}(P(o)) \neq \phi$. Thus o satisfies cnd_{PE}.

The strength of the criteria is decided by implication of cnd_{LE}, cnd_{PE}, cnd_{PN}, and cnd_{LN} as shown by Lemmas 2, 3, and 4.

Theorem 2. *For cnd_{LE}, cnd_{PE}, cnd_{PN}, and cnd_{LN}, $cnd_{LE} < cnd_{PE} < cnd_{PN} < cnd_{LN}$.*

Proof. $cnd_{LN} \Rightarrow cnd_{PN} \Rightarrow cnd_{PE} \Rightarrow cnd_{LE}$ because $cnd_{LN} \Rightarrow cnd_{PN}$, $cnd_{PN} \Rightarrow cnd_{PE}$, and $cnd_{PE} \Rightarrow cnd_{LE}$ by Lemmas 3, 4, and 2, respectively. Thus $cnd_{LE} < cnd_{PE} < cnd_{PN} < cnd_{LN}$ by Theorem 1.

Since Theorem 2 shows the strength of the criteria, the strongest criterion satisfied by o is to express the strength of relationship between o and $\mathcal{L}$, which is defined as the level of o for $\mathcal{L}$. Levels of objects enable us to evaluate the strength of the objects for $\mathcal{L}$.

Example 5. For $\mathcal{L}_1 = \{Transportation, Electronics\}$, object o_5' such that $P(o_5') = \{Finance\}$ and $S(o_5') = \{Automobile, Mobile\ Phone\}$ satisfies only cnd_{LE} and o_5' is at the lowest or the weakest level on the strength. Since object o_5'' such that $P(o_5'') = \{Automobile, Finance\}$ and $S(o_5'') = \{Mobile\ Phone\}$ includes primary label *Automobile* for $\mathcal{L}_1$, o_5'' satisfies cnd_{PE} too, namely, o_5'' is at the second level on the strength. Moreover, object o_5''' such that $P(o_5''') = \{Automobile, Mobile\ Phone\}$ and $S(o_5''') = \{Finance\}$ satisfies cnd_{PN} because o_5''' does not have the primary labels which relate to other labels than $\mathcal{L}_1$, and o_5''' is at the third level on the strength. Finally, object o_4' ($P(o_4') = \{Automobile, Mobile\ Phone\}$ and $S(o_4') = \phi$) satisfies cnd_{LN} because o_4' has no label which relates to other labels than $\mathcal{L}_1$, and o_4' is at the highest or the strongest level on the strength. Thus $o_5' < o_5'' < o_5''' < o_4'$.

By Lemma 1, the inclusion relation of objects according to the levels is shown in Fig. 1 and users can select the range of the objects on their purposes.

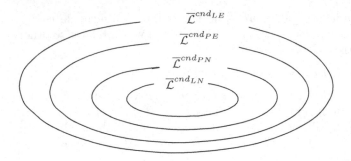

Fig. 1. Inclusion relation of objects satisfying each of the criteria

5 k Ranks

The discussion for two rank objects is extended to k rank objects. Let k ranks be $R_1, \cdots, R_i, \cdots, R_k$ $(1 \leq i \leq k?$jwhere R_i is stronger than R_j $(i < j)$. In the case of $k = 2$, $R_1 = P$ and $R_2 = S$. For an object o, let $R_i(o)$ be the set of labels of $L(o)$ whose rank is R_i, and $R_i^*(o) = \bigcup_{j=1,i} R_j(o)$ be the set of labels of $L(o)$ whose ranks are stronger than or equal to R_i.

The properties of set labels of two rank objects in Sect. 3 are extended to k ranks.

Property 4. $L(o) = \bigcup_{i=1,k} R_i(o)$.

Property 5. $R_i(o) \cap R_j(o) = \phi$ $(i \neq j)$.

Property 6. $R_1(o) \neq \phi$.

The rest of this section discusses the criteria for k rank objects. The criteria for the strength of relationship between a set of labels $\mathcal{L}$ and the set labels of an object o can be divided into two types, which are the criteria for relationship between $\mathcal{L}$ and the labels of $L(o)$ and the criteria for relationship between $\mathcal{L}$ and other labels than $L(o)$. Each of them is extended for k rank.

$cnd_{R_i E}$ $(1 \leq i \leq k)$: For a set of labels $\mathcal{L}$ and an object o, there exists a label of $L(o)$ which relates to $\mathcal{L}$ and whose rank is stronger than or equal to R_i, that is, $Rel_{\mathcal{L}}(R_i^*(o)) \neq \phi$.

$cnd_{R_i N}$ $(1 \leq i \leq k)$: For a set of labels $\mathcal{L}$ and an object o, there does not exist a label of $L(o)$ which relates to other labels than $\mathcal{L}$ and whose rank is stronger than or equal to R_i, that is, $Rel_{\mathcal{L}}(R_i^*(o)) = R_i^*(o)$.

Lemmas 2, 3, and 4 correspond to the following lemmas for k rank objects.

Lemma 5. *For* $cnd_{R_i E}$ $(2 \leq i \leq k)$, $cnd_{R_{i-1} E} \Rightarrow cnd_{R_i E}$.

Proof. For an object o which satisfies $cnd_{R_{i-1} E}$, $Rel_{\mathcal{L}}(R_{i-1}^*(o)) \neq \phi$. Since $R_{i-1}^*(o) \subseteq R_i^*(o)$, $Rel_{\mathcal{L}}(R_i^*(o)) \neq \phi$, and o satisfies $cnd_{R_i^* E}$.

Lemma 6. *For cnd_{R_iN} $(2 \leq i \leq k)$, $cnd_{R_iN} \Rightarrow cnd_{R_{i-1}N}$.*

Proof. For $Rel_{\mathcal{L}}(R_i^*(o)) = R_i^*(o)$. Since $R_{i-1}^*(o) \subseteq R_i^*(o)$, $Rel_{\mathcal{L}}(R_{i-1}^*(o)) = R_{i-1}^*(o)$, and that o satisfies $cnd_{R_{i-1}^*N}$.

Lemma 7. *For cnd_{R_1N} and cnd_{R_1E}, $cnd_{R_1N} \Rightarrow cnd_{R_1E}$.*

Proof. For an object o which satisfies cnd_{R_1N}, $Rel_{\mathcal{L}}(R_1(o)) = R_1(o)$, in other words, $R_1(o)$ does not include a label relating to other labels than $\mathcal{L}$. Since $R_1(o) \neq \phi$ by Property 6, there always exists a label of $R_1(o)$ which relates to $\mathcal{L}$, and $Rel_{\mathcal{L}}(R_1(o)) \neq \phi$. Thus o satisfies cnd_{R_1E}.

Since implication of the criteria is shown by Lemmas 5, 6, and 7, the following theorem on the strength of the criteria is satisfied.

Theorem 3. *For cnd_{R_iE} and cnd_{R_iN} $(1 \leq i \leq k)$, $cnd_{R_kE} < cnd_{R_{k-1}E} < \cdots < cnd_{R_1E} < cnd_{R_1N} < \cdots < cnd_{R_{k-1}N} < cnd_{R_kN}$.*

Proof. $cnd_{R_kN} \Rightarrow cnd_{R_{k-1}N} \Rightarrow \cdots \Rightarrow cnd_{R_1N} \Rightarrow cnd_{R_1E} \Rightarrow \cdots \Rightarrow cnd_{R_{k-1}E} \Rightarrow cnd_{R_kE}$ because $cnd_{R_iN} \Rightarrow cnd_{R_{i-1}N}$, $cnd_{R_1N} \Rightarrow cnd_{R_1E}$, and $cnd_{R_{i-1}E} \Rightarrow cnd_{R_iE}$ by Lemmas 6, 7, and 5, respectively. Thus $cnd_{R_kE} < cnd_{R_{k-1}E} < \cdots < cnd_{R_1E} < cnd_{R_1N} < \cdots < cnd_{R_{k-1}N} < cnd_{R_kN}$ by Theorem 1.

6   Conclusion

This paper introduced the criteria for the strength of relationship between an object o and a set of labels $\mathcal{L}$, which are cnd_{LE}, cnd_{PE}, cnd_{PN}, and cnd_{LN}. o satisfies cnd_{LE}, cnd_{PE}, cnd_{PN}, and cnd_{LN} if o relates to $\mathcal{L}$, $\mathcal{L}$ mainly, and only $\mathcal{L}$, respectively. Referring to the strength of the criteria, it was shown that $cnd_{LE} < cnd_{PE} < cnd_{PN} < cnd_{LN}$. Thus the strongest criterion which o satisfies can be used as the levels to express the degree of the strength. Those results can be applied to k rank objects.

The strength of the criteria is decided by implication of the criteria. If one criterion implies another criterion, both of them can be used to evaluate the strength of relationship between objects and sets of labels because their criteria are based on the same point of view. The criteria proposed in this paper enable to evaluate data with ranks qualitatively and consistently. Thus users can select the range of data at each of levels based on the criteria according to the purpose of the utilization of data. In general, the range of data is decided by changing the set of labels to identify the data. For example, if users want to utilize data widely, lower concept labels are replaced by higher concept labels or additional labels are inserted. In such utilization of data, originally intended purpose may not be realized because the set of labels itself has been changed. The levels based on the criteria solve this issue because the range of data can be changed according to the levels even if the set of labels is no change.

References

1. Cardoso-Cachopo, A., Oliveira, A.: Semi-supervised single-label text categorization using centroid-based classifiers. In: Proceedings of Symposium on Applied Computing, SAC 2007, pp. 844–851 (2007)
2. Chakrabarti, K., Ganti, V., Han, J., Xin, D.: Ranking objects by exploiting, relationships: computing top-k over aggregation. In: Proceedings of ACM SIGMOD International Conference on Management of Data, SIGMOD 2006, pp. 371–382 (2006)
3. Ding, B., Wang H., Jin, R., Han, J., Wang, Z.: Optimizing index for taxonomy keyword search. In: Proceedings of ACM SIGMOD International Confernce on Management of Data, SIGMOD 2012, pp. 493–504 (2012)
4. Fazzinga, B., Flesca, S., Furfaro, F.: RFID-data compression for supporting aggregate queries. ACM Trans. Database Syst. **38**(2), 11–45 (2013)
5. Kim, J., Croft, B.: Ranking using multiple document types in desktop search. In: Proceedings of ACM International Confernce on Research and Development in Information Retrieval, SIGIR 2010, pp. 50–57 (2010)
6. Lopez, V., Prieta, F., Ogihara, M., Wong, D.: A model for multi-label classification and ranking of learning objects. Expert Syst. Appl. **39**(10), 8878–8884 (2012)
7. Lu, J., Senellart, P., Lin, C., Du, X., Wang, S., Chen, X.: Optimal top-k generation of attribute combinations based on ranked lists. In: Proceedings of ACM SIGMOD International Confernce on Management of Data, SIGMOD 2012, pp. 409–420 (2012)
8. Silla, C., Freitas, A.: A survey of hierarchical classification across different application domains. Data Min. Knowl. Disc. **22**(1–2), 31–72 (2011)
9. Tang, L., Rajan, S., Narayanan, V.: Large scale multi-label classification via metalabeler. In: Proceedings of the International Confernce on World Wide Web, WWW 2009, pp. 211–220 (2009)
10. Wang, H., He, X., Chang, M., Song, Y., White, R., Chu, W.: Personalized ranking model adaptation for web search. In: Proceedings of ACM International Confernce on Research and Development in Information Retrieval, SIGIR 2013, pp. 323–332 (2013)
11. Zhang, X., Yang, Y., Han, Z., Wang, H., Gao, C.: Object class detection: a survey. ACM Comput. Surv. **46**(1), 10–53 (2013)
12. Zhu, X., Song, S., Lian, X., Wang, J., Zou, L.: Matching heterogeneous event data. In: Proceedings of ACM SIGMOD International Confernce on Management of Data, SIGMOD 2014, pp. 1211–1222 (2014)

Online Ad-fraud in Search Engine Advertising Campaigns

Prevention, Detection and Damage Limitation

Andreas Mladenow[1], Niina Maarit Novak[2(✉)], and Christine Strauss[3]

[1] Secure Business Austria, Favoritenstr. 16, 1040 Vienna, Austria
amladenow@sba-research.org
[2] Institute of Software Technology and Interactive Systems, Vienna University
of Technology, Favoritenstr. 9-11, 1040 Vienna, Austria
niina.novak@ifs.tuwien.ac.at
[3] Department of e-Business, Faculty of Business, Economics and Statistics,
University of Vienna, Oskar-Morgenstern-Platz 1, 1090 Vienna, Austria
christine.strauss@univie.ac.at

Abstract. Search Engine Advertising has grown strongly in recent years and amounted to about USD 60 billion in 2014. Based on real-world data of online campaigns of 28 companies, we analyse the incident of a hacked campaign-account. We describe the occurred damage, i.e. (1) follow-up consequences of unauthorized access to the account of the advertiser, and (2) limited availability of short-term online campaigns. This contribution aims at raising awareness for the threat of hacking incidents during online marketing campaigns, and provides suggestions as well as recommendations for damage prevention, damage detection and damage limitation.

Keywords: Online advertising · Online Ad-fraud · Search engine marketing, SEM · Search engine advertising, SEA · Paid-Search · Security · Availability · Reliability · Online campaigns · Typology

1 Introduction

From the viewpoint of information economics peoples' attention is seen as a scarce commodity [1–4]. Through the use of search engine advertising (SEA), companies aim at improving their visibility among the search engine results in order to attract the attention of potential customers [5]. It is a global phenomenon that companies tend to invest more and more in sponsored search in electronic markets. It is estimated that in 2014 businesses have spent USD 60 billion in Search Engine Marketing (SEM) [6]. From an international perspective, Google was the undisputed global leader in 2014 with a market share of more than 90 % in Germany and 65 % in the US, which allowed the company to increase its revenues from advertising by 17 % compared to the prior year [6].

Quality, costs and time are major drivers on key success factors. For this reason, it is for many companies one of the main motivational reasons to perform online-campaigns [7–9]. Unlike traditional marketing campaigns, online campaigns provide

© IFIP International Federation for Information Processing 2015
I. Khalil et al. (Eds.): ICT-EurAsia 2015 and CONFENIS 2015, LNCS 9357, pp. 109–118, 2015.
DOI: 10.1007/978-3-319-24315-3_11

the advertiser with fast information on the campaign's effectiveness. Moreover, online campaigns are highly flexible and allow a custom-tailored and targeted advertising approach. The flexibility and the time savings of online campaigns rely on fast transaction processes, based on the usage of tools such as Google *AdWords* [10] and Bing *Ads* [11] which allow to create online campaigns within a couple of minutes, and which allow to evaluate the campaigns' success within a few hours by means of predefined and built-in analysis functions [10, 11].

However, whereas these advantages seem to be quite obvious for the success of a marketing campaign, dealing with online campaigns often results in facing different kinds of problems such as trust and security issues. In this regard, advertisers and search engines representatives are confronted with the topic of ad-frauds. In the literature, this subject has mainly focussed on the so-called "click-fraud" problem [12–16], while other issues concerning ad-frauds have been neglected.

Against this background, this paper contributes in filling this research gap by providing a typology covering current types of ad-frauds as well as analysing the neglected topic of ad-frauds caused by unauthorized access to campaign accounts, so-called "hacks". What happens to hacked advertising accounts in the context of short-term online campaigns using the example of Google *AdWords*? What are the alternatives of action for campaign providers in the event of a hacker attack? Are there any prophylactic security controls to be set? Hence, this paper is structured as follows: the next section pinpoints theoretical insights of both, online ad-campaigns using the Google search engine tool *AdWords* as well as a typology of ad-fraud. Section 3 analyses scenarios based on real-world data. Section 4 provides a discussion, and the final section summarizes major findings and gives a brief outlook on future developments.

2 Online Campaigns and Ad-Fraud Using AdWords Accounts

2.1 Online Ad-Campaigns

When battling for customers' attention, businesses seek for the best ranking position – and thus visibility – in the results' list of search engine queries. In addition to the possibility of improving the organic search results through search engine optimization (SEO), which very often turns out to be highly time-consuming, search-engine advertisements (SEA) allow to address the customer in a rapid and targeted manner. The display of advertisements in search engines follows the keyword-principle, which allows buying an advertisement-position on the first page of the search engine results based on specific keywords. In the case of the big players, including Google, Yahoo and Bing, paid advertisements are grouped together in a commercial advertisement-block and are thus visually separated and highlighted from the unpaid (organic) results [cf. 10, 11].

Since the beginnings of text-based advertisement in search engines, advertisers aim to create specific advertisements matching query results, hoping to create a highly effective advertising tool. In contrast to traditional advertising (where costs incur when placing an advertisement) in SEA one does not pay for impressions, but for clicks made. This is referred to as cost per click (CPC) or pay per click (PPC) [7, 9].

Paying for SEA is performance-based advertising [8]. Thus, the advertiser has to pay only for the click, and – as a consequence – only if a user visits the advertised website. Impressions are free of charge. This concept seems to be highly effective as auction-based text advertisements are by far the largest source of income for search engines, and there are still no signs indicating that this will change in the foreseeable future [8].

In the case of Google the *AdWords* tool supports the development of effective SEA-campaigns. When it comes to SEA, the positioning of an advertisement-candidate related to a specific search term is based on the willingness of the advertiser to pay a certain amount, previously specified by the advertiser. The entire set of advertiser candidates takes part in an auction for the entered search term of the Internet user. The order of display, or the positioning of advertisements is (for example in the case of Google) determined through an "advertisement-ranking procedure", a weighted second price auction. This ranking-position is further determined by the maximum amount for the homepage visit set by the advertiser and by Google's advertisement quality score (QS), an indicator which is highly influenced by the performance of the advertiser.

Typical advantages of online campaigns include factors such as elimination of geographic barriers, cost-efficiency, target group precision, measurability of the response, and personalization [8]. But what are the challenges and limitations of online marketing campaigns for companies? Experts agree that the integration of search engine marketing and more traditional forms of marketing is one of the biggest challenges [17]. Multi-channel marketing often require coordinated action in terms of content and time. In this regard, the design and creation of online marketing campaigns require specific competences and different strategic and operational approaches compared to conventional marketing. In their effort to reach potential consumers, advertisers are facing several risks. Besides the possibility to have advertisements blocked by the consumer, e.g. through software-based AdBlocker applications, online-advertising accounts may be the target of unauthorized usage through hacking activities leading to considerable loss of money and/or reputation. In the case of a hacker attack advertisers are confronted with problems of loss of integrity and reputation, lack of face-to-face communication, violation of privacy-issues, lack of trust and security. Moreover, advertisers and clients depend on the availability and reliability of the provided online tools.

2.2 Types of Ad-Fraud

Two types of ad-fraud in the context of online campaigns are to be distinguished, i.e. hacking and click-fraud. A third type of ad-fraud are so-called customer-misleading ads, which is beyond the scope of this paper due to the fact, that it is not directly targeting a certain advertiser. Furthermore, we refer to the most widely used search engine, i.e. Google (cf. Fig. 1).

Hence, Fig. 1 locates the two types of online ad-fraud in the case of *AdWords* within the pattern of interaction of four involved parties: the advertiser, the consumers,

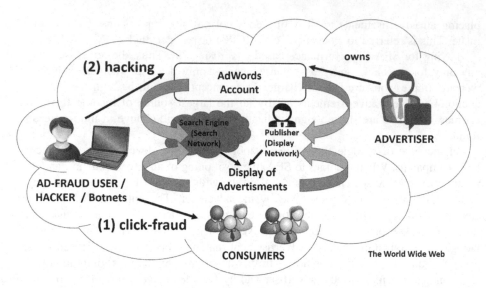

Fig. 1. Click-fraud and hacking

the publisher, and the hacker. The advertiser holds a Google *AdWords* account. Consumers surf on websites or use the search engine to perform search queries. Advertisements are displayed either via the search engine network or via website or blog of a publisher from the display network. Ad-fraud in such a context may include one or both of the two following activities: (1) hacking and/or (2) click-fraud. Hacking refers to a direct attack on an advertiser's *AdWords* account aiming at taking over control on that account. Click-fraud in contrast, involves taking on the role of a consumer either directly (personally) or indirectly (software-supported). In the case of click-fraud the goal of the attacker is an increase of the advertisers' costs by artificially increasing the number of clicks per ad. Click-fraud is a method frequently used by both, publishers and competing businesses, with the intention to significantly damage and downgrade a competitors ranking-position or/and improving one's own search engine ranking-position.

3   Ad-Fraud by Hacking Online-Campaign Accounts

Whereas click-frauds are difficult to be detected and revealed by the advertiser, hacking very often implies the difficulty for the advertiser to regain access to his/her own account, third party control through account blocking and limited or no access to the online campaigns. This may result in disrupting short-term online-campaigns, which might have been carefully orchestrated with other marketing activities e.g. in multi-channel campaigns, or which were launched with the intention to promote a specific time-dependent event.

Against this background, we analyse an ad-fraud scenario, which is based on real-world data selected from a set of a total of 28 online campaigns that were performed between 2013 and 2015 from the Google online marketing challenge [18] each during a three-week period. In the following selected companies and their usage of SEA will be described in detail, based on their necessity for marketing campaigns with short-term availability. During these campaigns, one account was hacked. Hence, we describe this event of campaign account hacking and the perceived difficulty to regain access [19–21] for the remaining campaign time in Subsect. 3.2. The selected cases had to be anonymised to protect the involved parties. The selected examples shall give an insight into the importance of time-critical availability of campaign-tools during certain time-windows due to either event-driven necessities (*Case3* and *Case4*) or multi-channel ad-strategies (*Case1* and *Case2*).

3.1   Four Exemplary Cases for Short-Term Online Campaign

Case1 is a family-owned brand of fur products based in Vienna, Austria, originally established in 1948 in Prague. The company's core business is the manufacturing of fur-based products, including coats, jackets, blankets, pillows, accessories and custom-tailored products. The company positions its own brand as a high quality brand and expert for fur products. Although the company possesses a license for trading its products online, the company's online presence and penetration could be described as modest mainly depending on the company's website created in 2008, a Facebook-fan page, Pinterest and Instagram accounts in addition to an email newsletter and a cooperation with the online shop platform *case1partner.com*. As *case1.com* relies heavily on the local customer base in its three main cities (Vienna, Budapest and Bratislava), the client database generated by using *case1partner's* online presence offers the company the possibility to acquire global customers.

Case2 was originally founded in August 2010 in order to satisfy the local demand for limited, exclusive and edition-specific sneakers in Vienna. Since April 2012 the business runs as well an online-shop. Besides sneakers the company sells a small selection of T-shirts, shoelaces and shoe-cleaning kits. In addition, customers have the possibility to sell and trade their private and limited editions of sneakers that are no longer commercially available for sale via the online-shop. This feature represents a marketing tool for case2.at and generates traffic for the online-shop. The company's website, customer-management and social media presence (including Facebook, Google+, Twitter, Tumblr, Instagram and Pinterest) is maintained by the company itself. Currently the larger amount of sales is done over-the-counter, highlighting the company's necessity for an online-marketing campaign with the goal of increasing online sales. Both case1.com and the *Case2* operate in a small but highly competitive niche segment of the fashion industry. In these niche segments companies rely strongly on local customer bases and word-of-mouth. A company such as *Case1*, having a long tradition of operating in the fur segment of the fashion industry, undergoes by definition some seasonality. *AdWords* campaigns are thus especially used to promote after-season products, as well as to announce sales and new season or product lines. Furthermore, they allow for targeting not only German-speaking customers but also customers e.g. from Czech Republic, Hungary, Slovakia and Russia. *Case2* utilizes *AdWords* campaigns to target specific consumer-groups and to promote their online shop as well as special sales and products, which allows the company to differentiate itself from big players of the industry segment (e.g., Zalando, Foot Locker, etc.).

Case3 is a website reporting on all games of the Austrian amateur soccer-league and is available free of charge. More than 100 private editors ("fans") cover the various national leagues. The company has four employees only who maintain the website and perform online marketing. This highlights that the website is fully dependent on the work of private individuals, or fans to report the latest news. The website has its own self-administered content management system, which delivers the latest information to readers (e.g., game reports, photos, previews, headlines, etc.). Particular attention should be paid to the so called "live ticker" covering even the smallest soccer-league-games in real time. The live ticker is also available as a mobile-app to keep readers 24/7 up-to-date. Since 2009 when *Case3* was founded, the number of users had continuously increased and large social media communities around the topic of the amateur-soccer-league with multiple thousands of participants had been formed. Besides the information-portal the company also operates a web-shop, selling soccer related sport products. As *Case3* is a website which heavily relies on advertising to finance itself, a high website traffic is crucial for its success. Thus targeted *AdWords* campaigns generating website-traffic through website promotion and its special features such as the live ticker, are of paramount importance. Furthermore, due to the fact that *AdWords* campaigns can be used to promote time- and date-specific events during a short time-window (e.g., final game of a sports tournament) emphasizes the importance of perpetual availability of this marketing tool.

Case4, is a famous and exquisite party and bar location offering a relaxed and beach-like atmosphere. At *Case4* one can enjoy delicious Israeli dishes together with various cocktails or drinks. The owners cooperate with an advertising agency to promote the location using various media channels. For restaurants no longer it is just about quality of food, beverages and services but also about location and about image and reputation. Diversification is an important strategy in a saturated market. One way to do so is to organize special events such as in the case of *Case4*, which organises special viewing parties, e.g. for the finals of the Eurovision Song Contest. These kind of events, which are planned on a short-term basis, are best promoted through short time advertisements. Based on the fact that individuals use online search engines in order to find out what is happening in town tonight and where to go, *AdWords* campaigns are the self-evident choice. Another argument strongly suggesting the use of *AdWords* campaigns is the fact that these events are weather-dependent open-air events.Thus, the chosen media channel needs to be very flexible in order to stop or change the advertisement in case the event has to be cancelled, substituted or postponed.

3.2   Hacking a Campaign-Account

In one of the described cases the campaign-account had been subject to unauthorized access, i.e. hacking. Due to the fact that the verification process of new advertisements and keywords normally takes some time the hacked account was not in use during a period of about 12 h. During this time window the account has been hacked and a new advertisement in Russian language and Cyrillic writing was implemented and approved by Google. The fast approval by Google was the result of setting the newly created advertisement budget as: 'Budget delivery method set to accelerated: show ads as quickly as possible', which in turn may accelerate the approval procedure of Google. The campaign created produced stunning numbers in less than 18 h: 1,646,824 impressions and 6,190 clicks, generating costs of 207.66$. Achieving these amazing performance index figures in such a short period of time reveals professional skills and malicious intentions as drivers of such an activity.

After reporting the attack to Google, the *AdWords* account was deactivated and all *AdWords* campaigns were put on hold. Since the investigation process lasted longer than the remaining campaign-window (i.e., two weeks) the campaigns could not be restarted until Google finished the investigation process and had re-credited the amount lost due to the attack. Creating a new account to run another short-term campaign would have involved considerable amount of additional time, effort and expenses. To put it in a nutshell: the attack resulted in the loss of potential sales revenues as the *AdWords* campaigns had to be suspended.

In addition to the experience gained by the advertisers, a desk research revealed that *AdWords* seems to be an attractive target for hacking activities as many entries on web pages, in blogs and IT journals can be found on the internet. It is to be assumed that security mechanisms have not provided sufficient protection for the advertisers of the hacked campaign-accounts.

4 Prevention, Detection and Damage Limitation

Since its launch in the year 2000 Google *AdWords* [22] developed into Google's main source of revenue but became at the same time a target for online ad-fraud. From various incident reports and forum entries can be concluded that in most cases the Gmail-account address and password were used for unauthorized access to the campaign-account. In the case of Google *AdWords* most hacks follow a simple but effectual pattern involving (i) brute-force login, (ii) phishing carried out via email spoofing and very similar looking phishing websites asking the user to sign-in, as well as (iii) spy- and malware tools in order to acquire the user's account details [23]. Once the fraudsters have gained access to a campaign-account they typically duplicate campaigns, add a vast variety of keywords aimed to generate high amounts of clicks and redirect the target URL to some African airfare company [24], a Spanish online shop or some Russian website advertising bracelets [25].These practices cause fraudulent charges on users' credit cards quite often in the amount of several thousand US-Dollars caused by a single fraud-campaign over a time frame of less than 24 h. Furthermore, for people and businesses depending on Google *AdWords* to generate traffic for example to their online shops for direct sale purposes, considerable amounts of money are also lost in terms of revenue, reputation and benefits from historical account performance [26].

What can be done to prevent an attack? Choosing strong passwords is the most obvious and effective measure. Choosing a complex and long password involving not only letters but also numbers and special characters as well as changing the password on a regular basis increases security and protects the account owner from simple attacks. Checking for spyware and using browsers with phishing filters [27], especially when signing into a Google-account from an unsecured Wireless Fidelity(WIFI) connection are highly recommended. Moreover, for businesses it is advised to have a contingency advertising-plan to be able to counter possible revenue drops caused by fraudulent campaigns [28].

How to detect an attack? Checking ones' account several times per day is not only a good practice to improve the performance and the cost-benefit ratio of the campaign itself. At the same time frequent checks protect from possible money and reputation losses caused by an attack. Best practice involves close monitoring and analysing the performance of each individual *AdWords* campaign several times per day.

How to behave during an attack? What happens after an attack? If the advertiser is able to access his/her own account the immediate activity is to change the password. This action will lock-out hackers. Ongoing campaigns shall be suspended or deleted. If access to the advertisers account is denied, the hacker may have changed the password, preventing the account owner from regaining access to his/her own account [29]. In such cases the account owner needs to contact the Google *AdWords* Support either per email or via the live help desk and report the incident. Google typically reimburses the fraud-victim for the money lost during the attack, following a thorough investigation. Moreover, it should be mentioned that Google *AdWords* has an inherent fraud-detection mechanism disabling the account [30] once a possible fraud is detected based on unusual activity, preventing both the display of campaigns created by hackers and further money loss of the user [30].

Based on our analysis of online campaigns of 28 companies in the following we suggest several methods, focusing on authentication, notification and budget limitation, aimed to increase the security of online campaigns and to protect users from ad-fraud.

Authentication. Unauthorized access to online advertising accounts could be impeded by use of encryption (adoption of best practice for security from online banking), digital signatures or a mandatory two-step verification process for each login-process (e.g., including username, password and for example a code sent to the user by email or SMS).

Notification. Push messages, SMS or E-Mail notifications for defined activities which are sent automatically and with the intention to inform advertisers about signification changes and performance details of their online campaigns could help to detect fraudulent activities in a timely manner and could thus prevent losses.

Budget limitation. Pre-setting a fixed daily maximum budget per campaign or a total maximum budget for the whole account prevents from considerable financial losses.

5   Conclusion and Outlook

Paid search marketing through Google *AdWords* exists now for more than 15 years and has been established as an essential and indispensable advertising channel. In every industry and every sector local, regional and global advertisements are placed in search engines, the majority of advertisements are placed in Google. *AdWords* has become a widespread and widely accepted tool characterized by high reliability and flexibility. The analysis provides a typology of occurring ad-frauds and points to potential flaws in account handling that might be used for hacker attacks. When it comes to the integration of online marketing activities temporarily blocked accounts can cause financial losses. Ultimately, the understanding of search engine developments dependent on the dominant search-engine market providers represents a challenge for companies.

In the future the risk of ad-fraud seems to remain a major challenge for advertising companies, search engines and ad campaigners. Whereas ad-centers from Google, Yahoo and Microsoft have developed large data mining systems to score traffic quality, some types of ad-fraud are still to be resolved. More research needs to be addressed to all types of occurring ad-fraud. In the context of online marketing campaigns this includes not only click-fraud, but also problems such as hacking ad-campaign accounts.

References

1. Goldhaber, M.H.: The attention economy and the net. First Monday **2**(4), 66–78 (1997)
2. Mladenow, A., Fröschl, K.A.: Kooperative Forschung. Lang, Frankfurt am Main (2011)
3. Mladenow, A., Bauer, C., Strauss, C.: Social crowd integration in new product development: crowdsourcing communities nourish the open innovation paradigm. Global J. Flex. Syst. Manage. **15**(1), 77–86 (2014)
4. Mladenow, A., Kryvinska, N., Strauss, C.: Towards cloud-centric service environments. J. Serv. Sci. Res. **4**(2), 213–234 (2012)
5. Ghose, A., Yang, S.: An empirical analysis of search engine advertising: Sponsored search in electronic markets. Manage. Sci. **55**(10), 1605–1622 (2009)
6. Statista. http://de.statista.com/statistik/daten/studie/75188/umfrage/werbeumsatz-von-google-seit-2001/. Accessed 22 May 2015
7. Goldfarb, A., Tucker, C.: Search engine advertising: channel substitution when pricing ads to context. Manage. Sci. **57**(3), 458–470 (2011)
8. Langville, A.N., Meyer, C.D.: Google's PageRank and beyond: the science of search engine rankings. Princeton University Press, Princeton (2011)
9. Xiang, Z., Pan, B.: Travel queries on cities in the United States: implications for search engine marketing for tourist destinations. Tour. Manage. **32**(1), 88–97 (2011)
10. AdWords. https://www.google.at/adwords/. Accessed 22 May 2015
11. Bing Ads. https://secure.bingads.microsoft.com/. Accessed 22 May 2015
12. Kitts, B., et al.: Click fraud detection: adversarial pattern recognition over 5 years at microsoft. In: Abou-Nasr, M., Lessmann, S., Stahlbock, R., Weiss, G.M. (eds.) Real World Data Mining Applications, vol. 17, pp. 181–201. Springer, Heidelberg (2015)
13. Immorlica, N., Jain, K., Mahdian, M., Talwar, K.: Click fraud resistant methods for learning click-through rates. In: Deng, X., Ye, Y. (eds.) WINE 2005. LNCS, vol. 3828, pp. 34–45. Springer, Heidelberg (2005)
14. Wilbur, K.C., Zhu, Y.: Click fraud. Mark. Sci. **28**(2), 293–308 (2009)
15. Haddadi, H.: Fighting online click-fraud using bluff ads. ACM SIGCOMM Comput. Commun. Rev. **40**(2), 21–25 (2010)

16. Liu, B., Nath, S., Govindan, R., Liu, J.: DECAF: detecting and characterizing ad fraud in mobile apps. In: Proceedings of NSDI (2014)
17. Statista. http://www.statista.com/statistics/248059/biggest-challenages-in-search-marketing-worldwide/. Accessed 22 May 2015
18. GOMC. https://www.google.com/onlinechallenge/. Accessed 22 May 2015
19. Strauss C.: Informatik-Sicherheitsmanagement: eine Herausforderung für die Unternehmensführung, Vieweg+Teubner Verlag (1991)
20. Strauss, C., Stummer, C.: Multiobjective decision support in IT-risk management. Int. J. Inf. Technol. Decis. Making 1(2), 251–268 (2002)
21. Kiesling E., Ekelhart A., Grill B., Stummer C., Strauss C.: Multi-objective evolutionary optimization of computation-intensive simulations: the case of security control selection. In: Proceedings of the 11th Metaheuristics International Conference (MIC 2015), forthcoming (2015)
22. GOOGLE Company – Our history in depth. http://www.google.com/about/company/history/#2000. Accessed 22 May 2015
23. LEFTY G BALOGH – Digital Marketing Testing Ground. http://www.leftygbalogh.com/2011/story-hacked-google-adwords-account/. Accessed 22 May 2015
24. MOZ – Blogs: AdWords Hackers – What a Nightmare. https://moz.com/ugc/adwords-hackers-what-a-nightmare/. Accessed 22 May 2015
25. GOOGLE – Official AdWords Community. https://www.de.adwords-community.com/t5/Grundlagen/Hilfe-Mein-Account-wurde-gehackt/td-p/44399/. Accessed 22 May 2015
26. ABEST WEB. http://www.abestweb.com/forums/showthread.php?113490-Google-AdA Words-account-hijacked/. Accessed 22 May 2015
27. GOOGLE – Official Blog – Insights from Googlers into our products, and technology. http://googleblog.blogspot.co.at/2008/04/how-to-avoid-getting-hooked.html/. Accessed 22 May 2015
28. GOOGLE Product Forums. https://productforums.google.com/forum/#!topic/gmail/A0wZmlrC0f8/. Accessed 22 May 2015
29. PPCDISCUSSIONS. http://www.ppcdiscussions.com/2008/09/my-personal-adwords-account-hacked.html/. Accessed 22 May 2015
30. SEARCH ENGINE Roundtable: Google AdWords Account Hacked: False Ads & False Charges. https://www.seroundtable.com/archives/017946.html/. Accessed 22 May (2015)

Applied Modeling and Simulation

Markov Chain Solution to the 3-Tower Problem

Guido David[(✉)]

Institute of Mathematics and National Sciences Research Institute,
University of the Philippines, Quezon City, Philippines
gdavid@math.upd.edu.ph
http://www.math.upd.edu.ph

Abstract. The 3-tower problem is a 3-player gambler's ruin model
where two players are involved in a zero information, even-money bet
during each round. The probabilities that each player accumulates all
the money has a trivial solution. However, the probability of each player
getting ruined first is an open problem. In this paper, the 3-tower problem recursions are modeled as a directed multigraph with loops, which
is used to construct a Markov chain. The solution leads to exact values, and results show that, unlike in other models where the first ruin
probabilities depend only on the proportion of chips of each player, the
probabilities obtained by this model depend on the number of chips each
player holds.

Keywords: Markov chains · Graph theory · Discrete mathematics ·
3-dimensional gambler's ruin · Applied probability · Tower of Hanoi

1 Introduction

The gambler's ruin problem for two players is solved using recursion when the
bets are even money. The solution gives the expected time until one player is
ruined, and the probabilities each player acquires all the money. The multiplayer
problem presents more difficulties. Consider a three-player game and let the
amount of money (or chips) of the players be S_1, S_2, S_3. Let $S = S_1 + S_2 + S_3$.
In each time step, a game is played, with winners and losers. Suppose that each
game involves exactly two players, each one having a 50 % chance of winning
the bet. The model goes as: f_{ij} is chosen randomly with probability 1/6, where
$i, j = 1, 2, 3$ and

$$f_{ij} : (S_i, S_j) \mapsto (S_i + b, S_j - b). \tag{1}$$

If the bet is fixed at $b = 1$ and the stacks are positive integers, the resulting model
is the 3-tower game. The 3-tower model is loosely based on the tower of Hanoi
problem, with no constraints on the order by which the chips are stacked. One
application of this model is tournaments that involve the accumulation of chips
or wealth, for example, poker tournaments. In such cases, a partial information
game may be modeled as a zero information games to determine players' equities
independent of skill. Other forms of the gambler's ruin for three players are the
symmetric problem [8,9] and the C-centric game [4]. The time until a player is
ruined in the 3-tower problem has been solved [1,2,10,11] and is given by

© IFIP International Federation for Information Processing 2015
I. Khalil et al. (Eds.): ICT-EurAsia 2015 and CONFENIS 2015, LNCS 9357, pp. 121–128, 2015.
DOI: 10.1007/978-3-319-24315-3_12

$$T = \frac{3S_1 S_2 S_3}{S}. \tag{2}$$

The probability that each player is ruined first is an open problem [4]. Ferguson used Brownian motion to numerically approximate the probability of ruin [3], and Kim improved on this by using numerical solutions to Markov processes [6]. An alternative method for calculating placing probabilities is the Independent Chip Model (ICM), credited to Malmuth-Harville [7], although no proofs of the method are found. Let n be the number of players, X_i be the random variable denoting the placing of Player i, and S_i be the current stack size of Player i. Then the probability of player i placing 1st is

$$P(X_i = 1) = S_i/S \tag{3}$$

where $S = S_1 + S_2 + \ldots + S_n$. To obtain the probability of placing 2nd, conditional probabilities are used for each opponent finishing 1st, and from the remaining players the probability of placing 2nd (which is essentially 1st among the remaining $n - 1$ players) is the proportion of player i's stack to the total stack not including the stack of the conditional 1st place finisher. Thus,

$$P(X_i = 2) = \sum_{j \neq i} P(X_j = 1) P(X_i = 2 | S_j = 0) = \sum_{j \neq} \frac{S_j}{S} \frac{S_i}{S - S_j}. \tag{4}$$

Continuing, the probability of Player i finishing 3rd is

$$P(X_i = 3) = \sum_{j \neq i} \sum_{k \neq i,j} \frac{S_j}{S} \frac{S_k}{S - S_j} \frac{S_i}{S - S_j - S_k}. \tag{5}$$

It should be emphasized that ICM does not make any assumptions about the bet amount, hence is slightly different from the 3-tower problem.

In the 3-tower model, the probability of finishing 1st is easily solved by recursion. The result is exactly the same as (3). A method of calculating 3rd place probabilities (and hence, 2nd place probabilities) for the 3-tower problem is presented here using Markov chains constructed using directed multigraphs with loops.

2   Methods

Consider a 3-player model where the players are involved in even money bets. We define a *state* as an ordered triple (x, y, z) with $x \geq y \geq z \geq 0$. Because the games in each round are all fair and random, the probabilities of becoming ruined first of each player depends only on the amount of money each player has in a given state. We also define *chip position* (or simply, *position*) to be the number of money (or chips) a player has in a given state. Let us also define the function $p(u|v, w)$ to be the probability that a player with a given chip position u in the state (u, v, w) will finish 3rd, or become ruined first. If the state is understood from context, we will simply write this as $p(u)$. If v and w are positions in the same state such that $v = w$, then it is assumed that $p(v) = p(w)$.

A *terminal state* is one wherein the probabilities of placing 3rd are known. There are two types of terminal states.

1. If one of the three positions is zero, i.e. $z = 0$
2. If all three positions are equal, i.e. $x = y = z$.

Note that for the terminal state $(x, y, 0)$, then $p(x) = p(y) = 0$ and $p(0) = 1$. For the terminal state (x, x, x), $p(x) = 1/3$ using the previous assumption.

A state (x, y, z) is adjacent to a state (u, v, w) if the former state can move to the latter state in one round. A state that is adjacent to a terminal state is called a *near-terminal state*.

Lemma 1. *A state (x, y, z) with $x \geq y \geq z$ that satisfies one of the following is a near-terminal state:*

(i) $z = 1$
(ii) $x = y + 1$ and $z = y - 1$.

In constructing the multigraph, all possible states of S are represented by nodes. The transitions between adjacent states are given by directed edges. The states are arranged such that all states (x, y, z) with a fixed value of z are aligned vertically, with the highest value of x in the topmost position, in decreasing order going down (i.e. from North to South), while y is increasing at the same time. All states (x, y, z) with fixed x are aligned horizontally, with y in decreasing order from left to right (i.e. West to East) and z increasing at the same time. Consequently, all states with fixed y are aligned diagonally, with x decreasing and z increasing as the states move from Northwest to Southeast. An example of the resulting multigraph is given in Figs. 1 and 2. From the construction, it is clear that for a given node, its adjacent nodes are the ones located to its immediate top, bottom, left, right, top left and bottom right positions (i.e. North, South, East, West, Northwest and Southeast). A state may be adjacent to itself if the following holds:

Lemma 2. *A state (x, y, z) is adjacent to itself if $y = x - 1$ and/or $z = y - 1$.*

In the "and" case in Lemma 2, the state is doubly adjacent to itself. The state is also doubly adjacent to itself for states of the form $(x, x, x-1)$ and $(x, x-1, x-1)$. This and the following Lemma can be proved using the definition of adjacent nodes and (1) with $b = 1$.

Lemma 3. *A state of the form (x, y, y) or (x, x, z) is doubly adjacent to its adjacent nodes.*

There is always at least one edge from a non-terminal state to its adjacent state. A state that is doubly adjacent to another state has two edges going to that other state. If a state A is doubly adjacent to a non-terminal state B, it does not follow that B is doubly adjacent to A.

3   Results and Discussion

Based on the multigraph, we construct the Markov chain. Let τ be a relation that maps a position from one state to a position in another non-terminal state. We can think of τ as directed edges that connect specific positions within states to other positions in other states (or possibly within the same state). Let the function ϕ denote the ruin probability of the position in one move. Note that the unique non-terminal positions are exactly the transient states in the Markov chain, while ϕ gives the probability of absorption to the first-ruined state. The Theorem below follows from the previous Lemmas.

Theorem 1. *Let the state corresponding to a non-terminal vertex be denoted by* (x, y, z) *where* $x \geq y \geq z$ *such that* $z \geq 1$. *Let* $S = x + y + z$ *and let* (u, v, w) *be an adjacent non-terminal vertex.*

  (i)   If $z = y - 1$, *then* $\tau(x) \to u, \tau(y) \to w, \tau(z) \to v$
  (ii) If $y = x - 1$, *then* $\tau(x) \to v, \tau(y) \to u, \tau(z) \to w$
  (iii) If $z = y$, *then* $\tau(x) \to u$ *twice,* $\tau(y) \to v$ *and* $\tau(y) \to w$
  (iv) If $y = x$, *then* $\tau(z) \to w$ *twice,* $\tau(x) \to u$ *and* $\tau(x) \to v$.

In all other cases, the transitions are $\tau(x) \to u$, $\tau(y) \to v$ *and* $\tau(z) \to w$.

Remark 1. If the state is self-adjacent, then the corresponding transition of positions within the same state in Theorem 1(*i*),(*ii*) are given by

(i) $\tau(x) \to x, \tau(y) \to z, \tau(z) \to y$
(ii) $\tau(x) \to y, \tau(y) \to x, \tau(z) \to z$.

Each mapping of positions by τ gives a transition probability of $1/6$, except when the mapping occurs twice, as in the 3rd and 4th cases in the Theorem, then the transition probability is $2/6$. These values are then used to generate the transient matrix $\mathbf{Q}$ in the Markov chain. For the absorption probabilities, we use the following:

Theorem 2. *Given a position* u, *then* $\phi(u) = 1/3$ *when* $u = 1$. *If* $u > 1$, *then* $\phi(u) = 0$, *the only exception is for the state* $(u + 1, u, u - 1)$, *wherein* $\phi(u + 1) = \phi(u) = \phi(u - 1) = 1/18$.

If $S = 6$, then in the state $(3, 2, 1)$, $\phi(1) = 1/3 + 1/18$, by combining the two cases in Theorem 2. The values of ϕ on the various positions are then used to construct the vector $\mathbf{r}$. Finally, we solve the system

$$(\mathbf{I} - \mathbf{Q})\mathbf{p} = \mathbf{r} \tag{6}$$

where the vector $\mathbf{p}$ gives the probabilities of first ruin for each position and $\mathbf{I}$ is the identity matrix with the same dimension as $\mathbf{Q}$. It is easy to show the transient matrix $\mathbf{I} - \mathbf{Q}$ is invertible [5].

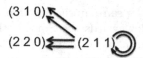

Fig. 1. Multigraph with loops for $S = 4$.

Example 1. To illustrate the method, we first consider the simplest case $S = 4$ with only one non-terminal state $(2, 1, 1)$ and two terminal states $(3, 1, 0), (2, 2, 0)$. The multigraph is shown in Fig. 1. Note that by Lemma 2, $(2, 1, 1)$ is adjacent to itself, and by Lemma 3, it is doubly adjacent to its adjacent nodes including itself. We use a combination of Remark 1 and Theorem 1 (*iii*) to get $\tau(2) \to 1$ twice, $\tau(1) \to \tau(2)$ once and $\tau(1) \to \tau(1)$ once. This generates our transient matrix **Q**. Using Theorem 2, $\phi(2) = 0$ and $\phi(1) = 1/3$. This produces the vector **r**. Thus

$$Q = \frac{1}{6}\begin{pmatrix} 0 & 2 \\ 1 & 1 \end{pmatrix}, \quad r = \begin{pmatrix} 0 \\ 1/3 \end{pmatrix}. \tag{7}$$

Substituting (7) in (6), we obtain the solution $\mathbf{p} = (1/7, 3/7)^T$, i.e. the probabilities of being ruined first are $p(2) = 1/7$, $p(1) = 3/7$. The 2nd place probabilities are thus $10/28$ and $9/28$ for positions 2 and 1, respectively. In comparison, [3] obtained $(0.35790, 0.32105)$ using a Brownian motion model, which are good approximations of the true values obtained by our method. The computed ICM values are $(1/3, 1/3)$, which are slightly different from the 3-tower values.

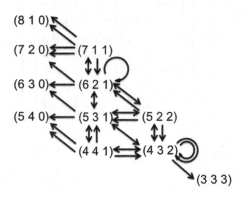

Fig. 2. Directed multigraph (with loops) of state transitions for $S = 9$.

Example 2. Figure 2 illustrates the various states for $S = 9$. In this example, there are 6 non-terminal states and a total of 15 unique positions. For labeling purposes, letters are affixed to the position in cases when there are two or more unique states with the same position value. Starting from the top left non-terminal state moving downwards (or South), the non-terminal states are $(7, 1a, 1a)$, $(6, 2a, 1b)$, $(5a, 3a, 1c)$, $(4a, 1d, 1d)$, $(5b, 2b, 2b)$, and $(4b, 3b, 2c)$. The unique positions are then arranged starting from the x positions in each of the states above, then the y positions, and then the z positions, skipping the non-unique positions as needed. Thus our indices correspond to 7, 6, 5a, 4a, 5b, 4b, 1a, 2a, 3a, 1d, 2b, 3b, 1b, 1c and 2c, respectively. For example, index $i = 1$ of $\mathbf{Q}$, $\mathbf{r}$ and $\mathbf{p}$ corresponds to values for position 7 from the state $(7, 1, 1)$, while index $i = 15$ corresponds to the state-position 2c from the state $(4, 3, 2)$. In constructing $\mathbf{Q}$, note that by Theorem $1(iii)$, $\tau(7) \rightarrow 6$ twice, and using the 1 and 2-index for positions 7 and 6, respectively, we have $Q_{12} = 2/6$. Because all other transitions of 7 are towards terminal states, then $Q_{1j} = 0$ for $j \neq 2$. From Theorem 2, $r_1 = \phi(7) = 0$ because 7 is not a near-terminal position. For position 6, we have $\tau(6) \rightarrow \{7, 6, 5a, 5b\}$ using Theorem $1(i)$, hence $Q_{21} = Q_{22} = Q_{23} = Q_{25} = 1/6$. For position 5a in the state $(5a, 3a, 1c)$, the 'regular' case of Theorem 1 applies, hence $\tau(5a) \rightarrow \{6, 5b, 4a, 4b\}$. The rest of the entries are computed similarly, using Theorems 1 and 2. The transient matrix $\mathbf{Q}$ and absorption vector $\mathbf{r}$ in (6) are obtained as follows:

$$\mathbf{Q} = \frac{1}{6} \begin{pmatrix} 0\,2\,0\,0\,0\,0\,0\,0\,0\,0\,0\,0\,0\,0\,0 \\ 1\,1\,1\,0\,1\,0\,0\,0\,0\,0\,0\,0\,0\,0\,0 \\ 0\,1\,0\,1\,1\,1\,0\,0\,0\,0\,0\,0\,0\,0\,0 \\ 0\,0\,1\,0\,0\,1\,0\,0\,1\,0\,1\,0\,0\,0\,0 \\ 0\,2\,2\,0\,0\,2\,0\,0\,0\,0\,0\,0\,0\,0\,0 \\ 0\,0\,1\,1\,1\,1\,0\,0\,0\,0\,1\,0\,0\,0\,0 \\ 0\,0\,0\,0\,0\,0\,0\,1\,0\,0\,0\,1\,0\,0\,0 \\ 0\,0\,0\,0\,0\,0\,1\,0\,1\,1\,0\,1\,0\,0\,0 \\ 0\,0\,0\,1\,0\,0\,0\,1\,0\,1\,1\,0\,0\,0\,0 \\ 0\,0\,0\,0\,0\,0\,0\,1\,1\,0\,1\,1\,1\,0\,1 \\ 0\,0\,0\,1\,0\,1\,0\,0\,1\,1\,0\,0\,0\,0\,1 \\ 0\,0\,0\,0\,0\,0\,1\,1\,0\,1\,0\,0\,1\,0\,0 \\ 0\,0\,0\,0\,0\,0\,0\,0\,1\,0\,1\,0\,1\,1 \\ 0\,0\,0\,0\,0\,0\,0\,0\,0\,0\,2\,0\,2 \\ 0\,0\,0\,0\,0\,0\,0\,0\,1\,1\,0\,1\,1\,1 \end{pmatrix} \tag{8}$$

and

$$\mathbf{r} = (0\ 0\ 0\ 0\ 0\ 1/18\ 1/3\ 0\ 0\ 1/18\ 0\ 1/3\ 1/3\ 1/3\ 1/18)^T. \tag{9}$$

The solution of (6) using (8) and (9) then produces the 3rd place probabilities of the various positions. For example, given the state $(5, 3, 1)$, the probabilities of placing 3rd are $p(5) = 0.075227$, $p(3) = 0.196310$, and $p(1) = 0.728463$. The results are similar to the values obtained using numerical solutions to Markov processes, which were given to 4 decimal places [6]. The corresponding ICM values are $(0.0972, 0.2083, 0.6944)$.

Unlike ICM or other methods, the actual number of chips of each player, rather than just the proportion of the chips to those of the other players, affects that player's probability of first ruin. The accuracy of the method allows very minute differences in probabilities to be observed. As an illustration, the 3rd place probabilities for states in multiples of $(3, 2, 1)$ are shown in Table 1. As x, y and z increase, the ruin probabilities approach a limiting value. The ICM values are shown for comparison.

Table 1. Probabilities of placing 3rd for given states (x, y, z), where $x : y : z$ are in the ratio $3 : 2 : 1$. The ICM values are shown for comparison.

(x, y, z)	$p(x)$	$p(y)$	$p(z)$
$(3, 2, 1)$	0.12690355	0.25888325	0.61421320
$(6, 4, 2)$	0.12672895	0.25857077	0.61470028
$(12, 8, 4)$	0.12671616	0.25854223	0.61474162
$(24, 16, 8)$	0.12671533	0.25854029	0.61474439
$(48, 32, 16)$	0.12671528	0.25854016	0.61474456
$(96, 64, 32)$	0.12671527	0.25854016	0.61474457
ICM	0.1500	0.2667	0.5833

The time until first ruin can also be calculated from the model. For this purpose, we adjust the transient matrix $\mathbf{Q}$ when $S \bmod 3 = 0$ by regarding the state $(S/3, S/3, S/3)$ as non-terminal. The time until ruin is calculated from the row sum of $\mathbf{N} = (\mathbf{I} - \mathbf{Q})^{-1}$. In Example 1, for the state $(2, 1, 1)$, $\mathbf{Q}$ given by (7) and $\mathbf{I}$ the 2×2 identity, we obtain

$$\mathbf{N} = \frac{1}{14} \begin{pmatrix} 15 & 6 \\ 3 & 18 \end{pmatrix} \tag{10}$$

and the row sum for both positions is $3/2$, exactly the same value using the time until ruin formula (2).

4   Conclusion

In this paper, a method of solving players' first-ruin probabilities in the 3-tower problem or gambler's ruin with three players was presented. The assumptions were that each player started with some nonzero number of chips and during each round, two players were randomly selected in an even-money bet with a randomly chosen winner winning one chip from the loser. One application of this is computing equities in a partial information game (e.g. poker tournaments) modeled as a random game. A multigraph of the various states given S total chips was constructed. The method specified how to obtain the state transitions and absorption probabilities, as given by Theorems 1 and 2. The resulting linear system of the Markov chain were then used to solve the 3rd place (and thus 2nd place) probabilities of any state in S. Although a closed form formula was not derived for the probabilities, the method produces exact solutions instead of numerical approximations. This made it possible to show subtle differences in probabilities of first ruin as S was increased, while preserving the relative chip ratios. In contrast, other methods, such as ICM or Brownian models, only depend on the proportion of chips each player has, thus are independent of any scaling factor. The calculated results were similar to previous numerical approximations using Brownian motion, but differed from ICM by up to 15 %, although as mentioned, ICM and the 3-tower problem do not use the same assumptions.

The 3-tower model may be extended to one wherein bet sizes are not fixed. The multigraph form of such a model would be much more complex because the number of edges and adjacent nodes is not limited to six. The model may also be applied to other forms of the three-player gambler's ruin such as player-centric and symmetric games. An extension to an N-tower problem may be done but the increase in complexity of the graph is expected to be significant.

Acknowledgments. This project was supported by the National Sciences Research Institute of the University of the Philippines, Project Reference No. 2008.149. A special thanks to Ramon Marfil of the Institute of Mathematics, University of the Philippines, for his assistance in the project.

References

1. Bruss, F.T., Louchard, G., Turner, J.W.: On the N-tower-problem and related problems. Adv. Appl. Probab. **35**, 278–294 (2003)
2. Engel, A.: The computer solves the three tower problem. Am. Math. Mon. **100**, 62–64 (1993)
3. Ferguson, T.S.: Gambler's Ruin in Three Dimensions (1995). http://www.math.ucla.edu/gamblers
4. Finch, S.: Gambler's Ruin (2008). http://www.people.fas.harvard.edu/sfinch/csolve/ruin.pdf
5. Grinstead, C.M., Snell, J.L.: Introduction to Probability, 2nd edn. American Mathematical Society, Providence (2006)
6. Kim, M.S.: Gambler's ruin in many dimensions and optimal strategy in repeated multi-player games with application to poker. Master's Thesis, UCLA (2005)
7. Roberts, B.: Ben Roberts ICM Model (2012). http://www.pokericmcalculator.com/en-us/articles/ben-roberts-icm-model
8. Rocha, A., Stern, F.: The gambler's ruin problem with n players and asymmetric play. Stat. Probabil. Lett. **44**, 87–95 (1998)
9. Rocha, A., Stern, F.: The asymmetric n-player gambler's ruin problem with equal initial fortunes. Adv. Appl. Math. **33**, 512–530 (2004)
10. Stirzaker, D.: Tower problems and martingales. Math. Sci. **19**, 52–59 (1994)
11. Swan, Y., Bruss, F.T.: A matrix-analytic approach to the n-player ruin problem. J. Appl. Probab. **43**, 755–766 (2006)

Fitness Function in ABC Algorithm
for Uncapacitated Facility Location Problem

Yusuke Watanabe[✉], Mayumi Takaya, and Akihiro Yamamura

Department of Computer Science and Engineering, Akita University, 1-1,
Tegata-Gakuenmachi, Akita, Japan
m9014090@ie.akita-u.ac.jp

Abstract. We study the fitness function of the artificial bee colony algorithm applying to solve the uncapacitated facility location problem. Our hypothesis is that the fitness function in the artificial bee colony algorithm is not necessarily suitable for specific optimization problems. We carry out experiments to examine several fitness functions for the artificial bee colony algorithm to solve the uncapacitated facility location problem and show the conventional fitness function is not necessarily suitable.

Keywords: Swarm intelligence · Artificial bee colony algorithm · Uncapacitated facility location problem · Fitness function

1 Introduction

Efficient supply chain management has led to increased profit, increased market share, reduced operating cost, and improved customer satisfaction for many businesses [8]. For this purpose, it is getting more and more important in information and communications technologies to solve optimization problem such as the *uncapacitated facility location problem* (UFLP) which is a combinatorial optimization problem. The objective of the UFLP is to optimize the cost of transport to each customer and the cost associated to facility opening, when the set of potential locations of facilities and the customers are given, whereas UFLP is known to be NP-hard (see [6]). In the context of performing economic activities efficiently, various objects have been considered as facilities, such as manufacturing plants, storage facilities, warehouses, libraries, fire stations, hospitals or wireless service stations. Several techniques have been applied to the UFLP such as the swarm intelligence algorithms or a meta-heuristics algorithm; *particle swarm optimization* (PSO) [3], *ant colony optimization* (ACO) [5], *artificial bee colony algorithm* (ABC) [9], and *genetic algorithm* [7].

The method of simulating swarm intelligence is inspired by the movement and foraging behavior in herd animals [10]. As typical examples, particle swarm optimization was inspired by the behavior of groups of birds and fish, ant colony optimization was inspired by the foraging behavior of ants. These have been applied to a wide range of computational problems like data mining and image

© IFIP International Federation for Information Processing 2015
I. Khalil et al. (Eds.): ICT-EurAsia 2015 and CONFENIS 2015, LNCS 9357, pp. 129–138, 2015.
DOI: 10.1007/978-3-319-24315-3_13

processing [1] in addition to numerous optimization problems like the traveling salesman problem and the flow shop scheduling problem.

Inspired by the foraging behavior of honey bee swarm, D. Karaboga [4] proposed the artificial bee colony (ABC) algorithm, which is an optimization algorithm developed for a function optimization. In the ABC algorithm model, a honey bee swarm consists of three types of bees which carry out different tasks. The first group of bees are called *employed bees*. They have a potential solution, evaluate its fitness value and keep the better solutions in their memory. The second group of bees are called the *onlooker bees*. They choose potential solutions on the basis of information provided by the employed bees. If a potential solution has high fitness value, many onlooker bees choose the solution. The third group of bees are called the *scout bees*. They explore new potential solutions randomly. An employed bee whose potential solution has been abandoned becomes a scout bee. The ABC algorithm is operated in an iterative manner by these three groups of artificial honey bees to search a better solution. The ABC algorithm is applied to many real-world problems, however, its mechanism has not been understood in detail. In this paper we examine the fitness function that is an important piece of the ABC algorithm by implementing several variants and comparing with the original fitness function.

The paper is organized as follows. In Sect. 2 we review the uncapacitated facility location problem and application of the ABC algorithm to the UFLP. In Sect. 3 we show the results of our experiments and we examine the fitness function of the ABC algorithm applied to the UFLP. In the last section, we summarize our findings.

2   Artificial Bee Colony Algorithm for the Uncapacitated Facility Location Problem

2.1   Uncapacitated Facility Location Problem

In the UFLP, a finite set F of facilities can be opened and a finite set D of customers are present. Each facility i in F has a fixed opening cost $f_i \in \mathbb{R}_+$, where $\mathbb{R}_+$ stands for the set of positive real numbers. For each pair of i in F and $j \in D$, a transport cost $c_{ij} \in \mathbb{R}_+$ for serving the customer j from facility i is specified. It is possible to open any number of facilities and to assign each user to any of the facilities opened that will serve for the user. The task of the UFLP is to minimize the sum of the opening costs of the facilities and the transport costs for each customer, that is, to minimize

$$\sum_{i \in X} f_i + \sum_{j \in D} c_{\sigma(j)j}$$

where $X \subseteq F$ is a subset of facilities to be opened and $\sigma : D \to X$ is an assignment of each customer to an appropriate facility.

2.2   Artificial Bee Colony Algorithm

In the UFLP with n potential facilities, that is $|F| = n$, for each employed bee k is given the *open facility vector* $Y_k = [y_{k1}, y_{k2}, y_{k3}, ..., y_{kn}]$ representing a potential solution, where $y_{ki} = 1$ if the i-th facility is open and $y_{ki} = 0$ otherwise.

For the open facility vector Y_k of an employed bee k, X is defined to be the set of facilities i in F such that $y_{ki} = 1$. Then the allocation $\sigma : D \to X$ for Y_k from each customer in D to an appropriate facility in X is uniquely determined for the transport costs c_{ij} as follows. For each j in D, $\sigma(j)$ is defined to be $i \in X$ so that c_{ij} is the smallest among $\{c_{hj} \mid h \in X\}$. If there are several such i, we choose one of them randomly. The total cost x_k for each employed bee k is computed as the sum of the fixed cost of opening facility determined by the open facility vector Y_k and the transport cost of each customer to the opened facilities.

Table 1. Open facility vector for an employed bee k

Facility		A	B	C	D	E
Open facility vector Y_k		1	0	0	1	1
Opening cost		10	8	4	7	3
Customer (Transportation costs)	a	1	4	3	10	12
	b	9	8	7	4	3
	c	8	12	6	5	7
	d	15	10	6	10	13

Let us see a concrete example shown in Table 1. In this example, 5 facilities A, B, C, D, E and 4 customers a, b, c, d are given and the open facility vector Y_k for an employed bee k is given as $[1, 0, 0, 1, 1]$. The total cost x_k for the employed bee k is calculated as follows:

x_k
= open facilities fixes costs
+ min (cost of supply from open facilities to customer)
= $(10 + 7 + 3)$ + min$(1, 10, 12)$
+ min$(9, 4, 3)$ + min$(8, 5, 7)$ + min$(15, 10, 13)$
= $(20) + (1 + 3 + 5 + 10)$=20 + 19=39.

The fitness value $fitness(x_k)$ of the potential solution of the employed bee k is calculated from its total cost x_k by the formula below that is given in [4].

$$fitness(x_k) \begin{cases} \frac{1}{1+x_k} & if \quad x_k \geq 0 \\ 1 + abs(x_k) & if \quad x_k < 0 \end{cases} \tag{1}$$

where $abs(x_k)$ stands for the absolute value of x_k. We remark that a larger fitness value is better.

Step 1: Initialization. First, each entry in the open facility vector Y_k of each employed bee k is initialized to either 0 or 1 at random. We compute the fitness value $fitness(x_k)$ by the formula (1) for each employed bee k in the population B_1 of employed bees. We remark that we do not use the later part $1 + abs(x_k)$ in the formula (1) because x_k is always a positive number in case of the UFLP.

Step 2: Employed Bee Phase. In each iteration, each employed bee k obtains a new potential solution candidate by manipulating the current potential solution. The open facility vector for k is updated by randomly selecting one facility i in F and switching the bit corresponding to the selected facility (see Fig. 1). If the fitness value of the new open facility vector for k is larger than the fitness value of the previous vector for k, we update the open facility vector for k.

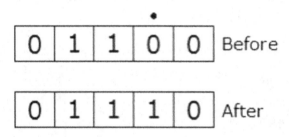

Fig. 1. Update of open facility vector

Step 3: Onlooker Bee Phase. To update onlooker bees, we select stochastically one of the potential solutions, that is, one of the open facility vectors of the employed bees, according to the probability p_k determined by the following formula:

$$p_k = \frac{fitness(x_k)}{\sum_{l=1}^{B_1} fitness(x_l)} \tag{2}$$

Note that the selection follows the probability above and so employed bees with larger fitness value have more bigger chance to be chosen. Like the process similar to Step 2, if the open facility vector of the selected employed bee has larger fitness value than the onlooker bee's current solution, then we replace the potential solution of the onlooker bee with the open facility vector of the selected employed bee. This procedure is repeated for all onlooker bees in the population B_2 of the onlooker bees.

Step 4: Scout Bee Phase. For a *cut limit* c which is determined in advance, if the fitness value of the open facility vector of an employed bee is not improved during c times iteration, then the employed bee is discarded. We harvest the employed bee whose open facility vector was discarded and turn it into a scout bee by giving a new random open facility vector. This operation prevents the search from falling into local optima.

Step 5: Termination Condition of Iteration. The termination condition is determined by the number N of iterations set in advance. When the program reaches N, it outputs the open facility vector whose fitness value is the largest and execution stops.

```
Begin
    Initialize solution randomly (Step1)
    Do
        For Each employ bee (Step2)
            search the new solution
            If the solution is improved
                Update the solution
        For Each Onlooker bee (Step3)
            Choice a solution by probability
            search the new solution
            If the solution is improved
                Update the solution
        For Each solution (Step4)
            If it is not updated
                search new solution randomly and update
    While (Maximum Iteration is not reached) (Step5)
End
```

Algorithm. Pseudocode of the ABC algorithm for UFLP.

3   Experimental Results

We examine the fitness function given by (1) when we implement the ABC algorithm for the UFLP to investigate the adequateness of the fitness function.

The ABC Algorithm was coded in C# language using Visual Studio and run on an Intel Core i3 3.07 GHz Desktop with 2.0 GB memory. We used 12 data sets (cap 71, 72, 73, 74, 101, 102, 103, 104, 131, 132, 133, 134) of benchmark problems from OR-Library [2] compiled by J.E. Beasley. UFLP is called Uncapacitated Warehouse Location Problem in the OR-Library. There are three groups of benchmark problems of size $m \times n$, where m is the number of customers and n is the number of facilities: 50×16 (cap 71, 72, 73, 74), 50×25 (cap 101, 102, 103, 104), 50×50 (cap 131, 132, 133, 134), and the optimal solutions for those instances are known. The performance of our program was evaluated by *average relative percent error* (ARPE), *hit to optimum rate* (HR) and *average computational processing time* (ACPU) that are introduced in [3].

ARPE is the average of the difference from the optimum expressed in percentages, and the lower ARPE shows it produces better solutions. HR represents the number that the algorithm finds the optimal solutions across all repetitions and the higher HR shows better performance. HR takes a value from 0.00 to 1.00 where 1.00 implies that the algorithm finds the optimal solution with probability 1. ACPU represents the time (in seconds) that the algorithm spends to output one solution and the lower ACPU shows better performance.

Table 2. Benchmark

Data set	Size(m × n)	Optimum
cap71	16×50	932615.75
cap72	16×50	977799.40
cap73	16×50	1010641.45
cap74	16×50	1034976.98
cap101	25×50	796648.44
cap102	25×50	854704.20
cap103	25×50	893782.11
cap104	25×50	928941.75
cap131	50×50	793439.56
cap132	50×50	851495.33
cap133	50×50	893076.71
cap134	50×50	928941.75

ARPE is defined by

$$ARPE = \sum_{i=1}^{R} \left(\frac{H_i - U}{U} \right) \times \frac{100}{R} \tag{3}$$

where H_i denotes the i-th replication solution value, U is the optimal value provided by [2], and R is the number of replications. In Table 2, we summarize the data sets we used for our experiments. It shows the size of data sets and the optimal solutions.

3.1 Experiment 1

We conducted an experiment to investigate 5 different candidates for fitness value as follows:

$$fitness(x_k) = 1 \tag{4}$$

$$fitness(x_k) = \frac{1}{1 + x_k} \tag{5}$$

$$fitness(x_k) = \frac{1}{1 + (x_k - x_*)} \tag{6}$$

$$fitness(x_k) = \frac{1}{1 + (x_k - x_*)^2} \tag{7}$$

$$fitness(x_k) = \frac{1}{1 + \sqrt{x_k - x_*}} \tag{8}$$

where x_* represents the best solution obtained so far. Note that the formula (5) is the original fitness function given in [4].

The results obtained in this experiment are shown in Figs. 2 and 3. For the benchmark problem cap131, we set a population of employed bees $B_1 = 50$, a population of onlooker bees $B_2 = 200$, and the number of repetitions $N = 100$ and the cut limit c ranges between 5 and 50. The x-axis of the graph represents the cut limit c and the y-axis of the graph represents HR in Fig. 2 and ARPE in Fig. 3, respectively. Comparing the formulas (4) and (5), we found that the two formulas show almost the same results. This implies that the formula (5) does not have a desired property as a fitness function. The formulas (6), (7) and (8) are designed so that the fitness value is affected largely by the value of x_k. If the cut limit c is set small, we obtain better results in the formulas (6), (7) and (8) than the formula (5), on the other hand, the cut limit c gets larger, then the formula (5) gives a better result. This indicates that we can obtain a better result in a shorter computation, although the search may fall in a local optimal.

Table 3. Experimental Results of the proposed fitness value

Problem	$fitness(x_k) = \frac{1}{1+x_k}$			$fitness(x_k) = \frac{1}{1000+(x_k-x_*)}$		
	ARPE	HR	ACPU	ARPE	HR	ACPU
cap71	0.000	1.00	0.1610	0.000	1.00	0.1674
cap72	0.000	1.00	0.1462	0.000	1.00	0.1490
cap73	0.000	1.00	0.1214	0.000	1.00	0.1215
cap74	0.000	1.00	0.1148	0.000	1.00	0.1173
cap101	0.000	1.00	0.2384	0.000	1.00	0.2482
cap102	0.000	1.00	0.2120	0.000	1.00	0.2231
cap103	0.000	1.00	0.2001	0.000	1.00	0.2061
cap104	0.000	1.00	0.1819	0.000	1.00	0.2065
cap131	0.349	0.06	0.5044	0.143	0.24	0.5357
cap132	0.214	0.03	0.4599	0.039	0.41	0.4976
cap133	0.173	0.04	0.4348	0.040	0.36	0.4501
cap134	0.039	0.73	0.4206	0.000	1.00	0.4360

3.2 Experiment 2

Considering the results of Experiment 1, we propose the following formula for the fitness value:

$$fitness(x_k) = \frac{1}{Q + (x_k - x_*)} \qquad (9)$$

where Q is an arbitrary constant, given as a parameter to the algorithm.

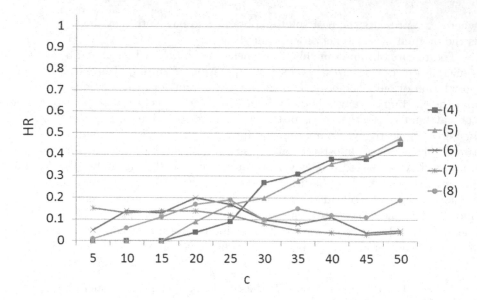

Fig. 2. Experiment 1: HR

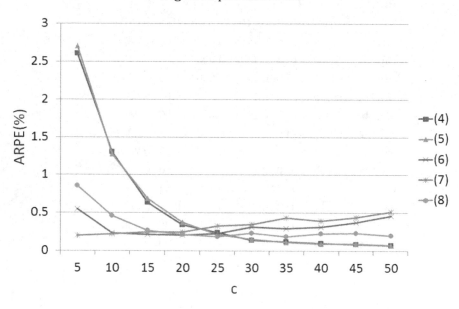

Fig. 3. Experiment 1: ARPE

Figures 4 and 5 show how the value of cut limit c between 5 and 50 affects HR and ARPE for the benchmark problem cap131 with bee populations $B_1 = 50$, $B_1 = 20$ and the number of iterations $N = 100$. If $Q = 10^6$ or 10^8, the fitness value of (5) is almost the same as the one for (9). If $Q = 1$, the fitness value of (9) is almost the same as the one for (6). If $Q = 10^4$, the fitness value of

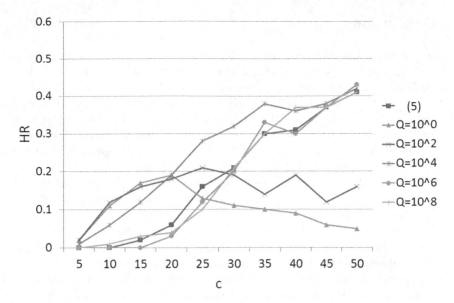

Fig. 4. Experiment 2: HR

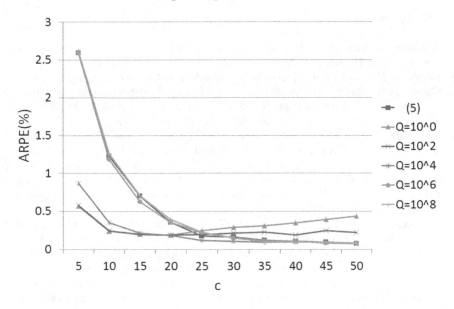

Fig. 5. Experiment 2: ARPE

(9) is better than (5). As a result of the experiment, we believe that the ABC algorithm operates more efficiently by the fitness formula (9) with $Q = 10^4$.

Finally, we show the result of performing the proposed fitness value and conventional fitness value for each set of benchmark problems in Table 3, where we set the population of employed bees $B_1 = 50$, the population of the onlooker bees $B_1 = 200$, the cut limit $c = 20$ and the number of repetitions $N = 100$.

4 Conclusions

In this paper we discussed the fitness function of the ABC algorithm for the UFLP by carrying out experiments of several variants and comparing with the original fitness function. Our experiment indicates the conventional formula (5) for the fitness value of the ABC algorithm is almost same as the fitness of a constant function given by (4) for the benchmark problems and so it seems inadequate for the UFLP. Therefore, we proposed a new formula (9) which can appropriately weight the fitness value according to problem instances. Using the formula (9) with a smaller value of Q, we can find more open facility vectors whose total costs are low and it makes the search efficient. However, we consider that the algorithm falls in a local optima when we use a too small value of Q and the algorithm does perform adequately. In our experiment, the ABC algorithm with the fitness function (9) with $Q = 10^4$ performs best and exceeds the original formula (5). The new candidate for the fitness function is worth being applied to other problems, although we do not know how to adjust the value of Q for specific optimization problem. It will be our future research to study how to adjust the value Q for a specific optimization problem such as TSP.

References

1. Abraham, A., Grosan, C., Ramos, V.: Swarm Intelligence in Data Mining. Springer-Verlag, Berlin Heidelberg (2006)
2. Beasley, J.E.: OR-Library (2005). http://www.brunel.ac.uk/mastjjb/jeb/info.html
3. Guner, A.R., Sevkli, M.: A discrete particle swarm optimization algorithm for uncapacitated facility location problem. J. Artif. Evol. Appl. **2008**, Article ID 861512, 9 p. (2008). http://dx.doi.org/10.1155/2008/861512
4. Karaboga, D.: An Idea Based on Honey Bee Swarm for Numerical Optimization. Erciyes University, Kayseri, Turkey, Technical report-TR06 (2005)
5. Kole, A., Chakrabarti, P., Bhattacharyya, S.: An ant colony optimization algorithm for uncapacitated facility location problem. Artif. Intell. Appl. **1**(1), 55–61 (2014)
6. Korte, B., Vygen, J.: Combinatorial Optimization: Theory and Algorithms. Springer, Heidelberg (2007)
7. Kratica, J., Tosic, D., Filipovic, V., Ljubic, I.: Solving the simple plant location problem by genetic algorithm. RAIRO Oper. Res. **35**, 127–142 (2001)
8. Simchi-Levi, D., Kaminsky, P., Simchi-Levi, E.: Designing and Managing the Supply Chain. Concepts, Strategies and Case Studies. McGraw-Hill, Boston (2000)
9. Tuncbilek, N., Tasgetiren, F., Esnaf, S.: Artificial bee colony optimization algorithm for uncapacitated facility location problems. J. Econ. Soc. Res. **14**(1), 1–24 (2012)
10. Yang, X., Cui, Z., Xiao, R., Gandomi, A.H., Karamanoglu, M.: Swarm Intelligence and Bio-Inspired Computation - Theory and Applications. Elsevier, Amsterdam (2013)

Comparative Study of Monte-Carlo Tree Search and Alpha-Beta Pruning in Amazons

Hikari Kato[✉], Szilárd Zsolt Fazekas, Mayumi Takaya, and Akihiro Yamamura

Department of Computer Science and Engineering, Akita University, 1-1, Tegata Gakuen-machi, Akita 010-8502, Japan
{m9014076,szilard.fazekas,msato,yamamura}@ie.akita-u.ac.jp

Abstract. The game of Amazons is a combinatorial game sharing some properties of both chess and Go. We study programs which play Amazons with strategies based on Monte-Carlo Tree Search and a classical search algorithm, Alpha-Beta pruning. We execute several experiments to investigate the effect of increasing the number of searches in a Monte-Carlo Tree Search program. We show that increasing the number of searches is not an efficient method to strengthen the program for Amazons. On the other hand, augmenting the algorithms with a choice of several evaluation functions fulfills has great influence on playing strength.

Keywords: Amazons · Two player games · Monte-Carlo tree search · UCT · Game programs · Playouts · Alpha-Beta pruning · Evaluation function

1 Introduction

Artificial intelligence is an important technology in our digitalized society. There are many applications of artificial intelligence to industry, e.g., data mining in big data processing, natural language processing, robotics, intelligent agents and machine learning, etc. One of the most important applications, as well as proving grounds for artificial intelligence methods is to create game playing programs for board games like chess or Go. Monte-Carlo Tree Search is one of the simple, yet often efficient approaches along this line. We shall study the performance of a simple Monte-Carlo Tree Search program playing Amazons compared with traditional artificial intelligence methods like Alpha-Beta pruning.

Alpha-Beta pruning is a search algorithm that applies an evaluation function to each leaf node in the game tree and selects the node with the highest evaluation based on the Mini-Max principle. It has been widely studied for a long time as a search program for two player games such as Shogi and Reversi. When applying this method, it is important to use strong evaluation functions [11] and enhanced pruning techniques of the game tree [10]. *Monte-Carlo Tree Search* (MCTS for short) is a search algorithm based on probability statistics,

© IFIP International Federation for Information Processing 2015
I. Khalil et al. (Eds.): ICT-EurAsia 2015 and CONFENIS 2015, LNCS 9357, pp. 139–148, 2015.
DOI: 10.1007/978-3-319-24315-3_14

and it can create a strategy without using an evaluation function which is first implemented by Coulom [6]. This property made it a prime candidate for games for which it is difficult to create an evaluation function such as Go [8] and Arimaa [20]. For instance, it was considered difficult to write a strong program for Go using conventional Mini-Max search technique. However, programs such as CrazyStone [7], based on MCTS, were able to win computer Go tournaments, proving the validity of the approach.

The game of Amazons (Amazons for short) is a two player game [24] sharing some attributes with both chess and Go, but also being different from them in crucial ways. There are more legal moves in each turn in the game of Amazons than in chess. A strong game playing program must explore the game tree to great depth. However, searching deeply in Amazons with a simple Alpha-Beta pruning is ineffective, because the state space is huge; the number of legal moves is so great that doing a full width search is impractical throughout at least the first two thirds of an Amazons game [3]. Therefore, creating a strong player using only Alpha-Beta pruning is impossible.

Amazons has been extensively studied, see, for instance, the analysis of $2 \times n$ Amazons [4], the analysis of endgames [5,13,14], the Amazons opening book [16], and a study of creating strong programs by combining an evaluation function and MCTS [12]. Nobody succeeded in creating a strong game playing program of Amazons based on simple MCTS. Kloetzer et al. [15,17] gave much stronger approaches by combining MCTS and an evaluation function in the search process. They also showed that the strength of MCTS combined with an evaluation function for Amazons can be enhanced by increasing the number of simulations. However, we are not aware of any previous analyses of direct play between simple MCTS not using an evaluation function and Alpha-Beta pruning. As such a study would emphasize the gain brought by combining evaluation functions with MCTS, we conducted experiments in this direction.

We will carried out experiments in which a simple MCTS program not using an evaluation function plays against an Alpha-Beta pruning program using the classical evaluation function. We recorded how many times the MCTS program won against the Alpha-Beta pruning program and the average time that each program took to output a move. Our experiment showed that Alpha-Beta pruning is stronger than the simple MCTS program and increasing the number of simulations in a simple MCTS is inefficient for strengthening the strategy for Amazons.

2   The Game of Amazons

The game of Amazons is a combinatorial two-player game invented in 1988 by Zamkauskas [24] and first published (in Spanish) in issue 4 of the puzzle magazine El Acertijo in 1992. Amazons is played on a 10×10 chess-style board. The game starts by placing four black and white queens on the specified cells on the board. The first player (P_W) selects and moves one of the white queens according to the movement of a queen in chess (vertical, horizontal and diagonal straight lines on the board). Then, P_W chooses any empty cell in the range of the queen moved and thwarts it. No piece can be placed on the thwarted cell nor pass through it thereafter. Similarly, the second player (P_B) selects and moves one of the black queens and chooses any empty cell in the range of the queen moved and thwarts it. The players P_W and P_B move alternately and the player who can no longer complete their moves (both moving a queen and thwarting a cell) loses the game. Amazons resembles Go in that it is considered good strategy for one to create their own territory, while the movement of the pieces on the board is borrowed from chess. It should be noted, that while Amazons originally uses a 10×10 board, the game can also be considered in a more general manner on an $n \times n$ board as a variant. Figure 1 shows the initial setting of an Amazons game and the board after the first player made their first move.

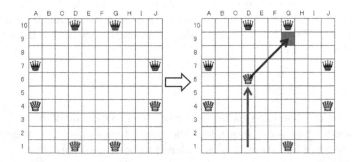

Fig. 1. From initial placement to the first movement of P_W

Amazons is known to have a very large number of legal moves in a given turn compared with other board games such as chess, Shogi or Go. For example, the number of legal moves of a player in their turn in chess is about 35 on average (see [1]), in Shogi it is 80 (see [22]) and in Go it is 361 on a 19×19 board. In contrast, in the first turn of Amazons the starting player has 2176 legal moves, and each player has 400 legal moves per turn on average even during the game. Therefore, the evaluation of the game tree involves many more states than in the case of previously mentioned board games and creating a strong computer player for Amazons is considered difficult [3].

3   Alpha-Beta Pruning

The game tree for a two-player game is a directed graph whose nodes are states in the game and whose edges are legitimate moves. Alpha-Beta pruning is an algorithm to find the best move from a state according to an evaluation function and the Min-Max principle (see [18]) by analyzing part of the game tree. The algorithm has been studied since J. McCarthy showed an idea in 1956. It is a widely used algorithm in the field of two player games; notable examples includes chess and Reversi. First, Alpha-Beta pruning expands the game tree until a specified search depth. After that, it applies the evaluation function to the child nodes of the portion of the game tree expanded up to then. The evaluation of the nodes higher up in the tree is done by the Mini-Max principle. After obtaining the evaluation of all the nodes, the algorithm selects the move leading to the child node with the highest value.

Alpha-Beta pruning can lead to a stronger strategy if one increases the allowed search depth. However, since Amazons has a very large number of legal moves on average, it is difficult to explore the game tree to a large depth because of time and memory limitations. The Alpha-Beta pruning program in our experiment used depth-first search for evaluating the nodes to a depth of 2. Several different heuristics for Amazons have already been studied [9]. For the Alpha-Beta pruning programs we used the three evaluation functions given in [21] and described below. In what follows, by *turn player* in a state we mean the player whose turn it is to move in that state and by *opponent* we mean the other. When not specified explicitly, by evaluating a state we mean evaluation from the point of view of the turn player.

3.1 Mobility Evaluation

In Amazons, it is advantageous to have more legal moves available in one's turn because players who cannot move, lose the game. Consequently, if the number of legal moves is small in a state, it is considered to be an unfavorable game-state for the player. In other words, reducing the number of legal moves of the opponent is considered as an effective strategy. Let *mobility evaluation* (ME) of a state be the value obtained by subtracting the number of legal moves of the opponent from the number of legal moves of the turn player in a given game state. For example, if P_W has 161 legal moves in a certain game state and P_B has 166 moves, then ME of the state X from P_W's point of view is $\mathrm{ME}_W(X) = 161 - 166 = -5$.

3.2 Territory Evaluation

The concept of territory is important in Amazons. A *territory* of a player is a cell which is reachable by the queens of only that player, so advantageous game states should have many of these. The player who has access to more empty cells is in advantage because the playing area is divided in several separated subareas in the end-game of Amazons.

Figure 2 shows the minimum number of moves required to reach each cell on the game board by any of the pieces of the players. The value in the upper left corner of each blank cell is the minimum number of moves needed for P_W to reach it, whereas the value in the lower right corner represents the corresponding number required for P_B. For example, to reach cell $C6$, player P_W needs at least four moves, e.g., $B8 \rightarrow A7 \rightarrow A6 \rightarrow B5 \rightarrow C6$. In contrast, P_B requires only two moves, $B3 \rightarrow A4 \rightarrow C6$. Therefore, P_B has a faster access to $C6$ than P_W so according to territory evaluation, cell $C6$ belongs to the territory of P_B. Let

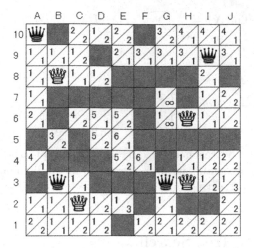

Fig. 2. Territory evaluation

$D_X(A)$ denote the minimum number of moves needed for player X to reach cell A. In the example above, $D_W(C6) = 4$ and $D_B(C6) = 2$.

We compute the minimum number of moves needed for each player in this manner for each blank cell on the board and take the sum over all blank cells to obtain the evaluation of the game-state based on the territories. We define territory evaluation of a state X for P_W as follows.

$$T_W(X) = \sum_{\text{empty cells } A} \Delta_1(D_W(A), D_B(A)),$$

where

$$\Delta_1(n, m) = \begin{cases} 0 & (n = m = \infty) \\ \frac{1}{5} & (n = m < \infty) \\ 1 & (n < m) \\ -1 & (n > m) \end{cases}$$

The evaluation value of the cells that both players reach in the same number of moves may be set to an arbitrary value; in setting it to $\frac{1}{5}$ we followed [21].

3.3 Relative Territory Evaluation

The basic idea of *relative territory evaluation* is similar to that of territory evaluation. In essence, territory evaluation counts the number of cells that can be reached by a player in less moves than by the other player, disregarding the actual difference in the number of moves. In contrast, relative territory evaluation assesses the difference in the number of moves needed by the two players to reach each blank cell. Let us define relative territory evaluation of state X for P_W as follows.

$$\mathrm{RT}_W(X) = \sum_{\text{empty cells } A} \Delta_2(D_W(A), D_B(A))$$

where

$$\Delta_2(n, m) = \begin{cases} 5 & (m = \infty, n < \infty) \\ -5 & (n = \infty, m < \infty) \\ 0 & (n = \infty, m = \infty) \\ m - n & (\text{otherwise}) \end{cases}$$

For a cell which can be reached by only one of the players, the difference in number of moves is by default infinite. However, for implementation purposes it is convenient to avoid treating infinity and so we set the difference to 5 in those cases.

4 Monte-Carlo Tree Search

A Monte-Carlo algorithm [23] is a randomized algorithm whose output is allowed to be incorrect with a certain probability. Even though the answer may be incorrect, in some cases this approach can be much more efficient than using deterministic algorithms. A Monte-Carlo tree search (MCTS) [6] is a Monte-Carlo algorithm suitable for certain decision processes, most notably employed in game playing. Random simulations in a game tree called *playouts* are employed to select the next move by game playing programs. MCTS has received considerable interest due to its great success in playing *Go* [7].

MCTS employs playouts, which are simulations to determine the outcome of a game played by two players who choose their moves randomly until the game ends. As a refinement of MCTS, the method of *upper confidence bounds applied to trees (UCT)* was introduced by Kocsis and Szepesvári [19] based on the *UCB1 algorithm* proposed by Auer et al. [2]. In a game state G with child states $G_1, \ldots, G_k$, a UCT algorithm selects a child state for which the UCB1 value is maximal among the ones computed for each G_i. The UCB1 value of each child state G_i is defined by the following equation:

$$\mathrm{UCB1}(G_i) = \overline{x_i} + \sqrt{\frac{\log n}{n_i} \min(\frac{1}{4}, \overline{x_i} - \overline{x_i}^2 + \sqrt{\frac{2 \log n}{n_i}})}$$

where

- n is the number of playouts executed from game state G,
- n_i is the number of playouts executed from child state G_i,
- $\overline{x_i} = \frac{x_i}{n_i}$ is the win-loss ratio of G_i, where x_i is the number of wins among playouts from G_i.

A UCT program does not necessarily have an evaluation function and its move selection depends only on the result of playouts.

Through selecting a child node, executing the playout, and repeatedly updating winning percentages, it is possible to find the most selected child node and recommend it as the final move. UCT explores the game tree to a great depth by repeating playouts, therefore it can be configured to be a strong player by increasing the number of searches (or the allowed search time).

5   Experiment

5.1   UCT vs. Alpha-Beta

We compared a UCT algorithm and Alpha-Beta pruning by letting these two programs play Amazons against each other. This experiment not only compared the relative strength of UCT and Alpha-Beta pruning in Amazons but also aimed to evaluate the improvement of the UCT program when increasing the number of allowed searches.

We employed a simple UCT program not using heuristic techniques such as pruning. The number of playouts performed was 10000, 30000, 50000, 100000, 200000. The Alpha-Beta pruning programs had maximum search depth 2 and used one of the three types of evaluation functions described in Sect. 4, respectively.

We executed the experiment on a 10×10 board. For each match-up, we performed 50-50 simulations with the UCT program being the first player and the second player, respectively, and we recorded the number of times the UCT program won. In addition, we recorded the average time taken by UCT and Alpha-Beta pruning to make one move and the average time it took to play one game. This experiment was performed by using an Amazons match simulator written in C#, developed by us. To be able to measure the times correctly, while one game playing program is searching for a move, the other does not compute anything. Our experiments were run on a computer with Windows 7 Professional(64bit), having an Intel(R) Xeon(R) CPU E31245(3.30 GHz) and memory of 16 GB.

5.2   Experimental Results

Table 1 shows the number of times that the UCT programs (with different number of playouts) won against the three Alpha-Beta pruning players out of 100 games (50-50 as first and second player, respectively). Figure 3 shows the average time taken for a move by the programs. The vertical axis of the graph is average search time for one move; the horizontal axis represents the number of playouts performed by the UCT. The time taken by the Alpha-Beta pruning algorithms to compute a move only depends on the depth (2) and on the individual states being evaluated. As the depth was fixed, the slight variations in average computing time for the Alpha-Beta pruning programs is probably due to having to evaluate different game states reached by the changing strategy of the UCT programs and to the relatively low number of matches between the programs. We expect that increasing the number of head-to-head matches would drive the averages closer to each other approximating a horizontal line.

Table 1. UCT vs Alpha-Beta: number of wins for the UCT.

		Mobility	Territory	Relative territory
UCT	10000	71	1	9
	30000	89	8	40
	50000	90	11	43
	100000	97	24	57
	200000	100	34	66

With respect to the number of wins of UCT against Alpha-Beta pruning, the winning percentages of UCT were very different depending on the evaluation function of the opponent. territory evaluation is strongest when comparing the three types of evaluation functions. Against TE, even the UCT program with 200000 playouts won only 34 out of 100. In contrast, when playing against mobility evaluation, the UCT gained significant strength by increasing the number of playouts, the strongest one (200000 playouts) winning all 100 matches.

There are clear differences in the number of wins against the three evaluation functions, but it can be clearly seen that even when the UCT performed poorly (vs. TE) its number of wins was much higher with 200000 playouts than with 10000.

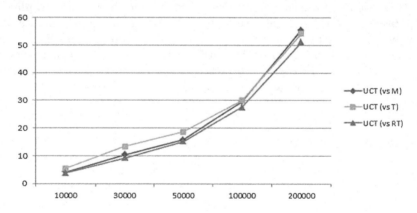

Fig. 3. UCT vs Alpha-Beta: the average time taken by the programs to make a move (sec).

Now let us see the computation time required to make one move by the programs. With 10000 playouts, the UCT needed on average 4 s to decide on a move and this is almost the same as for Alpha-Beta pruning. However, the required time increased in accordance with the increase in the number of playouts. The UCT program with 100000 playouts needed on average 30 s, while the UCT with 200000 playouts took on average 55 s. The UCT program with 200000 playouts had less wins than losses against Alpha-Beta pruning using territory evaluation, even though it required more than 30 times the computation time of the Alpha-Beta pruning program.

Meanwhile, among the three versions of Alpha-Beta pruning there was only a small difference in computing time due to the difference in the evaluation function. Alpha-Beta pruning using mobility evaluation did not record a single win against the UCT with 200000 playouts. However, against relative territory evaluation under the same conditions the UCT won only 34 times. This means that while increasing the number of playouts improved the UCT program, the gain depended heavily on the evaluation function of the opponent, while Alpha-Beta pruning was greatly enhanced by changing the heuristic. Moreover, the increase in playouts caused a significant increase in computing time for UCT, whereas the computing time for Alpha-Beta pruning was not greatly influenced by the change in the evaluation function.

6 Conclusions

We conducted an experiment in which we set UCT based strategies against Alpha-Beta pruning ones in Amazons matches. We showed that even Alpha-Beta pruning with territory evaluation is faster than the simple UCT. Increasing the number of playouts (and thus computing time, too) led to improvements in the UCT. However, with 200000 playouts allowed, the UCT program consumed 30 times more computation time and still only won 34 out of 100 games against Alpha-Beta pruning using territory evaluation. In conclusion, it looks like there is more to gain in playing strength for Amazons programs by improving the evaluation function and using classical methods like Alpha-Beta pruning than by increasing the number of playouts using the MCTS strategy.

References

1. Allis, L.V.: Searching for Solutions in games and Artificial Intelligence. Ph.D. thesis, Maastricht, Rrijksuniversiteit Limburg (1995)
2. Auer, P., Cesa-Bianchi, N., Fischer, P.: Finite-time analysis of the multiarmed bandit problem. Mach. Learning **47**(2–3), 235–256 (2002)
3. Avetisyan, H., Lorentz, R.J.: Selective search in an Amazons program. In: Schaeffer, J., Müller, M., Björnsson, Y. (eds.) CG 2002. LNCS, vol. 2883, pp. 123–141. Springer, Heidelberg (2003)
4. Berlekamp, E.R.: Sums of $N \times 2$ Amazons. Institute of Mathematical Statistics Lecture Notes - Monograph Series, vol. 35 (2000)
5. Buro, M.: Simple Amazons endgames and their connection to Hamilton circuits in cubic subgrid graphs. In: Marsland, T., Frank, I. (eds.) CG 2001. LNCS, vol. 2063, pp. 250–261. Springer, Heidelberg (2002)
6. Coulom, R.: Efficient selectivity and backup operators in Monte-Carlo tree search. In: van den Herik, H.J., Ciancarini, P., Donkers, H.H.L.M.J. (eds.) CG 2006. LNCS, vol. 4630, pp. 72–83. Springer, Heidelberg (2007)

7. Coulom, R.: Computing Elo ratings of move patterns in the game of Go. ICGA J. **30**, 198–208 (2007)
8. Gelly, S., Wang, Y., Munos, R., Teytaud, O.: Modification of UCT with patterns in Monte-Carlo Go. Technical Report PR-6062, INRIA (2006)
9. Hensgens, P.: A Knowledge-based Approach of the Game of Amazons. Master's thesis, Maastricht University (2001)
10. Hoki, K., Muramatsu, M.: Efficiency of three forward-pruning techniques in Shogi: futility pruning, null-move pruning, and late move reduction (LMR). Entertainment Comput. **3**, 51–57 (2012)
11. Kaneko, T.: Evaluation functions of computer Shogi programs and supervised learning using game records. J. Jpn. Soc. Artif. Intell. **27**, 75–82 (2012)
12. Kloetzer, J., Iida, H., Bouzy, B.: The Monte-Carlo approach in Amazons. In: Computer Games Workshop, pp. 185–192, Amsterdam, The Netherlands (2007)
13. Kloetzer, J., Iida, H., Bouzy, B.: A comparative study of solvers in Amazons endgames. In: IEEE 2008 Symposium on Computational Intelligence in Games, Perth, Australia (2008)
14. Kloetzer, J., Iida, H., Bouzy, B.: Playing Amazons endgames. ICGA J. **32**, 140–148 (2009)
15. Kloetzer, J.: Experiments in Monte-Carlo Amazons. IPSJ SIG Technical Report, vol. 2010-GI-24 No. 6, pp. 1–4 (2010)
16. Kloetzer, J.: Monte-Carlo opening books for Amazons. In: 7th Conference on Computer and Games (2010)
17. Kloetzer, J.: Monte-Carlo techniques: application to Monte Carlo tree search and Amazon (2011). http://hdl.handle.net/10119/8867
18. Knuth, D., Moore, R.: An analysis of alpha-beta pruning. Artif. Intell. **6**, 293–326 (1975)
19. Kocsis, L., Szepesvári, C.: Bandit based Monte Carlo planning. In: 17th European Conference on Machine Learning (ECML 2006), pp. 282–293 (2006)
20. Kozelek, T.: Methods of MCTS and the game Arimaa. Master's thesis, Charles University in Prague (2009)
21. Lieberum, J.: An evaluation function for the game of Amazons. Theoret. Comput. Sci. **349**, 230–244 (2005)
22. Matsubara, H., Iida, H., Grimbergen, R.: Chess, Shogi, Go, natural developments in game research. ICCA J. **19**, 103–112 (1996)
23. Motwani, R., Raghavan, P.: Randomized Algorithms. Cambridge University Press, Cambridge (1995)
24. Zamkauskas, W.: Amazons. http://www.chessvariants.org/other.dir/amazons.html

Network Security

Can We Securely Use CBC Mode in TLS1.0?

Takashi Kurokawa[(✉)], Ryo Nojima, and Shiho Moriai

National Institute of Information and Communications Technology (NICT),
4-2-1, Nukui-Kitamachi, Koganei, Tokyo 184-8795, Japan
{blackriver,ryo-no,shiho.moriai}@nict.go.jp

Abstract. Currently, TLS1.0 is one of the most widely deployed protocol versions for SSL/TLS. In TLS1.0, there are only two choices for the bulk encryption, i.e., RC4 or block ciphers in the CBC mode, which have been criticized to be insecure.

In this paper, we explore the current status of the CBC mode in TLS1.0 and prove theoretically that the current version of the (patched) CBC mode in TLS1.0 satisfies *indistinguishability*, which implies that it is secure against BEAST type of attacks.

Keywords: TLS1.0 · The BEAST attack · Security

1 Introduction

1.1 CBC Mode in TLS1.0

The SSL/TLS is one of the most widely deployed cryptographic protocols used in the network. In fact, SSL/TLS is employed in almost all the popular services for online shopping and online banking. At the same time, many cryptographic attacks against SSL/TLS have been found, e.g., CRIME, Lucky Thirteen [2], BEAST [5], POODLE [7] and RC4 bias attacks [1,6].[1]

In SSL/TLS, many cryptographic primitives have been employed, e.g., RSA, DH(E), AES, RC4, CBC mode, and HMAC. Among them, we are going to focus on the *CBC mode* in *TLS 1.0*, which is one of the most problematic cryptographic primitives in SSL/TLS. To see this, let us introduce how the CBC mode is used in SSL/TLS. In SSL/TLS, a plaintext is "tagged" before the encryption. That is, to encrypt a plaintext M, the tag t is firstly generated and then the message

$$M' = M \| t$$

is encrypted by the CBC mode. Then, the ciphertext of the (tagged) message $M' = (M'[0], M'[1], \ldots, M'[m-1])$ is encrypted as

$$\text{IV}, \mathcal{F}_K(\text{IV} \oplus M'[0]), \ldots, \mathcal{F}_K(C[m-2] \oplus M'[m-1]\|\text{PAD}\|\text{PAD\_LEN}), \quad (1)$$

where $\mathcal{F}_K : \{0,1\}^\lambda \to \{0,1\}^\lambda$ is a block cipher modeled as the pseudorandom permutation, λ is the block length, IV is an initial vector, PAD is a padding,

---

[1] For the overview of the recent attacks, see [9].

I. Khalil et al. (Eds.): ICT-EurAsia 2015 and CONFENIS 2015, LNCS 9357, pp. 151–160, 2015.
DOI: 10.1007/978-3-319-24315-3_15

PAD_LEN is the length of PAD, $C[0] = \mathcal{F}(\text{IV} \oplus M[0])$ and $C[i] = \mathcal{F}_K(C[i-1] \oplus M'[i])$ for $1 \leq i \leq m - 1$.

The CBC mode in TLS1.0 has two potential weaknesses: one is in the padding and the other is in the choice of the initial vector IV [13].

Padding: In the encryption of the form Eq. (1), which is known as Mac-then-Enc, the message authentication code is not applied to the padding. That is, the padding is appended after the generation of the tag. Accordingly, we can consider two errors: the error of the padding and that of the message authentication code. If the adversary can distinguish these two errors, an attack known as the *padding oracle attack* [10] works. For a concrete example, there exists a timing analysis [4] which enables the adversary to distinguish these two errors. However, this problem has been repaired in some implementations of SSL/TLS, e.g., OpenSSL 0.9.6c, 0.9.6i, and 0.9.7a. There is a possibility that other side channel information can be used to attack the CBC mode. In fact, for SSL3.0, the Möller et al. [7] showed a practical attack against the CBC mode in SSL3.0, named the POODLE attack. However, this attack cannot be applied directly to the CBC mode in TLS1.0 since a different padding scheme is employed.

Choice of IV: In TLS1.0, the initial vector IV is chosen from the last block of the ciphertext, therefore the adversary who can eavesdrop the ciphertexts knows the IV before the next plaintext is encrypted [8]. Since this means that IV is predictable from the adversary's viewpoint, the CBC mode in TLS1.0 does not satisfy indistinguishability.

However, this does not immediately imply that the adversary can recover the whole plaintext and moreover it was expected that the time complexity of the recovering the plaintext would be $O(2^\lambda)$ for one block of ciphertexts. Unfortunately, such an idea was not true. Duong and Rizzo demonstrated the BEAST attack [5] whose time complexity is $O(\lambda)$.

1.2 On BEAST Attack

To launch the BEAST attack, two underlying conditions must be satisfied. One is that there exists a software bug on Same Origin Policy (SOP) in the browser and the other is the predictability of IV, which is the case of the CBC mode in TLS1.0. The attack has huge impact since Duang and Rizzo found the software bug on SOP in Java. At present, a software patch for Java is released but there is a possibility that there are many software bugs. Hence, browser vendors such as Microsoft, and Mozilla released a software patch for the CBC mode in addition to the patch for Java [9].

1.3 Contributions

According to [14], currently, TLS1.0 is the most widely deployed protocol version in SSL/TLS, and the CBC mode is used in many ciphersuites. Although the software patch is released for the CBC mode, there has been a problem remained. That is, it is not clarified whether or not the patched CBC mode is secure against BEAST type of attacks. In this paper, we show that the patched CBC mode satisfies the indistinguishability, which implies that the CBC mode is secure against BEAST type of attacks. As far as we know, this is the first time to show that the current version of the CBC mode in the TLS1.0 satisfies the indistinguishability despite the fact that TLS1.0 is widely used in practice.

2   Preliminaries

2.1   Definition

Let λ, τ denote security parameters, where each of them represents the length in byte. The length is often considered in byte, and hence λ, τ are multiple of eight. The negligible function is denoted by $\epsilon(\lambda)$, or simply by ϵ.

Pseudorandom Function and Permutation: A pseudorandom function (PRF) $\mathcal{P}$ consists of a pair of algorithms $(\mathcal{K}, \mathcal{F})$:

- The key generation algorithm $\mathcal{K}$ is a PPT   (probabilistic polynomial time) algorithm and generates a key K.
- The evaluation algorithm $\mathcal{F}$ is a deterministic polynomial time algorithm. It generates $\mathcal{F}(K, x)$ given the key K and a point x.

Definition 1 (Pseudorandom Function, PRF). *We say that* $\mathcal{P} = (\mathcal{K}, \mathcal{F})$ *is PRF if for any* PPT   *algorithm A,*

$$\left| Pr[K \xleftarrow{\$} \mathcal{K} : A^{\mathcal{F}(K, \cdot)} = 1] - Pr[\mathcal{F}' \xleftarrow{\$} \mathcal{R} : A^{\mathcal{F}'(\cdot)} = 1] \right| \leq \epsilon_{\mathrm{PRF}}(\lambda),$$

where $\mathcal{R}$ *is a set of all functions such that both the domain and the range are the same as* $\mathcal{F}(K, \cdot)$, *respectively.*

If the function $\mathcal{F}_K(\cdot) := \mathcal{F}(K, \cdot)$ is a permutation, then we say that $\mathcal{P}$ is a pseudorandom permutation (PRP). In this case, we denote the negligible function by ϵ_{PRP}.

Symmetric Key Encryption: The symmetric key encryption (SKE) scheme $\mathcal{SE}$ consists of a triple of algorithms $(\mathcal{K}, \mathcal{E}, \mathcal{D})$:

- The key generation algorithm $\mathcal{K}$ is a PPT   algorithm which generates a key K.
- The PPT   encryption algorithm $\mathcal{E}$ takes a key K and a plaintext M as input, and outputs a ciphertext C. If we consider a *stateful* SKE, then $\mathcal{E}$ has additional input st as a state, and outputs a new state st$'$ as well.
- The decryption algorithm $\mathcal{D}$ is a deterministic polynomial time algorithm. This algorithm takes a ciphertext C and a key K as input and outputs a plaintext M or $\perp$ representing an invalid ciphertext. If we consider a stateful SKE then $\mathcal{D}$ is given a state st and outputs a new state st$'$ in addition.

The SKE scheme must be "decryptable." That is for any key K and any plaintext M,

$$\mathcal{D}(K, \mathcal{E}(K, M)) = M$$

must be satisfied.

To define the security, we consider the function $\mathsf{LR}_{K,b}(M_0, M_1) = \mathcal{E}(K, M_b)$, where $b \in \{0, 1\}$.

Definition 2 (IND-CPA). *We say that the SKE* $\mathcal{SE} = (\mathcal{K}, \mathcal{E}, \mathcal{D})$ *satisfies the* $(\epsilon_{\mathrm{IND}}, q)$ *IND-CPA if for any* PPT *algorithm A,*

$$\mathsf{Adv}_{\mathrm{IND}}(\lambda) = \left| Pr[K \xleftarrow{\$} \mathcal{K}, b \xleftarrow{\$} \{0, 1\}, b' \xleftarrow{\$} A^{\mathsf{LR}_{K,b}(\cdot, \cdot)} \mid b = b'] - \frac{1}{2} \right| \le \epsilon_{\mathrm{IND}}(\lambda),$$

where q is the number of queries to LR *oracle.*

Message Authentication Code (MAC): The message authentication code (MAC) scheme $\mathcal{MA}$ consists of a triple of algorithms $(\mathcal{K}, \mathcal{T}, \mathcal{V})$.

- The key generation algorithm $\mathcal{K}$ is a PPT algorithm and outputs a key K.
- The tag generation algorithm $\mathcal{T}$ is a deterministic polynomial-time algorithm. This algorithm takes a key K and a plaintext M as input and outputs a tag t of length τ.
- The verification algorithm $\mathcal{V}$ is a deterministic polynomial-time algorithm. This algorithm takes a key K, a message M, and a tag t as input, and outputs 0 or 1.

We say that $\mathcal{MA}$ satisfies the completeness if $\mathcal{V}(K, M, t) = 1$ is equivalent to $t = \mathcal{T}(K, M)$. We assume that, for a randomly chosen key K, $\mathcal{T}(K, \cdot)$ is a pseudorandom function. The negligible function will be denoted as ϵ_{PRF}.

2.2 The Format in SSL/TLS

In the CBC mode of SSL/TLS, to encrypt the plaintext CONTENT, some additional information for maintaining the SSL/TLS session is appended. That is,

$$\mathsf{CONTENT}, \mathsf{MAC}, \mathsf{PAD}, \mathsf{PAD\_LEN}$$

are encrypted, simultaneously. Here PAD is a padding, PAD_LEN is the length of the padding, and MAC is a tag of

$$\mathsf{SEQ\_NUM}, \mathsf{CONTENT\_TYPE}, \mathsf{LEN}, \mathsf{CONTENT}$$

generated by the message authentication code HMAC.

A sequence number SEQ_NUM is a binary sequence of length 64 in bit. This is a counter starting from 0, and the length of the message CONTENT is incremented for every encryption. This is originally for preventing the replay attack, but we show later that this counter makes the "patched" CBC mode in TLS1.0 indistinguishable.

There is other information such as CONTENT_TYPE, but these are not related to our security analysis.

Table 1. The original CBC mode in TLS1.0 (WeakCBC mode)

Algorithm $\mathcal{K}_{\text{WeakCBC}}$	**Algorithm** $\mathcal{E}_{\text{WeakCBC}}(K, M; \mathbf{st})$
$K \xleftarrow{\$} \mathcal{K}_{\text{PRP}}$	$\mathbf{IV} \leftarrow \mathbf{st}$
Output K	$M[0], \ldots, M[n-1] \leftarrow M$
	$C[0] \leftarrow \mathcal{F}_{\text{PRP}}(K, M[0] \oplus \mathbf{IV})$
	For $i = 1$ to $n - 1$
	$\quad C[i] \leftarrow \mathcal{F}_{\text{PRP}}(K, M[i] \oplus C[i-1])$
	Output $C = (\mathbf{IV}, C[0], \ldots, C[n-1])$ and $\mathbf{st} = C[n-1]$

3 The Effect of the Patch

Let λ be a block length of the underlying block cipher (in byte), and let $\parallel$ be concatenation. Then, for a binary sequence X, we define $X[i]$ as

$$X = \overbrace{X[0]}^{\lambda \text{ byte}} \parallel \overbrace{X[1]}^{\lambda \text{ byte}} \parallel \cdots \parallel \overbrace{X[n-1]}^{\leq \lambda \text{ byte}}, X[i..] = \overbrace{X[i]}^{\lambda \text{ byte}} \parallel \cdots \parallel \overbrace{X[n-1]}^{\leq \lambda \text{ byte}}.$$

Hence, except for the last block $X[n-1]$, $X[i]$ is λ byte. Let $X[i]$ be a byte sequence of $\lambda'(\leq \lambda)$ byte. Then we define $X[i][j]$ as

$$X[i] = \overbrace{X[i][0]}^{1 \text{ byte}} \parallel \cdots \parallel \overbrace{X[i][\lambda'-1]}^{1 \text{ byte}}, X[i][j..] = X[i][j] \parallel \cdots \parallel X[i][\lambda-1] \parallel X[i+1..].$$

3.1 Weak CBC Mode in TLS1.0

Let $\mathcal{P} = (\mathcal{K}_{\text{PRP}}, \mathcal{F}_{\text{PRP}})$ be a PRP. The CBC mode in TLS1.0 is implemented as Table 1, where we assume that the length of the message M is multiple of λ, and the initial vector $\mathbf{IV}$ is chosen random at the beginning. The decryption algorithm $\mathcal{D}_{\text{WeakCBC}}$ is not described since it is trivial.

We call this version of the CBC mode as the WeakCBC mode. Clearly, in the WeakCBC mode, since the adversary knows $\mathbf{IV}(= C[n-1])$ in advance, it does not satisfy the IND-CPA security. This is the reason why the original CBC mode (WeakCBC) is vulnerable to the BEAST attack.

3.2 Unpatched CBC

In TLS1.0, the encryption is done by Mac-then-Enc. Hence, the tag is generated before the message is encrypted in the CBC mode. (See Table 2.) In Table 2, c plays the role of the counter which starts from 0. The counter represents the sequence number SEQ_NUM in Sect. 2.2. Other information such as TYPE is not related in our security analysis, and hence we remove from this algorithm.

The algorithm Pad is the padding algorithm which is defined as Eq.(1), and Pad^{-1} is the algorithm which removes the padding.

Table 2. Unpatched CBC (WeakTLS1.0)

Algorithm $\mathcal{K}_{\mathtt{WeakTLS1.0}}$	**Algorithm** $\mathcal{D}_{\mathtt{WeakTLS1.0}}(K, C; \mathtt{st})$
$K_{\mathtt{WeakCBC}} \xleftarrow{\$} \mathcal{K}_{\mathtt{WeakCBC}}$	Parse $\mathtt{st}$ as c
$K_{\mathtt{MA}} \xleftarrow{\$} \mathcal{K}_{\mathtt{MA}}$	Parse K as $(K_{\mathtt{WeakCBC}}, K_{\mathtt{MA}})$
$K \leftarrow (K_{\mathtt{WeakCBC}}, K_{\mathtt{MA}})$	$M' \leftarrow \mathcal{D}_{\mathtt{WeakCBC}}(K_{\mathtt{WeakCBC}}, C)$
Output K	$M'' \leftarrow \mathsf{Pad}^{-1}(M')$
	If $M'' \neq \bot$ then parse M'' as $M\|t$
Algorithm $\mathcal{E}_{\mathtt{WeakTLS1.0}}(K, M; \mathtt{st})$	else output $\bot$
Parse $\mathtt{st}$ as $(\mathtt{st}_{\mathtt{WeakCBC}}, c)$	If $\mathcal{T}(K_{\mathtt{MA}}, c\|\|M\|\|M) = t$,
Parse K as $(K_{\mathtt{WeakCBC}}, K_{\mathtt{MA}})$	output $(M, c + |M|)$
$t \leftarrow \mathcal{T}(K_{\mathtt{MA}}, c\|\|M\|\|M)$	else output $\bot$
$(C, \mathtt{st}_{\mathtt{WeakCBC}}) \leftarrow \mathcal{E}_{\mathtt{WeakCBC}}(K_{\mathtt{WeakCBC}}, \mathsf{Pad}(M\|t); \mathtt{st})$	
Output $(C, (\mathtt{st}_{\mathtt{WeakCBC}}, c + |M|))$	

Table 3. Patched CBC (SplTLS1.0)

Algorithm $\mathcal{K}_{\mathtt{SplTLS1.0}}$	**Algorithm** $\mathcal{E}_{\mathtt{SplTLS1.0}}(K, M; \mathtt{st})$
$K \xleftarrow{\$} \mathcal{K}_{\mathtt{WeakTLS}}$	$(C_0, \mathtt{st}) \leftarrow \mathcal{E}_{\mathtt{WeakTLS1.0}}(K, M[0][0]; \mathtt{st})$
Output K	If M is one byte then output $(C_0, \mathtt{st})$
	else $(C_1, \mathtt{st}) \leftarrow \mathcal{E}_{\mathtt{WeakTLS1.0}}(K, M[0][1..]; \mathtt{st})$
	and output (C_0, C_1) and $\mathtt{st}$

Note that $\mathcal{MA} = (\mathcal{K}_{\mathtt{MA}}, \mathcal{T}, \mathcal{V})$ is the message authentication code. We say that the authenticated encryption of Table 2 as WeakTLS1.0.

Since IV is predictable, WeakTLS1.0 does not satisfy the IND-CPA property as well.

3.3   Patched CBC

By the BEAST attack, some software patches for the WeakTLS1.0 described in Sect. 3.2 are released by browser vendors. Since some patches are not sufficient for the practical use due to the lack of the interconnectivity, they are no longer used. At present, the software patch named $1/n-1$ *Record Splitting Patch* [11] is widely used, which is implemented as Table 3, and Fig. 1. We call the authenticated encryption scheme described in Table 3 as SplTLS1.0. For the decryption, the algorithm outputs the plaintexts using $\mathcal{D}_{\mathtt{WeakTLS1.0}}$ multiple times.

In SplTLS1.0, the encryption algorithm for WeakTLS1.0 is invoked two times to encrypt the message M. For the first time, the first byte of the message $M[0][0]$ is encrypted, and for the second time the remained message $M[0][1..]$ is encrypted. The security proof of SplTLS1.0 is given as follows:

Theorem 1. *If $\mathcal{P}$ is PRP, and $\mathcal{MA}$ is (complete) PRF, then SplTLS1.0 satisfies $(\epsilon_{\mathrm{IND}}, q)$ IND-CPA security, where*

$$\epsilon_{\mathrm{IND}} = 2\epsilon_{\mathrm{PRF}} + 2\epsilon_{\mathrm{PRP}} + \frac{q'(q'-1)}{2^{8\lambda}} + \epsilon_{\mathrm{G4}} + \frac{q'^2}{2^{8\lambda}}.$$

$M[0][0]$, $\mathrm{T}(c \| \mathrm{len}(M[0][0]) \| M[0][0])$ $M[0][1..]$, $\mathrm{T}(c + \mathrm{len}(M[0][1..]) \| \mathrm{len}(M[0][1..]) \| M[0][1..])$

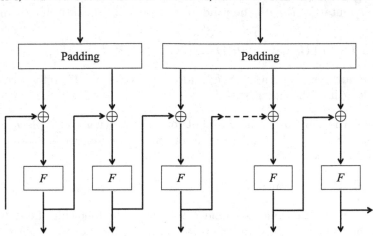

‖ is concatenation, len(x) is length of x

Fig. 1. Patched CBC: $1/n - 1$ Record Splitting Patch Applied WeakTLS1.0 (SplTLS1.0)

and $8\lambda q'$ is the bit-length of all the ciphertexts generated by LR oracle. For ϵ_{G4},

- if $\lambda - 1 \leq \tau$ then, $\epsilon_{\mathrm{G4}} = \frac{q(q-1)}{2^{8\lambda-7}}$
- else $\epsilon_{\mathrm{G4}} = \frac{q(q-1)}{2^{8\tau-1}}$.

Therefore, the indistinguishability of the patched CBC mode depends on the tag length. For example, if AES and HMAC-SHA1 are employed then $\lambda = 16$, $\tau = 20$ and hence $\epsilon_{\mathrm{G4}} = q(q-1)/2^{121}$. However, if the truncated message authenticated code is used instead (as RFC 6066 [15]), then $\tau = 10$ and hence $\epsilon_{\mathrm{G4}} = q(q-1)/2^{79}$.

4   Security Proof of Theorem 1

We define a sequence of games and prove its IND-CPA security. In Game i, the probability of the adversary D outputting 1 is described by

$$\Pr[D = 1 \mid \text{Game } i].$$

<u>Game 0</u>: In this game, we set $b = 0$ in the definition of IND-CPA. Therefore,

$$\Pr[D = 1 \mid \text{Game } 0].$$

<u>Game 1</u>: This is the same as Game 0 except for the following. The modification is to replace the PRP $\mathcal{F}$ with the random permutation. By the definition of PRP,

$$|\Pr[D = 1 \mid \text{Game } 0] - \Pr[D = 1 \mid \text{Game } 1]| \leq \epsilon_{\mathsf{PRP}}.$$

Game 2: This game is the same as Game 1 except for the following. We replace the random permutation $\mathcal{P}$ with the random function. By the switching lemma of [3],

$$|\Pr[D = 1 \mid \text{Game } 1] - \Pr[D = 1 \mid \text{Game } 2]| \leq \frac{q'(q'-1)}{2^{8\lambda+1}},$$

where q' is the number of queries to the random permutation. Therefore, this is a total block length of the ciphertexts.

Game 3: This is the same as Game 2 except for the following. We replace $\mathcal{MA}$ modeled as the PRF with the random function. Since the difference is bounded by the definition of the PRF,

$$|\Pr[D = 1 \mid \text{Game } 2] - \Pr[D = 1 \mid \text{Game } 3]| \leq \epsilon_{\text{PRF}}.$$

Game 4: This game is the same as Game 3 except for the following. Let M_i be the i-th message to be encrypted in LR oracle, and let c_i be its counter. Also we define

$$I_i = \mathsf{Pad}(M_i[0][0] \| \mathcal{T}(c_i \| M_i[0][0] \| M_i[0][0])).$$

In this game, if there exists a pair (i, j) $(i \neq j)$ such that $I_i[0] = I_j[0]$ then LR oracle stops. Let $\mathtt{Coll}_{i,j}$ be the event that there exists a pair (i, j) $(i \neq j)$ such that $I_i[0] = I_j[0]$. Then, if for every i, j $(i \neq j)$, $\mathtt{Coll}_{i,j}$ does not occur then the probability that D outputs 1 in Game 3 and in Game 4 are the same.

Let us estimate the amount of $\Pr[\mathtt{Coll}_{i,j}]$. Depending on the length of the tag τ, we consider two cases $\lambda - 1 \leq \tau$ and $\lambda - 1 > \tau$.

Case $\lambda - 1 \leq \tau$ in Game 4 : Since $M[0][0]$ is 1 byte which can be controlled by the adversary, and $\lambda - 1 \leq \tau$, the input to $\mathcal{F}_K$ is

$$A = \mathbf{IV} \oplus M[0][0] \| t[0][0] \| \cdots \| t[0][\lambda - 2],$$

where $t = \mathcal{T}(c_i \| M_i[0][0] \| M_i[0][0])$.

Further, since c_i is a counter, the input $c_i \| M_i[0][0] \| M_i[0][0]$ to $\mathcal{T}$ is not duplicate. Hence, $A[0][1..]$ is random since $\mathcal{T}$ is a random function. Therefore, for every i, j $(i \neq j)$, $\Pr[\mathtt{Coll}_{i,j}] \leq 1/2^{8\lambda-8}$. Taking the union bound, we have

$$|\Pr[D = 1 \mid \text{Game } 3] - \Pr[D = 1 \mid \text{Game } 4]| \leq \epsilon_{\text{G4}}$$

where $\epsilon_{\text{G4}} = \frac{q(q-1)}{2^{8\lambda-7}}$, and q is the number of queries to LR oracle.

Case $\lambda - 1 > \tau$ in Game 4: By the similar discussion as above, we can estimate the difference as

$$|\Pr[D = 1 \mid \text{Game } 3] - \Pr[D = 1 \mid \text{Game } 4]| \leq \epsilon_{\text{G4}},$$

where $\epsilon_{\text{G4}} = \frac{q(q-1)}{2^{8\tau-1}}$.

Game 5: This game is the same as Game 4 except for $b = 1$. We prove that the difference of probability D outputting 1 in Game 5 and in Game 4 is

$$|\Pr[D = 1 \mid \text{Game 4}] - \Pr[D = 1 \mid \text{Game 5}]| \leq \frac{q'^2}{2^{8\lambda}}. \tag{2}$$

If the input to the random function $\mathcal{F}_K$ is not duplicate, then a bit b is information theoretically hidden. Therefore, we estimate the probability that the input to $\mathcal{F}_K$ duplicates. Let Bad be the event that input to the random function duplicates. Then, the left-hand side of inequality (2) is bounded by $\Pr[\text{Bad}]$.

The oracle LR encrypts M_0 or M_1. From the previous game we know that the first query $I_i[0]$ to $\mathcal{F}_K$ is not duplicated. Hence, we can estimate the probability of Bad happens as

$$\Pr[\text{Bad}] \leq \frac{q+1}{2^{8\lambda}} + \frac{q+2}{2^{8\lambda}} + \cdots + \frac{q'}{2^{8\lambda}} \leq \frac{q'^2}{2^{8\lambda}}$$

Game 6: This game is the same as Game 5 except for the followings. Firstly we replace the random function $\mathcal{T}$ in $\mathcal{MA}$ with the PRF, and then replace the random function $\mathcal{F}_K$ with the PRP. Since this modification implies going the reverse direction in the sequence of games, we have

$$|\Pr[D = 1 \mid \text{Game 5}] - \Pr[D = 1 \mid \text{Game 6}]|$$

$$\leq \epsilon_{\text{PRF}} + \epsilon_{\text{PRP}} + \frac{q'(q'-1)}{2^{8\lambda+1}}.$$

Since Game 0 is $b = 0$ in the game IND-CPA and Game 6 is $b = 1$ in the game IND-CPA, we have

$$|\Pr[K \overset{\$}{\leftarrow} \mathcal{K}_{\text{Spl TLS1.0}}, b \overset{\$}{\leftarrow} \{0, 1\}, b' \overset{\$}{\leftarrow} A^{\text{LR}_{K,b}(\cdot,\cdot)} \mid b = b'] - \frac{1}{2}|$$

$$\leq 2\epsilon_{\text{PRF}} + 2\epsilon_{\text{PRP}} + \frac{q'(q'-1)}{2^{8\lambda}} + \epsilon_{\text{G4}} + \frac{q'^2}{2^{8\lambda}},$$

where if $\lambda - 1 \leq \tau$ then, $\epsilon_{\text{G4}} = \frac{q(q-1)}{2^{8\lambda-7}}$, and else $\epsilon_{\text{G4}} = \frac{q(q-1)}{2^{8\tau-1}}$. This concludes the proof.

5 Conclusion

We have proved that the patched CBC mode which is currently recommended by major browser vendors satisfies indistinguishability. The security is guaranteed if the length of the tag is longer than the block length of the underlying block cipher. However, there are some situations that the tag length τ is shorter than the block length λ. For example, the truncated HMAC defined in RFC 6066 [15] uses the short tag. In this special case, the security bound is not tight enough for the real use.

References

1. AlFardan, N.J., Bernstein, D.J., Paterson, K.G., Poettering, B., Schuldt, J.C.N.: On the security of RC4 in TLS and WPA. In: USENIX Security Symposium (2013)
2. AlFardan, N.J., Paterson, K.G.: Lucky thirteen: breaking the TLS and DTLS record protocols. In: IEEE Symposium on Security and Privacy 2013, pp. 526–540 (2013)
3. Bellare, M., Rogaway, P.: The security of triple encryption and a framework for code-based game-playing proofs. In: Vaudenay, S. (ed.) EUROCRYPT 2006. LNCS, vol. 4004, pp. 409–426. Springer, Heidelberg (2006)
4. Canvel, B., Hiltgen, A.P., Vaudenay, S., Vuagnoux, M.: Password interception in a SSL/TLS channel. In: Boneh, D. (ed.) CRYPTO 2003. LNCS, vol. 2729, pp. 583–599. Springer, Heidelberg (2003)
5. Duong, T., Rizzo, J.: Here Come The ⊕ Ninjas (2011). http://nerdoholic.org/uploads/dergln/beast_part2/ssl_jun21.pdf
6. Isobe, T., Ohigashi, T., Watanabe, Y., Morii, M.: Full plaintext recovery attack on broadcast RC4. In: Moriai, S. (ed.) FSE 2013. LNCS, vol. 8424, pp. 179–202. Springer, Heidelberg (2014)
7. Möller, B., Duong, T., Kotowicz, K.: This POODLE Bites: Exploiting The SSL 3.0 Fallback. https://www.openssl.org/~bodo/ssl-poodle.pdf
8. Rogaway, P.: Problems with Proposed IP Cryptography (1995). http://www.cs.ucdavis.edu/~rogaway/papers/draft-rogaway-ipsec-comments-00.txt
9. Sarkar, P.G., Fitzgerald, S.: Attacks on SSL a Comprehensive Study of BEAST, CRIME, TIME, BREACH, LUCKY 13 & RC4 BIASES (2013). https://www.isecpartners.com/media/106031/ssl_attacks_survey.pdf
10. Vaudenay, S.: Security flaws induced by CBC padding - applications to SSL, IPSEC, WTLS. In: Knudsen, L.R. (ed.) EUROCRYPT 2002. LNCS, vol. 2332, pp. 534–546. Springer, Heidelberg (2002)
11. Bug 665814. https://bugzilla.mozilla.org/show_bug.cgi?id=665814#c59
12. Information Security, Is BEAST really fixed in all modern browsers? http://security.stackexchange.com/questions/18505/is-beast-really-fixed-in-all-modern-browsers
13. Security of CBC Ciphersuites in SSL/TLS: Problems and Countermeasures. http://www.openssl.org/~bodo/tls-cbc.txt
14. SSL Pulse, Survey of the SSL Implementation of the Most Popular Web Sites. https://www.trustworthyinternet.org/ssl-pulse/
15. Transport Layer Security (TLS) Extensions: Extension Definitions. http://tools.ietf.org/html/rfc6066

Key Agreement with Modified Batch Rekeying for Distributed Group in Cognitive Radio Networks

N. Renugadevi$^{(\boxtimes)}$ and C. Mala

Department of Computer Science and Engineering,
National Institute of Technology, Tiruchirappalli, Tamil Nadu, India
nrenu79@gmail.com, mala@nitt.edu

Abstract. Cognitive radio networks have received more research interest in recent years as they can provide a favourable solution to spectrum scarcity problem prevailing in the wireless systems. This paper presents a new key agreement protocol called 'TKTOFT' with modified batch rekeying algorithm for distributed group oriented applications in cognitive radio networks by integrating a ternary key tree and an one way function. It is inferred from the experimental results that TKTOFT outperforms the existing one way function based protocol both in terms of computation and communication overhead. Hence, TKTOFT is suited for establishing secure and quick group communication in dynamic groups in cognitive radio networks.

Keywords: Distributed group · Ternary key tree · One way function · Batch rekeying · Cognitive radio networks

1 Introduction

The group oriented applications are in the rise due to rapid developments in internet technology and mobile computing technology. The distributed collaborative applications such as video conferencing, online games and pay-per-view have received special interest in recent years [1]. The unlicensed frequency spectrums are heavily congested due to rapid proliferation of wireless mobile devices working in these spectrum bands.

Cognitive Radio (CR) [2] can resolve the spectrum scarcity problem present in the existing wireless networks through dynamic operations such as spectrum sensing, spectrum mobility, etc. The concepts such as *Dynamic Spectrum Access* [3] and *Secondary Spectrum Access* [4] used in *CR Networks (CRNs)* allow the unlicensed or *CR Users (CRUs)* to access the free portions of licensed spectrum bands without disturbing the operations of licensed or *Primary Users (PUs)*.

To ensure privacy [5] and data confidentiality in distributed and collaborative groups in CRNs, a secure group communication should be provided by establishing the common group key for all the CRUs or members. *Group Key Management*

© IFIP International Federation for Information Processing 2015
I. Khalil et al. (Eds.): ICT-EurAsia 2015 and CONFENIS 2015, LNCS 9357, pp. 161–172, 2015.
DOI: 10.1007/978-3-319-24315-3_16

(GKM) is a building block for providing security in group oriented applications. The distributed GKM or key agreement protocol is suitable for providing security in group communication of distributed and dynamic networks [6,7] such as CRNs rather than centralized and decentralized GKM techniques [8].

Batch Rekeying (BR) approach reduces the total rekeying cost than Individual Rekeying (IR) as it performs rekeying operations for a batch of join and leave requests at a time to compute the new group key [9]. The tree based GKM protocols also help in minimizing both computation and communication cost during rekeying [10].

An alternative method of developing key agreement protocols is to employ an *One Way Function (OWF)* [11] rather than a standard Diffie-Hellman primitive to get the group key. OWF helps to achieve computational savings by eliminating the expensive modular exponentiations [12] and therefore OWF is a best candidate for smaller and portable mobile devices in CRNs. Hence, this paper proposes a *Ternary Key Tree based OFT (TKTOFT)* protocol which integrates OWF, tree based distributed GKM and BR approach to improve the efficiency of both computation and communication involved in tree based GKM protocols.

The rest of the paper is organized as follows. Section 2 explains briefly about the existing OWF based research work. The proposed TKTOFT protocol is discussed in Sect. 3. The performance of proposed TKTOFT protocol is analysed in Sect. 4. Section 5 concludes this paper.

2   Literature Review

This section discusses about available OWF based research work and GKM protocols which can be adopted for CRNs.

An efficient authentication algorithm [13] based on OWF and symmetric key cryptography was proposed for authenticating local sensing reports in cooperative spectrum sensing in CRNs. In sensing assignment phase, each user generates two one-way chains both for empty decision and occupied decision for each channel.

Sherman and McGrew presented a novel centralized algorithm based on OWF tree namely OFT [14] for dynamic large groups. The bottom-up construction of key tree halves the number of bits to be broadcast during rekeying.

A key distribution protocol which uses parametric OWF and Euler's totient function [15] for achieving high level of security with reduced computation time was developed for secure multicast communication. This paper uses an N-ary tree to minimize the number of multiplications performed during leave operation in the group which in trun reduces the computation complexity.

Zhou et al. proposed a multicast key management technique called Threshold based OFT (TOFT) [16]. In this paper, threshold-key mechanism and quad tree were employed to improve the security of algorithm and to reduce the storage as well as rekeying cost.

An efficient centralized GKM was proposed which integrates key trees with one-way key derivation in order to reduce the communication complexity during rekeying operations [17]. The member itself can derive the key by itself and hence, the total number of keys to be transmitted by the server, i.e., bandwidth of rekeying message was reduced.

A Hash-chain based Authentication Protocol (HAP) [18] was designed for vehicular communication in which vehicle can be verified by combining its public key and its hash code. A new GKM for dynamic access control in a large leaf class hierarchy was proposed [19] which improves previous related research works by using symmetric key cryptography and OWF with less computational and storage overheads.

An image based group key agreement protocol [20] was designed which employs OWF as an image morphing operation to hide the secret information of each member in the morphed image. An Extended Chaotic Map and password based three Party Authenticated Key Exchange (ECM-3PAKE) [21] was developed which provides both implicit and explicit key confirmation.

Li et al. proposed a secure BR scheme which employs two algorithms namely, Distributed BR Marking (DBRM) and Secure Distributed BR (SDBR) [22] for marking the key tree and re-computing the group key respectively.

3   Proposed TKTOFT Protocol

Subsection 3.1 explains briefly about OWF and Subsect. 3.2 discusses about BR scheme used in the existing SDBR algorithm [22]. The proposed protocol which uses an improved BR scheme is described in Subsect. 3.3.

3.1   One Way Function (OWF)

An n-bit hash (h) is a map from a binary string of any arbitrary length to n-bit binary string and the properties of OWF are as follows [23].

1. Preimage resistance: It is easy to compute y for the given x, such that y=h(x). But it is not possible to find x given h(x).

2. Second Preimage resistance: Given an input x, it is not possible to find different y, such that h(y)=h(x).

3. Collision resistance: It is not possible to find any two different x and y, such that h(x)=h(y). The security of proposed TKTOFT protocol is based on one way property of hash function.

3.2   Existing SDBR and DBRM Algorithms

The SDBR algorithm [22] uses a combination of binary key tree and OWF for generating the group key in a distributed dynamic collaborative group. It avoids a renewed node to be rekeyed more than once. In DBRM marking algorithm, four cases of join and leave possibilities are discussed.

The distributed OWF based key tree (OFT) used in SDBR is shown in Fig. 1. The leaf nodes in the key tree store individual members' keys as they represent group members. An unique secret key 'k_i' of the member 'i' is generated using the pseudo random number generator and OWF is used to compute its corresponding Blinded Key, BK_i, such that $BK_i = f(k_i)$, where f is an OWF. The secret key of parent node is computed from the blinded keys of its children, i.e., parent's secret key $= F(BK_{2i+1}, BK_{2i+2})$, where F is a mixing function.

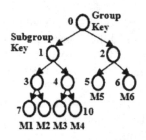

Fig. 1. Distributed OFT

Each member in the key tree maintains the secret keys of nodes in its keypath and also blinded keys of sibling of nodes in its keypath in order to compute the group key. The four cases of DBRM algorithm are discussed as follows.

Case 1. $J = L$: Join members replace all the leave members. The algorithm marks nodes in the path from sibling nodes of all the leave members to root node as UPDATE.

Case 2. $J < L$: The locations of J number of leave members with minimum height are selected to replace them with join members. The nodes associated with the remaining leave members are removed from the key tree. The nodes in the path from sibling nodes of replaced and remaining nodes to the root are marked as UPDATE.

Case 3. $J > L$ & $L = 0$: Create a key tree 'STB' for new joining members and a new root node. Connect the existing key tree 'STA' as left child of newly created root node and STB as its right child. The root of STA and nodes in the path from sponsor of STB to its root are marked as UPDATE.

Case 4. $J > L$ & $L > 0$: All the leave members are replaced by join members. Then, Case 3 is applied for remaining J-L joining members.

The DBRM algorithm has some limitations. In Case 3, insertion of STB as a right child of new root node increases the height of key tree which is shown in Fig. 2. Whenever the system has $J > L$ & $L = 0$, this algorithm repeats the same operation which causes the increase in height of key tree. This step may significantly degrade the performance of BR algorithm when the system has only less number of joining members.

There may be a situation in which the system may have only join members without any leave members. If this happens repeatedly, then after a few rekeying operations, the key tree will become either skewed or unbalanced. The high

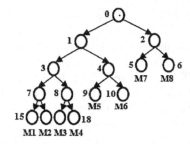

Fig. 2. OFT after inserting joining members

rekeying cost will be the consequence, irrespective of the relationship between join and leave members in future rekey operation.

Though the system may have one or more leave members in Case 4, after replacing the leave memebrs with L join members, again it will have only join members, i.e., $J > L$ & $L = 0$. This will make the system to follow Case 3 which will result in further performance degradation.

An Efficient Distributed Key Agreement Scheme (EDKAS) [24] also uses a binary key tree and SDBR outperforms well than EDKAS by modifying all blinded keys which are known to leaving members. The efficiency of BR algorithm depends on the structure of key tree being used. An unbalanced key tree leads to increased number of operations which in turn increases the total rekeying cost. The limitations of DBRM algorithm explained above are overcome in the proposed algorithm and is explained in the next subsection.

3.3 Proposed TKTOFT Protocol

The efficiency of BR method in this type of tree based GKA depends on the structure of key tree [10]. An efficient BR algorithm should maintain the balanced key tree in order to reduce the rekeying cost. Li et al. proved that the optimal key tree to provide a minimal rekeying cost in the group with unrestricted size during batch update is a *ternary key tree* [25]. Therefore, the proposed TKTOFT uses the ternary key tree to organize the members in the group which is depicted in Fig. 3.

The leaf nodes indicate CRUs in distributed dynamic group in CRNs, i.e., members in the group. As ternary key tree is being used in the proposed protocol, each set of maximum of three CRUs can form a subgroup which corresponds to a subtree in the key tree.

The Subgroup Key (SK) is stored in the intermediate nodes whereas the root node has key for the entire group of CRUs. The rightmost nodes both in subtrees and entire key tree act as sponsors. The subgroup sponsor generates the sub group key and the sponsor of entire group establishes the Group key (G). This paper uses the terms 'members' and 'CRUs' alternatively to mean the group members.

An algorithm for *Batch Process (BP)* operation of the proposed protocol called *TKTOFT_BP* is given in Algorithm 1. It considers each specific case with the appropriate number of join and leave requests. This BP algorithm improves the Cases 3 and 4 and the remaining Cases are same as in DBRM. The abbreviations used in TKTOFT_BP are Key Tree (KT), Sub Key Tree (SKT), Root Node (RN), Link (LK), Internal Node (IN), Closest IN (CIN), Insertion Location (IL), Height (Ht), Minimum Height (MinHt), Node ID (NID), Minimum ID (MinID), New KT (NKT), Leave Members (LMs) and First ID (FID).

SKT is created for new joining members. Case 3 searches for an appropriate IL and inserts SKT, where the height of KT is not increased. First, it checks the links of root node. If the root has null links, then SKT is inserted as a subtree to the root. If the root is full, i.e., if it has three children, then TKTOFT_BP() searches the IN which is closest to root node (CIN).

If CINs in key tree have null links, then CIN with minimum ID is selected as an IL. Else, CIN with minimum height is selected at which SKT can be inserted into KT. After selecting IL, unlike exisiting methods, TKTOFT_BP() checks whether the insertion of SKT into KT at this IL will increase the height of KT

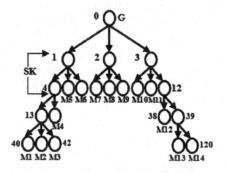

Fig. 3. Ternary OFT

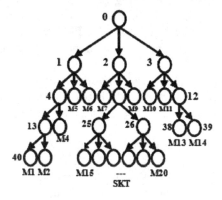

Fig. 4. Merging SKT with KT

Algorithm 1. TKTOFT_BP(KT, J, L)

This algorithm modifies only Cases 3 & 4 discussed in subsection 3.2

Begin
  Step 1 % Modified Case 3
    If $(J > L$ & $L = 0)$ **then**
    Begin Case
        Create a SKT
  5:      **If** $(LK(RN) = \phi)$ then
          IL=LK(RN)
        Else
          If $(LK(CIN) = \phi)$ then
            $IL \leftarrow CIN_{MinID}$
          Else
            $IL \leftarrow CIN_{MinHt}$
          Endif
          If $(Ht(NKT) > Ht(KT))$ **then**
            $IL \leftarrow RN$
          Endif
        Endif
      End Case
    Endif
  Step 2 % Modified Case 4
    If $(J > L$ & $L > 0)$ **then**
    Begin Case
        Create a SKT
        $NID \leftarrow$ Node IDs (LMs)
        $IL \leftarrow$ FID in sorted NID
        If $(Ht(NKT) > Ht(KT))$ **then**
          IL= go to 5
        Endif
      End Case
    Endif
  End

or not. It will be merged with KT only when there is no increase in height. Otherwise, the root node will be selected as IL.

In Case 4, the location of leave member which is closest to root node is selected first as an IL. If the insertion of SKT at this IL increases the height of KT, then an appropriate IL is chosen using Case 3. Else, SKT is inserted at this selected IL. In Fig. 3, when the system has 3 leave members (M3,M8,M12) and 6 join members, it results in a key tree shown in Fig. 4. The location of M8 is selected as an IL, where the SKT created for 6 join members is inserted without increase in height of KT.

Thus, the proposed BR algorithm always chooses the correct IL in order to maintain the balanced key tree. It will select the root of KT as IL only after checking all the possibilities for inserting SKT into KT without increasing the height of KT. Thus, the number of operations to generate the group key tree will be reduced.

If selected IL has null link, then SKT is inserted as its child node. Else, a new IN is generated. The member stored at IL is connected as a left child and root of SKT is connected as a middle child of newly created IN. In all the cases of algorithm, the sponsor nodes are selected based on the group operations (i.e., join and leave) and positions of both join and leave members in the key tree. All the sponsors in the key tree recompute the group key by updating their secret key. The remaining members will compute the new group key after receiving the broadcast message from the sponsor.

4   Results and Discussion

The performance of proposed TKTOFT protocol is analysed and compared with the existing SDBR protocol. The computation complexity is decided based on (a) time to generate initial group key and (b) number of secret key computation of parent node. The communication complexity is determined based on the number of renewed nodes generated in the key tree [6,22] which are non-leaf nodes whose keys are modified during BR operation.

A group with size 3^5 (243 members) was considered for generating the initial group key. In Figs. 5 and 6, x-axis represents the group size. Figure 5 compares the time to compute the initial group key which is represented in y-axis between SDBR and TKTOFT. From the figure it is inferred that TKTOFT takes less time to generate the group key than SDBR for the same group size.

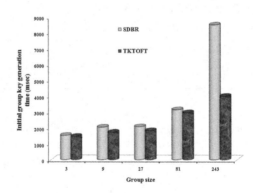

Fig. 5. Group size Vs Initial group key generation time

Figure 6 depicts the performance analysis between the existing and proposed protocols based on the number of secret key computation of parent node in the key tree. As the number of internal nodes in the ternary key tree is less than binary key tree for the same group size, TKTOFT performs less number of key computations when compared to SDBR protocol.

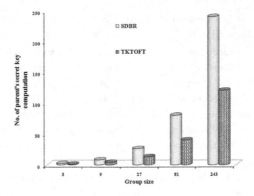

Fig. 6. Group size Vs Number of parent's secret key computation

It is clearly seen from Figs. 5 and 6 that, initially there is no big difference between SDBR and proposed TKTOFT. But, when the group is increased, both key generation time and the number of secret key computation in SDBR are also increased. As SDBR uses a binary key tree, the height of key tree is increased even for a small change in group size. The increase in height leads to performance degradation in SDBR.

As proposed TKTOFT uses ternary key tree, its key tree height is minimum when compared to SDBR for the same group size. This reduced height of the key tree helps in minimizing the group key generation time and number of key computation of parent nodes in the key tree. The difference in values of y axis both in SDBR and TKTOFT is more prominent when the group has more number of members. From Figs. 5 and 6, it is concluded that the proposed TKTOFT protocol has reduced computation complexity than SDBR protocol.

As ternary key tree is being used in this paper, a group with 243 (3^5) members was considered during each iteration of batch rekeying. The values for number of join and leave members in the group were varied between 0 and 81 for measuring the total number of renewed nodes which indicates the communication complexity. In Fig. 7, the total number of join members (J) and total number of leave members (L) are represented in x and y-axis respectively. The total number of renewed nodes created in the key tree are mentioned in z-axis of Fig. 7.

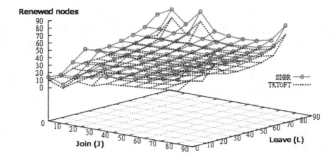

Fig. 7. No. of Join and Leave operations vs Renewed nodes

From the graph, it is understood that TKTOFT has generated less number of renewed nodes than SDBR. The reasons are, (a) the height of key tree is minimum, (b) maintaining the same key tree height even when J is large with no leave members by choosing the correct insertion location for the sub key tree and (c) pruning the leave members and choosing the appropriate location for merging. These prevent increase in key tree height which in turn minimizes the number of nodes to be renewed in the key tree. In this figure also, the significant difference in total renewed nodes can be clearly seen when J and L are large. Because, SDBR replaces the leave members with join members which result in the same key tree height instead of pruning them.

In Case 3 of SDBR, SKT is inserted at the root node without checking the status of KT. This leads to an unbalanced key tree with increased height. These limitations have been overcome in the proposed TKTOFT BP algorithm which gives an improved performance. TKTOFT protocol reduces the number of renewed nodes by choosing the appropriate insertion location to merge the key tree created for joining members and by pruning the leave members when $J > L$ & $L > 0$.

From the experimental analysis, it is concluded that the modified Cases 3 and 4 of the proposed protocol improves the performance in terms of both computation and communication complexities. Hence, this proposed TKTOFT can be adopted for a distributed group with highly dynamic scenarios in CRNs.

5   Conclusion

Cognitive radio network can help in providing a quick communication as its nodes solve spectrum scarcity problem prevalent in the present wireless systems. An improved distributed group key agreement called TKTOFT has been proposed in this paper which integrates ternary key tree, one way function and modified batch rekeying algorithm. The experimental results show that TKTOFT improves the efficiency of both computation and communication. Hence, this proposed protcol is suited for providing quick and secure group communication among cognitive radio devices in distributed collaborative applications in cognitive radio networks.

References

1. Daghighi, B., Kiah, M.L.M., Shamshirband, S., Rehman, M.H.U.: Toward secure group communication in wireless mobile environments: issues, solutions, and challenges. J. Netw. Comput. Appl. **50**, 1–14 (2015)
2. Mitola, J., Maguire Jr, G.Q.: Cognitive radio: making software radios more personal. IEEE Pers. Commun. **6**(4), 13–18 (1999)
3. Grandblaise, D., Bourse, D., Moessner, K., Leaves, P.: Dynamic spectrum allocation (DSA) and reconfigurability. IEEE Commun. Mag. **42**, 72–81 (2004)
4. Wyglinski, A.M., Nekovee, M., Hou, T.: Cognitive Radio Communications and Networks: Principles and Practice. Academic Press, New York (2009)

5. Armando, A., Bocci, G., Chiarelli, G., Costa, G., De Maglie, G., Mammoliti, R., Merlo, A.: Mobile App security analysis with the MAVeriC static analysis module. J. Wirel. Mob. Netw., Ubiquitous Comput., Dependable Appl. (JoWUA) **5**(4), 103–119 (2014)
6. Kiyomoto, S., Fukushima, K., Miyake, Y.: Design of categorization mechanism for disaster-information-gathering system. J. Wirel. Mob. Netw. Ubiquitous Comput. Dependable Appl. **3**(4), 21–34 (2012)
7. Pokrić, B., Krčo, S., Drajić, D., Pokrić, M., Rajs, V., Mihajlović, Ž., Knežević, P., Jovanović, D.: Augmented reality enabled IoT services for environmental monitoring utilising serious gaming concept. J. Wirel. Mob. Netw., Ubiquitous Comput., Dependable Appl. (JoWUA) **6**(1), 37–55 (2015)
8. Zou, X., Ramamurthy, B., Magliveras, S.S.: Secure group communications over data networks. Springer Science & Business Media, Newyork (2007)
9. Lee, P.C., Lui, C.S., Yau, K.Y.: Distributed collaborative key agreement and authentication protocols for dynamic peer groups. IEEE/ACM Trans. Networking **14**(2), 263–276 (2006)
10. Kim, Y., Perrig, A., Tsudik, G.: Simple and fault-tolerance key agreement for dynamic collaborative groups. In: 7th ACM Conference on Computer and Communications Security, pp. 235–244 (2000)
11. Diffie, W., Hellman, M.E.: New directions in cryptography. IEEE Trans. Inf. Theory **22**(6), 644–654 (1976)
12. Boyd, C., Mathuria, A.: Protocols for Authentication and Key Establishment. Springer, Heidelberg (2003)
13. Rifá-Pous, H., Garrigues, C.: Authenticating hard decision sensing reports in cognitive radio networks. Comput. Netw. **56**(2), 566–576 (2012)
14. Sherman, A.T., McGrew, D.A.: Key establishment in large dynamic groups using one-way function trees. IEEE Trans. Software Eng. **29**(5), 444–458 (2003)
15. Vijayakumar, P., Bose, S., Kannan, A., Subramanian, S.S.: An effective key distribution protocol for secure multicast communication. In: IEEE 2010 Second International Conference on Advanced Computing (ICoAC), pp. 102–107 (2010)
16. Zhou, F., Xu, J., Lin, L., Xu, H.: Multicast key management scheme based on TOFT. In: 10th IEEE International Conference on HPCC 2008, pp. 1030–1035 (2008)
17. Lin, J.C., Lai, F., Lee, H.C.: Efficient group key management protocol with one-way key derivation. In: IEEE Conference on Local Computer Networks, pp. 336–343 (2005)
18. Sulaiman, A., Raja, S.K., Park, S.H.: Improving scalability in vehicular communication using one-way hash chain method. Ad Hoc Netw. **11**(8), 2526–2540 (2013)
19. Odelu, V., Das, A.K., Goswami, A.: A secure effective key management scheme for dynamic access control in a large leaf class hierarchy. Inf. Sci. **269**, 270–285 (2014)
20. Mao, Q., Chang, C.C., Harn, L., Chang, S.C.: An image-based key agreement protocol using the morphing technique. Multimedia Tools Appl. **74**, 3207–3229 (2013)
21. Islam, S.H.: Design and analysis of a three party password-based authenticated key exchange protocol using extended chaotic maps. Inf. Sci. **312**, 104–130 (2015)
22. Li, B., Yang, Y., Lu, Z., Yuan, B., Long, T.: Secure distributed batch rekeying algorithm for dynamic group. In: 2012 IEEE 14th International Conference on Communication Technology (ICCT), pp. 664–667 (2012)
23. Rogaway, P., Shrimpton, T.: Cryptographic hash-function basics: definitions, implications, and separations for preimage resistance, second-preimage resistance, and

collision resistance. In: Roy, B., Meier, W. (eds.) FSE 2004. LNCS, vol. 3017, pp. 371–388. Springer, Heidelberg (2004)

24. Zhang, J., Li, B., Chen, C.X., Tao, P., Yang, S.Q.: EDKAS: a efficient distributed key agreement scheme using one way function trees for dynamic collaborative groups. IEEE IMACS Multiconference Comput. Eng. Syst. Appl. **2**, 1215–1222 (2006)

25. Li, M., Feng, Z., Zang, N., Graham, R.L., Yao, F.F.: Approximately optimal trees for group key management with batch updates. Theoret. Comput. Sci. **410**(11), 1013–1021 (2009)

Secure Mobility Management for MIPv6 with Identity-Based Cryptography

Nan Guo$^{(\boxtimes)}$, Fangting Peng, and Tianhan Gao

Northeastern University, No. 3-11, Wenhua Road, Heping District,
Shenyang, People's Republic of China
{guonan,pengft,gaoth}@mail.neu.edu.cn

Abstract. Mobile IPv6 is an improvement of the original IPv6 protocol, and provides mobility support for IPv6 nodes. However, the security of mobility management is one of the most important issues for MIPv6. Traditional MIPv6 uses IPSec to protect the mobility management, while the dependence on the mechanism of the pre-shared key or certificate limits its applicability. This paper proposes an improved scheme for the original method based on IBC, to protect the mobility management signaling for MIPv6.

Keywords: Mobile IPv6 · IPSec · IBC · Mobility management

1 Introduction

The development of IPv6 [11] has leaded to the rapid popularization of Mobile IPv6 (MIPv6). MIPv6 is a protocol to provide mobile support for IPv6, and it was standardized by IETF in 2004. The security problem has been exposed at the devising of MIPv6. The primary threat comes from fake binding update messages, replay attack and route attack which mainly manifest in the mobility management procedure [1,10]. The main reason derives from no efficient authentication approach between the communication entities. In this paper, we propose a novel encryption and authentication scheme to guarantee the security of MIPv6 mobility management.

In the literatures, [2] shows that MIPv6 adopts IPSecurity(IPSec) protocol and Internet Key Exchange(IKE) protocol to protect mobile management signaling between mobile node and home agent. However, the method is not efficient as required. [3] shows that pre-shared key or certificate adopted by the first stage of IKE is not suitable under the mobile environment. It is not realistic to build the infrastructure to satisfy IKE. Besides, using IPSec with IKE would add extra burden for mobile nodes. To solve the problem, [4] utilizes multilevel IPSec in MIPv6 to protect mobility management procedure; [5] suggests that a secure association between mobile node and home agent should be built in advance. However, this will bring more cost of security management. Thus, the efficiency of the above schemes still need to be improved.

© IFIP International Federation for Information Processing 2015
I. Khalil et al. (Eds.): ICT-EurAsia 2015 and CONFENIS 2015, LNCS 9357, pp. 173–178, 2015.
DOI: 10.1007/978-3-319-24315-3_17

In traditional public key cryptography, the public key is a string of random characters without any practical information. The Certificate Authority(CA) in PKI infrastructure takes the responsibility of publishing certificates. As a result, the expense of release, storage, verification and revocation is enormous. To solve the problem, the Identity-Based Cryptography(IBC) uses IP address, Email address or any other string that represents the users identity as public keys. Shamir first proposed Identity-Based Encryption(IBE) in 1984. Then in 2001, Boneh and Franklin proposed BF-IBE scheme [7]. Later, Identity-Based Signature(IBS) was proposed. In IBS, every communication entity owns a pair of public key and private key. Public key is the identity of the entity and private key is generated and allocated by the trusted third party, Private Key Generator(PKG). Certificate is not necessary during communication, which relieves the computation and storage cost in encryption and authentication. IBC is thus suitable for the security of mobile network [9].

In this paper, we discuss the typical security protocols in MIPv6 and propose a novel identity-based security scheme for MIPv6 mobility management. The scheme can protect the mobility management signaling among mobile node, home agent and correspondent node in an efficient way.

2   Preliminaries

2.1   MIPv6 Protocol

According to the standardization document RFC3775, MIPv6 protocol is the mobility extension solution for IPv6. It is composed of four entities, Mobile Node(MN), Home Agent(HA), Correspondent Node(CN) and Access Router (AR). MN is allocated a permanent address, i.e. Home of Address(HoA) at the home network, and will get a temporary address, i.e. Care-of Address(CoA), from AR and register it to HA when moving to a foreign network [6].

2.2   IPSec Protocol

IPSec protocol provides confidentiality, data integrity, data authentication and anti-replay services at IP layer. It is an open framework applied widely in a variety of operating environments including mobile network. IPSec supports IKE protocol, which means that key negotiation can be implemented. Besides, encryption and authentication in IPSec guarantee the security of IP data packet. As shown in Fig. 1, IPSec owns a set of approaches for data security such as Authentication Header(AH), Encapsulating Security Payload(ESP), as well as the related cryptography algorithms.

2.3   Identity-Based Cryptography

An IBE scheme is generally defined as follows.

IBE.Setup: given a security parameter k as input, output PKG's public key mpk and private key msk.

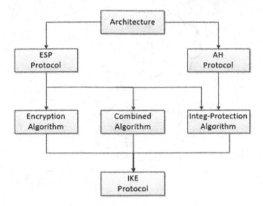

Fig. 1. The architecture of IPSec

IBE.Extract: given msk and user's id as input, output user's private key usk.

IBE.Encrypt: given msk, id, and message m as input, output the encryption δ on m.

IBE.Decrypt: given usk and δ as input, output 1 if δ is valid or 0 otherwise.

In an IBS scheme, IBS.Setup and IBS.Extract are identical to IBE.Setup and IBE.Extract respectively. The other algorithms are defined as follows.

IBS.Sign: given usk and message m as input, output the signature σ on m.

IBS.Verify: given mpk, id, m and σ as input, output 1 if σ is valid or 0 otherwise.

3 Our Solution

In this chapter, we propose a secure mobility MIPv6 management scheme based on BF-IBE scheme [7] and BF-IBS Scheme [8]. The network architecture and intra-domain security management solution are given in detail.

3.1 Network Architecture

In our scheme, the security of the mobility management signaling among MN, CN and HA is guaranteed by IBC. NAI acts as the identifier for every entity. The format of NAI is as user@domain, which would be kept fixed even when the location of MN has changed.

As shown in Fig. 2, the proposed network architecture can be divided into several domains according to the trajectories of MN's roaming. The architecture is composed of CA, PKG, MN, HA and CN. CA is in charge of issuing certificates for PKGs and providing identity authentication service for the communication among them. PKG takes the responsibility of security management in each domain. It maintains public parameters and generates private keys for entities in its domain.

In order to simplify the descriptions of the relevant protocol, Table 1 shows the notations and explanations used in our scheme.

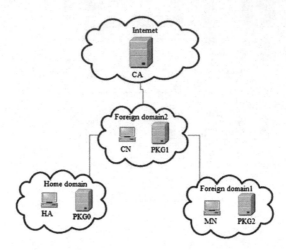

Fig. 2. Network Architecture

Table 1. Notations and Explanations

Notations	Explanations
$Msg_1 \| Msg_2$	Msg_1 connects to Msg_2
$S_{x,y}$	Entity X's private key generated by PKG_Y
$SK_{x,y}$	Symmetric key between entity X and entity Y
ID_x	Entity X's ID
$Enc(Msg, ID_x)$	Msg is encrypted by Entity X's public key ID_x by BF-IBE
$Sig(Msg, S_{x,y})$	Msg is signed by Entity X's private key $S_{x,y}$ by BF-IBS
$Code$	Global unique message type for message handling
$Source$	The source of message
$Destination$	The final destination of message
$Payload$	The load of message
$Time$	The message's generation time and allowable maximum delay

3.2 Secure Mobility Management Scheme

There are two states in our scheme in terms of MN's location: When MN is at home domain, the scheme is on the initial state, and when MN moves to foreign domain, the scheme is on the mobile state.

As shown in Fig. 3 MN and HA execute Diffie-Hellman key exchange to negotiate the shared symmetric key, which is the same as IKE key agreement that can provide encryption key for IPSec.

At the initial state, key negotiation is relatively simple and there are only two messages because MN and HA are both at the home domain.

(1) MN → HA: Key Exchange Request

Message format in detail:

$Code||MN||HA||Enc(Sig(g^m, S_{MN,0}), ID_{HA})||Time$

Key Exchange Request is generated by MN and sent to HA. *Code* is the message type. MN is *Source* and HA is *Destination*. g^m is the parameter of Diffie-Hellman key exchange in the *Payload*, where g is public parameter in the home domain and m is the secret value chosen by MN. After sending the message, MN expects to get reply within *Time*.

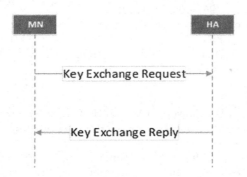

Fig. 3. Intra-domain Secure Mobile Management Scheme

(2) HA → MN: Key Exchange Reply

Message format in detail:

$Code||MN||HA||Enc(Sig(g^h, S_{HA,0}), ID_{MN})||Time$

Key Exchange Reply is generated by HA and acts as the reply for MN's Request. *Code* is the message type. HA is *Source* and MN is *Destination*. g^h is the parameter of Diffie-Hellman key exchange in the *Payload*, where h is the secret value chosen by HA.

After the exchange of the above two messages, MN and HA have achieved Diffie-Hellman key exchange through IBC. They compute the same symmetric key respectively, $SK_{MN,HA} = SK_{HA,MN} = (g^m)^h = (g^h)^m$. The symmetric key can work for the following IPSec stage.

4   Conclusion and Future Work

In this paper, we first analyze a series of threats on MIPv6, then propose a secure mobility management scheme based on IBC to protect the signaling among MN, HA and CN. The details of the scheme are explained.

For the next step, we plan to discuss inter-domain secure mobile management scheme and add a new method Return Routability to guarantee the security of MIPv6. Further security analysis is also required to demonstrate the robustness of our scheme.

Acknowledgments. This work was supported by National Natural Science Foundation of China under [Grant Number 61402095] and [Grant Number 61300196], China Fundamental Research Funds for the Central Universities under [Grant Number N120404010] and [Grant Number N130817002].

References

1. Tian, Y., Zhang, Y., Zhang, H.: Identity-based hierarchical access authentication in mobile IPv6 networks. In: IEEE International Conference on Communications, ICC 2006, vol. 5, pp. 1953–1958. IEEE (2006)
2. Elgoarany, K., Eltoweissy, M.: Security in mobile IPv6: a survey. Inf. Secur. Tech. Rep. **12**(1), 32–43 (2007)
3. Aura, T., Roe, M.: Designing the mobile IPv6 security protocol. Annales Des Télécommunications **61**(3–4), 332–356 (2006)
4. Choi, H., Song, H., Cao, G., et al.: Mobile multi-layered IPsec. Wirel. Netw. **3**(6), 1929–1939 (2005)
5. Yebin, Y., Qingxian, W., Junyong, L., Luzi, H.: Optimized method of constructing IPSec SA between MN and HA in MobileIPv6. J. Inf. Eng. Univ. (2), 222–224 (2008)
6. Conta, A., Deering, S.: Generic Packet Tunneling in IPv6 Specification, RFC 2473. OverDRiVE 102 Description and Validation of Mobile Router and Dynamic IVAN Management, 3/31/04 OverDRiVE WP3 D17 (1998)
7. Boneh, D., Franklin, M.: Identity-based encryption from the weil pairing. SIAM J. Comput. **32**(3), 213–229 (2001)
8. Barreto, P.S.L.M., Kim, H.Y., Lynn, B., Scott, M.: Efficient algorithms for pairing-based cryptosystems. In: Yung, M. (ed.) CRYPTO 2002. LNCS, vol. 2442, pp. 354–369. Springer, Heidelberg (2002)
9. Sun, K., Kim, Y.: Flow mobility management in PMIPv6-based DMM (Distributed Mobility Management) networks. J. Wirel. Mob. Net., Ubiquit. Comput., Dependable Appl. (JoWUA) **5**(4), 120–127 (2014)
10. Andersson, K., Elkotob, M.: Rethinking IP mobility management. J. Wirel. Mob. Net., Ubiquit. Comput., Dependable Appl. (JoWUA) **3**(3), 41–49 (2012)
11. Jara, A.J., Ladid, L., Skarmeta, A.: The internet of everything through IPv6: an analysis of challenges, solutions and opportunities. J. Wirel. Mob. Net., Ubiquit. Comput., Dependable Appl. (JoWUA) **4**(3), 97–118 (2013)

Investigation of DDoS Attacks by Hybrid Simulation

Yana Bekeneva[1], Konstantin Borisenko[1], Andrey Shorov[1],
and Igor Kotenko[2,3(✉)]

[1] Department of Computer Science and Engineering,
Saint Petersburg Electrotechnical University "LETI", Professora Popova Str. 5,
Saint Petersburg, Russia
{yana.barc,borisenkoforleti,ashxz}@mail.ru
[2] St. Petersburg Institute for Informatics and Automation, 14th Liniya, 39,
Saint Petersburg, Russia
ivkote@comsec.spb.ru
[3] St. Petersburg National Research University of Information Technologies,
Mechanics and Optics, 49, Kronverkskiy Prospekt, Saint Petersburg, Russia

Abstract. At present protection against distributed attacks of the type "denial of service" (DDoS) is one of the important tasks. The paper considers a simulation environment for DDoS attacks of different types using the combination of a simulation approach and real software-hardware testbeds. In the paper we briefly describe the system architecture and a series of experiments for DDoS attack simulation on transport and application levels. The experimental results are provided, and the analysis of these results is performed.

Keywords: Network security · DDoS attacks · Simulation · Flooding

1 Introduction

The main goal of DDoS attacks is to make a network resource unavailable to its users. Every year there is an increase in the number DDoS attacks, their power and complexity and hence the harm they can do. According to the report of the Arbor Network [1], more than 60 % of companies that have been questioned detected more than 10 DDoS attacks per month in 2014. By the year 2015 the main victims of such attacks are not only servers of different companies and Internet providers, but also their clients. New types of DDoS attacks appear and one of destroyable type of attacks is so called Reflection attacks. These attacks use servers to reflect and amplify the malicious traffic. Nowadays Network Time Protocol (NTP) Reflection attacks using NTP servers became very popular. This means that it is necessary to develop new efficient protection mechanisms against DDoS attacks. Development of new protection systems and testing of real networks for stability to DDoS attacks requires significant hardware, temporal, and financial costs. For this reason in order to perform such experiments we suggest using computer simulation techniques.

As against of our previous papers [2, 3] we would like to present the system, having included the possibility of using real nodes connected to a virtual network. Such an

© IFIP International Federation for Information Processing 2015
I. Khalil et al. (Eds.): ICT-EurAsia 2015 and CONFENIS 2015, LNCS 9357, pp. 179–189, 2015.
DOI: 10.1007/978-3-319-24315-3_18

approach has made it possible to significantly increase the adequacy of DDoS attack simulation on transport and application levels. The system has been verified for a real network. The paper is devoted to the experiments for simulating different types of DDoS attacks in the developed environment. The authors have conducted the experiments of simulating DDoS attacks on transport and application levels. We have simulated the attacks using the protocols of TCP (for SYN-flooding) and UDP (for Chargen and Echo attacks). Attack simulation on an application level has been performed. Section 2 discusses related work. Section 3 specifies formal models of main components. In Sect. 4 we briefly represent the architecture and implementation. Sections 5 and 6 consider examples of experiments. Section 7 and Conclusion outline application of the developed system, main results and further research.

2 Relevant Works

Nowadays a large number of researches and companies are looking for the most efficient ways of service protection against DDoS attacks [3]. In [4] one can get acquainted with a system that uses Spirent Test Center [5] as a device generating traffic. This work contains templates for setting IP-address configurations and attack scenarios. In order to deal with similar tasks it is also possible to use the environment produced in 2014 by the company MazeBolt's Team [6]. Using this environment we can generate different types of DDoS attacks of the power up to 20 000 Mbit/sec. [7] considers a system developed by Ixia [8]. The authors point out that the system makes it possible to provide protection against DDoS attacks of the power of 70 Gbits/sec. In real time. ViSe [9] is a system for simulating the main most widespread attacks (40 different scenarios). In [2] we can read about a DDoS attack simulation system, which allows us to simulate a network with different behavior of clients inside it.

The system introduced in our paper allows us to construct virtual networks with a high degree of adequacy. Furthermore, the system makes it possible to introduce any known protection mechanism or the one created by the user. Protection mechanisms can be architecture-dependent, which also allows us to conduct experiments in the way most close to a real network. An important advantage is the possibility of connecting real nodes to a virtual network, which will make it possible to improve the accuracy of the experiments and also to test various settings and types of servers.

3 Specification of Simulation Components

In order to understand the structure of the developed simulation components, it is necessary to specify the parameters of their models. The formal model of the network is defined as follows: $Network = \langle NetConf, Router_{1..q}, Host_{1..n}, Server_{1..m} \rangle$, where $NetConf$ — network configuration, $Router$ — routers, $Host$ — hosts, $Server$ — servers.

Network configuration $NetConf = \langle IPStart, ExtIP, ServPath, NetPar \rangle$, where $IPStart$ — initial IP-address for assignment to hosts, for example, if $IPStart$ = "1.0.0.1", and a network consists of 20 hosts (personal computers (PCs), routers, servers), then the IP address of the last host is 1.0.0.20; $ExtIP$ — IP address of the external server;

ServPath — the path to the virtual server, which will be a plug (it reflects the position of the real server) for the virtual network; *NetPar* — on the basis of the above components each network host will receive its interface settings and routing tables.

Model of the router $Router_k = \langle NetPar, NPcap, Def_{0..n}, ExtDevN_{0..q}, DelConf \rangle$, where *NetPar* — router's parameters obtained during initialization of Netconf; *NPcap* — the number of modules to account the traffic flow; *Def* — a protection algorithm running on the router, this algorithm is implemented in software, the router may use any number of algorithms; *ExtDevN* — the number of interfaces connected to the external network, required for routers which contain an external host in their local network; *DelConf* — configuration of packets delay, it is used that the virtual network would have the characteristics of the real network. Model of virtual clients $Host_k = \langle NetPar, DDoSApp_{0..1} \rangle$, where *NetPar* — client's settings received under initialization of *Netconf*; *DDoSApp* — an application that will perform the attack for a given scenario. Model of attacks against the server includes the following options: $DDoSApp = \langle VictimPath, AType, Lvl, Dport, DeltaT, AStart, AEnd, MaxP, SpecialP \rangle$, where *VictimPath* — a path to the victim server (to empower attacks against several servers); *Atype* — type of the attack against the server: 1 — HTTP Flooding, 2–7 — different variants of TCP Flooding (SYN, SYN-ACK, RST, UDP, etc.); *Lvl* — the percent of clients involved in the attack;; *Dport* — destination port, it is defined in a random manner; *DeltaT* — the time between packets (in the case of HTTP Flooding it is the time between sessions); *AStart, AEnd* — start and end time of the attack; various conditions for this interval can be set; *MaxP* — the maximum number of packet sendings (in the case of HTTP attacks — sessions); *SpecialP* — specific attack parameters, i.e. for HTTP it is a string of the HTTP query, for TCP — the type of the sender's IP address spoofing. The developed models allow connecting any number of external servers to the virtual network. In the router it is also possible to configure the attack scenarios and the DDoS protection methods.

4 Architecture and Implementation of a Simulation System

The architecture of the developed system can be represented as a set of several components (Fig. 1). On the first level of the component hierarchy we can find a discrete-event simulation system OMNeT++ [10]. The second level of hierarchy is represented by a model of a computer network. In order to adjust the network and set package switching the INET library is used [11]. The library ReaSE [12] has been completed for topology settings. The authors ceased to support it in 2011 and therefore it was renewed for working with the version OMNeT++4.5. The third level contains the models of hosts and routers that are included in the network. The server model is related to both this level and the next one. The fourth level contains the following models developed: an application for performing attacks according to the given scenario; traffic accounting modules; a container for protection algorithms, which can be installed at different network nodes. The models and architecture that have been created were used for developing a hybrid simulation system. In order to provide virtualization of operating systems and computational resources, VirtualBox и Vmware [13, 14] have been applied. The possibilities for risk analysis [15, 16] can be added.

Examples of settings for created components are shown below. Figure 2 depicts an example of the topology which includes models *Network, NetConf, NetPar*. This topology contains a Web-server, routers, gateways and hosts. Every node can be configured by user any time. Example of settings for NetConf is shown in Fig. 3.

				Real server	IV
DDoSapp	Pcap	Def	ExtDev	Server	III
Host	Router				
Network settings			Topology settings		II
OMNeT++					I

Fig. 1. Common architecture of modeling system

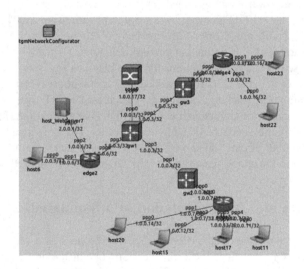

Fig. 2. Example of the created topology

```
#interface and route settings
**.ExtServerIP = "2.0.0.1"        #ip of real server
**.ExtServerNedPath = "InetVerific.host_WebServer7.ppp0"
**.IniIp = "1.0.0.2"
```

Fig. 3. An example of settings for the network configuration model

It should be noted that the range of addresses, the real IP address of the server belongs to, must not overlap with IP addresses of virtual PC. This is to ensure that the server's responses are forwarded to computer of the virtual network. For the experiments we used a computer with the following characteristics: processor is Intel Core i7-3770, 3,4 Ghz, 8 cores; RAM is 15, 6 GB DDR3 1600 MHz; Operating system is Ubuntu 14.04 64-bit. The developed system can also be deployed on the Windows computers. The system currently operates in a single-threaded simulation mode. More than 200 virtual desktops are used, they can attack with the delay of 10 ms. During attack simulations the capacity of the core is 50 %.

5   Experiments with Attacks on Transport Level

The authors have conducted a series of 10 experiments devoted to simulating an attack of the type SYN-Flooding In order to successfully perform a SYN-flooding attack, SYN cookies were switched off on a server. The attack involves 200 hosts generating packages with a frequency of 2 packages per second. 3 hosts are attacking throughout the whole experimental time; the rest are included in an attack in a distributed way from the 10th to the 35th second of the experiment and stop package generation in the interval from the 50th to the 70th seconds. Figure 4 shows SYN packages sent to a server from a virtual network; the line shows the mean value for 10 experiments and errors are also demonstrated. Server responses are represented in a similar way without repeated sending of SYN-ACK for semiopen connections that have already been established.

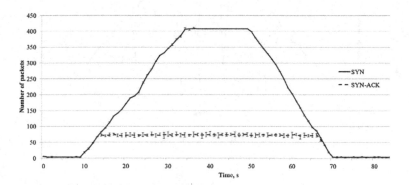

Fig. 4. Plot of the traffic log for SYN flooding against the server

Only 3 clients applied to the server prior to the 10th second. At the beginning of an attack, on the 10th second, the number of server applications increases because more and more virtual clients are beginning to take part in the attack. Till the 14th second the server manages to process all messages and after that the TCP-stack is overfilled and the server is unable to deal with an increasing flow of applications. Then, beginning from the 50th second and ending with the 70th second virtual clients are leaving the attack. 3 clients are applying to the server again from the 70th on the 88th second. Simulation was stopped at the 88th second. In the period from the 14th second till the 68th second the server did not respond to SYN-packages.

The experiments devoted to attack simulation and based on the UDP-protocol used the network consisting of 100 computers. The attacking packages were sent at a rate of 2 packages per second. The nodes started generation of malicious packages from the 1st to the 20th seconds and terminated the attack from the 40th to the 60th seconds. The Chargen attack is performed by sending a large number of packages to the UDP-port of the 19th victim computer. This causes the server to generate responses consisting of a random set of symbols. Thus, it is possible to reboot the server and reduce its efficiency. The solid line in Fig. 5 shows malicious traffic arriving at an attacking server. Prior to the 20th second we can notice traffic rise, which remains invariable till the 40th second. Then, the number of malicious packages starts to decrease. The dashed line shows server responses (chargen). After sending some number of responses the server becomes inactive and instead of UDP-packages generates ICMP-messages about the server unavailability. ICMP-messages are shown in the plot by the dot-and-dash line. Traffic resending is reached when a server being attacked has to send return packages to the UDP-port of the 19th sender, which generates return chargen packages to the server.

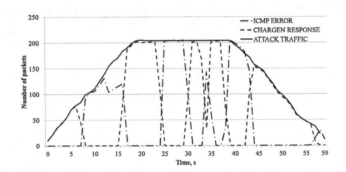

Fig. 5. Server traffic for a chargen attack

Figure 6 shows server traffic during an attack with resending. The solid line indicates incoming malicious packages coming from different UDP-ports except the 19th one. The dot line shows incoming UDP-packages sent from the 19th port of attacking nodes, i.e. obtained during resending. The dashed line (short dashes) shows chargen server responses. The curve of chargen responses almost completely coincides with the curve of resent packages. The line with long dashes shows ICMP-messages of the server telling us that the server is currently unavailable.

Attack Echo is carried out by sending a large number of packets on the UDP port 7 of a victim computer. This causes the server to generate responses that mimic the incoming packet. As Chargen, this attack leads to overload of the server, and reduces its productivity.

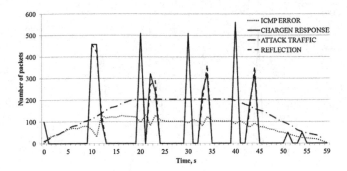

Fig. 6. Server traffic for a chargen attack with resending

Figure 7 outlines by the solid line the malicious traffic directed to the target server. The traffic increases up to 20 s, then it remains unchanged up to 40 s, and further the number of malicious packets is reduced. The dashed line shows the server's response (echo). After sending a certain number of responses the server becomes inactive and generates ICMP packets (instead of UDP ones) that the service is not available. The graph demonstrates the ICMP packets by the dotted line. Bounced traffic is generated when the attacked server needs to send response packets to the UDP port 7 of the sender, which in turn generates echo response packets to the server. However, the implementation of such an attack cannot achieve infinite loop, as the server, as in the previous case, at some time becomes inactive and does not respond to incoming traffic.

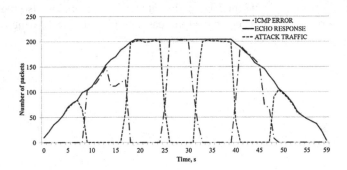

Fig. 7. Server traffic under an echo attack

Figure 8 depicts by solid line the incoming UDP packets to the server, including bounced traffic. The dotted line shows Echo responses of the server. It can be seen that when the server responds to Echo requests the incoming traffic includes balanced Echo messages from attacking hosts. Dotted line represents the ICMP packets, indicating that the server is currently inactive.

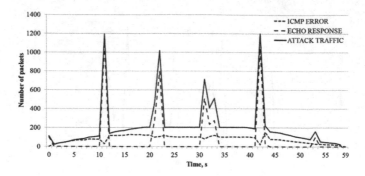

Fig. 8. Server traffic under an echo attack with bounced traffic

6 Experiments with Attacks on Application Level

An HTTP-Flooding attack is reached by sending a large number of GET queries to the port 80 and as a result the server becomes incapable of processing other queries. A series of 10 experiments has been conducted and 200 hosts are involved in the attack. Each host initiates a TCP-connection with an HTTP-query at a rate of 2 packages per second. The queries are processed by the server using the PHP script, which increases the server load. Due to increasing load the server response time increases with the increase of the number of hosts. The host studied is participating in the attack during the whole experiment; other hosts are included in the attack in a distributed way from the 10th to the 40th seconds and stop package generation from the 70th to the 90th second. The plot (Fig. 9) shows the dependence of session duration from its number. The line shows the mean value for 10 experiments and the errors are also indicated. As can be seen from the plot, the server load increases during an attack, which makes query processing time longer.

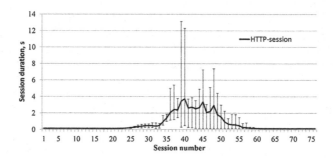

Fig. 9. Traffic log plot for HTTP flooding against the server

Next NTP Reflection Attack was simulated. It is based on an NTP vulnerability consisting in the fact that if the packet with the request on the latest hosts, which asked for his time, was sent, the NTP-server will send the list of these hosts.

Attack of the type NTP Reflection Attack is implemented the following way. The attacking nodes send the queries get_monlist to an NTP-server; at the same time the source address is replaced with the address of a victim computer. In response to this command the server sends a package containing 600 IP-addresses applying to it earlier. We can gain 500 times attack increase. Consider a scenario when 30 % of computers included in a network are participating in the attack (Fig. 10).

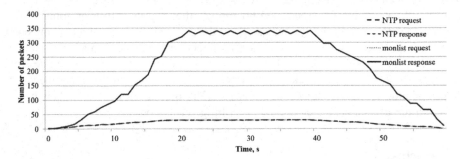

Fig. 10. Server traffic for an NTP-attack (30 % of network computers are in an attack)

Each of the attacking nodes generated 2 packages per second. One of the packages was a legitimate query to an NTP-server, i.e. a query for time synchronization. Address substitution has not been used. The second package contained the command get_monlist, and the IP-address of the source was replaced with the IP-address of a server being attacked. The nodes started sending packages in a distributed way from the 1st to the 20th seconds and terminated the attack from the 40th to the 60th seconds. The plot (Fig. 10) shows time dependencies of the number of queries and responses. The curves of legitimate queries and NTP responses and also get_monlist queries coincide completely and are shown by the solid line. Server responses to the command get_monlist are shown by the dashed line.

7 Discussion

There are many systems that can simulate DDoS attacks [3–9, etc.], including systems that generate real traffic for malicious attacks against legitimate sites. But they all have drawbacks that make it difficult to use them. The system presented in [5] cannot be applied to create defense mechanisms. The systems [6, 8] can provide protection against the attacks with limited power; moreover, these systems are very expensive. ViSe [9] requires a lot of hard disc space as well as a rather large number of settings for starting and repeating the tests. Our system can be considered not only as a packets generator for various types of DDoS attacks, but also as a research laboratory to investigate existing DDoS attacks and methods of protection against them. The main advantage of the developed system is that it allows creating and testing new distributed architecture specific defense mechanisms against DDoS attacks. This is achieved by the fact that by using this laboratory it is possible to create a large-scale computer networks consisting of thousands of nodes, generating as attacks as well as the legitimate traffic. The ability to use real hosts allows to work not only with the web server, but with any network services without the need for simulation, for example, with cloud computing systems.

The ability to use not emulated, but real software is very important to simulate DDoS attacks with the highest power, as different software can react differently to events taking place in its environment. For example, if the attacked host is an actual web server, it can have different hardware configurations, settings, software installed on it, so that the reaction of one attacked host may differ significantly from others. The virtual (simulated) part of the system also gives the possibilities to configure parameters of network interfaces for clients and routers (connection speed, performance of routers, etc.). Experiments have shown that the developed system allows quite accurate simulation of the behavior of attacked web servers. For example, in the experiments on SYN Flooding the server stops processing all SYN packets from clients. This corresponds to the official CERT document describing SYN Flooding [17].

8 Conclusion

In the present paper we have introduced the experiments devoted to simulation of different types of DDoS-attacks. The experiments were conducted in the modeling environment developed by the authors with the possibility of connecting real nodes. In the paper we have provided the experiments for attack simulation at transport and application levels. The experiments have shown that the developed system performs adequate simulation of the processes occurring in computer networks. The behavior of a server being attacked when it is overloaded corresponds to a real server. All the results and plots obtained during simulation in the developed environment are almost identical to the results that could have been achieved in a real network. The developed system can be used in the field of computer security for creating and testing protection mechanisms against DDoS attacks. In future we plan to use this environment for developing new protection techniques against DDoS attacks.

Acknowledgements. This research is being supported by grants of RFBR (projects 13-01-00843, 13-07-13159, 14-07-00697 and 14-07-00417), state project "Organization of scientific research" of the main part of the state plan of the Board of Education of Russia, project part of the state plan of the Board of Education of Russia (task # 2.136.2014/K) as well as by Government of the Russian Federation, Grant 074-U01.

References

1. Worldwide Infrastructure Security Report. ARBOR Networks reports 2014 (2014). http://www.arbornetworks.com/resources/infrastructure-security-report
2. Konovalov, A., Kotenko, I., Shorov, A.: Simulation-based study of botnets and defense mechanisms against them. J. Comput. Syst. Sci. Int. **52**(1), 43–65 (2013). Pleiades Publishing Ltd

3. Kotenko, I., Konovalov, A., Shorov, A.: Agent-based modeling and simulation of botnets and botnet defense. In: Conference on Cyber Conflict, Proceedings 2010. CCD COE Publications. Tallinn, Estonia (2010)
4. Wang, J., Phan, R., Whitley, J., Parish, D.: Advanced DDoS attacks traffic simulation with a test center platform. Int. J. Inf. Secur. Res. (IJISR), 1(4) (2011)
5. Spirent TestCenter. http://www.spirent.com/Ethernet_Testing/Software/TestCenter
6. MazeBolt developer. https://mazebolt.com
7. Butler, B.: Interop network squares off against controlled 70G bit/sec DDoS attack (2013). http://www.networkworld.com/article/2166091/data-center/interop-network-squares-off-against-controlled-70g-bit-sec-ddos-attack.html
8. About Ixia. http://www.ixiacom.com/about-us/company
9. Årnes, A., Haas, P., Vigna, G., Kemmerer, R.A.: Using a virtual security testbed for digital forensic reconstruction. DIMVA 2006, pp. 144–163. Springer-Verlag, France (2006)
10. OMNeT ++ Discrete Event System Simulator. http://www.omnetpp.org/intro
11. INET Framework. http://inet.omnetpp.org/
12. ReaSE, developer web-site. https://i72projekte.tm.uka.de/trac/ReaSE
13. VirtualBox, developer site. https://www.virtualbox.org/wiki/Technical_documentation
14. VMware, developer site. www.vmware.com
15. Kotenko, I., Doynikova, E.: Evaluation of computer network security based on attack graphs and security event processing. J. Wireless Mob. Netw. Ubiquitous Comput. Dependable Appl. (JoWUA) 5(3), 14–29 (2014)
16. Fedorchenko, A., Kotenko, I., Chechulin, A.: Integrated repository of security information for network security evaluation. J. Wireless Mob. Netw. Ubiquitous Comput. Dependable Appl. (JoWUA) 6(2), 41–57 (2015)
17. TCP SYN Flooding and IP Spoofing Attacks. CA-1996–21. http://www.cert.org/historical/advisories/CA-1996-21.cfm

Dependable Systems and Applications

Secure Database Using Order-Preserving Encryption Scheme Based on Arithmetic Coding and Noise Function

Sergey Krendelev$^{(\boxtimes)}$, Mikhail Yakovlev, and Maria Usoltseva

Novosibirsk State University, Pirogova str. 2, 630090 Novosibirsk, Russia
{s.f.krendelev,m.o.yakovlev,m.a.usoltseva}@gmail.com

Abstract. Order-preserving symmetric encryption (OPE) is a deterministic encryption scheme which encryption function preserves numerical order of the plaintexts. That allows comparison operations to be directly applied on encrypted data in case, for example, decryption takes too much time or cryptographic key is unknown. That's why it is successfully used in cloud databases as effective range queries can be performed based on. This paper presents order-preserving encryption scheme based on arithmetic coding. In the first part of it we review principles of arithmetic coding, which formed the basis of the algorithm, as well as changes that were made. Then we describe noise function approach, which makes algorithm cryptographically stronger and show modifications that can be made to obtain order-preserving hash function. Finally we analyze resulting vulnerability to chosen-plaintext attack.

Keywords: Cloud computing security · Order-preserving encryption · Symmetric-key cryptosystems · Order-preserving hash functions

1 Introduction

Nowadays, the amount of information stored in various databases steadily increases. In order to store and effectively manage large amounts of data it is needed to increase data storages capacity and allocate funds for its administration. Another way that was chosen by many companies is to give the database management to a third-party. Such service is managed by a cloud operator and is called Database as a Service, DBaaS.

Obviously, this approach has its own flaws. And the most important of them is security issue. Data can be stolen by the service provider itself or by someone else from its storage. Fortunately, this problem can be solved by encryption. Of course if we just encrypt the whole database with a conventional encryption algorithm, we'll have to encrypt and decrypt it each time we need something. So, all advantages will be lost. That's why special encryption schemes, such as homomorphic encryption and order-preserving encryption, are developed. The first one allows us to handle encrypted data, and the second – to sort them and select the desired.

All known order-preserving schemes have significant problems, such as low level of security (polynomial monotonic functions [1], spline approximation [2], linear functions with random noise [3]), low performance (summation of random numbers

© IFIP International Federation for Information Processing 2015
I. Khalil et al. (Eds.): ICT-EurAsia 2015 and CONFENIS 2015, LNCS 9357, pp. 193–202, 2015.
DOI: 10.1007/978-3-319-24315-3_19

[4], B-trees [5]) or too-large numbers proceeding (scheme by Boldyreva [6]). Proposed scheme doesn't have these disadvantages and, furthermore, unlike all the others can be used to encrypt real numbers. Also it can be used to obtain order-preserving hash function.

This algorithm combines two main ideas, which the majority of OPE schemes operate with: monotonic functions design and elements of coding theory (implicit monotonic functions design). It is claimed that scheme is based on arithmetic coding and noise function, but, in fact, this article considers only the case with binary alphabet. In theory, nothing prevents the use of an arbitrary one.

First, let's give a definition of order-preserving encryption. Assume there are two sets A and B with order relation $<$. Function $f : A \rightarrow B$ is strictly increasing if $\forall x, y \in A, x < y \Leftrightarrow f(x) < f(y)$. Order-preserving encryption is deterministic symmetric encryption based on strictly increasing function.

The described order-preserving encryption scheme was developed in Laboratory of Modern Computer Technologies of Novosibirsk State University Research Department as a part of "Protected Database" project[1] and is based on arithmetic coding and noise function. Let us consider them precisely.

2 Splitting Procedure of Arithmetic Coding

Suppose c is non-negative integer number requiring for its representation n bits, i.e.

$$c = \sum_{i=1}^{n} \alpha_i 2^i$$

where $(\alpha_1, \alpha_2, \ldots, \alpha_n)$ is a bit string, α_1 is the MSB. Let us define the bijection f. Assume that the string $(\alpha_1, \alpha_2, \ldots, \alpha_n)$ defines certain real number $s \in [0, 1)$ as follows:

$$s = \frac{c}{2^n}.$$

Let us find another representation for the number s. In order to do it, we use the idea of arithmetic coding. Notice that the number s satisfies the equation $2^n s = c$. The equation

$$G(x) = 2^n x - c = 0$$

has only one solution on the interval $[0, 1)$. If we solve this equation using a standard binary search, we get the initial number s after n steps. The main idea of arithmetic coding is that intervals can be split into parts randomly. In this case approximate solution of the equation can be found after the less number of steps. That allows us to

[1] This research is performed in Novosibirsk State University under support of Ministry of Education and Science of Russia (contract no. 02.G25.31.0054).

achieve compression of data while using arithmetic coding. First of all, let us consider the splitting procedure.

Suppose $\gamma = \frac{p}{p+q}$, $\mu = \frac{q}{p+q}$, where p, q are random natural numbers. Obviously, $\gamma + \mu = 1$. Let us split the interval $[0, 1)$ into two parts $\left[0, \frac{p}{p+q}\right)$, $\left[\frac{p}{p+q}, 1\right)$. If $G\left(\frac{p}{p+q}\right) > 0$, the interval $\left[0, \frac{p}{p+q}\right)$ is selected, and the output is 0-bit ($\beta_1 = 0$). If $G\left(\frac{p}{p+q}\right) < 0$, the interval $\left[\frac{p}{p+q}, 1\right)$ is selected, and $\beta_1 = 1$. Let us denote $[a_1, b_1)$ the interval was selected.

This interval is again split into parts in the ratio $\gamma : \mu$. According to the sign of function $G(x)$ in the splitting point, one of the segments is selected. Proceeding by induction, the interval $[a_k, b_k)$ can be calculated for $\forall k$. Its length is $\gamma^r \mu^{n-r}$, where r is the number of zeros in string β. If $\forall r : \frac{1}{2^n} < \gamma^r \mu^{k-r}$, then $s \in [a_k, b_k)$ and $c = 2^n s$ are uniquely defined by $\beta = (\beta_1, \ldots, \beta_k)$. It is also obvious that this mapping preserves an order.

Generalizing used in the adaptive arithmetic coding, as well as in the proposed algorithm, is that it is possible to use different ratio on each step. This allows us to achieve stronger security of encryption.

3   Noise Function

It is known that the composition of two strictly increasing functions strictly increases. Therefore, to provide stronger security of cryptographic algorithm special random strictly increasing function is used in addition to the splitting procedure. In fact, we use inverse function of the one that was generated.

It was proved [6] that OPE schemes cannot satisfy the standard notions of security, such as indistinguishability against chosen-plaintext attack (IND-CPA) [7], since they leak the ordering information of the plaintexts. If an adversary knows plaintexts p_1, p_2 and corresponding ciphertexts c_1, c_2 and c, such that $c_1 < c < c_2$, it is obvious that the plaintext for c lies in the interval (p_1, p_2). In addition, the adversary can always find the decryption function in some approximation, for instance, using linear interpolation.

And moreover, in case of using, for example, encryption method developed by David A. Singer and Sun S. Chung [1], where strictly increasing polynomial functions $f(x) = a_0 + a_1 x + \ldots + a_n x^n$ are used for encryption, the adversary can calculate the exact encryption function if he has $(n + 1)$ arbitrary pairs (plaintext, ciphertext). It is enough to solve the system of equations:

$$\begin{cases} a_0 + a_1 x_0 + \ldots + a_n x_0^n = y_0 \\ a_0 + a_1 x_1 + \ldots + a_n x_1^n = y_1 \\ \quad \vdots \\ a_0 + a_1 x_n + \ldots + a_n x_n^n = y_n \end{cases}$$

Thus, the adversary can get $(a_0, \ldots a_n)$ and correspondingly encryption function $f(x)$.

In order to complicate his task it is necessary to maximize the amount of pairs required for this attack and complexity of the system of equations $f(x_i) = y_i$. Therefore, it was decided to generate noise function from class of function

$$f(x) = \int_c^x (a_0 + a_1 t + a_2 t^2)(a_3 + a_4 \sin(a_5 + a_6 t) + a_7 \cos(a_8 + a_9 t)) dt,$$

where c is an arbitrary constant and coefficients a_i are selected so that

$$(a_0 + a_1 t + a_2 t^2)(a_3 + a_4 \sin(a_5 + a_6 t) + a_7 \cos(a_8 + a_9 t)) > 0$$

for $\forall t \in (c; x_{max})$. In this case $f(x)$ is strictly increasing function (see Fig. 1). This integral can be calculated explicitly, which increases the speed of function value calculation. Nevertheless, the system of equations

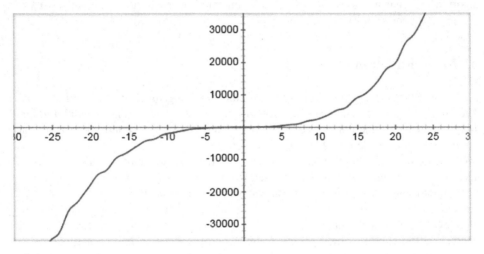

Fig. 1. Example of the correct noise function from the class. Due to such combination of sine and cosine, its behavior is hard to predict without $(a_0, \ldots a_9)$ coefficients knowledge.

$$\begin{cases} \int_c^{x_0} (a_0 + a_1 t + a_2 t^2)(a_3 + a_4 \sin(a_5 + a_6 t) + a_7 \cos(a_8 + a_9 t)) \, dt = y_0 \\ \int_c^{x_1} (a_0 + a_1 t + a_2 t^2)(a_3 + a_4 \sin(a_5 + a_6 t) + a_7 \cos(a_8 + a_9 t)) \, dt = y_1 \\ \quad\quad\quad\quad\quad\quad \vdots \\ \int_c^{x_k} (a_0 + a_1 t + a_2 t^2)(a_3 + a_4 \sin(a_5 + a_6 t) + a_7 \cos(a_8 + a_9 t)) \, dt = y_k \end{cases}$$

is difficult to solve, which indicates that proposed algorithm is cryptographically strong against this type of attack.

4 Cryptographic Scheme

4.1 Key Generation

As a private key of encryption algorithm we consider noise function $f(x) = \int_c^x (a_0 + a_1 t + a_2 t^2)(a_3 + a_4 \sin(a_5 + a_6 t) + a_7 \cos(a_8 + a_9 t))dt$ and a set of ratios (p_i, q_i).

In order for an encrypted n-bit number to be uniquely decrypted, the length of intervals computed during decryption has to be less than $\frac{1}{2^n}$. The largest length of the interval that can be obtained during decryption is $\prod_i \frac{\max(p_i, q_i)}{p_i + q_i} f'_{max}(x)$. So the algorithm of calculation the set of ratios is:

1. Generate random ratios p_i, q_i.
2. Check the condition

$$\prod_i \frac{\max(p_i, q_i)}{p_i + q_i} f'_{max}(x) < \frac{1}{2^n}$$

   If this conditions if satisfied, go to the step 3, else go back to the step 1.
3. Output the set of ratios $(p_1, q_1), (p_2, q_2), \ldots, (p_k, q_k)$.
   The key is the set $K = [(a_0, \ldots, a_9), (p_1, q_1), (p_2, q_2), \ldots, (p_k, q_k)]$.

4.2 Encryption

Assume we need to encrypt n-bit integer s with the key $K = [f(x), (p_1, q_1), (p_2, q_2), \ldots, (p_k, q_k)]$, where $f(x)$ is a noise function, $f(a_0) = 0$, $f(b_0) = 2^n$, and (p_i, q_i) is a set of ratios. Consider the i-th iteration of algorithm.

The current interval $[a_{i-1}, b_{i-1})$ is split in the ratio $p_i : q_i$. Let it be split at the point $x \in [a_{i-1}, b_{i-1})$, i.e.

$$x = a_{i-1} + \frac{(b_{i-1} - a_{i-1})p_i}{p_i + q_i}.$$

If $f(x) > s$, then $\beta_i = 0$, $a_i = a_{i-1}$, $b_i = x$. Otherwise, $\beta_i = 1$, $a_i = x$, $b_i = b_{i-1}$.

Notice that $\forall i, f^{-1}(s) \in [a_i, b_i)$ according to the selection of a_i and b_i. After performing k iterations, (where k is the size of the key, i.e. the number of ratios) we obtain the bit sequence $\beta = (\beta_1, \ldots, \beta_k)$, $\beta_i \in \{0, 1\}$, which is a ciphertext for s.

4.3   Decryption

Suppose there is a bit sequence $\beta = (\beta_1, \ldots, \beta_k), \beta_i \in \{0, 1\}$, which is the ciphertext for s, encrypted with some key K. Let us consider the i-th iteration of the algorithm.

Similar to the encryption algorithm, current interval $[a_{i-1}, b_{i-1})$ is split in the ratio $p_i : q_i$. Let it be split at the point $x \in [a_{i-1}, b_{i-1})$, i.e.

$$x = a_{i-1} + \frac{(b_{i-1} - a_{i-1})p_i}{p_i + q_i}.$$

If $\beta_i = 0$, then $a_i = a_{i-1}, b_i = x$. Otherwise, $a_i = x, b_i = b_{i-1}$.

After performing k iterations, we obtain the interval $[a_k, b_k)$ and the condition $(f(b_k) - f(a_k)) < \frac{1}{2^n}$ is satisfied according to the key selection. As $s \in [f(a_k), f(b_k))$, the s is uniquely decoded as follows:

$$s = 2^n f(a_k) + 1,$$

where $\lfloor x \rfloor$ is the largest integer, which comes before x.

5   Scheme Modifications

5.1   Application of the Scheme for Fixed-Point Arithmetic

It is easy to see that this scheme can be generalized to the set of rational numbers. Encryption and decryption algorithms are the same except for the final operation – the length of the segment $[a_k, b_k)$ that determines encrypted number is reduced to 2^l times, where l is the number of bit decimal places. It should be known at the stage of key generation and condition from point 2 takes the following form:

$$\prod_i \frac{\max(p_i, q_i)}{p_i + q_i} * f'_{max}(x) < \frac{1}{2^{n+l}}$$

After key generation number l can't be modified and is a part of the key. So, the secret key K now is the set $[l, (a_0, \ldots, a_9), (p_1, q_1), (p_2, q_2), \ldots, (p_k, q_k)]$.

5.2   Strictly Increasing Hash Function

This algorithm can also be modified to produce a strictly increasing hash function. It can be used, for example, in encrypted database, if it stores two entities for each data: ciphertext, that was obtained from cryptographically strong algorithm and hash value returned by hash function. This allows both to be sure that the data won't be decrypted by adversary (first entity is secure and the second can't be decrypted at all) and apply comparison operations on encrypted data to some extent.

To begin, we note that output has the same bit size as the number of ratios p_i, q_i from the secret key. So, in order to obtain a hash function, it is enough to change the procedure of key generation, and more precisely, its ratios generation part.

Instead of the condition checking from the point 2, satisfaction of which guaranteed that the data can be decrypted, now we need to perform the first point – pair p_i, q_i generation – a number of times. This number, evidently, is equal to the number of bits that hash function returns.

Thus, the key generation algorithm for order-preserving m-bit hash function is:

1. Select strictly increasing noise function $f(x)$. To do this, generate $(a_0, \ldots a_9)$ so that

$$\left(a_0 + a_1 t + a_2 t^2\right)\left(a_3 + a_4 \sin(a_5 + a_6 t) + a_7 \cos(a_8 + a_9 t)\right) > 0$$

for $\forall t \in (c; x_{max})$, where c is a fixed constant.
2. Generate random set of ratios $(p_1, q_1), (p_2, q_2), \ldots, (p_m, q_m)$.
3. The key is the set $K = [(a_0, \ldots, a_9), (p_1, q_1), (p_2, q_2), \ldots, (p_m, q_m)]$.

To get rid of the big numbers processing, for instance, if we need to get hash of a large file, it is possible to split input data into parts with acceptable size and calculate hash for each of them. The result hash value of the whole file can be found as their concatenation. This approach allows us to hash data of any predetermined dimension.

So, there are three parameters that we can select arbitrarily depending on our purpose: s_1 – size of the processed parts, s_2 – hash size for each of them ($s_2 < s_1$), and s_3 – maximum file size. Obviously, final hash is $\frac{s_2 s_3}{s_1}$-bit.

Since encryption algorithm remains the same, the hash function running time depends linearly on its output size (it is equal to the number of algorithm iterations). Therefore, it is not recommended to choose too-big s_2 number.

In order to process files smaller than the maximum size, they can be padded with zeros on the left. In this case, order is still preserves. Since this is a hash function algorithm, decryption is no longer exists.

6 Encryption Security

As we have seen (see Sect. 3) OPE schemes cannot satisfy the standard notions of security against chosen-plaintext attack. Different methods of cryptoanalysis are considered to determine the notion of order-preserving encryption security [2, 8–10]. Generally, the security of such schemes is based on the fact that monotonic function, the scheme is based on, must be completely indistinguishable from truly random monotonic function. This means that only an access to the private key allows performing accurate data decryption.

So let us check this algorithm for this condition in practice. To do that, we encrypted all 16-bit numbers (from 0 to 65535) with the same random key and analyzed the results.

As a subject of analysis we chose the difference between two ciphertexts for nearby integers. For example, if $f(x) = 2186003864819$ and $f(x + 1) = 2186004033407$, where $f(x)$ is encryption function, then $f(x + 1) - f(x) = 168588$ is considered. One of the reasons for this choice was the fact that success of chosen-plaintext attack by interpolation depends on this differences (see Fig. 2).

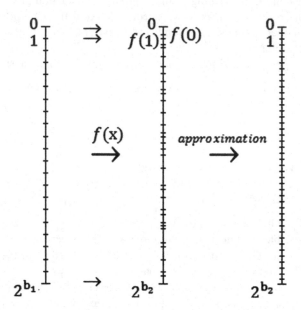

Fig. 2. Chosen-plaintext attack using values interpolation. Ciphertext for some b_1-bit plaintext x is approximated by the value of $\frac{X}{2^{b_2}}$, where b_2 is size of ciphertext. Approximation in the other direction is counted similarly.

As a result, we obtained the following data (see Fig. 3). In this chart the Y-axis displays the difference value between two ciphertexts (higher values were rounded), and the X-axis shows the number of them was found.

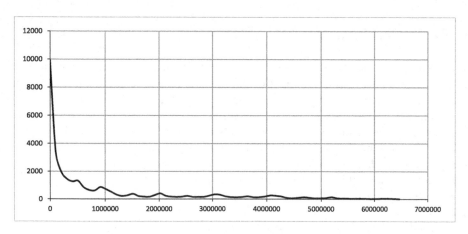

Fig. 3. Frequency distribution of the differences between ciphertext.

As we see, this chart and right hyperbola $y = \frac{1}{x}$ are alike. It is typical for monotonic functions that were generated randomly and indicates that the maximum available security of the algorithm was achieved.

But the distribution of the differences itself is also important (see Fig. 4). The Y-axis displays $f(x + 1) - f(x)$ when the X-axis shows x (from 0 to 65535).

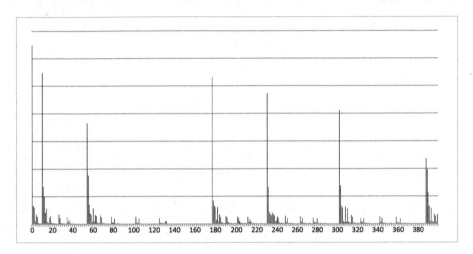

Fig. 4. Distribution of the differences on the interval.

We can see that the differences are distributed very irregularly. As it is a feature of secure encryption, we can claim that proposed algorithm is cryptographically strong.

References

1. Ozsoyoglu, G., Singer, D.A., Chung, S.S.: Anti-tamper databases: querying encrypted databases. EECS Department, Math Department, Case Western Reserve University, Cleveland, OH 44106. doi:http://dx.doi.org/10.1109/ICDEW.2006.30
2. Agrawal, R., Kiernan, G.G., Srikant, R., Xu, Y.: System and method for order-preserving encryption for numeric data
3. Kerschbaum, F.: Commutative order-preserving encryption. Karlsruhe, United States Patent 20120121080, DE, 17 May 2012
4. Bebek, G.: Anti-tamper database research: Inference control techniques. Technical Report EECS433 Final Report, Case Western Reserve University (2002)
5. Popa, R.A., Li, F.H., Zeldovich, N.: An ideal-security protocol for order-preserving encoding, MIT CSAIL (2011). doi:http://dx.doi.org/10.1109/CISS.2012.6310814
6. Boldyreva, A., Chenette, N., Lee, Y., O'Neill, A.: Order-preserving symmetric encryption. In: Joux, A. (ed.) EUROCRYPT 2009. LNCS, vol. 5479, pp. 224–241. Springer, Heidelberg (2009)
7. Shnayder, B.: Applied Cryptology, 816 pp. Triumph, Moscow (2002)

8. Boldyreva, A., Chenette, N., O'Neill, A.: Order-preserving encryption revisited: improved security analysis and alternative solutions. In: Rogaway, P. (ed.) CRYPTO 2011. LNCS, vol. 6841, pp. 578–595. Springer, Heidelberg (2011)
9. Martinez, S., Miret, J.M., Tomas, R., Valls, M.: Security analysis of order preserving symmetric cryptography. Appl. Math. Inf. Sci. 7(4), 1285–1295 (2013)
10. Xiao, L., Bastani, O., Yen, I.: Security analysis for order preserving encryption schemes. Technical Report UTDCS-01-12 (2012). https://utd.edu/~ilyen/techrep/OPE-proof1.pdf

An Approach for Evaluating Softgoals Using Weight

Shuichiro Yamamoto[✉]

Strategy Office, Information and Communications Headquarters,
Nagoya University, Nagoya, Japan
syamamoto@acm.org

Abstract. The resolution of conflicts among non-functional requirements are difficult problem during the analysis of non-functional requirements. To mitigate the problem, the weighted softgoal is proposed based on the Softgoal Interdependency Graphs (SIG) that help engineers resolve conflicts among non-functional requirements. It is also shown evaluation results of the weighted SIG applications to develop non-functional requirements and choose alternative design decisions.

Keywords: Non-functional requirements · NFR framework · Softgoal Interdependency Graphs · Softgoal weight

1 Introduction

Non-functional requirements are used to define qualities and validate that system architectures achieve the quality requirements. NFR framework is traditionally focusing on qualitative evaluation of softgoals, and different kinds of softgoals are evaluated separately. For example, it is difficult to evaluate security and safety softgoals in the integrated way. Therefore, conflicts between safety and security softgoals should resolve implicitly.

This paper discusses the effectiveness of a softgoal weight extension based on SIG diagrams of the NFR framework. The weight values are assigned to softgoal decompositions and contributions link. The new main top goal is introduced to resolve conflicts between security and safety softgoals that are decomposed from the main softgoal. The weights assigned to each link define clearly priority between decomposed softgoals.

Section 2 describes related work of non-functional requirements approach based on softgoals. Section 3 proposes an approach to introduce quantitative weights to SIG diagrams. Section 4 describes examples of applying the proposed approach to evaluate operationalization softgoals for simple cases. In Sect. 5, we discuss the effectiveness of the proposed approach. Section 6 concludes the paper and shows future work.

2 Related Work

The NFR framework [1] is a Goal Oriented Requirements Engineering method can be used to evaluate architecture by defining levels of safety and security requirements. The SIG (Softgoal Interdependency Graph) is used to represent security and safety

© Springer International Publishing Switzerland 2015
I. Khalil et al. (Eds.): ICT-EurAsia 2015 and CONFENIS 2015, LNCS 9357, pp. 203–212, 2015.
DOI: 10.1007/978-3-319-24315-3_20

goals. The NFR soft goals are non-functional requirements softgoals, operationalization softgoals, and claim softgoals. First, constraints of target systems are clarified by non-functional requirements softgoals. Softgoals are, then, decomposed into sub softgoals to develop SIG. NFR softgoals are allocated to operationalization softgoals for describing target system functions.

In SIG the design decisions for the target system are represented by operationalization softgoals. The operationalization softgoals are validated for satisfying parent soft goals.

For analysing functional requirements, alternative requirements are selected to satisfy non-functional softgoals. If the conflict between non-functional softgoals is occurred, the conflict should be resolved by using the criteria whether non-functional requirements are satisfied.

To evaluate the quality of architecture, the following methods are proposed.

(1) Check list based method

The operationally critical threat, asset, and vulnerability evaluation (OCTAVE) for security provides the check list to evaluate vulnerability [2].

However, the standard check list did not satisfy every safety requirements and security requirements. The check list also have the problem that it cannot be applied to resolve conflicts and interactions between safety and security requirements.

(2) Scenario based method

Scenarios can be developed to describe critical factors that impact on architectures significantly. The scenarios are used to identify important factors that affect high priority requirements. Utility trees are used to define scenarios in ATAM (Architecture Trade off Analysis Method) [3]. ATAM provides the quality trade off analysis method to analyze safety and security requirements.

(3) Subramanian method

Subramanian proposed the following method that NFR framework is applied to analyse safety and security [4]. Safety and security are decomposed by using non-functional softgoals. The target architecture is decomposed by operationalization softgoals. The contribution relationship from operationalization softgoals to non-functional softgoals are defined. By using propagation rules, labels of softgoals are investigated to evaluate safety and security of the target architecture. However their approach did not consider quantitative relationship between values of child softgoals. And they evaluate safety and security softgoals independently.

To analyse system faults, FTA (Fault Tree Analysis) has been used [5]. Although the fault tree of FTA can be considered as an AND/OR goal graph, nodes of the fault tree represent fault events and logic gates. An upper event is resulted from a combination of lower events through a logic gate. The lowest events are primary events that require no further logical decomposition.

3   Softgoal Weight

In case of introducing weights to SIG, nodes and relationships are candidates to assign weights. Names are assigned to SIG nodes, but SIG relationships do not have names. Therefore, we consider to add weights as the attributes of node names. This approach is comfortable because it does not affect the SIG grammar syntax. Attributes are not assigned for the SIG relationship, because attributes for the relationship between softgoals can be represented by node attributes.

In NFR framework, the achievement of soft goals are shown by the check symbol for each soft goal. Figure 1 shows an example portion of NFR framework to assure the safety of elevator control. The buffer device evades a car collision to the ground when the car is going down. This supports the claim that the down movement of the elevator is safe.

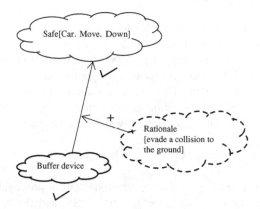

Fig. 1. A portion of NFR framework to assure safety of elevator control

3.1   AND Decomposition Weight

If a softgoal decomposed by the AND relationship, then the AND decomposition weight label $<W_1,...,W_k>$ is appended to the parent softgoal name.

Where k is the number of sub softgoals, and Wi are defined to satisfy $\Sigma_{i=1,k} Wi = 1$.

3.2   OR Decomposition Weight

If a softgoal decomposed by the OR relationship, then the OR decomposition weight label $<max(W_1,...,W_k)>$ is appended to the parent softgoal name, where W_i is the weight of the i-th sub softgoal.

3.3   Operationalization Weight

If a softgoal is related to operationalization softgoals, then the weight ratio label $<W_1, ...,W_k>$ is appended to the parent softgoal name.

Where k is the number of operationalization softgoals that are related to the soft-goal, and Wi are defined to satisfy $\Sigma_{i=1,k}$ Wi = 1.

3.4 Contribution Weight

There are positive and negative contributions in SIGs. The weights of positive and negative contributions are +N and −N, respectively. N is either 1 or 2. 1 and 2 also mean weak and strong contribution, respectively. The positive and negative contributions can be represented by styles of relation lines. The solid and dotted lines show positive and negative contributions, respectively.

3.5 Weight Propagation Rules

There are two rules for operationalization and decomposition. The operationalization propagation rule is defined as follows.

Let a parent softgoal is contributed by k operationalization goals. And let <P> be the weight of the softgoal. Let $<Q_1,...,Q_k>$ be the operationalization weight ratio of the softgoal. Let <Ri> be the weight of i-th operationalization goal, and Ci be the contribution weight of the operationalization goal to the softgoal, respectively. Then the weight value P of the softgoal is calculated by the following equation.

$$P = \left(\Sigma_{i=1,k} Q_i^* R_i^* C_i\right), \text{ where } \Sigma_{i=1,k} Q_i = 1$$

The Fig. 2 shows an example of the operationalization propagation. Suppose the weights of operationalization goals are <Q>, <R>, <S>, and the contribution weight ratio is <1/3, 1/3, 1/3>, then the weight P of the softgoal is Q/3 + R/3–S/3, where Q and R are the positive, but S is the negative contribution.

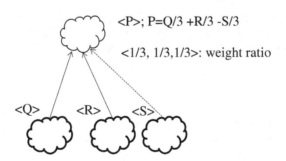

Fig. 2. Operationalization propagation

In the same way, the decomposition propagation rule can be defined as follows. Let a parent softgoal is decomposed by k sub softgoals with AND decomposition. Let <P> be the weight of the softgoal. Let $<Q_1,...,Q_k>$ be the AND decomposition weight ratio of the softgoal. Let <Ri> be the weight of i-th sub softgoal. Then the weight value P of the softgoal is calculated by the following equation.

$$P = (\Sigma_{i=1,k} Q_i^* R_i), \text{ where } \Sigma_{i=1,k} Q_i = 1$$

The Fig. 3 shows an example of the AND decomposition propagation. Suppose the weights of sub softgoals are <Q>, and <R>. And the contribution weight ratio is <1/2, 1/2>, then the weight P of the softgoal is Q/2 + R/2.

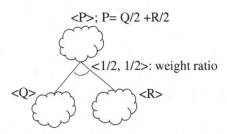

Fig. 3. AND decomposition propagation example

In case of OR decomposition, P is also calculated by the following equation.

$$P = \max(R_1, \ldots, R_k)$$

The Fig. 4 shows an example of the OR decomposition propagation. Suppose the weights of sub softgoals are <Q>, and <R>. Then the weight P of the softgoal is the max(Q, R).

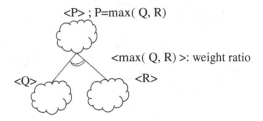

Fig. 4. OR decomposition propagation example

4 Examples of Weighted SIG

4.1 Credit Card Account

The credit card system shall manage customer accounts. The NFR of the customer accounts consists of good performance, security, and accessibility.

The weighted SIG for the customer accounts of a credit card system is shown in Fig. 5. The main NFR is decomposed into the above three softgoals. The top softgoal of the figure integrates these softgoals as well as defines that these softgoals have the same priority by using the weight attribute clause <1/3, 1/3, 1/3>.

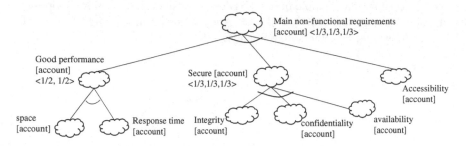

Fig. 5. Decomposition of a main NFR with weights

The impact of the operationalization softgoals to achieve the above NFRs can be evaluated by adding operationalization softgoals to the weighted SIG. An example of the interrelationship between NFR and operationalization softgoals are shown in Fig. 6.

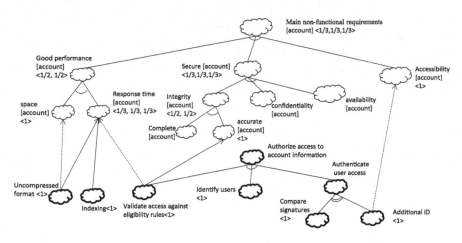

Fig. 6. Evaluation of the decision impact

There are 8 operationalization softgoals. The Authorize access to account information softgoal is decomposed into Validate access against eligibility rules, Identify users, and Authenticate user access softgoals by AND decomposition. Authenticate user access softgoal is also decomposed into Compare signatures and Additional ID softgoals by OR decomposition. The Uncompressed format operationalization have the positive and negative contribution to the Space and Response time softgoals, respectively. The indexing operationalization has the positive contribution to the Response time softgoal. The Validate access against eligibility rules operationalization has negative and positive contribution to the Response time and accurate softgoals, respectively. Additional ID operationalization has negative contribution to the Accessibility softgoal.

The impact of the operationalization can be evaluated as follows.

$$(-1/2 + (1/3 + 1/3 - 1/3)/2)/3 + ((0 + 1/2)/3 + 0 + 0)/3 + (-1)/3$$
$$= (-1/2 + 1/6)/3 + 1/18 - 1/3$$
$$= -1/9 - 5/18 = -7/18$$

Therefore the operationalization is not a good decision in total. It is difficult to evaluate the total impact of the operationalization without the top main softgoal.

4.2   Alternative Design Decision

Figure 7 shows the comparison of alternative operationalization to manage the system data. The top NFR softgoal is decomposed into comprehensibility, modifiability, performance, and reusability softgoals. The shared data and abstract data type are two operationalization alternatives.

The total impact value of the quality requirements for shared data is calculated as follows.

$$(1/2 - 1/2)/6 + (-1/3 - 1/3 + (1/2 + 0)/3)/3 + (1/2 + 0)/3 - 1/6$$
$$= 0 + (-2/3 + 1/6)/3 + 1/6 - 1/6 = -1/6$$

The total impact value of the main non-functional requirements for Abstract Data Type is calculated as follows.

$$1/6 + (-1/3 + 1/3 + 0)/3 - (1/2)/3 + 1/6 = 1/6 + 0 - 1/6 + 1/6 = 1/6$$

The result shows that Abstract data type is better than shared data.

It is worth to remark that contribution weight are not assigned to the bottom level non-functional requirement softgoals in Fig. 7. Because the shared data and abstract data type softgoals are different alternative operationalization softgoals, therefore the bottom level non-functional requirement softgoals have no weight value list.

The impact evaluation can also be represented by tabular form. Table 1 shows the tabular evaluation of Abstract Data Type solution for the SIG diagram. The column values of the Abstract Data Type shows the contribution values for NFR softgoals.

On the top left first column corresponds to the main softgoal. The value in the next row of the same top left column is the total evaluation value for the selected alternative solution. The second column shows the decomposition coefficient values.

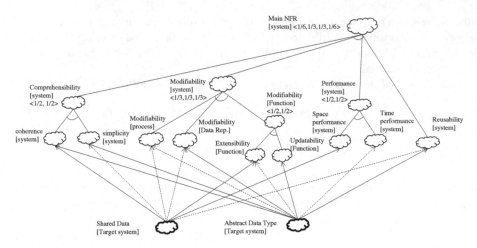

Fig. 7. Evaluating the impact of solution alternatives on the integrated NFR

Table 1. Tabular evaluation of Abstract Data Type solution

SIG decomposition structure								AbstractDataType
Main NFR 0.16667	1/6	Comprehensibility 1	1/2	Coherence 1				1
			1/2	Simplicity 1				1
	1/3	Modifiability 0	1/3	Modifiability [Process] -1				-1
			1/3	Modifiability [Data Rep.] 1				1
			1/3	Modifiability [Function] 0	1/2	Extensibility [Function] -1		-1
					1/2	Updatability [Function] 1		1
	1/3	Performance -1/2	1/2	Space 0				0
			1/2	Time -1				-1
	1/6	Reusability 1						1

The table shows the coefficient vector <1/12, 1/12, 1/6, 1/6, 1/6, 1/6, 1/4, 1/4, 1/6> for the SIG decomposition. The summation of the multiplication of the contribution vector and coefficient vector becomes the evaluation value for the selected alternative solution.

5 Discussion

5.1 Effectiveness of Argument Patterns

As examples showed, the weighted SIG approach was useful to analyze the satisfing relationship between non-functional softgoals and operationalization softgoals. This showed that the effectiveness of the weight propagation method. Although the evaluation was only executed for small examples, it is clear the same results can be derived for other applications.

The conflict among different quality characteristics can be resolved by using decomposition weight list defined by decomposition link of SIGs. The mechanism is generic and widely applicable to quantitative evaluation of the validity of various architectures. The proposed approach can be applicable for evaluating not only software architectures, but also business and technology architectures [6, 7].

5.2 Limitation

This paper only examines the effectiveness of the proposed method for a simple example SIG diagrams. It is necessary to show the effectiveness of the method by evaluating more number of applications. This paper qualitatively examines the effectiveness of the weighted SIG approach. Quantitative evaluations of the proposed method are also necessary.

6 Conclusion

This paper introduced the softgoal weight for evaluating NFRs. Evaluation examples of the approach was also shown for quantitatively validating quality satisfying levels of solutions represented by operationalizing softgoals. The example evaluations showed the effectiveness of the approach.

Future work includes more experimental evaluation of the proposed approach, comparative analysis of different quantitative extensions to the NFR framework. The claim softgoals are not mentioned in this paper. It is also necessary to consider the effect of introducing weight for claim softgoals.

Acknowledgment. This work was supported by KAKENHI (24220001).

References

1. Chung, L., Nixson, B.A., Yu, E., Mylopoulos, J.: Non-Functional Requirements in Software Engineering. Kluwer Academic Publishers, Boston (2000)
2. OCTAVE: Operationally Critical Threat, Asset, and Vulnerability Evaluation, Software Engineering Institute. http://www.cert.org/octave/

3. Bass, L., Clements, P., Kazman, R.: Software Architecture in Practice, 2nd edn. Addison-Wesley, Reading (2003)
4. Subramanian, N., Zalewski, J.: Quantitative assessment of safety and security of system architectures for cyberphysical systems using the NFR approach. IEEE Syst. J. (2014)
5. Leveson, N.: Safeware - System Safety and Computers. Addison-Wesley, Reading (1995)
6. Josely, A., et al.: TOGAF® Version 9.1 A Pocket Guide (2011)
7. Josely, A., et al.: ArchiMate®2.0, A Pocket Guide, The Open Group, Van Haren8 Publishing `(2013)

An Efficient Unsavory Data Detection Method for Internet Big Data

Peige Ren[1(✉)], Xiaofeng Wang[1], Hao Sun[1], Fen Xu[2],
Baokang Zhao[1], and Chunqing Wu[1]

[1] College of Computer, National University of Defense Technology,
Changsha 410073, China
renpeige@163.com, sunhao4257@gmail.com,
{xf_wang,bkzhao,chunqingwu}@nudt.edu.cn
[2] China Aerodynamics Research and Development Center,
Hypervelocity Aerodynamics Institute, Mianyang, China
fenxl5@163.com

Abstract. With the explosion of information technologies, the volume and diversity of the data in the cyberspace are growing rapidly; meanwhile the unsavory data are harming the security of Internet. So how to detect the unsavory data from the Internet big data based on their inner semantic information is of growing importance. In this paper, we propose the i-Tree method, an intelligent semantics-based unsavory data detection method for internet big data. Firstly, the internet big data are mapped into a high-dimensional feature space, representing as high-dimensional points in the feature space. Secondly, to solve the "curse of dimensionality" problem of the high-dimensional feature space, the principal component analysis (PCA) method is used to reduce the dimensionality of the feature space. Thirdly, in the new generated feature space, we cluster the data objects, transform the data clusters into regular unit hyper-cubes and create one-dimensional index for data objects based on the idea of multi-dimensional index. Finally, we realize the semantics-based data detection for a given unsavory data object according to similarity search algorithm and the experimental results proved our method can achieve much better efficiency.

Keywords: High-dimensional feature space · Principal component analysis · Multi-dimensional index · Semantics-based similarity search

1 Introduction

In recent years, with the era of Internet big data coming, the volume and diversity of internet data objects in the cyberspace are growing rapidly. Meanwhile, more and more various unsavory data objects are emerging, such as various malwares, violent videos, subversive remarks, pornographic pictures and so on [1–3]. The unsavory data are harming our society and network security, so efficiently detecting the unsavory data objects from the Internet big data is of growing importance. But the traditional accurate matching based data detection methods cannot identify the inner semantic information of various internet data objects and cannot realize intelligent data detection.

© IFIP International Federation for Information Processing 2015
I. Khalil et al. (Eds.): ICT-EurAsia 2015 and CONFENIS 2015, LNCS 9357, pp. 213–220, 2015.
DOI: 10.1007/978-3-319-24315-3_21

To realize the intelligent semantics-based data detection, we need to extract the features of internet data collection to construct a high-dimensional feature space [4], and the data objects are expressed as high-dimensional points in the feature space, so we can discover the data objects semantics-similar to a given query data object (unsavory data) based on the distances between high-dimensional points. While the efficiency of semantics-based similarity search in feature space is sensitive to the dimensionality of the space, when the dimensionality is too high, the efficiency of similarity search can be so worse that cannot meet our needs.

In the other hand, when searching the semantics-similar data objects to a given query point in feature space, the multi-dimensional indexes [5] can prune away the data objects semantics-irrelevant (with large distance) to the query point, reducing the searching zone and searching paths and increasing the efficiency of similarity search. While the existing multi-dimensional indexes have several shortcomings for processing the internet big data: Firstly, the multi-dimensional indexes are influenced by the dimensionality of feature space, when the dimensionality is very high, the efficiency of multi-dimensional indexes might become worse than sequential scan; Secondly, most existing multi-dimensional indexes are proposed in some particular situations. For instance, the Pyramid-Technique [6] is efficient at processing uniformly distributed data set but inefficient when data set is irregularly distributed, while the iDistance [7] method is efficient at kNN query but cannot carry out range query; Thirdly, for the semantics-based similarity searching in feature space, the semantic information of data set is usually embedded in a lower-dimensional subspace so the original high-dimensional feature space can be compressed. Besides, there are many correlated features, noise and redundant information in the original feature space, which can impair the efficiency of semantics-based similarity search.

To realize intelligent and efficient unsavory data detection for internet big data, we proposed the i-Tree method, a semantics-based data detection method. The method firstly utilize the PCA [8] method to reduce the dimensionality of original high-dimensional feature space, eliminating ill effects of "curse of dimensionality" meanwhile diminishing the redundant and noise interference; secondly, we adopt a multi-dimensional index which is robust for arbitrarily distributed data set in the feature space, the index can effectively divide, organize and map multi-dimensional data objects into one-dimensional values; finally, to validate the validity of our method, we realize similarity search algorithm using our method and compare our method with other classic methods. Our method can avoid "curse of dimensionality", and the method is adaptive for various distributed data set, which can provide inspiration to efficient unsavory data detection for internet big data.

The rest of the paper is organized as follows. Section 2 introduced the related technologies and methods of this paper. Section 3 proposed the semantics-based unsavory data detection method for internet big data based on PCA and multi-dimensional indexes. Section 4 presents the experimental results of our method. Finally we conclude in Sect. 5.

2 Related Work

2.1 Principal Component Analysis

Principal component analysis (PCA) is widely used in analyzing multi-dimensional data set, which can reduce the high dimensionality of original feature space to a lower intrinsic dimensionality, and can realize redundancy removal, noise elimination, data compression, feature extraction, etc. The PCA is widely employed in many actual applications with linear models, such as face recognition, image processing, sex determination, time series prediction, pattern recognition, communications, etc.

The basic idea of PCA is representing the distribution of original date set as precisely as possible using a set of features that containing more amount of information, in other words, it computes an orthogonal subspace with lower dimensionality to represent the original high-dimensional data set.

For an N-dimensional data set X containing M data objects (expressed as N-dimensional vectors): $x_k \in R^{N \times 1} (k = 1, 2, \ldots, M)$, let m represent the mean vector: $m = \frac{1}{M} \sum_{i=1}^{M} x_k$, and the covariance matrix can be represented as $S_i = \frac{1}{M} \sum_{k=1}^{M} (x_k - m)(x_k - m)^T \in R^{N \times N}$. Let $Z = [x_1 - m, x_2 - m, \ldots, x_M - m] \in R^{N \times M}$, then $S_i = \frac{1}{M} ZZ^T \in R^{N \times N}$.

The optimal projected vectors of PCA are a set of orthonormal vectors (u_1, u_2, ..., u_d) when the evaluation function $J(u) = u^T S_i u$ attends its maximal value, and the retained variance in the projection is maximal. In fact, the vectors u_1, u_2, ..., u_d are the corresponding orthonormal eigenvectors of d larger eigenvalues of S_i ($\lambda_1 \geq \lambda_2 \geq \ldots \geq \lambda_d$), the vector u_i is also called the i-th principal component. The evaluation function of PCA can also be represented as $J(W) = tr(W^T S_i W)$, where the optimal projection matrix is $W_{opt} = \arg \max_W J(W) = (u_1, u_2, \ldots, u_d)$.

The contribution rate (energy) of k-th principal component u_k can be defined as: $\frac{\lambda_k}{\lambda_1 + \lambda_2 + \ldots + \lambda_n}$, that is the rate of the k-th principle component variance in the sum of all principle component variances. Owing to $\lambda_1 \geq \lambda_2 \geq \ldots \geq \lambda_n$, the contribution rate of anterior principal component is greater than the contribution rate of latter principal component. When the contribution rate sum of d anterior principal components: $\eta_k = \frac{\lambda_1 + \lambda_2 + \ldots + \lambda_d}{\lambda_1 + \lambda_2 + \ldots + \lambda_k + \ldots + \lambda_n}$ is large enough (such as $\geq 90\%$), then we can think that the d principal components almost contain all the useful information of original features. When d<< n, we can achieve the goal of dimensionality reduction of original feature space, then we can construct a lower-dimensional feature space using the eigenvectors: u_1, u_2, ..., u_d.

2.2 Multi-dimensional Indexes

The multi-dimensional indexes can efficiently divide and organize the data objects in feature space, making sure data objects that close to each other are likely to be stored in the same page, so the useless data zones can be pruned away in advance for processing similarity queries. So far, a series of multi-dimensional indexes have been proposed, the typical ones include Pyramid-Technique, iDistance, and so on.

The partitioning strategies of multi-dimensional indexes can be divided into space-based partitioning and data-based partitioning. The Pyramid-Technique is based on the space-based partitioning strategy. It firstly divides the d-dimensional feature space into 2d subspaces such that the resulting subspaces are shaped liked pyramids with the center-point of the feature space as their common top, and then every subspace is cut into slices that are parallel to the pyramid's basis to form data pages. The technique defines a pyramid number for each subspace. For a d-dimensional data object, the technique determines the pyramid number i in which the data object is located and computes the height h of the data object to the pyramid top. So we can obtain the one-dimensional mapping value of the data object through adding the pyramid number i and the height h of the data object.

The partitioning strategy of the iDistance method can be space-based partitioning strategy or data-based partitioning strategy. The iDistance firstly divides the feature space into subspaces equally or according to the distribution of the data objects and determines a subspace number i for each subspace; secondly, selects a reference point for each subspace and computes the distance d of a given data object p to its nearest reference point; finally, the data object can be mapped into a one-dimensional value y based on the formula: $y = i \times c + d$, where c is a constant to make sure that the data objects in different subspaces are mapped into different one-dimensional intervals. Finally the iDistance uses a B+-tree to index the resulting one-dimensional space.

3   The Overview of Our Method

To realize intelligent semantics-based unsavory data detection, we proposed the i-Tree method, and our method consists of the following three phases:

- Dimensionality reduction of feature space based on PCA;
- Adaptive multi-dimensional index for data distribution;
- Semantics-based similarity search.

3.1   Dimensionality Reduction of Feature Space Based on PCA

The dimensionality of internet big data's feature space is usually too high to easily cause the "curse of dimensionality". In this section we realize the dimensionality reduction of the original feature space using the PCA method, eliminating the ill effects of "curse of dimensionality" and the redundant and noise interference.

Firstly we use the PCA to compute the features of a new feature space, the features (vectors) of the new space are in the direction of the largest variance of the original internet data. Then we use the new features to construct a lower-dimensional feature space, and the internet data set are expressed in this new feature space by their feature coefficients (weights). A user query is also projected into the feature space generated by PCA, and we can find semantics-similar internet data by searching the internet data near it; if the query is not projected into the feature space, we can conclude that there is no semantics-similar internet data to the query.

By means of the PCA method, we can realize the dimensionality reduction of the original feature space, which can eliminate the impact of "curse of dimensionality", remove the noisy and redundancy information during the similarity search and reduce the complexity of computation and storage for further data processing.

3.2   Adaptive Multi-dimensional Index for Data Distribution

In this section we divide and manage the data objects in feature space based on the idea of multi-dimensional indexes. For the internet data objects irregularly distributed in feature space, we proposed an adaptive multi-dimensional index. Our index can be realized by the following three steps: 1, partitioning the data set according to the data distribution to form a series of data clusters; 2, transforming the data clusters into regular-shaped data subspaces; 3, mapping the high-dimensional data objects into one-dimensional values and index them using a B+-tree.

Firstly, we partition the data set according to their distribution to form data clusters. The data objects distribute irregularly in feature space, usually semantics-similar data objects gather together. So we here employ the data-based partitioning strategy to partition the feature space. Specifically, we utilize the K-means clustering algorithm to cluster the data objects into a series of data clusters, the data objects in a same cluster are near to each other, having similar semantic information.

Secondly, we transform the data clusters into regular-shaped subspaces. To utilize the Pyramid-Technique to process each data cluster, we transform the data clusters into unit high-dimensional hyper-cube shaped subspaces and move the cluster centers to the centers of the unit subspaces. For the data objects in each data clusters, the transformation is a one-to-one mapping [6], so we can perform similarity search algorithm based on the Pyramid-Technique. Figure 1 shows the process of data clustering and transforming.

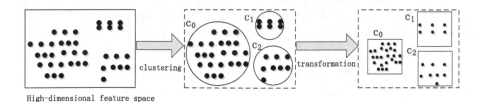

High-dimensional feature space

Fig. 1. The process of data clustering and transforming

Thirdly, we map high-dimensional data objects in each subspace into one-dimensional values and index them. For each hyper-cube shaped subspace, we utilize the Pyramid-Technique to map the data objects. We firstly number each subspace with subspace number i. Then we use the Pyramid-Technique to map data objects in each subspace respectively. For an m-dimensional subspace C_i, we partition the subspace into 2 m hyper-pyramids with the subspace center as their common top, and number the pyramids counterclockwise with pyramid-number j. For a high-dimensional data object v in pyramid j of subspace i, we compute the height h_v (to its top) and map v into a one-dimensional value $p_v = i + j + (0.5 - h_v)$. Using the above method, we can map all data objects in feature space into a one-dimensional space. Finally, we index the one-dimensional space using the B+-tree, the high-dimensional data objects and the corresponding one-dimensional keys are stored in the data pages of the B+-tree. The mapping of the data objects is shown in the Fig. 2.

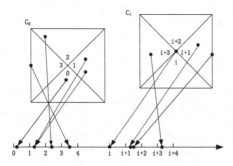

Fig. 2. Mapping of the data objects

3.3   Semantics-Based Similarity Search

In the feature space, the semantics-similar data objects are near to each other, so we can utilize the distance information to discover data objects that are semantics-similar to a given query q. In this section, we mainly study the range query.

The range query is a very popular similarity search algorithm. In this paper, the range query can be realized as follows: firstly extract the features of the query and express it as a multi-dimensional point in feature space; secondly determine the searching spaces and abandon the space that does not intersected with the query range; finally scan the data objects in searching spaces to find the right answers. The range query can be realized by the following algorithm:

Algorithm 1 Semantics-based range search

---

1.   Read the range query RangeQuery (D, q, r, M).

2.   Map the query range to one-dimensional space.

3.   Determine which subspaces are affected with the range query according to the intersected zone in one-dimensional space.

4.   Determine the searching spaces by reversely mapping the intersected zone to multi-dimensional feature space.

5.   Scan the data objects in the searching spaces, find the final answers to the query q.

---

4 Performance Evaluation

In this section, we evaluate the effectiveness and efficiency of our method by analyzing the experimental results. We implement the range query based on our method in C, and chose the sequential scan and Pyramid-Technique as the reference algorithms. We choose a computer with Intel(R) Core (TM) 2 Quad CPU Q8300 2.5 GHz and 4 GB RAM, and the operating system is CentOS 5. For each experiment, we run 20 times and computed the average results as the final experimental results. For the input data set, we generate synthetically a series of clustered data sets of different data sizes and different dimensionality. The dimensionalities of the data sets are respectively 16, 32, 64 and 128, and the data size of them varies from 100000 to 2000000. We compare the response time of our method with the two reference algorithms in the same conditions. The experimental results are shown in the Figs. 3 and 4.

As shown in the Fig. 3, the input data set is a clustered 32-dimensional data set with data size varying from 100000 to 2000000, and the data set has 8 natural clusters. We can observe from the Fig. 3 that the response time of the three methods increases with the data size, while the response time of our method is less than the sequential scan and the Pyramid-Technique.

As shown in the Fig. 4, we observe the response time with the dimensionality of feature space varying from 16 to 128. Here we choose the input data set with 1000000 data objects and 8 natural clusters. We can observe that the response time of three methods increases with the dimensionality of feature space, and the sequential scan may be faster than the Pyramid-Technique when the dimensionality is high enough, but our method is more efficient than the other methods. The experimental results from Figs. 3 and 4 show that our method can effectively find the semantics-similar data objects to a given query.

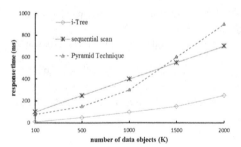

Fig. 3. Effects of data size

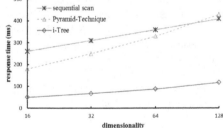

Fig. 4. Effects of dimensionality

5 Conclusion

In this paper, we proposed an efficient unsavory data detection method for Internet big data. To realize semantics-based similarity search of various unsavory data, we express the data objects as high-dimensional points in feature. To solve the problem of "curse of dimensionality" caused by the high dimensionality of feature space, we used the PCA to reduce the dimensionality of feature space. By partitioning the feature space into subspaces and transform them into unit hyper-cubes, we could utilize the Pyramid-Technique to index the data objects and realize efficient semantics-based similarity search. Finally, the performance evaluation results revealed that our method could efficiently discover the semantics-similar data objects to a given query.

Acknowledgment. The work described in this paper is partially supported by the grants of the National Basic Research Program of China (973 project) under Grant No. 2009CB320503, 2012CB315906; the project of National Science Foundation of China under grant No. 61070199, 61103189, 61103194, 61103182, 61202488, 61272482; the National High Technology Research and Development Program of China (863 Program) No. 2011AA01A103, 2012AA01A506, 2013AA013505, the Re-search Fund for the Doctoral Program of Higher Education of China under Grant No. 20114307110006, 20124307120032, the program for Changjiang Scholars and Innovative Research Team in University (No. IRT1012), Science and Technology Innovative Research Team in Higher Educational Institutions of Hunan Province ("network technology").

References

1. Fedorchenko, A., Kotenko, I., Chechulin, A.: Integrated repository of security information for network security evaluation. JoWUA **6**(2), 41–57 (2015)
2. Shahzad, R.K., Lavesson, N.: Comparative analysis of voting schemes for ensemble-based malware detection. JoWUA **4**(1), 98–117 (2013)
3. Skovoroda, A., Gamayunov, D.: Securing mobile devices: malware mitigation methods. JoWUA **6**(2), 78–97 (2015)
4. Zhan, Y., Yin, J., Liu, X.: A convergent solution to matrix bidirectional projection based feature extraction with application to face recognition. Int. J. Comput. Intell. Syst. **4**(5), 863–873 (2011)
5. Bohm, C.: Searching in high-dimensional spaces: index structures for improving the performance of multimedia databases. ACM Comput. Surv. **33**, 322–373 (2001)
6. Zhang, R., Ooi, B.C., Tan, K.L.: Making the pyramid technique robust to query types and workloads. In: Data Engineering 2004, p. 313 (2006)
7. Jagadish, H.V., Ooi, B.C.: iDistance techniques. In: Encyclopedia of GIS, pp. 469–471. Springer, New York (2008)
8. Zhan, Y., Yin, J.: Robust local tangent space alignment via iterative weighted PCA. Neurocomputing **74**(11), 1985–1993 (2011)

Identification of Corrupted Cloud Storage in Batch Auditing for Multi-Cloud Environments

Sooyeon Shin, Seungyeon Kim, and Taekyoung Kwon[✉]

Graduate School of Information, Yonsei University, Seoul 120-749, Korea
{shinsy80,tribunus000,taekyoung}@yonsei.ac.kr

Abstract. In cloud storage services, users can store their data in remote cloud servers. Due to new and challenging security threats toward outsourced data, remote data integrity checking has become a crucial technology in cloud storage services. Recently, many integrity checking protocols have been proposed. Several protocols support batch auditing, but they do not support efficient identification when batch auditing fails. In this paper, we propose a new identification method for the corrupted cloud in multi-cloud environments without requiring any repeated auditing processes.

Keywords: Cloud computing · Provable data possession · Public auditing · Batch auditing · Identification for the corrupted clouds

1 Introduction

In cloud storage service, users' outsourced data can be lost or corrupted due to outside and inside threats [2,5] but cloud servers might hide data loss incidents by claiming that the data are still correctly in the cloud in order to maintain their reputation. Thus, users need to be able to verify that their outsourced data are correctly stored in the cloud. Recently, many remote integrity checking protocols have been proposed to support public auditability that allows a third party auditor to verify the correctness of outsourced data on demand without retrieving a copy of the whole data [1,3,6–12]. As cloud computing has been widely adopted, a third party auditor may take charge of multiple auditing delegations from different users. To improve auditor efficiency, several protocols support batch auditing, which allows the auditor to simultaneously handle multiple auditing delegations from a large number of different users [3,8–10,12]. For batch auditing, multiple proofs on distinct data of different users are aggregated into a single proof. If a single data block or authenticator has been corrupted or discarded, batch auditing will fail and the benefits of batch auditing could

This research was supported by the MSIP(Ministry of Science, ICT and Future Planning), Korea, under the ITRC(Information Technology Research Center) support program (IITP-2015-H8501-15-1008) supervised by the IITP(Institute for Information & communications Technology Promotion).

© IFIP International Federation for Information Processing 2015
I. Khalil et al. (Eds.): ICT-EurAsia 2015 and CONFENIS 2015, LNCS 9357, pp. 221–225, 2015.
DOI: 10.1007/978-3-319-24315-3_22

be canceled out. Wang et al. suggested a divide-and-conquer approach (e.g., binary search) in order to identify the corrupted data [9] and Kai et al. recommended an encoding and decoding approach to reduce communication overhead when batch auditing fails [3]. However, both approaches are inefficient because repeated auditing processes are needed.

To address these problems, in this paper, we propose a new identification method for the corrupted cloud based via two batch auditing schemes [9,10] in multi-users and multi-cloud environments. When the data of users on the single cloud are corrupted, our protocol can identify the corrupted cloud without requiring any repeated auditing processes by utilizing an unique indexing value assigned to each cloud server.

We briefly introduce batch auditing and describe our identification method for the corrupted cloud server in Sects. 2 and 3, respectively. In Sect. 4, we conclude this paper.

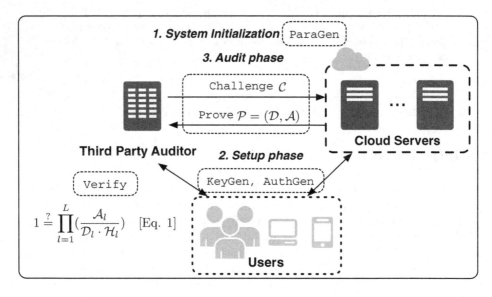

Fig. 1. System model of batch auditing.

2   Batch Auditing

We consider batch auditing for multi-cloud data storage systems involving multi-users and L multi-cloud servers, and the third-party auditor (TPA), as illustrated in Fig. 1. The users store their data in the remote cloud servers and rely on them for data maintenance. Each cloud server $CS_l (1 \leq l \leq L)$ provides powerful storage, computational resources, and the data access to users. The TPA has the expertise and capability to audit data storage on behalf of the user upon request. For batch auditing, we take two batch auditing schemes into consideration: Wang et al's privacy-preserving public auditing scheme (hereafter, W-BA) [9] and

Yang & Jia's efficient and secure dynamic auditing scheme. The original W-BA provides batch auditing for multi-users of single cloud server but it is possible to extend W-BA to support batch auditing for multi-users of multi-cloud servers.

Batch auditing consists of three phases: system initialization, setup, and audit. The system initialization phase involves a ParaGen step to generate system parameters and the setup phase involves KeyGen and AuthGen steps. In KeyGen step, a user generates a key pair (public key and secret key) used for computing authenticators of data. In AuthGen step, the user computes authenticators used for further auditing then stores them with the data in the remote cloud servers. When multi-users of multi-cloud servers request auditing to the TPA, the TPA performs an audit phase through Challenge, Prove, and Verify steps. In Challenge, the TPA randomly selects the number of data blocks for each user and sends a challenge message C to each cloud server involved in batch auditing. In Prove, upon receiving a challenge message, each cloud server sends a response message P as a proof of possession to the TPA. The proof P includes the data proof D and the authenticator proof A. In Verify, upon receiving the proofs from the challenged servers, the TPA performs batch verification to check the correctness of all proofs at the same time. The TPA firstly computes the challenged hash H_l for each cloud server in the challenged servers and simultaneously verifies all proofs via [Eq. 1] in Fig. 1. If the batch verification holds, it means that all challenged servers correctly maintain the data of users.

3   Identification for Single Corrupted Cloud

Batch verification only holds when all of the proofs are valid and fails when there is even one invalid proof of single user in batch auditing. In many situations, a proof collection may contain invalid proofs caused by malicious cloud server or accidental data corruption. If the batch verification equation ([Eq. 1]) fails, it means that a proof of single cloud server is invalid. In this case, the TPA runs Identify step to determine which server's proof is invalid.

1. The TPA sequentially allocates an index $I_l(I_l = 1, \cdots, \pi)$ to each CS_l, where π is the number of challenged cloud servers. For example, the second server in the challenged servers has 2 as the index.
2. Let T is the right side of [Eq. 1]. By exponentiation of the corresponding index I_l for each cloud server CS_l, the TPA computes T' as

$$T' = \prod_{l=1}^{L}(\frac{A_l}{H_l \cdot D_l})^{I_l}   [Eq. 2].$$

3. When the data of a single server CS_o are corrupted, T will be Δo, the difference between the original data and the corrupted data . Similarly, T' will be Δo^{I_o}, the I_o-th power of Δo. The TPA can identify the corrupted server by multiplying T by T until the result equals to T' where $T' \overset{?}{=} \prod_{i=1}^{I_l} T$. Consequentially, $M - 1$ will be the index for the corrupted server CS_o, where M is the number of multiplications.

There can be several cases of corruption as follows: only data blocks are corrupted or discarded, only authenticators are corrupted or discarded, and both data blocks and authenticators are corrupted or discarded. To hide those corruptions and to deceive the TPA, the malicious cloud server may generate the proof using the user's another valid and uncorrupted pairs (data block and the corresponding authenticator), another user's pairs, random data blocks, or the previous proof. Δo can have several forms according to the above cases. However, it is possible for the proposed method to identify the corrupted server regardless of the forms of Δo.

4   Conclusion and Future Work

In this paper, we proposed a new identification method for the corrupted cloud in multi-users and multi-cloud environments. When the data of users on the single cloud are corrupted and thus batch auditing fails, our method can identify the corrupted cloud without requiring any repeated auditing processes by utilizing an unique index for each cloud server.

As part of future work, we would analyze the performance of the proposed identification method and compare it with the divide-and-conquer approach [9] and sequential re-verification for each server one by one.

References

1. Ateniece, G., Burns, R., Curtmola, R., Herring, J., Kissner, L., Peterson, Z., Song, D.: Provable data possession at untrusted stores. In: CCS 2007, pp. 598–609. ACM press (2007)
2. Claycomb, W.R., Legg, P.A., Gollmann, D.: Guest editorial: emerging trends in research for insider threat detection. J. Wirel. Mob. Networks Ubiquitous Comput. Dependable Appl. (JoWUA) 5(2), 1–6 (2014)
3. Kai, H., Chuanhe, H., Jinhai, W., Hao, Z., Xi, C., Yilong, L., Lianzhen, Z., Bin, W.: An efficient public batch auditing protocol for data security in multi-cloud storage. In: IEEE ChinaGrid Conference, pp. 51–56. IEEE press (2013)
4. Kammüller, F., Probst, C.W.: Invalidating Policies using Structural Information. J. Wirel. Mob. Networks Ubiquitous Comput. Dependable Appl. (JoWUA) 5(2), 59–79 (2014)
5. Lindauer, B., Glasser, J., Rosen, M., Wallnau, K.: Generating Test Data for Insider Threat Detectors. J. Wirel. Mob. Networks Ubiquitous Comput. Dependable Appl. (JoWUA) 5(2), 80–94 (2014)
6. Shacham, H., Waters, B.: Compact proofs of retrievability. In: Pieprzyk, J. (ed.) ASIACRYPT 2008. LNCS, vol. 5350, pp. 90–107. Springer, Heidelberg (2008)
7. Wang, Q., Wang, C., Li, J., Ren, K., Lou, W.: Enabling public verifiability and data dynamics for storage security in cloud computing. In: Backes, M., Ning, P. (eds.) ESORICS 2009. LNCS, vol. 5789, pp. 355–370. Springer, Heidelberg (2009)
8. Wang, C., Wang, Q., Ren, K., Lou, L.: Privacy-preserving public auditing for data storage security in cloud computing. In: IEEE INFOCOM 2010, pp. 525–533. IEEE Press, New York (2010)

9. Wang, C., Chow, S.S.-M., Wang, Q., Ren, K., Lou, W.: Privacy- preserving public auditing for secure cloud storage. IEEE Trans. Comput. **62**(2), 362–375 (2013)
10. Yang, K., Jia, X.: An efficient and secure dynamic auditing protocol for data storage in cloud computing. IEEE Trans. Parallel Distrib. Syst. **24**(9), 1717–1726 (2013)
11. Zhu, Y., Wang, H., Hu, Z., Ahn, G.-J., Hu, H., Yau, S.S.: Dynamic audit services for integrity verification of outsourced storages in clouds. In: ACM Symposium Applied Computing, pp. 1550–1557. ACM press (2011)
12. Zhu, Y., Hu, H., Ahn, G.-J., Yu, M.: Cooperative provable data possession for integrity verification in multicloud storage. IEEE Trans. Parallel Distrib. Syst. **23**(12), 2231–2244 (2012)

Multimedia Security

Face Recognition Performance Comparison Between Real Faces and Pose Variant Face Images from Image Display Device

Mi-Young Cho[✉] and Young-Sook Jeong

Electronics and Telecommunications Research Institute (ETRI), Daejeon, Korea
{mycho,ysjeong}@etri.re.kr

Abstract. Face recognition technology, unlike other biometric methods, is conveniently accessible with the use of only a camera. Consequently, it has created an enormous interest in a variety of applications, including face identification, access control, security, surveillance, smart cards, law enforcement, human computer interaction. However, face recognition system is still not robust enough, especially in unconstrained environments, and recognition accuracy is still not acceptable. In this paper, to measure performance reliability of face recognition systems, we expand performance comparison test between real faces and face images from the recognition perspective and verify the adequacy of performance test methods using an image display device.

Keywords: Face recognition · Image display device · Performance evaluation

1 Introduction

Face recognition is a widely used biometric technology because it is more direct, user friendly, and convenient to use than other biometric approaches. Face recognition technology is now significantly advanced, has great potential in the application systems. However, it is difficult to guarantee of performance due to insufficient test methods in real environment. The best method is direct evaluation from human subjects in real environment. Unfortunately, in this case, it would be considered impossible to consistently obtain the same way for a lengthy period of time a certain number of persons. That is, it's difficult to guarantee objectivity and reproducibility.

There are many approaches for performance evaluation of the face recognition in the system level including methods using an algorithm [1], a mannequin [2], and a high-definition photograph [3]. The first method simply evaluates the performance of an algorithm installed in a face recognition system. However, the performance of an algorithm cannot guarantee the performance of a face recognition system. The second method uses mannequin instead of real human face. This method has a number of problems because the material coating the mannequin is not the same as human skin. Last, the method using a high-definition photograph has overcome some of the existing problems. However, it still experiences minor difficulties with automatic control interoperation with a computer, and a lack of reproducibility in real situations.

I. Khalil et al. (Eds.): ICT-EurAsia 2015 and CONFENIS 2015, LNCS 9357, pp. 229–234, 2015.
DOI: 10.1007/978-3-319-24315-3_23

In this paper, we expand performance comparison test between real faces and face images from the recognition perspective and verify the adequacy of performance test methods using an image display device. The paper is organized as follows: in Sect. 2, we explain limitation of precious works. Section 3 describes how to construct the facial DB. In Sect. 4, we show and analyze the experimental results. Section 5 concludes this paper.

2 Previous Works

In the previous works, we have introduced performance evaluation method of face recognition using face images from a high definition monitor and prove similarity between real faces and face images [4, 10]. However, the previous work has a limitation to reflect performance in real environments as it is a test only using frontal pose images.

Recognizing faces reliably across changes in pose and illumination has proved to be a much more difficult problem [11]. So, we need verification about the proposed test method according to not only illumination but also pose. In this paper, we expand previous works and compare face recognition performance according to various poses (Fig. 1).

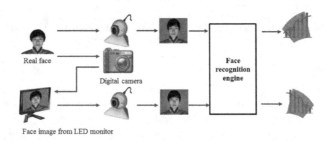

Fig. 1. Previous works.

3 Facial DB

The majority of facial images used to evaluate face recognition algorithms such as Feret [5], PF07 [6], and CMU PIE [7] could be used for the proposed test method. However, most images are not adequate because of the low-resolution output of the image display device. To overcome this challenge, high-resolution facial DB was required.

To obtain subject images under various pose conditions, seven cameras were used. The locations of cameras are shown in Fig. 2. We took ultra-high definition images using a Sony Nex 7 so that the face area took up at least two thirds of the whole area of the image. The height of the camera was fixed, and we controlled the height of the chair depending on the subject's height.

We captured 4200 real face images from 60 subjects, which were captured under ten different lighting directions and seven pose for each subject. Figure 3 shows sample images for one subject.

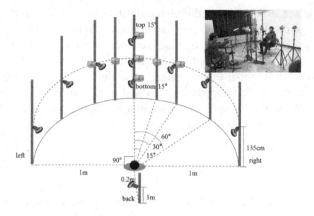

Fig. 2. Environment for capturing real face images.

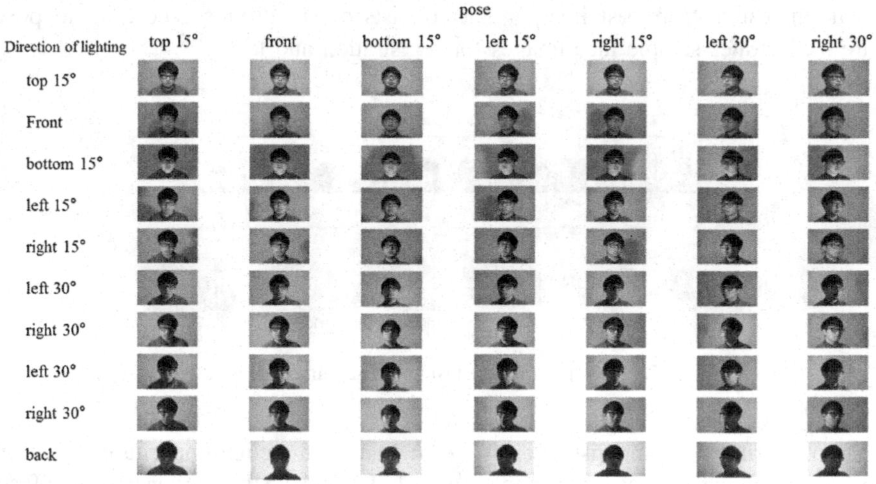

pose

Direction of lighting	top 15°	front	bottom 15°	left 15°	right 15°	left 30°	right 30°
top 15°							
Front							
bottom 15°							
left 15°							
right 15°							
left 30°							
right 30°							
left 30°							
right 30°							
back							

Fig. 3. Sample images for one subject.

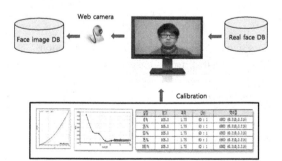

Fig. 4. Procedure for building face image DB.

To the re-capture, we displayed the high definition images captured with a camera on a 27-inch image display device to provide an output similar to a real face. The image display device was calibrated and characterized according to the ISO 15076-1:2010 standard [8], which contains the criteria for color management and standard image reproduction. To ensure proper display output, we used 2.2 gamma tone reproduction curve, D65 whitepoint color temperature as stated in IEC 61966-2-1:1999 [9], which contains the sRGB and HDTV color space standards. The procedure for the face image DB construction is presented in Fig. 4.

4   Experiment

This experiment verifies the similarity of real faces and face images from an image display device from the perspective of face recognition performance. In particular, we focused on changes in face recognition performance according to pose. The test engines registered ten frontal pose images under ten lighting conditions and obtained recognition results from test images that consists of six groups according to pose. Figure 5 illustrates sample face images for registration and test.

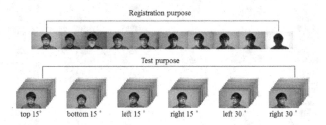

Fig. 5.   Registration and test purpose sample images.

The performance comparison results from four face recognition engines that are used for commercial purposes are shown Table 1. To analyze the similarity of real faces and the facial images captured from the image display device, recognition rate deviations were analyzed. As a result, the maximum deviation between the real facial and face images is 1.56.

Table 1.   Overall results.

Engine	Face recognition rate(%)		deviation
	Real faces	Face images	
A	97.09	95.90	1.19
B	98.96	99.01	0.05
C	97.78	98.23	0.45
D	87.62	86.06	1.56

Figure 6 shows performance changes according to the pose for each engine. Engine A and B get results from all test images, other engines get those from face images of only 4 poses(top/bottom/left/right 15°) because of coverage. The x-axis represents recognition rate and the y-axis represents pose. The number means recognition rate deviations between real faces and face images. Although each engine exhibited different recognition performance according to pose, the deviations between the real face and face images were all less than 3 %. In other words, there is no significant difference in face recognition performance when using face images instead of real faces.

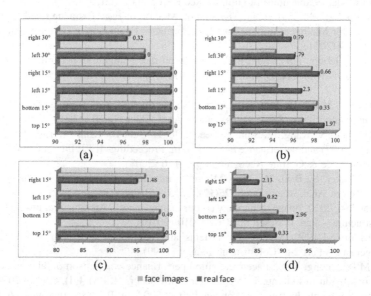

Fig. 6. Performance changes according to the pose for (a) Engine A. (b) Engine B. (c) Engine C. (d) Engine D.

5 Conclusion

In this paper, we expand the previous works and verified the similarity of real face and face images from an image display device by comparing face recognition performance changes according to pose. Based on the comparison results using an image display device, the proposed method can be applied to the face recognition performance evaluation in system level.

Acknowledgments. This work is partly supported by the R&D program of the Korea Ministry of Trade, Industry and Energy (MOTIE) and the Korea Evaluation Institute of Industrial Technology (KEIT). (Project: Technology Development of service robot's performance and standardization for movement/manipulation/HRI/Networking, 10041834).

References

1. TTAK.KO-10.0418, Performance Evaluation Method of Face Extraction and Identification Algorithm for Intelligent Robots: Part 1 Performance Evaluation of Recognition Algorithm (2010)
2. TTAK.KO-10.0419, Performance Evaluation Method of Face Extraction and Identification Algorithm for Intelligent Robots: Part 2. System Level Performance Evaluation using Human Model (mannequin) of Human Face Recognition (2010)
3. TTAK.KO-10.0507, Performance Evaluation Method of Face Extraction and Identification Algorithm for Intelligent Robots: Part 3. Performance Evaluation of Face Recognition using Face Photos (2011)
4. Cho, M.Y., Jeong, Y.S., Chun, B.T.: A study on face recognition performance comparison of real images with images from LED monitor. J. Inst. Electron. Eng. Korea **50**(5), 1164–1169 (2013)
5. Phillips, P.J., Moon, H., Rauss, P.J., Rizvi, S.: The FERET evaluation methodology for face recognition algorithms. IEEE Trans. Pattern Anal. Mach. Intell. **22**(10), 1090–1104 (2000)
6. Lee, H., Park, S., Kang, B., Shin, J., Lee, J., Je, H., Jun, B., Kim, D.: The POSTECH face database (PF07) and performance evaluation. In: Proceedings IEEE International Conference Automatic Face & Gesture Recognition, pp. 1–6 (2008)
7. Sim, T., Baker, S., Bsat, M.: The CMU pose, illumination, and expression database. IEEE Trans. Pattern Anal. Mach. Intell. **25**(12), 1615–1618 (2003)
8. ISO 15076-1:2010, Image technology colour management – Architecture, profile format and data structure – Part 1: Based on ICC.1:2010 (2010)
9. IEC 61966-2-1:1999, Multimedia systems and equipment – Colour measurement and management – Part 2-1: Colour management (1999)
10. Cho, M.-Y., Jeong, Y.-S.: Face recognition performance comparison of fake faces with real faces in relation to lighting. J. Internet Serv. Inf. Secur. (JISIS) **4**(4), 82–90 (2014)
11. Phillips, P.J., et al.: Face recognition vendor test 2002. In: IEEE International Workshop on Analysis and Modeling of Faces and Gestures, AMFG 2003. IEEE (2003)

A Lossless Data Hiding Strategy Based on Two-Dimensional Side-Match Predictions

Chi-Yao Weng[1], Sheng-Jie Wang[2], and Shiuh-Jeng Wang[2(✉)]

[1] Department of Computer Science,
National Pingtung University, Pingtung 90004, Taiwan
[2] Department of Information Management,
Central Police University, Taoyuan 33304, Taiwan
sjwang@mail.cpu.edu.tw

Abstract. The histogram-based reversible data hiding scheme (RDH) generated a one-dimensional (1D) histogram distribution. In this article, based on two-dimensional (2D) histogram distribution, a framework of reversible data hiding is proposed by using two side-match predictors, called as Forward side-match (FSM) and Backward side-match (BSM). First, by considering each predicted pixel value, we use two side-match predictors to obtain two prediction error distributions. A slope meter is computed by the differencing of two distributions. Then, a two dimensional histogram is generated by composing of BSM distribution and slope meter. Based on the 2D, more specified spaces can be found to enhance the performance. The experimental results demonstrated that our proposed scheme can achieve better performance in terms of both marked image quality and embedding capacity than that of conventional works.

Keywords: Reversible data hiding (RDH) scheme · Two dimensional histogram distribution · Side-match predictor

1 Introduction

Data hiding is an advanced technology for protecting the message with integrity and security from data transmission in a public network [1]. The secret information is capable of being hidden into some media, such as an image, audio or video data, using the well-known data hiding scheme. In general, for different target, the data hiding scheme can be classified into two categories. One is non-reversible data hiding scheme [2–4]. The non-reversible data hiding scheme aims to protect the hidden data for secret communication. The conventional LSBs (least signification bit substitution) is a simple and easy technology of non-reversible data hiding scheme. For example of 1-bit LSBs method, a secret bit is to be embedded into 1-rightmost bit of the cover pixel. The other is reversible data hiding (RDH) scheme [5–16]. The goal of RDH algorithm is to obtain both cover media and hidden data that can be recovered and extracted from stego media. It indicates that the distortion of cover media is intolerable when secret message is extracted. RDH can be widely applied into some applications, such as military, medical, or legal document.

Many RDH techniques have been developed in present. It can be divided into three categories, namely, histogram-based [5–8], difference expansion [9–12], and prediction

© IFIP International Federation for Information Processing 2015
I. Khalil et al. (Eds.): ICT-EurAsia 2015 and CONFENIS 2015, LNCS 9357, pp. 235–242, 2015.
DOI: 10.1007/978-3-319-24315-3_24

error [13–16]. Ni et al. first proposed a reversible data hiding based on histogram shifting in 2006 [5]. In their method, the histogram distribution is fist generated from an input image. After that, shift and conceal the secret bits into the selected range from histogram distribution. Ni's approach performed a good quality in the stego image because pixel shifting and data concealing are only shifted by one unit. Although histogram-based approach is simplicity and provides high image quality, the number of embedding capacity is limited in the height of peak point. Later on, more efficient algorithms have been invented for improving the embedding capacity limitation [6–8].

The second category is difference expansion. In 2003, Tian proposed a reversible data hiding scheme based difference expansion (DE) [9]. Tain's method expands the two pixel differencing for data concealing. The maximal embedding ratio based on DE is near to 0.5 bpp (bit per pixel) for one layer embedding. Some researchers are focused on investigation and developing high-fidelity reversible data hiding scheme [10–12].

The histogram-based approach and difference expansion method can perform lossless data hiding, but their performance might be limited within the media context. A basic idea is to review their drawback and develop suitable strategy for promoting the performance in terms of embedding capacity and image quality. The prediction error is a good strategy for both histogram-based approach and difference expansion method to devise a new method of improving the performance. A local prediction reversible data hiding combined prediction error and difference expansion is proposed by Drago and Coltur in 2014 [13]. Drago and Colutr's approach utilized least square predictor to obtain the prediction error, then, expend the prediction error for data hiding. This approach has better performance than that of DE method. Later on, more researchers are developed the efficient approaches for obtaining higher performance [14–16].

In reviewing above-mention reversible data hiding scheme, a framework of reversible data hiding is proposed. Our main contribution is to build 2D histogram distribution based on two side-match predictors and slope meter. 2D histogram distribution can collect more information and find out more spaces for date embedding, resulting in high embedding capacity. Our proposed can be extended into multi-dimensional framework in future.

The rest of the paper is organized as follows. The related works about histogram shifting scheme are briefly introduced in Sect. 2. Section 3 presents our proposed scheme in detail. The experimental result is illustrated in Sect. 4. Finally, the conclusion is concludes in Sect. 5.

2   Related Works

In this subsection, we will review the reversible data hiding scheme based on histogram shifting. The histogram shifting scheme, named as histogram-based, is introduced in 2006. Ni et al.'s approach found out that each cover image has its pixel distribution. Firstly, they applied the statistic function to account each pixel number, the histogram distribution is thus generated. Next, find out the range of peak point and zero point from this distribution. In the end, shift and conceal the data into the range of peak point and zero point. The detail algorithm of histogram-based is shown as below.

Input: Cover image CI, each pixel value $x \in [0.255]$, secret message $SM = b_1b_2b_3 \ldots b_n$, $b_i \in \{0,1\}$.
Output: Stego image SI, a pair information (peak point, zero point).

Step 1: Generate a histogram distribution $H(x)$ from an inputted image. Where, Fig. 1 is an example of histogram distribution using Lena image.

Step 2: Find out a pair-data (P, Z) from the histogram distribution. Notable, P indicates the maximum number of pixels in this distribution. Z means no pixel or minimum pixel in this distribution.

Step 3: Shift all the pixels x within the range of peak point and zero point by one unit. Note, the Fig. 2 shows the result after pixel shifting operation. The shifting function is given as following.

$$\begin{cases} x' = x + 1, \text{if } Z > P \text{ and } x \in [P + 1, Z] \\ x' = x - 1, \text{if } P > Z \text{ and } x \in [Z, P - 1] \end{cases} \quad (1)$$

Step 4: Scan all pixels in the cover image, once the pixel value meets the P value, and then, check the secret bits. If the secret bit is "0", the pixel value remains unchanged. If the secret bit is "1", the pixels value is changed by one unit according to following data concealing function

$$\begin{cases} x' = x + 1, \text{if } Z > P \\ x' = x - 1, \text{if } P > Z \end{cases} \quad (2)$$

Finally, output all the scanned pixel as the stego pixel (stego image). Notably, the stego pixel can be performed the processes of data extracting and pixel recovering since a pair-data (P, Z) is received. For the data extracting, the secret bit will be extracted when the inputted pixel meets the value of P or $P + 1$. In other words, the hidden bits can be successfully retrieved. For the concept of pixel recovering, each inputted pixel can run the inverse of shifting operation to recover the pixel value as an original pixel.

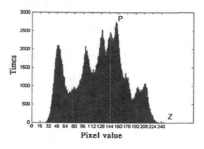

Fig. 1. The example of pixel distribution using Lena as cover image

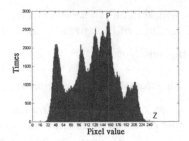

Fig. 2. The example of pixel shifting using Fig. 1.

3   Our Proposed Method

In this section, we introduce our reversible data hiding scheme based on 2D histogram modification in detail. The 1D histogram-based approach applied one factor, such as pixel value or prediction error, to generate a factor histogram distribution. Then, modify the highest value in the factor distribution for data concealing. For receiving more efficiency, our proposed scheme uses two prediction error to produce a 2D histogram distribution. More specified cases are to be considered for pursuing more spaces for promoting the embedding capacity. The detail of our data embedding algorithm is shown as below.

Input: Cover image CI with size $M \times N$, $CI = I_{i,j}$, $i = 0$ to $M\text{-}1$, $j =$ to $N\text{-}1$, secret message $SMsg = b_1 b_2 b_3 \dots b_n$, $b_i \in \{0,1\}$.

Output: Marked-image MI, two pair information (PP_0, PZ_0) and (NP_0, NZ_0).

Step 1:   Scan the cover image and run two side-match predictor methods, Forward side-match (FSM) and Backward side-match (BSM), to predict the pixel vale in the image.

Step 1.1:   The FSM prediction algorithm is shown the subsection, and then, compute the prediction error PE_FSM$_{i,j}$ = $PI_{i,j}$ - $I_{i,j}$.

Step 1.1.a: If $i = 0$ and $j = 0$, then $PI_{i,j} = I_{i,j}$ -128.

Step 1.1.b: If $i = 0$, then $PI_{i,j} = I_{i,j} - I_{i,j\text{-}1}$.

Step 1.1.c: If $j = 0$, then $PI_{i,j} = I_{i,j} - I_{i\text{-}1,j}$.

Step 1.1.d: Else, $PI_{i,j} = I_{i,j}$ - int (average $(I_{i\text{-}1,j} + I_{i\text{-}1,j\text{-}1} + I_{i,j\text{-}1})$).

Step 1.2:   The Backward side-match (BSM) prediction algorithm is shown the subsection, and calculate the prediction error PE_BSM$_{i,j}$ = $PI_{i,j}$ - $I_{i,j}$.

Step 1.2.a: If $i = 0$ and $j = M\text{-}1$, then $PI_{i,j} = I_{i,j}$ -128.

Step 1.2.b: If $i = 0$, then $PI_{i,j} = I_{i,j} - I_{i,j+1}$.

Step 1.2.c: If $j = 0$ and $j \neq 0$, then $PI_{i,j} = I_{i,j} - I_{i\text{-}1,j}$.

Step 1.2.d: Else, $PI_{i,j} = I_{i,j}$ - int (average $(I_{i\text{-}1,j} + I_{i,j\text{-}1})$).

Step 1.3:   Obtain each slope meter SM from computing the difference of PE_BSM$_{i,j}$ and PE_FSM$_{i,j}$, where $SM_{i,j}$ = PE_FSM$_{i,j}$ — PE_BSM$_{i,j}$.

Step 2: Let $(SM_{i,j}, PE\_FSM_{i,j})$ denotes a 2D value, and collect all 2D values to generate a 2D histogram distribution, $H(SM_{i,j}, PE\_FSM_{i,j})$.

Step 3: Find two pair information (PP_0, PZ_0) and (NP_0, NZ_0) from 2D histogram distribution. Where a pair information (PP_0, PZ_0) is selected in the positive regions of 2D histogram distribution. In the same way, a pair information (NP_0, NZ_0) is picked by the negative positive regions of 2D histogram distribution.

Step 4: Shift all the prediction error $PE\_FSM_{i,j}$ by 1 unit according to following function.

$$PE\_FSM'_{i,j} = \begin{cases} PE\_FSM_{i,j} + 1, PE\_FSM_{i,j} \in [PP_0 + 1, PZ_0] \\ PE\_FSM_{i,j} - 1, \quad PE\_FSM_{i,j} \in [NZ_0, NP_0 - 1] \end{cases} \quad (3)$$

Step 5: Scan all the $PE\_FSM_{i,j}$ and fetch each secret bits from secret message $SMsg$, and then, conceal the secret bitstring into $PE\_FSM_{i,j}$ value while $SM_{i,j}$ precisely equals to "0" and the $PE\_FSM_{i,j}$ equals to the peak values, PP_0 and NP_0. The data concealing function is listing as below.

$$PE\_FSM'_{i,j} = \begin{cases} PE\_FSM_{i,j} + 1, PE\_FSM_{i,j} = PP_0 \text{ and } b_i = 1 \\ PE\_FSM_{i,j}, PE\_FSM_{i,j} = PP_0 \text{ and } b_i = 0 \\ PE\_FSM_{i,j}, PE\_FSM_{i,j} = ZP_0 \text{ and } b_i = 0 \\ PE\_FSM_{i,j} - 1, PE\_FSM_{i,j} = ZP_0 \text{ and } b_i = 1 \end{cases}$$

$$PE\_FSM'_{i,j} = \begin{cases} PE\_FSM_{i,j} + 1, PE\_FSM_{i,j} = PP_0 \text{ and } b_i = 1 \\ PE\_FSM_{i,j}, PE\_FSM_{i,j} = PP_0 \text{ and } b_i = 0 \\ PE\_FSM_{i,j}, PE\_FSM_{i,j} = ZP_0 \text{ and } b_i = 0 \\ PE\_FSM_{i,j} - 1, PE\_FSM_{i,j} = ZP_0 \text{ and } b_i = 1 \end{cases} \quad (4)$$

Step 6: Recover the marked prediction error value ($PE\_FSM_{i,j}$) to be a stego-pixel (SPI) according the inverse of Forward side-match (FSM) predictor, where the inverse algorithm is given as below.

Step 6.1: If $i = 0$ and $j = 0$, then $SPI_{i,j} = PE\_FSM_{i,j} + 128$.

Step 6.2: If $i = 0$, then $SPI_{i,j} = PE\_FSM_{i,j} + I_{i,j-1}$.

Step 6.3: If $j = 0$, then $SPI_{i,j} = PE\_FSM_{i,j} + I_{i-1,j}$.

Step 6.4: Else, $SPI_{i,j} = PE\_FSM_{i,j} + int$ (average $(I_{i-1,j} + I_{i-1,j-1} + I_{i,j-1})$).

All the marked prediction error values are fully to be recovered, the marked image (MI) is therefore outputted.

The data extracting procedure is similar with the data embedding procedure. Two prediction methods, FSM and BSM, are also used in the extracting process. The extracting process is the inverse of the data embedding procedure. After running the data extracting procedure, the secret message is completely obtained and the image is successfully recovered.

4   Experiment Results

In section, we demonstrate the simulations of our proposed scheme. Five 512 × 512 images, including Lena, Airplane, Pepper, Boat, and Goldhill (See Fig. 3) are used in our simulations. The secret bitstring in our simulation is generated by the random number generator. We also employ the commonly measure function peak-signal-to-noise-ratio (PSNR) and MSE as a evaluate tool for comparing the visual quality between the cover image and marked image. The measure functions are given as following.

$$PSNR(db) = 10 \times log_{10}\left(\frac{Max^2}{MSE}\right) \quad (5)$$

$$MSE = \frac{1}{W \times H}\sum_{x=1}^{W}\sum_{y=1}^{H}\left((I(x,y)) - (I'(x,y))\right)^2 \quad (6)$$

where W and H are defined as the width and height of the image. $I(x, y)$ and $I'(x, y)$ indicates the values of cover image and marked image, respectively. The Max means the maximum value of cover image. Here, our cover image is gray level image, thus, the Max value in gray level is 255(= 2^8).

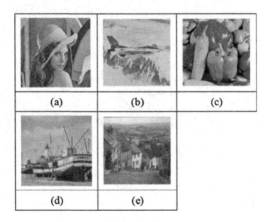

Fig. 3. The five cover images. (a)Lean; (b)Airplane; (c)Pepper; (d)Boat; (e)Goldhill

To obtain a better knowledge of how different cover image impact the performance of the proposed RDH scheme, we compare our experimental results with the recent RDH scheme, the comparison result is illustrated in Table 1. From this comparison, our scheme has better performance in terms of high embedding capacity and good image quality than that of existing RDH methods. The side match predictor applied the neighbor pixels to predict the prediction value. Generally speaking, in a nature image, the current pixel is very similar with its neighbor pixels. Assume that we use side match manner to predict the value, we can obtain an accuracy prediction. It leads that more and more prediction errors are falling into zero space. This is a reason that our side match predictor explores the advantage of prediction error to create more space for data concealing.

Table 1. The performance comparison with various approaches

	Ni et al.'s [5]	Tsai et al.'s [7]	Li et al.'s [14]	Our approach
Lean	0.02	0.18	0.23	0.25
Airplane	0.07	0.25	0.30	0.29
Pepper	0.02	0.18	0.24	0.23
Boat	0.04	0.17	0.19	0.22
Goldhill	0.02	0.13	0.19	0.17
Avag. Capacity (bpp)	0.034	0.182	0.230	0.232
Avag. PSNR (db)	48.30	48.7+	48.47	49.32

5 Conclusion

In this paper, based on two side match predictors and two peaks histogram embedding, an efficient reversible data hiding scheme is proposed. The key point is to build 2D histogram based on two side match predictors and slope meter. The slope meter is used to estimate the differencing of two prediction errors. Based on accurate prediction and selecting two peak points, our proposed scheme provides more spaces for enhancing embedding capacity, the evidence can be seen in the performance evaluation. From the experimental result, it shows that our proposed approach is superior over some histogram-based works.

Acknowledgment. This work was supported in part by the Ministry of Science and Technology, Taiwan, under Contract MOST 103-2221-E-015-002- and MOST 104-2221-E-015-001-.

References

1. Bender, W., Gruhl, D., Morimote, N., Lu, A.: Techniques for data hiding. IBM Syst. J. **35**(3–4), 313–316 (1996)
2. Chan, C.K., Chen, L.M.: Hiding data in images by simple LSB substitution. Pattern Recogn. **37**(3), 469–474 (2004)
3. Sun, H.M., Weng, C.Y., Wang, S.J., Yang, C.H.: Data embedding in image-media using weight-function on modulo operation. ACM Trans. Embed. Comput. Syst. **12**(2), 1–12 (2013)
4. Maleki, N., Jalail, M., Jahan, M.V.: Adaptive and non-adaptive data hiding methods for grayscale images based on modulus function. Egypt. Inform. J. **15**(2), 115–127 (2014)
5. Ni, Z.C., Shi, Y.Q., Ansari, N., Su, W.: Reversible data hiding. IEEE Trans. Circuits Syst Video Technol. **16**(3), 354–362 (2006)

6. Tai, W.L., Yeh, C.M., Chang, C.C.: Reversible data hiding based on histogram modification of pixel differences. IEEE Trans. Circuits Syst. Video Technol. **19**(6), 906–910 (2009)
7. Tsai, P., Hu, Y.C., Yeh, H.L.: Reversible image hiding scheme using predictive coding and histogram shifting. Sig. Process. **89**(6), 1129–1143 (2009)
8. Tain, J.: Reversible data embedding using a difference expansion. IEEE Trans. Circuits Syst. Video Technol. **13**(8), 890–896 (2003)
9. Kim, H.J., Sachnev, V., Shi, Y.Q., Nam, J., Choo, H.G.: A novel difference expansion transform for reversible data embedding. IEEE Trans. Inf. Forensics Secur. **3**(3), 456–465 (2008)
10. Alattar, M.: Reversible watermark using the difference expansion of a generalized integer transform. IEEE Trans. Image Process. **13**(8), 1147–1156 (2004)
11. Sachnev, V., Kim, H.J., Nam, J., Suresh, S., Shi, Y.Q.: Reversible watermarking algorithm using sorting and prediction. IEEE Trans. Circuits Syst. Video Technol. **19**(7), 989–999 (2009)
12. Wu, H.C., Lee, C.C., Tsai, C.S., Chu, Y.P., Chen, H.R.: A high capacity reversible data hiding scheme with edge prediction and difference expansion. J. Syst. Softw. **82**(12), 1966–1973 (2009)
13. Dragoi, I., Coltuc, D.: Local-prediction-based difference expansion reversible watermarking. IEEE Trans. on Image Processing **23**(4), 1779–1790 (2014)
14. Li, X., Yang, B., Zeng, T.: Efficient reversible watermarking based on adaptive prediction-error expansion and pixel selection. IEEE Trans. Image Process. **20**(12), 3524–3533 (2011)
15. Yang, C.H., Tsai, M.H.: Improving histogram-based reversible data hiding by interleaving predictions. IET Image Process. **4**(4), 223–234 (2010)
16. Wang, S.Y., Li, C.Y., Kuo, W.C.: Reversible data hiding based on two-dimensional prediction errors. IET Image Process. **7**(9), 805–816 (2013)

Secure Image Deduplication in Cloud Storage

Han Gang[1], Hongyang Yan[2(✉)], and Lingling Xu[3]

[1] Admission Office of the Graduate School, Jinan University, Guangzhou, China
[2] School of Mathematics and Information Science, Guangzhou University,
Guangzhou, China
Hyang.Yan@foxmail.com
[3] School of Computer Science and Engineering,
South China University of Technology, Guangzhou, China
1882646352O@163.com

Abstract. With the great development of cloud computing in recent years, the explosive increasing of image data, the mass of information storage, and the application demands for high availability of data, network backup is facing an unprecedented challenge. Image deduplication technology is proposed to reduce the storage space and costs. To protect the confidentiality of the image, the notion of convergent encryption has been proposed. In the deduplication system, the image will be encrypted/decrypted with a convergent encryption key which is derived by computing the hash value of the image content. It means that identical image copies will generate the same ciphertext, which used to check the duplicate image copy. Security analysis makes sure that this system is secure.

Keywords: Cloud computing · Image deduplication · Cloud storage · Security

1 Introduction

With the great development of cloud computing in recent years, the application of information and communication in the Internet has drew more and more attentions. Cloud computing [1] is a new computing paradigm with the dynamic extension ability, through the Internet to on-demand and extensible way of obtaining computing resources and services. It attracts much concern because of its unique technique and the emerging business computing model from the academic and industry.

However, with the explosive increasing of data, the mass of information storage, and the application demands for high availability of data, network backup is facing an unprecedented challenge. On the one hand, human society produce the data information from the Internet. On the other hand, we get the information from the daily production and kinds of scientific experiments (e.g. scientific computing and simulation, flight dynamics, a nuclear blast simulation, space exploration, and medical image data.). The growth of data information produced each day is to the impressive degree. According to the resent analysis

I. Khalil et al. (Eds.): ICT-EurAsia 2015 and CONFENIS 2015, LNCS 9357, pp. 243–251, 2015.
DOI: 10.1007/978-3-319-24315-3_25

report of IDC (International Data Corporation), the whole world produced 281 EB data in 2007, it is corresponded to everyone in the world owns 45 GB data. The world produced the amount of data will be close to 1800 EB, it is ten times than the amount of data in 2006 [2]. And the volume of data in the world is expected to reach 40 trillion GB in 2020 [3].

For above situation, data deduplication technology is proposed recently. Data deduplication technology [4] is a lossless data compression technology, mainly based on the principle of repeated data will be delete. This technology could reduce the cost of data transmission and storage [5]. Especially the image files in the social network, in most cases a celebrity public a message, it will be forwarded more than one thousand times soon. And popular images are also repeated many times. If such store operations occur every time, it certainly will cause waste of storage space. So simple to increase storage capacity does not solve the problem. Image deduplication have to be applied to the social network.

To protect the confidentiality of the image, the notion of convergent encryption [6] has been proposed. In the deduplication system, the image will be encrypted/decrypted with a convergent encryption key which is derived by computing the hash value of the image content [6–8]. It means that identical image copies will generate the same ciphertext, which allows the cloud storage server perform deduplication on the ciphertexts. Furthermore, image user make use of attribute-based encryption scheme to share images with friends by setting the access privileges.

In the rest of the paper is organized as follows. We introduce related work about deduplication in Sect. 2. Some preliminary works are introduced in Sect. 3. The architecture of image deduplication cloud storage system including security analysis will be described in Sect. 4. Finally, we include this paper in Sect. 5.

2   Related Work

There have been a number of deduplication technologies proposed recently. Most researchers focuss on text deduplication like [9]. They proposed a scheme to address the key management in deduplication system. There are different ways according techniques.

Technique based on the file-level deduplication is to delete the same file to reduce the data storage capacity, save storage space. It uses a hash function for each file to compute a hash value. Any two files with the same hash value is considered to be the same file. For example, SIS [10], FarSite [11], EMC Center [12] systems use this method.

Technique based on the block-level deduplication is to delete the same data block to reduce storage space [13]. This method is to divide a file into some data blocks [14], and uses hash functions compute the hash value, which be named as block fingerprint. Any two data block with the same block fingerprint are defined duplicate data block [15].

Based on the deduplication delete time, deduplication technology could divided to on-line deduplication [16] and post-processing deduplication [17].

On-line deduplication is to delete the duplicate data before storing, the storage service always stores a unique data copy. Post6-processing deduplication needs additional storage buffer to realize delete repeated data.

Based on the deduplication delete place, it can be divided to client deduplication [18] and service deduplication [19]. Client deduplication is before transferring the data copy to cloud server, user check and delete duplicate data. Service deduplication is performing duplicate data check and delete with service's resource in cloud server.

However, multi-media data like images, videos are larger than text. So image deduplication is becoming more important. Researchers have pay attention to this field like [20]. We have to handle the images before uploading them to server, a general way is watermarking [21, 22]. Compression technique save the space of cloud storage in some way, but deduplication will address this problem from the root.

3 Preliminaries

3.1 Bilinear Mapping

Definition 1. Let G_1, G_2 be two cyclic groups of the number q(q is a prime number.), g is a generating element of G_1, a bilinear map is a map $e : G_1 \times G_1 \rightarrow G_2$ which satisfies the following three properties:

- Bilinear: $e(g_1^a, g_2^b) = e(g_1, g_2)^{ab}$ for all $a, b \in \mathbb{Z}_p$ and $g_1, g_2 \in G_1$.
- Non-degenerate: $e(g, g) \neq 1$
- computable: $e(g_1, g_2)$ can be computed effectively with an algorithm for all $g_1, g_2 \in G_1$. so e is an efficient bilinear mapping from G_1 to G_2.

3.2 Access Structure

Let $P = \{P_1, P_2, \cdots, P_n\}$ be a set of parties. A collection $\mathbb{A} \subseteq 2^P$ is monotone. If $\forall B, C$, if $B \in \mathbb{A}$ and $B \subset C$, then $C \in \mathbb{A}$. An access structure(respectively, monotone-access-structure) is a collection(respectively,monotone collection)$\mathbb{A} \subseteq 2^P \setminus \phi$. The set in $\mathbb{A}$ are called the authorized sets, and the sets not in $\mathbb{A}$ are called the unauthorized sets. In this context, the attributes decide the role of the parties. So the authorized sets of attributes are included in $\mathbb{A}$.

3.3 Convergent Encryption

Convergent encryption [6,23] provides image confidentiality in deduplication. Because it uses the image content to compute encryption Hash value as the image encryption key. It makes sure that the key is directly related to the image content. The encryption key will not be leak under the condition of no leaking of the content of the image. And at the same time, because of the one-way operation of hash function, the image content will not be leaked when the key is leaked. Above all, it also can ensure the ciphertext is only related to the image content, but has nothing to do with the user.

In addition, we have to compute a tag to support deduplication for the image and use it to detect duplicate copy in the cloud storage server. If two image copies are the same, then their tags are the same. The user first sends the tag to the cloud storage server to check if the image copy has been already stored. We can not guess the convergent key in terms of the tag because they are derived independently. In a general way, the convergent encryption scheme has four primitive functions:

- $KeyGen_{CE}(M) \rightarrow K_M$ This algorithm computes a convergent key K_M which maps an image copy M to a key.
- $Encrypt_{CE}(K_M, M) \rightarrow C$ This algorithm uses symmetric encryption algorithm outputs a ciphertext C, with taking both the convergent key K_M and the image copy M as inputs.
- $TagGen_{CE}(M) \rightarrow T(M)$ This is the tag generation algorithm that maps the image copy M to a tag $T(M)$. We make $TagGen_{CE}$ to generate a tag from the corresponding ciphertext as index, by using $T(M) = TagGen_{CE}(C)$, where $C = Encrypt_{CE}(K_M, M)$.
- $Decrypt_{CE}(K_M, C) \rightarrow M$ This is the decryption algorithm which outputs the original image M, with taking both the convergent key K_M and the ciphertext C as inputs.

3.4   KP-ABE Scheme

This scheme is used to encrypt the K_M, which computed from image content called convergent key. As the same time we delete the duplicate copy, the image owner wants some other friends access this image file. In key-policy ABE(KP-ABE) scheme [24,25], the access policy is embedded into the decryption key. The image owner signs the K_M ciphertexts with a set of attributes, when a user wants to access the image, the cloud storage server judges the user's attribute and decides which type of ciphertexts the key can decrypt.

We show the KP-ABE scheme by the following four polynomial algorithms.

- Setup(1^n) $\longrightarrow$ (parameters,msk): The probabilistic polynomial time(PPT) algorithm takes a security parameter n as input. It outputs the public parameters and the master secret key(msk) which is known only to the trusted the cloud storage server.
- Encrypt(m, parameters, μ)$\longrightarrow$ c: The PPT encryption algorithm takes as a input with a message m, the public parameters and a set of attributes mu. It outputs the ciphertext c.
- KeyGen(parameters, msk, $\mathbb{A}$) $\longrightarrow$ SK_w: The PPT key generation algorithm takes as a input with the public parameters, the master secret key and an access structure $\mathbb{A}$. It outputs the decryption key $D_{\mathbb{A}}$.
- Decrypt(parameters, c, $D_{\mathbb{A}}$) $\longrightarrow$ m or $\perp$: The Decryption algorithm takes as a input with c, the public parameters and the decryption key. It outputs the message m if $\mu \in \mathbb{A}$ or else it outputs an error message.

Here we note that the convergent key k_M is seen as the message m in this paper.

3.5   Proof of Ownership

Proof of ownership [26] is a protocol to be used to prove the user indeed has the image to the cloud storage server. This is to solve the problem of using a small hash value as a proxy for the whole image in client side deduplication. In order to describe the proof of ownership in details, we suppose a prover (i.e. a user) and a verifier (i.e. the cloud storage server). The verifier derives a short value $\phi(M)$ from an image copy M. And the prover needs to send ϕ' and run a proof algorithm to prove the ownership of the image copy M. It is passed if and only if $\phi' = \phi(M)$.

Fig. 1. Deduplication cloud storage system

4   Architecture of Image Deduplication System

4.1   System Participants

In this paper, we consider a deduplication cloud system consisting of image owner, image user, cloud service provider. The image is assumed to be encrypted by the image owner before uploading to the cloud storage server. We assume the authorization between the image owner and users is appropriately done with some authentication and key-issuing protocols. After uploading the encrypted image to the cloud server, image users who are authorized could access the encrypted image. In more details, an authorized image user send a request to the cloud storage server, the server will verify the proof of ownership. The image user needs to send ϕ' and run a proof algorithm to prove the ownership of the image copy M. It is passed if and only if $\phi' = \phi(M)$. It is passed if and only if $\phi' = \phi(M)$.

- **Image Owner.** The image owner is an entity that send the image to the cloud service to storage, share and access again. In order to protect the image content, the owner have to encrypt the image before uploading to the cloud.

In a client side image deduplication system, only the first image owner could store in the cloud. If it is not the first one, then the storage server will tell the owner this image is duplicate. So there is only one image copy in the cloud storage.

- **Image User.** The image user is an entity that has privileges to access the same image by passing the proof of ownership in the deduplication cloud system. And image user also includes the friends of image owner who shared the image resource in the cloud storage.

- **Deduplication Cloud Service Provider.** The entity of deduplication cloud storage server provides the image storage service for the image owners and users. Moreover, the cloud storage server will also play the role of performing duplicate image before users upload their images. The users couldn't upload the image again if there is an identical content image stored in the cloud storage server, and then they will get the privileges of accessing the same image by using the proof of ownership.

4.2   Deduplication Cloud System

Figure 1 shows the participants of deduplication cloud system and the specific work process. It goes as follows:

- **System Setup:** Define the security parameter 1^λ and initialize the convergent encryption scheme. We assume that there are N encrypted images $C = (C_{M_1}, C_{M_2}, \cdots, C_{M_N})$ stored in the cloud server by a user. Then we could compute $K_M = H_0(M)$ and $C_M = Enc_{CE}(K_M, M)$. The user also could compute a tag $T_M = H(C)$ for duplicate check.

- **Image Upload:** Before uploading an image M, the user interacts with the cloud server and use the tag to check if there is any duplicate copy stored in the cloud storage server. The image tag will be computed $T_M = H(C)$ to check the duplicate image. If the image is the first time to upload, then the cloud storage server will receive the image ciphertext. At the same time, image owner could set the attributes to control access privileges.

  • If there is a duplicate copy founded in the storage server, the user will be asked to verify the proof of ownership, if the user pass, then he will be assigned a pointer, which allows him to access the image. In details, the image user needs to send ϕ' and run a proof algorithm to prove the ownership of the image copy M. It is passed if and only if $\phi' = \phi(M)$. It is passed if and only if $\phi' = \phi(M)$. By using proof of ownership, users have privileges to access the same image.

  • Otherwise, if there is no duplicate images in the storage server, the user computes the encrypted image $C_M = Enc_{CE}(k_M, M)$ with the convergent key $K_M = H_0(M)$, and uploads C_M to the cloud server. The user also encrypts the convergent key K_M with attributes for setting the access privileges. He will get the $C_{K_M} = Enc(sk, K_M)$ also be uploaded to the cloud server.

- **Image Retrieve:** Supposing that a user wants to download an image M. He first sends a request and the image names to the cloud storage server. When the cloud storage server receive the request and the image name, it will check whether the user is eligible to download the files. If pass, the cloud server returns the ciphertext C_M and C_{K_M} to the user. The user decrypts and gets the key K_M by using sk which stored locally. If the user's attributes match the owner setting, then the cloud storage server will send the corresponding sk. With the convergent encryption key, the user could recover the original images. If failed, the cloud storage server will send an abort signal to user to explain the download failure.

4.3   Security Analysis

In this section, we present the security analysis for the deduplication cloud system.

- Confidentiality: The image user stored in the cloud will not be read because the image have to be encrypted to $C_M = Enc_{CE}(K_M, M)$ with the convergent key $K_M = H_0(M)$. Therefore, we couldn't get the content of the image which stored in the cloud from a ciphertext.
- Privacy protection: Because it uses the image content to compute encryption Hash value as the image encryption key. It makes sure that the key is directly related to the image content, it will not be leak under the condition of no leaking of the contents of the image. And at the same time, because of the one-way operation of hash function, the image content will not be leaked when the key is leaked. Above all, it also can ensure the ciphertext is only related to the image content, but has nothing to do with the user. Therefore, it can protect the privacy of users as more as possible.
- Completeness: We suppose that if the images have been successfully uploaded to the cloud server, the image owner can retrieve them from the cloud storage server and decrypt the ciphertext by using the correct convergent encryption key. Furthermore, a user who has the same image wants to upload to the cloud server, will perform the proof of ownership and get the privilege to access the stored image.

5   Conclusion

In this paper, we propose the image deduplication cloud storage system. To protect the confidentiality of sensitive image content, the convergent encryption has been used while supporting image deduplication. Owner could download the ciphertext again and retrieve the image with secret key, as the same time, image owner makes use of attribute-based encryption scheme to share images with friends by setting the access privileges. A user who has the same image copy could get the privilege to access the ciphertext by passing the proof of ownership and delete his duplicate copy. If a user's attributes match the owner's setting access control, then he also could download the images. Security analysis makes sure that this system is secure in confidentiality, privacy protection and completeness.

Acknowledgement. This paper is supported by Fundamental Research Funds for the Central Universities (South China University of Technology) (No. 2014ZM0032), the Guangzhou Zhujiang Science and Technology Future Fellow Fund (Grant No. 2012J2200094), and Distinguished Young Scholars Fund of Department of Education (No. Yq2013126), Guangdong Province.

References

1. Mell, P., Grance, T.: The NIST Definition of Cloud, vol. 53, issue 6, p. 50 (2009)
2. Gantz, J.F., Ghute, C., Manfrediz, A., Minton, S., Reinsel, D., Schilchting, W., Toncheva, A.: The diverse and exploding digital universe: an updated forecast of world wide information growth through 2010. IDC white paper, pp. 2–16, March 2008
3. Gantz, J., Reinsel, D.: The digital universe in 2020: big data, bigger digital shadows, and biggest growth in the far east, December 2012. http://www.emc.com/collateral/analyst-reports/idc-the-digital-universe-in-2020.pdf
4. Asaro, T., Biggar, H.: Data De-duplication and Disk-to-Disk Backup Systems: Technical and Business Considerations, pp. 2–15. The Enterprise Strategy Group, July 2007
5. Tolia, N.: Using content addressable techniques to optimize client-server system. Doctoral thesis (2007)
6. Douceur, J.R., Adya, A., Bolosky, W.J., Simon, D., Theimer, M.: Reclaiming space from duplicate files in a serverless distributed file system. In: ICDCS, pp. 617–624 (2002)
7. Sabzevar, A.P., Sousa, J.P.: Authentication, authorisation and auditing for ubiquitous computing: a survey and vision. In: IJSSC, ser (2014). doi:10.1504/IJSSC.2011.039107
8. Yuriyama, M., Kushida, T.: Integrated cloud computing environment with it resources and sensor devices. In: IJSSC, ser (2014). doi:10.1504/IJSSC.2011.040342
9. Li, J., Chen, X., Li, M., Lee, P.P.C., Lou, W.: Secure deduplication with efficient and reliable convergent key management. IEEE Trans. Parallel Distrib. Syst. **25**, 1615–1625 (2013)
10. Bolosky, W.J., Corbin, S., Goebel, D.: Single instance storage in windows 2000. In: Proceedings of the 4th USENIX Windows Systems Symposium, pp. 13–24. Seattle, WA, USA (2000)
11. Adya, A., Bolosky, W.J., Castro, M.: Federated, available, and reliable storage for an incompletely trusted environment. In: Proceedings of the 5th Symposium on Operating Systems Design and Implementation, pp. 1–14. Boston, MA, USA (2002)
12. EMC Centera: Content Addressed Storage System. EMC CORPORATION (2003)
13. Policroniades, C., Pratt, L.: Alternative for detecting redundancy in storage systems data. In: Proceedings of the 2004 USENIX Annual Technical Conference, pp. 73–86. Boston, MA, USA (2004)
14. Rabin, M.O.: Fingerprinting by random polynomials. Technical report, Center for Research in Computing Technology, Harvard University (1981)

15. Henson, V.: An analysis of compare-by-hash. In: Proceedings of The 9th Workshop on Hot Topics in Operating Systems, pp. 13–18. Lihue, Hawaii, USA (2003)
16. Ungureanu, C., Atkin, B., Aranya, A.: A high-throughput file system for the HYDRAstor content-addressable storage system. In: Proceedings of the 8th USENIX Conference on File and Storage Technologies, pp. 225–238. San Jose, CA, USA (2010)
17. Clements, A.T., Ahmad, I., Vilayannur, M.: Decentralized deduplication in SAN cluster file systems. In: Proceedings of the 2009 USENIX Annual Technical Conference, pp. 101–114. San Diego, CA, USA (2009)
18. Fu, Y., Jiang, H., Xiao, N.: AA-Dedupe: an application-aware source deduplication approach for cloud backup services in the personal computing environment. In: Proceedings of the 2011 IEEE International Conference on Cluster Computing, pp. 112–120. Austin, TX, USA (2011)
19. Tan, Y., Feng, D., Zhou, G.: DAM: a data ownership-aware multi-layered deduplication scheme. In: Proceedings of the 6th IEEE International Conference on Networking. Architecture and Storage (NAS2010), pp. 403–411. Macau, China (2006)
20. Li, X., Li, J., Huang, F.: A secure cloud storage system supporting privacy-preserving fuzzy deduplication. Soft Computing (2015). doi:10.1007/s00500-015-1596-6
21. Pizzolante, R., Carpentieri, B., Castiglione, A.: A secure low complexity approach for compression and transmission of 3-D medical images. In: Broadband and Wireless Computing, Communication and Applications (BWCCA), pp. 387–392 (2013)
22. Pizzolante R., Castiglione A., Carpentieri B., De Santis A., Castiglione A.: Protection of microscopy images through digital watermarking techniques. In: Intelligent Networking and Collaborative Systems (INCoS), pp. 65–72 (2014)
23. Bellare, M., Keelveedhi, S., Ristenpart, T.: Message-locked encryption and secure deduplication. In: Proceedings of IACR Cryptology ePrint Archive, pp. 296–312 (2012)
24. Goyal, V., Pandey, O., Sahai, A., Waters, B.: Attribute based encryption for fine-grained access conrol of encrypted data. In: ACM conference on Computer and Communications Security, pp. 99–112 (2006)
25. Ostrovsky, R., Sahai, A., Waters, B.: Attribute-based encryption with non-monotonic access structures. In: the 14th ACM Conference on Computer and Communications Security, pp. 195–203 (2007)
26. Halevi, S., Harnik, D., Pinkas, B., Shulman-Peleg, A.: Proofs of ownership in remote storage systems. In: Chen, Y., Danezis, G., Shmatikov, V. (eds.) Proceedings of ACM Conference on Computer and Communication Security, pp. 491–500 (2011)

Cryptography

Hybrid Encryption Scheme Using Terminal Fingerprint and Its Application to Attribute-Based Encryption Without Key Misuse

Chunlu Chen[1,2(✉)], Hiroaki Anada[2], Junpei Kawamoto[1,2], and Kouichi Sakurai[1,2]

[1] Kyushu University, Fukuoka, Japan
chenchunlu@itslab.inf.kyushu-u.ac.jp,
{kawamoto,sakurai}@inf.kyushu-u.ac.jp
[2] Institute of Systems,
Information Technologies and Nanotechnologies, Fukuoka, Japan
anada@isit.or.jp

Abstract. Internet services make sharing digital contents faster and easier but raise an issue of illegal copying and distribution of those digital contents at the same time. A lot of public key encryption schemes solve this issue: However, the secret key is not completely protected i.e. these kinds of encryption methods do not prevent illegal copying and distribution of secret keys. In this paper, we propose a hybrid encryption scheme that employ terminal fingerprints. This scheme is a template to avoid such misuse of secret keys, and can be applied to, for example, attribute-based encryption schemes. There terminal fingerprint information is used to create a second encryption key and secret key. Since the terminal fingerprint is assumed to be unchangeable and unknowable, we ensure that our secret keys are valid in the terminal where such secret keys were created.

Keywords: Key misuse · Terminal fingerprint · Re-encryption

1 Introduction

In the last few years, the amount of data stored in the cloud server has been increasing day by day with the rapid development of the Internet in order to reduce the cost of using local storage and data sharing. However, information disclosure and trust issues arise in third party management cloud servers. Therefore, improving the security of the data stored in the cloud became a critical task. Typically, data stored in the cloud must be encrypted in order to achieve this goal of ensuring data security. Public-key cryptography is one of the methods to encrypt data, which uses a pair of keys, a secret key (SK) and a public key (PK). Although, public key encryption can enhance security, the complexity of key management is a big issue in this kind of cryptography.

Although public key cryptography can help us to protect the message, it also can be used to make illegal acts such as transferring and copying secret key unauthorized.

I. Khalil et al. (Eds.): ICT-EurAsia 2015 and CONFENIS 2015, LNCS 9357, pp. 255–264, 2015.
DOI: 10.1007/978-3-319-24315-3_26

Furthermore, it is possible to copy secret key from other users illegally. It is difficult to identify the source of leaking or the responsible entity if the secret key leaks. Various methods are proposed to utilize unique information for secret key generation to prevent this behavior, but the leakage of secret key is still a weak point of encryption waiting to be solved in the near future. Three related technologies are introduced as follows.

Hardware Certification

Physical Unclonable Function (PUF) achieved by a physical device using differential extraction of the chip manufacturing process inevitably leads to generate an infinite number, unique and unpredictable "secret key" [1]. PUF system receives a random code, and generates a unique random code as a response. Due to differences in the manufacturing process, the produced chip cannot be imitated and copied.

Kumar et al. [2] designed a system, where PUF output defines and gives a certain input, while other PUFs produce different outputs. According to the uniqueness of this chip output, it can be widely utilized in smart cards, bank cards and so on. In this way, we can protect message through the uniqueness of the secret key from copying and other illegal activities.

Biometric Authentication

Biometric technology consists of using computers and optics, acoustics, biosensors and other high-tech tools to retrieve the body's natural physiological characteristics (such as a fingerprint, finger vein, face, iris, etc.) and behavioral characteristics (e.g. handwriting, voice, gait, etc.) to identify personal identity. Biometric technology is not easy to forget, good security performance, and not copy or stolen "portable" and can be used anywhere [3]. Furthermore, biometric can be used as a unique, unalterable secret key but the safety is still taken seriously.

Jain, Anil et al. [4] analyzed and evaluated these biometric authentication systems. Moreover, biometric authentication is also used in various fields, for example, Uludag et al. [5] proposed the biometric authentication, which can be used to construct a digital rights management system.

In fact, in the present life, the biometric authentication has been very widely utilized, such as bank card fingerprint authentication, and face authentication in customs. Although biometrics brought us convenience, biometrics privacy protection has become an important research challenge.

Terminal Fingerprint

In general, the type of font, screen resolution and network environment are different for each browser terminal that is used to receive fingerprint information. This information can be used as the feature points to identify the terminal. The various sets of features possessed by the browser in this way is referred as browser fingerprint [6–8]. In this paper the terminal fingerprint is assumed to be unchangeable and unextractable.

Terminal fingerprint has been applied in a variety of locations. For example, terminal fingerprint is used to track the behavior of users on the web by collecting the trend of web sites that the user has accessed. As a result, it is possible to provide advertisements tailored to the interest and favorite of the user. It has also been made applicable to the risk-based authentication. The authentication terminal fingerprints are taken at the time of login of the user, and save. The terminal fingerprints are compared with those of the previous log. If it is significant difference, it will be determined that there is a high possibility of access from another terminal, which causes a higher strength authentication.

The hardware based authentication and Biometric based authentication methods mentioned above ensure the uniqueness of the key. These still cannot guarantee the security of keys. The update of hardware based authentication requires the replacement of the hardware itself, which will increases system cost. Biometric based authentication is impossible to alter but it is possible to be copied.

In order to meet the point, this paper utilizes the terminal fingerprint information because every terminal fingerprint information is different for an attacker. Even if attacker launches a collusion attack, it still cannot be decoded. Hence, in the proposed scheme, the terminal fingerprint information of the user can be utilized as a secret key, and it is never revealed outside even once. Unless the owner leaks information, otherwise the security of the key is guaranteed. Safety of the secret key is increased in this way.

For this purpose, we propose a hybrid encryption scheme that consists of a common-key encryption scheme and two public key encryption schemes. The hash value of a terminal fingerprint will be used as a secret key in the second public key scheme. In this paper, we employ Waters' CP-ABE [9] as the first encryption scheme, but any public key encryption scheme could be used as the first. Our scheme does not only utilize terminal fingerprint for generating unique secret key, but also updates itself according to user settings with relatively low cost to keep the freshness of the terminal fingerprint.

The rest of this paper is structured as follows. Section 2 introduces background information, formal definitions and CP-ABE scheme. Section 3 describes our encryption scheme. Section 4 discusses the security and advantage of the proposed scheme. Finally, conclusion and future work in Sect. 5.

2   Preliminaries

In this section, we give background information on bilinear maps and our cryptographic assumption.

2.1   Bilinear Maps

We present a few facts related to groups with efficiently computable bilinear maps. Let G_1 and G_2 be two multiplicative cyclic groups of prime order p. Let g be a generator of G_1 and e be a bilinear map $e : G_1 \times G_1 \to G_2$. The bilinear map e has the following properties:

1. Bilinearity: for all $u, v \in G_1$ and, $b \in Z_p$, we have $e(u^a, v^b) = e(u, v)^{ab}$,
2. Non-degeneracy: $e(g, g) \neq 1$.

2.2   Access Structure and Linear Secret Sharing Scheme

We will review here the definition of access structure and Linear Secret Sharing Schemes (LSSS) [10].

Definition 1 (Access Structure). *Let $P = \{P_1, P_2, \ldots, P_n\}$ be a set of attributes. A collection $\Gamma \subset 2^P$ is said to be monotone if Γ is closed under superset, i.e. if $\forall B, C$ if $B \in \Gamma$ and $B \subset C$, then $C \in \Gamma$. An access structure (respectively, monotone assess structures) is a collection (respectively, monotone collection) Γ of nonempty subsets of P, i.e., $\Gamma \subset 2^P \setminus \{\emptyset\}$. The members of Γ are called authorized sets, and the sets not in Γ are called unauthorized sets.*

Definition 2 (Linear Secret Sharing Schemes (LSSS) [10]). *A secret-sharing scheme $\prod$ over a set of parties $\mathcal{P}$ is called linear (over Z_p) if*

1. *The shares for each party form a vector over Z_p,*
2. *There exists a matrix M with ℓ rows and n columns called the share-generating matrix for $\prod$. For all $i = 1, \ldots, \ell$, the i-th row of M, we let the function ρ defined the party labeling row i as $\rho(i)$. When we consider the column vector $\mathbf{r} = (s, r_2, \ldots, r_n)$, where $s \in Z_p$ is the secret to be shared, and $r_2, \cdots, r_n \in Z_p$ are randomly chosen, then $M\mathbf{r}$ is the vector of ℓ share of the secret s according to $\prod$. The share $(M\mathbf{r})_i$ belongs to party $\rho(i)$.*

Here the $\prod$ is a Linear Secret Sharing Schemes(LSSS) composed of Γ. Let s be any attribute set of authenticated user, and define $I \subset \{1, 2, \ldots, \ell\}$ as $\{i; \rho(i) \in S\}$. For $\prod$, there exist a structure $\{\omega_i \in Z_p\}$ that if $\{\lambda_i\}$ are valid shares of any secret s, than $\sum_{i \in I} \omega_i \lambda_i = s$.

2.3   CP-ABE

There are a lot of studies on enhance the security of system. Cheung and Newport [11] proposed CP-ABE scheme based on DBDH problem using the CHK techniques [12], which satisfies IND-CPA secure and pioneers the achievement of IND-CCA secure. In this method, a user's secret key is generated by calculating user attributes and system attributes. Naruse et al. [13] proposed a new CP-ABE mechanism with re-encryption. Their method is based on the CP-ABE scheme to make the cipher text and has re-encryption phase to protect the message. Li et al. [14] proposed an encryption system using trusted third party, who issues authentication information embed user key to achieve better safety in decryption phase than CP-ABE. However, it is difficult to implement due to the complexity of the computational process required from the third party. Finally, Li et al. [15] proposed encryption scheme crowded included in the *ID* of the user *attribute*, decrypts it when ID authentication is also carried out at the same time, although this scheme can improve the safety, but the public key distribution center will increase the workload. Hinek et al. [16] proposed a *tk*-ABE(token-based attribute-based encryption) scheme that includes a token server to issue a token for a user to decrypt the cipher text, thus making the key cloning meaningless.

Our proposal scheme aims to increase the safety of the secret key without third party. When the cipher text corresponds to an access structure and secret key corresponds to a set of attributes, only if the attributes in the set of attributes is able to fulfill the access structure.

An (Ciphertext-policy) Attribute Based Encryption scheme consists of four fundamental algorithms: Setup, Encrypt, KeyGen, and Decrypt.

Setup $(\lambda, \mathbf{U}) \rightarrow (\mathbf{PK}, \mathbf{MK})$: The Setup algorithm takes security parameter λ and an attribute universe U as input. It outputs the public parameter PK and the system master secret key MK.

Encrypt $(\mathbf{PK}, \mathbf{M}, \mathbf{W}) \rightarrow \mathbf{CT}$: The Encrypt algorithm takes the public parameter PK, a message M, and an access structure was input. It output a cipher text CT.

KeyGen $(\mathbf{MK}, \mathbf{S}) \rightarrow \mathbf{SK}$: The KeyGen algorithm takes the master secret key MK and a set S of attributes as input. It output a secret key SK.

Decrypt $(\mathbf{CT}, \mathbf{SK}) \rightarrow \mathbf{M}$: The Decrypt algorithm takes as input the cipher text CT and the secret key SK. If the set S of attributes satisfies the access structure W then the system will output the message M.

3   Our System Model

In this section, we propose a hybrid encryption scheme. Then, we propose an attribute-based encryption scheme without key misuse. Finally, we provide a concrete realization of our attribute-based encryption scheme without key misuse.

Our system consists of three parts:

- *User* needs to provide their attributes information and legitimate manner to use the content. They also need to manage the terminal fingerprint information that their own;
- *Data server* needs to manage the attribute information, a common key and public parameter PK and issue the secret key that contains the attribute information of the user;
- *Document sender* needs to issue the common key and encrypt the contents.

3.1   Our Hybrid Encryption Scheme

We propose a hybrid encryption scheme HybENC that uses terminal fingerprint. HybENC consists of a common-key encryption scheme, CKE, two public key encryption schemes, PKE1 and PKE2, and a hash function, H : HybENC = (CKE, PKE1, PKE2, H). Informally, CKE is used for fast encryption and decryption of data of large size such as pictures and movies. PKE1 is used to encrypt the common key of CKE. Later, PKE1 will be replaced with an attribute-based encryption.

And Finally, PKE2 is used to *re-encrypt the common key* of CKE; fingerprint is used here as the secret key of PKE2 through a hash function.

Formally, our HybENC is described as follows.

HybENC.Key(λ) $\rightarrow$ FK, (PK1, SK1), (PK2, SK2): The HybENC.Key algorithm takes a security parameter λ as input. It calculates keys as follows; CKE.Key(λ) $\rightarrow$ FK, PKE1.Key(λ) $\rightarrow$ (PK1, SK1), H_λ(fingerprint) $\rightarrow$ SK2, PKE2.Key(SK2) $\rightarrow$ PK2. Then it outputs keys; FK, (PK1, SK1), (PK2, SK2).

HybENC.Enc(FK, PK1, PK2, m) $\rightarrow$ CT, CT2: The HybENC.Enc algorithm takes keys FK, PK1, PK2 and a plaintext m as input. It calculates cipher texts as follows; CKE.Enc(FK, m) $\rightarrow$ CT, PKE1.Enc(PK1, m1 := FK) $\rightarrow$ CT1, PKE2.Enc(PK2, m2 := CT1) $\rightarrow$ CT 2. Then it outputs cipher texts; CT, CT2.

HybENC.Dec(FK, SK1, SK2, CT, CT2) $\rightarrow$ m : The HybENC.Dec algorithm takes keys FK, SK1, SK2 and cipher texts CT, CT1, CT2 as input. It executes decryption as follows; PKE2.Dec(SK2, CT2) $\rightarrow$ m2 = CT1, PKE1.Dec(SK1, CT1) $\rightarrow$ m1 = FK, CKE.Dec(FK, CT) $\rightarrow$ m. Then it outputs the decryption result m.

3.2 Our Concrete Construction of ABE Without Key Misuse

We apply the above template of our hybrid encryption scheme to a scheme in the attribute-based setting. Plaintext is encrypted by using the *attribute* information and *terminal fingerprint* information. The advantages of this scheme, confirmation of the terminal fingerprint information is difficult to use except by authorized users.

We now give our construction by employing Water's CP-ABE as PKE1 in our hybrid encryption in Sect. 3.1.

In our construction the set of users is $U = \{1, 2, \cdots, n\}$ and the attribute universe is $A = \{1, 2, \cdots, \ell\}$. A random exponent for encryption is denoted as $s \in Z_p$. Note that secret keys below are randomized to avoid collusion attacks.

DO.Setup $(v, w) \rightarrow$ FK: The DO.Setup algorithm will choose a prime order p with generator q in the system. Next it will choose two random exponents $v, w \in Z_p$ as input. The common key is published by the Diffie-Hellman key exchange

$$FK = (q^v)^w mod\ p = (q^w)^v mod\ p$$

C.Enc $(FK, m) \rightarrow$ CT: The common-key encryption, C.Enc algorithm takes FK and a plaintext m as input. It outputs a ciphertext CT.

Auth.Setup $(\lambda) \rightarrow$ PK, MK: The Auth.Setup algorithm will choose a bilinear group G_1 of prime order p with generator g, and e be a bilinear map, $e: G_1 \times G_1 \rightarrow G_2$. It then chooses two random exponents $a, b \in Z_p$ and hash function $H : \{0, 1\}^* \rightarrow G$ as input. The Common key is published as

$$PK = g, g^b, e(g, g)^a$$

The system master secret key is published as

$$MK = g^a$$

Auth.Ext $(MK, S) \rightarrow$ **SK**: The Auth.Ext algorithm takes the master secret key MK and a set of attributes S as input. And algorithm chooses a random $t \in Z_p$ for each user. It creates the secret key as

$$SK = \left(g^{a+bt}, g^t, (K_X)_{X \in S}\right), \quad \forall_{X \in S} K_X = H(X)^t$$

U.Setup $(SK, f) \rightarrow$ **F, D**: The U.Setup algorithm takes user's fingerprint information f. Then it calculates the hash value $H(f) = D$ (in this paper we use the RSA encryption for our re-encryption). It chooses two primes p, q. Make $N = pq$. Next it computes E s. t. $DE \equiv 1 \bmod (p - 1)(q - 1)$. The user's terminal-fingerprint public key is $F = (N, E)$. The user keeps D as the user's terminal-fingerprint secret key.

Auth.Enc $(PK, FK, W) \rightarrow$ **FT**: The Auth.Enc algorithm takes the public parameter PK, common key FK, and an access structure (W, ρ) over the all of attributes to encrypts a message M. The function ρ associates row of W to attributes.
Where W is an $\ell \times n$ matrix. First the algorithm generates a vector $\mathbf{x} = (s, y_2 \cdots, y_n) \in Z_p^n$ and $r_1, r_2, \cdots, r_\ell \in Z_p$ randomly. The vector is made for sharing the encryption exponent s. Then W_i is the vector corresponding to the i-th row of W, calculates $\lambda_i = \mathbf{x} \cdot W_i$ from 1 to ℓ.
It output a ciphertext FT as

$$FT = (FKe(g, g)^{as}, g^s, \widehat{CS}),$$
$$\widehat{Cs} = \left(g^{b\lambda_1} H(X_{\rho_1})^{r_1}, g^{r_1}\right), \left(g^{b\lambda_2} H(X_{\rho_2})^{r_2}, g^{r_2}\right), \,,\, \left(g^{b\lambda_\ell} H(X_{\rho_\ell})^{r_\ell}, g^{r_\ell}\right).$$

Auth.ReEnc $(FT, F) \rightarrow$ **FT'**: The Auth.ReEnc algorithm takes the cipher text FT and user's terminal-fingerprint public key F as input.
The re-cipher text is published as

$$FT' = (FT)^E \bmod N,$$

$$\text{Where } (FT)^E = \left(FKe(g, g)^{asE}, g^{sE}, (\widehat{Cs})^E\right).$$

U.Dec $(FT', D) \rightarrow$ **FT**: The U.Dec algorithm takes as input the cipher text FT' and D. The decryption algorithm first computes.
The decryption algorithm computes

$$\left(FT'\right)^D = (FT^E)^D = FT \bmod N.$$

U.ReDec $(FT, SK) \rightarrow$ **FK**: The U.ReDec algorithm takes the cipher text FT and secret key SK as input. The secret key for an attribute set S, and the cipher text FT for access structure (W, ρ). Suppose that S satisfies the access structure and define I as

$\{i = \rho(i) \in s\}, I \in \{1,2,\ldots, \ell\}$ for $\prod$, there exist a structure $\{\omega_i \in Z_p\}$ that if $\{\lambda_i\}$ are valid shares of any secret s, than $\sum_{i \in I} \omega_i \lambda_i = s$. The U.ReDec algorithm will output the common key FK.

The re-decryption algorithm computes

$$\frac{e\left(g^s, g^{a+bt}\right)}{\prod_{i \in I}\left(e\left(g^{b\lambda_i} H\left(X_{\rho_i}\right)^{r_i}, g^t\right) e\left(H\left(X_{\rho_i}\right)^t, g^{r_i}\right)\right)^{\omega_i}} = \frac{e(g,g)^{as} e(g,g)^{bts}}{\prod_{i \in I} e(g,g)^{bt\omega_i \lambda_i}} = e(g,g)^{as}$$

$$\frac{FK e(g,g)^{as}}{e(g,g)^{as}} = FK$$

C.Dec $(\mathbf{FK, CT}) \to \boldsymbol{m}$: The C.Dec algorithm takes the common key FK and the cipher text CT as input. It output the message m.

4 Discussion

This paper shows that confidentiality of the shared data that has been encrypted can be protected and it is difficult to reveal the secret keys in the proposed scheme. The proposed scheme is secure against chosen-plaintext attacks because the underlying ABE scheme is secure against chosen-plaintext attacks. If the encrypted data is published, our scheme also resists attacks from colluding users. If the attacker did not know the terminal fingerprint information of the legitimate user, they wouldn't be able to get the secret key.

In this study, we proposed a cryptosystem to improve security. In the proposed method, the data server only sends re-cipher text and private information to the user, while the data server has to send both cipher text and secret key. In addition, the user creates secret key and re-encrypt key using the private information. Henceforth, user keeps the secret key and sends the re-encrypt key to the data server, and then the data server use the re-encrypt key to re-encrypt cipher text. Finally, data server sends back the re-cipher text to the user.

The proposed cryptosystem utilizes the terminal fingerprint information of the user. The terminal fingerprint is assumed to be unchangeable and unknowable. Also, only the key generation, encryption and decryption programs running on the trusted terminal can get the value of the fingerprints. The proposed scheme is built on the above-mentioned conditions. Here, the terminal fingerprint information is different for each user. It can be used as a user ID, and you can guarantee the anonymity of the user's own information. Misuse of the terminal fingerprint, such as transfer of the secret key, is incorrect behavior and meaningless,. Since the secret key that has legitimate user includes their terminal fingerprint information, the terminal fingerprint information is different in the other terminal, and the secret key is revoked. Safety of the secret key is increased in this way.

We proposed a hybrid encryption scheme in which a public key encryption scheme can be utilized. It is also easy to add, update and delete user's information. Then, we do not need a credible third party to guarantee the security of encryption and authenticate a user.

In this scheme, the secret key is generated and stored by the user, protecting the secret key against communication channel attack.

Our scheme requires that each user provide their own encryption terminal information to key management center. If there is large number of simultaneous user application, the workload of management center can be quite heavy. So in the future we should consider decreasing the computational complexity of re-encrypted.

Finally, the system ensures that the key cannot be copied, forwarded and etc. If there the safety of the security key is provided.

5   Conclusion and Future Work

In this study, we combine user terminal fingerprint data with a public key and secret key pair. Furthermore, we proposed a cryptographic scheme to update the secret key during decryption phase using terminal fingerprint information. As a result, the secret key is protected by ensuring that it does not operate except in the generated terminal key pair, even if an attacker eavesdrops the user secret key.

The encryption and decryption time can be optimized by proposing suitable algorithm as the future work. Furthermore, the security issue of our proposed method is that if the user connects to the Internet, the terminal fingerprint can be eavesdropped by an attacker. Hence, the proper solution should be proposed to mitigate this issue.

Acknowledgements. The second author is partially supported by Grants-in-Aid for Scientific Research of Japan Society for the Promotion of Science; Research Project Number:15K00029.

The fourth author is partially supported by Grants-in-Aid for Scientific Research of Japan Society for the Promotion of Science; Research Project Number: 15H02711.

(Authors: Chunlu Chen, Hiroaki Anada, Junpei Kawamoto, Kouichi Sakurai)

References

1. Suh, G.E, Devadas, S.: Physical unclonable functions for device authentication and secret key generation. In: Proceedings of the 44th Annual Design Automation Conference. ACM (2007)
2. Kumar, S.S., et al.: The butterfly PUF protecting IP on every FPGA. In: IEEE International Workshop on Hardware-Oriented Security and Trust, 2008. HOST 2008. IEEE (2008)
3. Jain, A., Hong, L., Pankanti, S.: Biometric identification. Commun. ACM **43**(2), 90–98 (2000)
4. Jain, A.K., Nandakumar, K., Nagar, A.: Biometric template security. EURASIP J. Adv. Signal Process. **2008**, 113 (2008)
5. Uludag, U., et al.: Biometric cryptosystems: issues and challenges. Proc. IEEE **92**(6), 948–960 (2004)
6. Nick Doty, W.C.: Fingerprinting Guidance for Web Specification Authors (Unofficial Draft) February 24 2015. available: http://w3c.github.io/fingerprinting-guidance/
7. Aggarwal, G., et al.: An Analysis of Private Browsing Modes in Modern Browsers. In: SENIX Security Symposium (2010)

8. Eckersley, P.: How unique is your web browser? In: Atallah, M.J., Hopper, N.J. (eds.) PETS 2010. LNCS, vol. 6205, pp. 1–18. Springer, Heidelberg (2010)

9. Bethencourt, J., Sahai, A., Waters, B.: Ciphertext-policy attribute-based encryption. In: IEEE Symposium on Security and Privacy, 2007. SP 2007, pp. 321–334 (2007)

10. Waters, B.: Ciphertext-policy attribute-based encryption: an expressive, efficient, and provably secure realization. In: Catalano, D., Fazio, N., Gennaro, R., Nicolosi, A. (eds.) PKC 2011. LNCS, vol. 6571, pp. 53–70. Springer, Heidelberg (2011)

11. Cheung, L., Newport, C.: Provably secure ciphertext policy ABE. In: Proceedings of the 14th ACM Conference on Computer and Communications Security, pp. 456–465 (2007)

12. Canetti, R., Halevi, S., Katz, J.: Chosen-ciphertext security from identity-based encryption. In: Cachin, C., Camenisch, J.L. (eds.) EUROCRYPT 2004. LNCS, vol. 3027, pp. 207–222. Springer, Heidelberg (2004)

13. Naruse, T., Mohri, M., Shiraishi, Y.: Attribute revocable attribute-based encryption with forward secrecy. In: Proceedings of the 2014 Information Processing Society of Japan. Japan (2014)

14. Li, J., Ren, K., Kim, K.: A2BE: accountable attribute-based encryption for abuse free access control. IACR Cryptology ePrint Archive, vol. 2009, p. 118 (2009)

15. Li, J., Ren, K., Zhu, B., Wan, Z.: Privacy-aware attribute-based encryption with user accountability. In: Samarati, P., Yung, M., Martinelli, F., Ardagna, C.A. (eds.) ISC 2009. LNCS, vol. 5735, pp. 347–362. Springer, Heidelberg (2009)

16. Hinek, M.J., et al.: Attribute-based encryption with key cloning protection. IACR Cryptology ePrint Archive 2008, p. 478 (2008)

Differential Fault Attack on LEA

Dirmanto Jap[1] and Jakub Breier[2]([✉])

[1] School of Physical and Mathematical Sciences,
Nanyang Technological University, Singapore, Singapore
dirm0002@e.ntu.edu.sg
[2] Physical Analysis and Cryptographic Engineering,
Temasek Laboratories at Nanyang Technological University,
Singapore, Singapore
jbreier@ntu.edu.sg

Abstract. LEA is a symmetric block cipher proposed in 2014. It uses ARX design and its main advantage is the possibility of a fast software implementation on common computing platforms.

In this paper we propose a Differential Fault Analysis attack on LEA. By injecting random bit faults in the last round and in the penultimate round, we were able to recover the secret key by using 258 faulty encryptions in average. If the position of faults is known, then only 62 faulty encryptions are needed in order to recover the key which surpasses the results achieved so far.

Keywords: LEA · Fault attack · DFA

1 Introduction

Today's applications require efficient ciphers that can run on small devices with constrained computing power. Recent trends show an increasing number of services intended for Internet of Things [5,8] requiring both high level of security and fast running speed on embedded devices. For such applications, lightweight cryptography is an ideal choice.

LEA [6] is a symmetric block cipher, using the ARX design (modular Addition, bitwise Rotation, and bitwise XOR). It offers fast software encryption, comparable to lightweight ciphers, and comes in the same key size variants as AES. There is an exhaustive security analysis report published by Bogdanov et al. [2], stating that the cipher is secure against known cryptanalysis attacks. So far, there was only one attempt to break the cipher using fault analysis method, which requires 300 chosen fault injections for recovering the 128-bit secret key.

In this paper we present a Differential Fault Analysis attack on LEA. We exploit properties of a non-linearity of modular addition operation used in a round function. To recover the key, our attack requires two different positions of fault injections - in the last round and in the penultimate round. By using a random bit-flip model, we were able to recover a 128-bit secret key by using $\approx$258 faulty ciphertexts in average. If the precise fault position is known, our attack

© IFIP International Federation for Information Processing 2015
I. Khalil et al. (Eds.): ICT-EurAsia 2015 and CONFENIS 2015, LNCS 9357, pp. 265–274, 2015.
DOI: 10.1007/978-3-319-24315-3_27

requires only ≈ 62 faulty ciphertexts in average. Thus, our method overcomes the fault attack on LEA published so far.

This paper is organized as follows. First, we provide an overview of related work in Sect. 2. LEA cipher is described in details in Sect. 3. Section 4 provides methodology of our fault attack, following by Sect. 5 which summarizes our simulation results. Finally, Sect. 6 concludes this work and provides motivation for further work.

2 Related Work

Since the first publication proposing a fault analysis as a method to retrieve the secret information from the encryption process proposed by Boneh, DeMillo, and Lipton in 1997 [3], this technique became very popular and testing of implementations against information leakage from fault attack has become a standard procedure.

Differential Fault Analysis technique was first introduced by Biham and Shamir [1], using this powerful technique for revealing the DES secret key. Many other techniques using fault injection have been proposed so far, e.g. Collision Fault Analysis (CFA), Ineffective Fault Analysis (IFA), and Safe-Error Analysis (SEA) [4].

There is only one fault attack on LEA published so far, using the Differential Fault Analysis technique. Myungseo and Jongsun [7] used 300 chosen fault injections in order to recover 128-bit secret key. They inject faults into three out of four words in the intermediate state at round 24.

From the attack methodology point of view, the closest attack proposal to this paper is the attack proposed by Tupsamudre et al. [9], aiming at SPECK cipher. Since SPECK uses the ARX structure as well, authors aimed at the only non-linear operation, at the modular addition. They were able to recover the n-bit secret key by using $n/3$ bit faults on average.

3 LEA Cipher

In this section we will describe a symmetric block cipher LEA, introduced by Hong et al. [6]. According to security evaluation report [2], LEA is secure against state-of-the-art cryptographic attacks.

The block size of this cipher is 128 bits, key sizes can be 128, 192, or 256 bits. Number of rounds for each key size is 24, 28, and 32, respectively. It is a pure ARX cipher, consisting of modular Addition, bitwise Rotation, and bitwise XOR operations on 32-bit words. We will further describe the design of the 128-bit key size version of the cipher.

3.1 Encryption Procedure

First, the 128-bit intermediate value X_0 is set to the plaintext P. Then, a key schedule process creates r round keys. The 128-bit output $X_{i+1} = (X_{i+1}[0], \ldots,$

$X_{i+1}[3]$) of i-th round is computed as:

$$X_{i+1}[0] \leftarrow ROL_9((X_i[0] \oplus RK_i[0]) \boxplus (X_i[1] \oplus RK_i[1]))$$
$$X_{i+1}[1] \leftarrow ROR_5((X_i[1] \oplus RK_i[2]) \boxplus (X_i[2] \oplus RK_i[3]))$$
$$X_{i+1}[2] \leftarrow ROR_3((X_i[2] \oplus RK_i[4]) \boxplus (X_i[3] \oplus RK_i[5]))$$
$$X_{i+1}[3] \leftarrow X_i[0]$$

The resulting ciphertext is then obtained after r rounds in the following way:

$$C[0] \leftarrow X_r[0], C[1] \leftarrow X_r[1], C[2] \leftarrow X_r[2], C[3] \leftarrow X_r[3].$$

The whole process is depicted in Fig. 1.

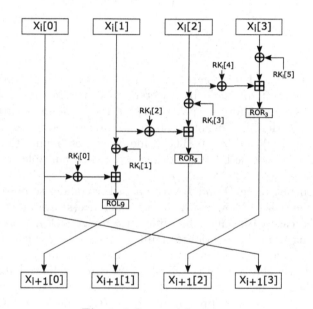

Fig. 1. i-th round function.

3.2 Key Schedule

Let $K = (K[0], K[1], K[2], K[3])$ be a 128-bit key. We set $T[i] = K[i]$ for $0 \leq i < 4$. Round keys $RK_i = (RK_i[0], \ldots, RK_i[5])$ for $0 \leq i < 24$ are then computed as follows:

$$T[0] \leftarrow ROL_1(T[0] \boxplus ROL_i(\delta[i \bmod 4]),$$
$$T[1] \leftarrow ROL_3(T[1] \boxplus ROL_{i+1}(\delta[i \bmod 4]),$$
$$T[2] \leftarrow ROL_6(T[2] \boxplus ROL_{i+2}(\delta[i \bmod 4]),$$
$$T[3] \leftarrow ROL_{11}(T[3] \boxplus ROL_{i+3}(\delta[i \bmod 4]),$$
$$RK_i \leftarrow (T[0], T[1], T[2], T[1], T[3], T[1]),$$

where $\delta[i]$ for $0 \leq i < 8$ are key generating constants, obtained from a hexadecimal expression of $\sqrt{766995}$, where 76, 69, and 95 are ASCII codes of 'L,' 'E,' and 'A.'

4   Attack Methodology

To perform a differential fault attack on LEA, we propose using two single bit flip faults, at $X_{22}[0]$ and at $X_{23}[2]$. The propagation of the faults can be observed in Fig. 2. We then retrieve the key by exploiting the modular addition operation.

To describe the proposed method, we first show how it works on a normal modular addition. First, let us assume that the operation is done on 32-bit values, A and B. The modular addition could then be expressed as:

$$D = (A \boxplus B),$$
$$D_j = (A_j \oplus B_j \oplus c_j),$$

where $j \in \{0, ..., 31\}$, and c_j is a carry bit from the previous addition with $c_0 = 0$. The idea is, that the fault could be injected at A, and by observing $(A \oplus A^*)$ and the pair of correct-faulty outputs (D, D^*), the attacker could retrieve the value of A and B. Here, A^* denotes the faulty value of A, where $A_k^* \neq A_k$ for $k \in \{j, j+1, ..., j+n\}$ and $n \geq 0$. The value k denotes the position of fault(s). If $n = 0$, then it is a single bit fault, otherwise, it is a multiple consecutive bit fault.

From the output value D and D^*, the attacker could also observe $D \oplus D^*$. The attacker then checks how many N bit difference(s) are in $D \oplus D^*$. First, we consider the case with only 1 bit difference in $(A \oplus A^*)$, more specifically, at bit j. Starting from the location of fault j, the attacker calculates N. If the value of $N = 1$, it can be concluded that the carry bit at bit $j+1$ is not flipped and hence, from the left part of the Table 1, we can conclude that the value of $B_j = c_j$ (highlighted with red color). However, if $N_1 > 1$, it can be concluded that the carry bit at $j+1$ is flipped, and thus, $B_j \neq c_j$. Note that this attack requires that the carry bit c_j is known and thus, it relies on the assumption that the 0-th bit could be faulted in the process (since $c_0 = 0$ is the only known carry from the beginning). Once the values of B_j, c_j and D_j are known, the value A_j could be determined $(A_j = D_j \oplus B_j \oplus c_j)$, as well as the value c_{j+1} (by observing the carry bit of $A_j + B_j + c_j$).

Next, we consider the case when there are multiple consecutive bit differences at $(A \oplus A^*)$, in bits $j, ..., j+n$. First, the attacker needs to determine if the carry bit at the bit $j+i$ ($i \in \{0, ..., n\}$) is flipped or not. The attacker observes $(D \oplus D^*)_{j+i}$.

$$(D \oplus D^*)_{j+i} = (A_{j+i} \oplus B_{j+i} \oplus c_{j+i}) \oplus (A_{j+1}^* \oplus B_{j+1} \oplus c_{j+1}^*)$$
$$(D \oplus D^*)_{j+i} = 1 \oplus c_{j+i} \oplus c_{j+i}^*$$

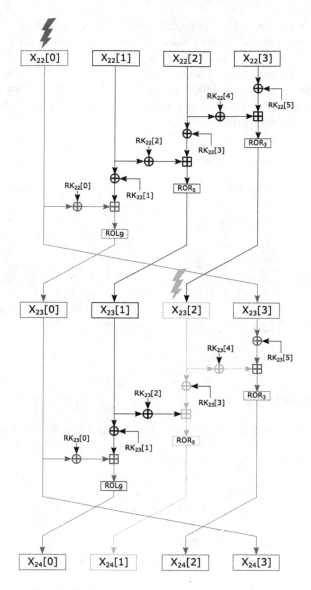

Fig. 2. Fault propagation in rounds 23 and 24.

So, if the value of $(D \oplus D^*)_{j+i} = 1$, it means that $c_{j+i} = c_{j+i}^*$, and similarly, if $((D \oplus D^*)_{j+i} \neq 1) \Rightarrow (c_{j+i} \neq c_{j+i}^*)$. Then, the attacker determines the value of the carry bit in the next bit $(j+i+1)$ using similar approach. The Table 1 summarizes the scenario when the carry values for the current bit and the consecutive bit are flipped or not. To highlight, if the value of the current bit is not flipped and if the value in the next carry bit is not flipped as well, then $B_{j+i} = c_{j+i}$ (left part, highlighted with red color). If the value of the current bit is not flipped and if the value in the next carry bit is flipped, then $B_{j+i} \neq c_{j+i}$ (left part). On the contrary, if the value of the current carry bit is flipped, and also the value in the next carry bit is flipped, then $A_{j+i} = c_{j+i}$ (right part). If the value of the current bit is flipped and if the value in the next carry bit is not flipped then $A_{j+i} \neq c_{j+i}$ (right part, highlighted with yellow color). Once the value of either A_{j+i}, or B_{j+i} is known, the other value and the next carry bit c_{j+i+1} could be determined.

Table 1. Changes of values in modular addition after a bit flip.

First faulty bit						Consecutive faulty bit						
A_j	A_j^*	B_j	c_j	c_{j+1}	c_{j+1}^*	A_j	A_j^*	B_j	c_j	c_j^*	c_{j+1}	c_{j+1}^*
0	1	0	0	0	0	0	1	0	0	1	0	1
0	1	0	1	0	1	0	1	0	1	0	0	0
0	1	1	0	1	0	0	1	1	0	1	0	1
0	1	1	1	1	1	0	1	1	1	0	1	1
1	0	0	0	0	0	1	0	0	0	1	0	0
1	0	0	1	1	0	1	0	0	1	0	1	0
1	0	1	0	0	1	1	0	1	0	1	1	1
1	0	1	1	1	1	1	0	1	1	0	1	0

5   Experiments

We tested the proposed method by conducting an experiment using simulated faults. Here, the attacker uses one fixed plaintext, measured multiple times, and injects fault at different bit locations. Then, he collects all the faulty ciphertexts. As mentioned earlier, the attacker has to inject faults at two different positions of different rounds. The main target is LEA-128, due to its key structure. Each of the round keys can be segmented into 6 parts, each part consists of 32 bits. In LEA-128, the second, the fourth and the last part ($RK_i[1], RK_i[3]$, and $RK_i[5]$) are identical, based on the key scheduling. In previous section, it is shown that the attack exploits the modular addition $D = (A \boxplus B)$.

5.1   Phase 1

First, the attacker injects single bit flip fault at $X_{22}[0]$, and the fault will propagate to $X_{24}[0]$, $X_{24}[2]$ and $X_{24}[3]$. The fault propagation will not be affected by the XOR operation with the round keys.

1. The attacker first exploits the difference $(X_{24}[3] \oplus X_{24}^*[3]) = (X_{23}[0] \oplus X_{23}^*[0])$. Then, he can pinpoint the location of initial fault injected by taking the last bit difference in $ROR_9(X_{23}[0]) \oplus ROR_9(X_{23}^*[0])$, since the attacker knows that the fault is a single bit flip and the locations of faults have been changed due to a rotation.

2. Then, the attacker can construct $(X_{22}[0] \oplus X_{22}^*[0])$. Here, the difference $(X_{24}[3] \oplus X_{24}^*[3])$ can be considered as caused by multiple consecutive bit flips injected at $X_{23}[0]$.

Input: $(X_{23}[0] \oplus X_{23}^*[0])$, $X_{24}[0]$, $X_{24}^*[0]$,

Output: estimated $(X_{23}[0] \oplus RK_{23}[0])$, $(X_{23}[1] \oplus RK_{23}[1])$.

However, since $X_{23}[0] = X_{24}[3]$, the round key $RK_{23}[0]$ can be calculated, and using the key schedule algorithm, $RK_{22}[0]$ can be determined as well from $RK_{23}[0]$.

3. Using the knowledge from the previous step, attacker can continue with revealing partial information.

Input: $(X_{22}[0] \oplus X_{22}^*[0])$, $X_{23}[0]$, $X_{23}^*[0]$,

Output: estimated $(X_{22}[0] \oplus RK_{22}[0])$, $(X_{22}[1] \oplus RK_{22}[1])$.

Since the attacker already knows $RK_{22}[0]$, he can reveal $X_{22}[0]$ based on the estimated output, which in turn reveals $X_{23}[3]$.

4. Here, $(X_{22}[0] \oplus X_{22}^*[0])$ is the same as $(X_{23}[3] \oplus X_{23}^*[3])$.

Input: $(X_{23}[3] \oplus X_{23}^*[3])$, $X_{24}[2]$, $X_{24}^*[2]$,

Output: estimated $(X_{23}[3] \oplus RK_{23}[5])$, $(X_{23}[2] \oplus RK_{23}[4])$.

However, as the $X_{23}[3]$ is known by previous step, the attacker obtains $RK_{23}[5]$, which, by key scheduling, is the same as obtaining $RK_{23}[1]$ and $RK_{23}[3]$.

By the end of phase 1, the attacker has obtained the values of $X_{22}[0](= X_{23}[3])$, $RK_{22}[0]$, $X_{23}[0]$, $RK_{23}[0]$, $X_{23}[1] \oplus RK_{23}[1]$, $RK_{23}[1]$, $X_{23}[2] \oplus RK_{23}[4]$, $RK_{23}[3]$ and $RK_{23}[5]$.

5.2   Phase 2

With the partial knowledge of the key and the intermediate states from phase 1, the attacker injects another single bit flip fault at $X_{23}[2]$.

1. By observing $(X_{24}[2] \oplus X_{24}^*[2])$, he can determine $(X_{23}[2] \oplus X_{23}^*[2])$, since it is a single bit flip fault.

Input: $(X_{23}[2] \oplus X_{23}^*[2])$, $X_{24}[1]$, $X_{24}^*[1]$,

Output: estimated $(X_{23}[1] \oplus RK_{23}[2])$, $(X_{23}[2] \oplus RK_{23}[3])$.

From the previous phase, $X_{23}[1]$ could be determined since $X_{23}[1] \oplus RK_{23}[1]$ and $RK_{23}[1]$ are known. Then, $RK_{23}[2]$ could be determined from $(X_{23}[1] \oplus RK_{23}[2])$ and $X_{23}[1]$.

2. Similarly, since $RK_{23}[3]$ is known from the previous phase, $X_{23}[2]$ can be calculated with $(X_{23}[2] \oplus RK_{23}[3])$, obtained in previous step.

3. Since $(X_{23}[3] \oplus RK_{23}[5])$ has been determined in previous phase, together with $X_{23}[2]$ from the previous step and $X_{24}[2]$, which is the output, the attacker can determine $RK_{23}[4]$.

Thus, the remaining of last round key, $RK_{23}[2]$ and $RK_{23}[4]$, can be retrieved in this phase.

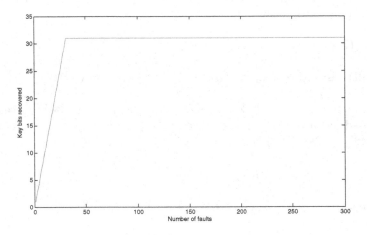

(a) Known position of faulty bits.

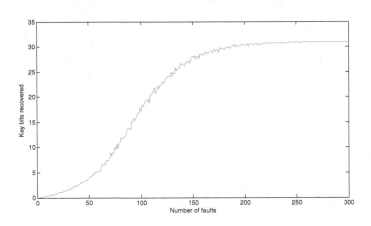

(b) Unknown position of faulty bits.

Fig. 3. Number of key bits retrieved.

5.3   Observations

One observation regarding the attack is that the last bit (MSB) could not be obtained because the next carry bit cannot be determined. This condition holds for each part of the key and hence, in total, 4 bits of the key could not be determined. Thus, these remaining key bits have to be brute-forced. Another problem could also occur due to the rotation of the bits. Due to rotation ROL_9, the resulting bit difference might not be consecutive, for example, $ROL_9(0\ldots01\ldots1) = (110\ldots01\ldots1)$. To mitigate this problem, it could be considered as separate multiple consecutive faults. From the example, the fault can be considered as $(110\ldots0)$ and $(0\ldots01\ldots1)$. Since the attack only considers bits of D and D^* which coincide with the faulty bits in A^*, the previous method still works.

In Fig. 3, we show the number of faults required to retrieve the value of the input of the modular addition. In the case where each bit could be flipped precisely, around 30 faults are required. However, if the bit could be flipped only randomly, more faults are required.

Based on the experiment, if the attacker cannot determine the location of a single bit flip fault, and hence, could only inject faults randomly at single bit, it requires ≈ 130 and ≈ 128 for the first and the second fault respectively in order to determine the last round key, minus the 4 bits mentioned earlier.

However, if the attacker could determine the precise location of a single bit flip, it requires only ≈ 31 and ≈ 31 faults for the first and the second fault respectively. This is because each fault reveals one bit of the key and in each attack, 2 parts of the last round key could be determined. For the previous attack model, more faults are required in order to obtain the value of each bit, similar to the coupon collector problem ($\Theta(n\log n)$). These results were verified by simulating 500 independent experiments on different scenarios.

6   Conclusions

In this paper we have proposed a differential fault attack on LEA. We used a random bit flip model, aiming at the last two rounds of the cipher. Using this model, we were able to retrieve the secret key with around 258 faulty encryptions in average. However, if the attacker can determine the position of faults, number of faults can be reduced to only 62 faulty encryptions in average. This result overcomes the only known fault attack on LEA published so far which needs 300 chosen faulty encryptions in order to reveal the key.

In the future, we would like to acquire practical results for our fault model, using the software implementation of LEA on a microcontroller, with the laser fault injection technique.

References

1. Biham, E., Shamir, A.: Differential fault analysis of secret key cryptosystems. In: Kaliski Jr, B.S. (ed.) CRYPTO 1997. LNCS, vol. 1294, pp. 513–525. Springer, Heidelberg (1997)

2. Bogdanov, A., Varici, K., Mouha, N., Velichkov, V., Tischhauser, E., Wang, M., Toz, D., Wang, Q., Rijmen, V.: Security evaluation of the block cipher LEA. Technical report, July 2011
3. Boneh, D., DeMillo, R.A., Lipton, R.J.: On the importance of checking cryptographic protocols for faults. In: Fumy, W. (ed.) EUROCRYPT 1997. LNCS, vol. 1233, pp. 37–51. Springer, Heidelberg (1997)
4. Clavier, C.: Attacking block ciphers. In: Joye, M., Tunstall, M. (eds.) Fault Analysis in Cryptography. Information Security and Cryptography, pp. 19–35. Springer, Heidelberg (2012)
5. Giang, N.K., Im, J., Kim, D., Jung, M., Wolfgang, K.: Integrating the EPCIS and building automation system into the internet of things: a lightweight and interoperable approach. J. Wirel. Mob. Netw. Ubiquit. Comput. Dependable Appl. **6**(1), 56–73 (2015)
6. Hong, D., Lee, J.-K., Kim, D.-C., Kwon, D., Ryu, K.H., Lee, D.-G.: LEA: a 128-bit block cipher for fast encryption on common processors. In: Kim, Y., Lee, H., Perrig, A. (eds.) WISA 2013. LNCS, vol. 8267, pp. 3–27. Springer, Heidelberg (2014)
7. Myungseo, P., Jongsung, K.: Differential fault analysis of the block cipher LEA. J. Korea Inst. Info. Secur. Cryptology **24**(6), 1117–1127 (2014)
8. Robles, T., Alcarria, R., Martín, D., Navarro, M., Calero, R., Iglesias, S., López, M.: An IoT based reference architecture for smart water management processes. J. Wirel. Mob. Netw. Ubiquit. Comput. Dependable Appl. **6**(1), 4–23 (2015)
9. Tupsamudre, H., Bisht, S., Mukhopadhyay, D.: Differential fault analysis on the families of simon and speck ciphers. In: 2014 Workshop on Fault Diagnosis and Tolerance in Cryptography (FDTC), pp. 40–48, September 2014

A Secure Multicast Key Agreement Scheme

Hsing-Chung Chen[1,2,3(✉)] and Chung-Wei Chen[4]

[1] Department of Computer Science and Information Engineering,
Asia University, Taichung City 41354, Taiwan
cdma2000@asia.edu.tw, shin8409@ma6.hinet.net
[2] Research Consultant with Department of Medical Research,
China Medical University Hospital, Taichung 40402, Taiwan, R.O.C.
[3] China Medical University Taichung, Taichung 40402, Taiwan, R.O.C.
[4] Institute of Communications Engineering, National Tsing Hua University,
Hsinchu City 30013, Taiwan
oliwad@gmail.com

Abstract. Wu et al. proposed a key agreement to securely deliver a group key
to group members. Their scheme utilized a polynomial to deliver the group key.
When membership is dynamically changed, the system refreshes the group key
by sending a new polynomial. We commented that, under this situation, the Wu
et al.'s scheme is vulnerable to the differential attack. This is because that these
polynomials have linear relationship. We exploit a hash function and random
number to solve this problem. The secure multicast key agreement (SMKA)
scheme is proposed and shown in this paper which could prevent from not only
the differential attack, but also subgroup key attack. The modification scheme
can reinforce the robustness of the scheme.

Keywords: Cryptography · Security · Secure multicast · Conference key · Key
distribution

1 Introduction

Many security protection schemes [1–11, 14] have been developed for an individual
multicast group. Some schemes address secure group communications by using secure
filter [1–4] to enhance performance of the key management. Wu et al. [4] proposed a
key agreement to securely deliver a group key to specific members efficiently. The
system conceals the group key within a polynomial consisting of the common keys
shared with the members. In the Wu et al.'s scheme, the polynomial is called as a
secure filter. Through their scheme, only the legitimate group members can derive a
group key generated by a central authority on a public channel. Nevertheless, for the
dynamic membership, the scheme is suffered from the differential attack which we
describe later. The dynamic membership means the addition and subtraction of the
group members. Naturally, the membership changes by the reason caused by network

---

This work was supported in part by the Ministry of Science and Technology, Taiwan, Republic of
China, under Grant MOST 104-2221-E-468-002.

I. Khalil et al. (Eds.): ICT-EurAsia 2015 and CONFENIS 2015, LNCS 9357, pp. 275–281, 2015.
DOI: 10.1007/978-3-319-24315-3_28

failure or explicit membership change (application driven) [5, 6]. If an adversary collects the secure filters broadcasted among the group members, as the membership changes, the group keys sent to the group members with the secure filter will be discovered through the differential attack [11].

The secure multicast key agreement (SMKA) scheme is proposed in this paper, which is a kind of secure filter to resist against the differential attack. The proposed secure filter is based on the properties of a cryptographically secure one-way hash function. Moreover, the complexity of the modified secure filter is almost the same with the complexity of the original one.

The rest of this paper consists of the following parts. The Sect. 2 gives an overview of the secure filter and the differential attack against the secure filter for the dynamic membership. The Sect. 3 introduces our scheme. The Sect. 4 gives the security proof of our scheme. Then we conclude our scheme in the Sect. 5.

2   The Secure Filter and the Differential Attack

2.1   Wu et al.'s Scheme

In Wu et al.'s Scheme [4], assume that there is a central authority which is in charge of distributing a group key to the group members, denoted as G, where $G = [M_1, M_2, \cdots M_n]$ in which the M_i indicates i-th group member. The M_i shares a common key k_i with the central authority. As the central authority starts to send a group key s to the members in the G, the central authority computes the secure filter as follows.

$$f(x) = \prod_{i=1,k_i \in K}^{n} (x - h(k_i)) + s \bmod p$$

$$= \sum_{i=1}^{n} a_i x^i \bmod p$$

Then the central authority broadcasts the coefficient of each item. For the M_i, upon receiving the coefficients, he can derive s by computing $f(h(k_i))$. Any adversary can not derive the s because he doesn't know any k_i, where $i = [1, 2, \cdots, n]$.

2.2   A Differential Attack on Wu et al.'s Scheme

The differential attack utilizes the linear relationship of the coefficients in the secure filter to compromise the group keys. The differential attack is described as follows. Assume that an adversary, Ad, where $Ad \notin G$. The Ad collects each secure filter used to send a group key at each session which means a period of the time for the membership unchanged. Observe that the coefficients of the secure filter, we learn the relationship as follows.

$$a_n = 1 \mod p,$$

$$a_{n-1} = \sum_{i=1}^{C_1^n} h(x_i) \mod p,$$

$$a_{n-2} = \sum_{i=1,i\neq j}^{C_2^n} h(x_i)h(x_j) \mod p,$$

$$\vdots$$

The coefficients of the secure filter are the linear relationship of the secure factors. As membership changes, the differential value of the coefficients will disclose the secure factors in the secure filter. For example, as the M_3 is excluded from the group, which may be caused by network failure, then the central authority re-computes the following secure filter to refresh the group key, where n' means the membership as the M_3 is excluded below.

$$f'(x) = \prod_{i=1,k_i \in K, i \neq 3}^{n'} (x - h(x_i)) + s' \mod p$$

$$= \sum_{i=1}^{n'} a_i x^i \mod p$$

For the coefficient $a_{n'-1}$, the adversary can compute $a_{n-1} - a_{n'-1}$ to derive $h(x_3)$. Through the $h(x_3)$, the adversary can derive the previous group keys through the preceding secure filters. Moreover, as the M_3 returns into the group, the central authority will refresh the group key through another secure filter composed of the secure factor $h(x_3)$. Then the adversary who already derives the $h(x_3)$ through the differential attack can derive any group key as long as the M_3 is in the group.

3   Our Scheme

In this section, we introduce our scheme. First, we define the environment and notation. And then we introduce our scheme. The notations used in the rest of this paper are shown in Table 1.

3.1   SMKA Scheme

The secure multicast key agreement (SMKA) scheme is proposed in this section. Assume that there are n group members at the session t. The set of these group members at the session t is denoted as G_t, where $G_t = [M_1, M_2, \cdots, M_n]$. The M_i denotes i-th group member, where $i \in [1, 2, \cdots, n]$. The set of the common keys is denoted as K_t, where $K_t = [k_1, k_2, \cdots, k_n]$. Before the CA starts to send the group key s_t for the session

Table 1. Notations

CA	central authority
n	number of the group members at the session t
$h(\cdot)$	cryptographically secure one-way function
c_t	random number used at the session t
s_t	group key for the session t
M_i	i-th group member
k_i	common key only shared with the CA and the i-th user
x_i	secure factor of the modified secure factors
$f_t(x)$	modified secure filter for the session t

t to the members in the G_t, the CA generates a random number c_t. Then the CA computes the secure factors below.

$$x_i = h(k_i \| c_t), \tag{1}$$

where $k_i \in K_t$ and $i = \{1, 2, \cdots, n\}$. Next, the CA generates a group key s_t and calculates the modified secure filter below.

$$f_t(x) = \prod_{i=1}^{n} (x - x_i) + s_t \bmod p. \tag{2}$$

Then the CA can derive the extension of the $f_t(x)$ as following.

$$f_t(x) = a_n x_n + a_{n-1} x_{n-1} + \cdots + a_0 \bmod p. \tag{3}$$

The CA broadcasts the set of the coefficients, denoted as A, and c_t, where $A = [a_n, a_{n-1}, \cdots, a_0]$. After receiving the A and the c_t, the group member M_i compute the secure factor, x_i through the procedure of (1) with the common key k_i and c_t. Next, the M_i derive s_t by calculating $f_t(x_i) = f_t(h(k_i\|c_t))$. In the next session $t + 1$, the CA generates a new random number c_{t+1} and repeats the procedures of (1) to (3) to send the secret s_{t+1} to the G_{t+1}, where the G_{t+1} may not be the same as G_t.

4   Security and Complexity Analyses

In this section, we show that the modified secure filter can resist against the differential attack. Moreover, we proof that the modified secure filter can also prevent from the subgroup key attack [13, 14] which could compromise other common keys through factorizing algorithm [15].

Proposition 1. *A cryptographically secure hash function $h(\cdot)$ has the properties: intractability, randomness, collision-free, unpredictability.*

The Proposition 1 is assumed commonly on cryptography [15]. The intractability means that, for only given a hash value y, where $y = h(x)$, the value of x is intractable.

The randomness means that, for a variable x, the elements in the set of the result $y = h(x)$, denoted as Y, are uniformly distributed. The collision free means that, given y, where $y = h(x)$, the probability of discovering x', where $x \neq x'$, that $h(x)$ equals $h(x')$ is negligible. The unpredictability means that hash functions exhibit no predictable relationship or correlation between inputs and outputs.

Theorem 1. *An adversary cannot discover the group keys through the differential attack.*

Proof: Assume that an adversary can know the membership of the group exactly. He records the distinct membership at different session. For the session t, the adversary can collect the modified secure filter below.

$$f_t(x) = a_n x_n + a_{n-1} x_{n-1} + \cdots + a_0 \bmod p. \tag{4}$$

The coefficient of $f_t(x)$ can be derived below.

$$a_n = \sum_{i=1}^{n} h(x_i || c_t) \bmod p, \tag{5}$$

$$a_{n-1} = \sum_{i=1, i \neq j}^{C_2^n} h(x_i || c_t) h(x_j || c_t) \bmod p,$$

$$\vdots$$

For any session t', where $t' \neq t$, the adversary can discover another modified secure filter for different membership in which the number of group member is n' below.

$$f_{t'}(x) = a_{n'} x_{n'} + a_{n'-1} x_{n'-1} + \cdots + a_0' \bmod p. \tag{6}$$

The coefficient of $f_{t'}(x)$ can be presented below.

$$a_{n'} = \sum_{i=1}^{n'} h(x_i || c_{t'}) \bmod p, \tag{7}$$

$$a_{n'-1} = \sum_{i=1, i \neq j}^{C_2^{n'}} h(x_i || c_{t'}) h(x_j || c_{t'}) \bmod p,$$

$$\vdots$$

According to the Proposition 1, we can learn that the coefficients in (5) and (7) are predictable for an adversary. Therefore, it induces that the adversary cannot predict the linear relationship between these coefficients. Hence, the adversary cannot engage the differential attack successfully to compromise the group key distributed within a secure filter.   □

Theorem 2. *A legitimate group member cannot discover other common keys shared between the CA and other group members.*

Proof: According to the Proposition 1, assume that a legitimate group member has enough ability to factorize the value of $f_t(0)$ and discover the other secure factors of the $f_t(x)$; he only can discover the hash values not tractable to the common keys. Therefore, the common keys cannot be discovered by the adversary. Then we prove that the modified secure filter can resist against the subgroup key attack.

According to Theorems 1 and 2, we proof that the modified secure filter can resist against the differential attack as well as the subgroup key attack [13, 14]. □

5   Conclusions

In this paper, the navel key agreement scheme by using the new secure filter to improve the robustness in order to support the security functionality on dynamically changing members in the Wu's secure filter [4]. The proposed secure filter is based on the properties of a cryptographically secure hash function. Via the security analysis, we proved that the modified secure filter can resist against the differential attack. More-over, the modified secure filter can prevent from the subgroup key attack. The modified secure filter almost has the same complexity with the original secure filter. For a group communication, the dynamic membership is an unavoidable issue. Though the secure filter proposed in [4] gave a simple and robustness distribution scheme for the group secret, it is suffered from the problems of the dynamic membership. The modified secure filter can enhance the secure filter for the dynamic membership and keep the efficiency.

References

1. Chen, H.-C., Wang, S.-J., Wen, J.-H.: Packet construction for secure conference call request in ad hoc network systems. Inf. Sci. **177**(24), 5598–5610 (2007)
2. Chen, H.-C.: Secure multicast key protocol for electronic mail systems with providing perfect forward secrecy. Secur. Commun. Netw. **6**(1), 100–107 (2013)
3. Chen, H.-C., Yang, C.-Y., Su, H.-K., Wei, C.-C., Lee, C.-C.: A secure E-mail protocol using ID-based FNS multicast mechanism. Comput. Sci. Inf. Syst. **11**(3), 1091–1112 (2014). Special Issue on Mobile Collaboration Technologies and Internet Services
4. Wu, K.P., Ruan, S.J., Lai, F., Tseng, C.K.: On key distribution in secure multicasting. In: Proceedings of 25th Annual IEEE International Conference on Local Computer Networks, p. 208 (2000)
5. Kim, Y., Perrig, A., Tsudik, G.: Communication-efficient group key agreement. IEEE Trans. Comput. **53**(7), 905–921 (2001)

6. Kim, Y., Perrig, A., Tsudik, G.: Tree-based group key agreement. ACM Trans. Inf. Syst. Secur. **7**(1), 60–96 (2004)
7. Fekete, A., Lynch, N., Shvartsman, A.: Specifying and using a partionable group communication service. ACM Trans. Comput. Syst. **19**(2), 171–216 (2001)
8. Chen, X., Lenzini, G., Mauw, S., Pang, J.: Design and formal analysis of a group signature based electronic toll pricing system. J. Wireless Mobile Netw. Ubiquitous Comput. Dependable Appl. (JoWUA) **4**(1), 55–75 (2013)
9. Craß, S., Dönz, T., Joskowicz, G., Kühn, E., Marek, A.: Securing a space-based service architecture with coordination-driven access control. J. Wireless Mobile Netw. Ubiquitous Comput. Dependable Appl. (JoWUA) **4**(1), 76–97 (2013)
10. Malik, S., Lee, J.-H.: Privacy enhancing factors in people-nearby applications. J. Wireless Mobile Netw. Ubiquitous Comput. Dependable Appl. (JoWUA) **6**(2), 113–121 (2015)
11. Kent, A.D., Liebrock, L.M., Wernicke, J.: Differentiating user authentication graphs. J. Wireless Mobile Netw. Ubiquitous Comput. Dependable Appl. (JoWUA) **5**(2), 24–38 (2014)
12. Moser, L.E., Amir, Y., Melliar-Smith, P.M., Agarwal, D.A.: Extended virtual synchrony. In: Proceedings of the IEEE 14th International Conference on Distributed Computing Systems, pp. 55–65 (1994)
13. Wen, J.H., Wu, M.C., Chen, T.S.: A novel elliptic curve method for secure multicast system. Far East J. Math. Sci. **28**(2), 449–467 (2008)
14. Wu, K.P., Ruan, S.J., Tseng, C.K., Lai, F.: Hierarchical access control using the secure filter. IEICE Trans. Inf. Syst. **E84-D**(6), 700–708 (2001)
15. Menezes, A.J., van Oorschot, P.C., Vanstone, S.A.: Handbook of Applied Cryptography. CRC Press, Boca Raton (1997)

Efficient Almost Strongly Universal Hash Function for Quantum Key Distribution

Extended Abstract

Bo Liu[1], Baokang Zhao[1(✉)], Chunqing Wu[1], Wanrong Yu[1],
and Ilsun You[2]

[1] School of Computer Science,
National University of Defense Technology, Changsha, Hunan, China
liubo.eecs@gmail.com,
{bkzhao,wuchunqing,wryu}@nudt.edu.cn
[2] School of Information Science, Korean Bible University, Seoul, Korea
isyou@bible.ac.kr

Abstract. Quantum Key Distribution (QKD) technology, based on principles of quantum mechanics, can generate unconditional security keys for communication parties. Information-theoretically secure (ITS) authentication, the compulsory procedure of QKD systems, avoids the man-in-the-middle attack during the security key generation. The construction of hash functions is the paramount concern within the ITS authentication. In this extended abstract, we proposed a novel Efficient NTT-based ε-Almost Strongly Universal Hash Function. The security of our NTT-based ε-ASU hash function meets $\varepsilon \leq L(n+1)/2^{n-2}$. With ultra-low computational amounts of construction and hashing procedures, our proposed NTT-based ε-ASU hash function is suitable for QKD systems.

Keywords: Almost strongly universal hash · Quantum key distribution

1 Introduction

With the rapid development of computing technologies, the importance of secure communication is growing daily [21–24]. Unlike conventional cryptography which based on the computational complexity, Quantum Key Distribution (QKD) can achieve the unconditional security communication [1, 2, 18–20]. By transmitting security key information with quantum states, the final key generated by QKD system is information-theoretically secure (ITS), which is guaranteed by the non-cloning theorem and measuring collapse theorem in quantum physics [3, 4]. Nowadays, QKD has been one of the research focuses around the world. In recent years, the famous QKD network projects mainly include SECOQC in Europe [5], UQCC in Tokyo [6] and NQCB in China [7] and so on.

ITS authentication is the compulsory procedure of QKD system and also the key procedure which ensures the security of generated keys between communication parties [4, 8]. Otherwise, QKD is vulnerable to the man-in-the-middle attack [9–11]. The main challenge about the research of ITS authentication is the construction of hash functions which are suitable for ITS authentication with less security key [9, 12–14].

© IFIP International Federation for Information Processing 2015
I. Khalil et al. (Eds.): ICT-EurAsia 2015 and CONFENIS 2015, LNCS 9357, pp. 282–285, 2015.
DOI: 10.1007/978-3-319-24315-3_29

Usually, ε-Almost Strongly Universal (ε-ASU) hash functions can be used to construct ITS authentication schemes in a natural way. Majority construction schemes focus on the ε-ASU$_2$ hash function families, such as Wegman-Carter's and Krawczyk's construction schemes [13, 14]. Nowadays, the photon transmission frequency has reached to about ten GHz [15, 16]. With heavy computational amounts, ITS authentication schemes which based on ε-ASU$_2$ hash functions cannot meet the high performance requirement of QKD systems [9, 13, 17].

In this extended abstract, with NTT technology, we proposed a novel Efficient ε-Almost Strongly Universal Hash Function. With the special features of number-theoretic transforms (NTT) technology, our ε-ASU hash function family is constructed in the prime ring $\mathbf{Z}_p^L$. In order to construct the NTT-based ε-ASU hash function efficiently, we assume that $L = 2^\lambda$, and the prime number $p = \upsilon L + 1$. We assume that the set of all messages is R, where $R \in \mathbf{Z}_p^L$ with length of L, and the length of authentication tag is n, where $n = \beta \lceil \log_2 p \rceil$. The security of our NTT-based ε-ASU hash function meets $\varepsilon \leq L(n+1)/2^{n-2}$ and the consumed key length of ITS authentication scheme is less than $3n + 1$.

2 NTT-Based Almost Strongly Universal Hash Function

Since the construction has to consume a very long key, Gilles's NTT-based almost universal hash function is not suitable for ITS authentication [18]. With a partially known security key and a LFSR structure [13], a random bit stream can be generated to construct the NTT-based almost strongly universal (NASU) hash functions.

Let R be the set of messages, where $R \in \mathbf{Z}_p^L$. We take only the first β elements of the hashing result. Let $f(x)$ be an irreducible polynomial with degree $\beta \lceil \log_2 p \rceil$ of $GF(2)$ and $s_{init} = (s_0, s_1, \cdots, s_{\beta \lceil \log_2 p \rceil - 1})^T$ be an initial state of the LFSR structure defined by the feedback function $f(x)$. s_{init} and $f(x)$ are both generated from the partially known key with length of $2\beta \lceil \log_2 p \rceil + 1$. Let $f = (f_0, f_1, \cdots, f_{\beta \lceil \log_2 p \rceil - 1})^T$ be the coefficient vector of $f(x)$ and $s_{[i-\beta\lceil \log_2 p \rceil, i-1]} = (s_{i-\beta\lceil \log_2 p \rceil}, s_{i-\beta\lceil \log_2 p \rceil + 1}, \cdots, s_{i-1})^T$, where $i \geq \beta \lceil \log_2 p \rceil$.

Thus, we can gain the random bit

$$s_i = s_{[i-\beta\lceil \log_2 p \rceil, i-1]}^T f \bmod 2. \tag{1}$$

Let $1 \leq \beta \leq L$ and $K = (2^0, 2^1, \cdots, 2^{\lceil \log_2 p \rceil - 1})$. For $C, R \in \mathbf{Z}_p^L$, let $h_C(R) = (F^{-1}(C \cdot R))_{0,1,\cdots,\beta-1}$ be the inverse NTT of their component-wise product, taking only the β first elements of the result. Assume that $u = \lceil \log_2 p \rceil$, we define that the set

$$H_{p,L,\beta,s,f} = \{h_C : C_i = Ks_{[(i+\beta)u,(i+\beta+1)u-1]} \bmod p, \forall i\} \tag{2}$$

is an almost strongly universal family of hash functions with $\varepsilon \leq (L + 2L\beta\lceil \log_2 p \rceil + 2)/2^{\beta\lceil \log_2 p \rceil}$. Assume that $n = \beta u$, we have $\varepsilon \leq (L + 2nL + 2)/2^n$.

3 Potential Advantages

Comparing with ASU_2 hash functions, our proposed NASU hash functions have the following potential advantages:

(a) NASU hash functions can be easily constructed with a partially known security key and a LFSR structure.
(b) With the special features of number-theoretic transforms (NTT) technology, the computational amounts of our NASU hashing procedure is much less than Krawczyk's scheme and other ASU_2 hash functions.
(c) Treating the elements of input messages as non-binary integers of the ring Z_p^L, our proposed NTT-based ε-ASU hash function is very suitable for ITS authentication in QKD systems.

In the future, we will explore the detailed security proof of NASU hash functions and its deployment within the QKD system.

References

1. Scarani, V., Bechmann-Pasquinucci, H., Cerf, N., Dušek, M., Lütkenhaus, N., Peev, M.: The security of practical quantum key distribution. Rev. Mod. Phys. **81**, 1301–1350 (2009)
2. Wang, L., Chen, L., Ju, L., Xu, M., Zhao, Y., Chen, K., Chen, Z., Chen, T.-Y., Pan, J.-W.: Experimental multiplexing of quantum key distribution with classical optical communication. Appl. Phys. Lett. **106**, 081108 (2015)
3. Bennett, C.H., Brassard, G.: Quantum cryptography: public key distribution and coin tossing. In: Proceedings of IEEE International Conference on Computers, Systems and Signal Processing, New York (Year)
4. Ma, X., Fung, C.-H.F., Boileau, J.C., Chau, H.F.: Universally composable and customizable post-processing for practical quantum key distribution. Comput. Securtiy **30**, 172–177 (2011)
5. Leverrier, A., Karpov, E., Grangier, P., Cerf, N.J.: Unconditional security of continuous-variable quantum key distribution. arXiv preprint arXiv:0809.2252 (2008)
6. Sasaki, M., Fujiwara, M., et al.: Field test of quantum key distribution in the Tokyo QKD Network. Opt. Express **19**, 10387–10409 (2011)
7. http://www.quantum2011.org/
8. Ma, X.: Practical Quantum key Distribution post-processing (2011)
9. Abidin, A.: Authentication in Quantum Key Distribution: Security Proof and Universal Hash Functions. Department of Electrical Engineering, vol. Ph.D. Linkoping University (2013)
10. Pacher, C., Abidin, A., Lorunser, T., Peev, M., Ursin, R., Zeilinger, A., Larsson, J.-A.: Attacks on quantum key distribution protocols that employ non-ITS authentication. arXiv preprint arXiv:1209.0365 (2012)
11. Ioannou, L.M., Mosca, M.: Unconditionally-secure and reusable public-key authentication. arXiv preprint arXiv:1108.2887 (2011)
12. Portmann, C.: Key Recycling in Authentication. arXiv preprint arXiv:1202.1229 (2012)
13. Krawczyk, H.: LFSR-based hashing and authentication. In: Desmedt, Y.G. (ed.) CRYPTO 1994. LNCS, vol. 839, pp. 129–139. Springer, Heidelberg (1994)

14. Wegman, M.N., Carter, J.L.: New hash functions and their use in authentication and set equality. J. Comput. Syst. Sci. **22**, 265–279 (1981)
15. Wang, S., Chen, W., Guo, J.: YIn, Z., Li, H., Zhou, Z., Guo, G., Han, Z.: 2 GHz clock quantum key distribution over 260 km of standard telecom fiber. Opt. Lett. **37**, 1008–1010 (2012)
16. Tanaka, A., Fujiwara, M., et al.: High-speed quantum key distribution system for 1-Mbps real-time key generation. IEEE J. Quant. Electron. **48**, 542–550 (2012)
17. Carter, J.L., Wegman, M.N.: Universal classes of hash functions. In: Proceedings of the Ninth Annual ACM Symposium on Theory of Computing, pp. 106–112. ACM (Year)
18. Liu, B., Zhao, B., Wei, Z., et al.: Qphone: a quantum security VoIP phone. In: Proceedings of the ACM SIGCOMM 2013 Conference on SIGCOMM. ACM, pp. 477–478 (2013)
19. Liu, B., Zhao, B., Liu, B., et al.: A security real-time privacy amplification scheme in QKD system. J. UCS. **19**(16), 2420–2436 (2013)
20. Sun, S., Jiang, M., Ma, X., Li, C., Liang, L.: Hacking on decoy-state quantum key distribution system with partial phase randomization, Scientific Reports (2013)
21. Liu, Y., Peng, W., Jinshu, S.: A study of IP prefix hijacking in cloud computing networks. Secur. Commun. Netw. **7**(11), 2201–2210 (2014)
22. Roland, R., Zhdanova, M., Repp, J.: Security compliance tracking of processes in networked cooperating systems. J. Wirel. Mob. Netw., Ubiquitous Comput., Dependable Appl. (JoWUA) **6**(2), 21–40 (2015)
23. Kotenko, I.: Guest editorial: security in distributed and network-based computing. J. Wirel. Mob. Netw., Ubiquitous Comput., Dependable Appl. (JoWUA) **6**(2), 1–3 (2015)
24. Skovoroda, A., Gamayunov, D.: Securing mobile devices: malware mitigation methods. J. Wirel. Mob. Netw., Ubiquitous Comput., Dependable Appl. (JoWUA) **6**(2), 78–97 (2015)

Big Data and Text Mining

DCODE: A Distributed Column-Oriented Database Engine for Big Data Analytics

Yanchen Liu[1], Fang Cao[1(✉)], Masood Mortazavi[1], Mengmeng Chen[1],
Ning Yan[1], Chi Ku[1], Aniket Adnaik[1], Stephen Morgan[1], Guangyu Shi[1],
Yuhu Wang[2], and Fan Fang[2]

[1] Huawei Innovation Center, Santa Clara, CA, USA
{Yanchen.Liu,Fang.Cao,Masood.Mortazavi,Mengmeng.Chen,Yan.NingYan,
Chi.Ku,Aniket.Adnaik,Steve.Morgan,shiguangyu}@huawei.com
[2] Huawei Incubation Center, Hangzhou, China
{wangyuhu,fangfan}@huawei.com

Abstract. We propose a novel Distributed Column-Oriented Database Engine (DCODE) for efficient analytic query processing that combines advantages of both column storage and parallel processing. In DCODE, we enhance an existing open-source columnar database engine by adding the capability for handling queries over a cluster. Specifically, we studied parallel query execution and optimization techniques such as horizontal partitioning, exchange operator allocation, query operator scheduling, operator push-down, and materialization strategies, etc. The experiments over the TPC-H dataset verified the effectiveness of our system.

Keywords: Distributed DBMS · Data processing · Query optimization

1 Introduction

With data collection methods continuously evolving, the demand for analytic results from the data we collect also increases. In scientific research, decision support, business intelligence, medical diagnosis, financial analysis, and numerous other fields it has become more crucial than ever to gain insights from organized data.

The sheer size of data in modern analytic tasks on large datasets makes using traditional row-based database systems quite impractical. On the other hand, column-based engines have shown better performance results for analytic queries [10,17] primarily due to two reasons:

1. Only the specific columns needed have to be retrieved, which significantly reduces the amount of I/O dead weight when compared with the traditional row-based query processing model.
2. More sophisticated optimizations such as cache-conscious processing, vector compression and vectorized execution can be used, resulting in better use of modern CPUs' capabilities.

© IFIP International Federation for Information Processing 2015
I. Khalil et al. (Eds.): ICT-EurAsia 2015 and CONFENIS 2015, LNCS 9357, pp. 289–299, 2015.
DOI: 10.1007/978-3-319-24315-3_30

As such, column storage techniques have been used not only in relational database systems (broadly supporting SQL) but also in other large-scale data processing systems, such as Google Dremel [16] and Apache Drill [1].

Many existing systems for large-scale data processing have been built using Hadoop. Hive [2] and YSmart [14] translate analytic queries into MapReduce jobs to be processed using Hadoop; others such as Cloudera Impala [3] and Facebook Presto [4] generate query equivalent operations directly over HDFS storage and bypass the MapReduce framework to improve query efficiency. While these systems achieve high scalability and reliability from their underlying Hadoop components, they nevertheless face the translation overhead from analytic queries to either MapReduce jobs or HDFS operations and miss many optimization opportunities frequently used by modern database systems. Moreover, these systems exhibit significant limitations on the types of SQL queries supported. Another system approaching scalable query processing is HadoopDB [9], which builds a hybrid engine taking advantage of the scalability of Hadoop as well as the full-fledged query processing capability of a DBMS but at the cost of maintaining two systems at the same time.

Motivated by pioneering work on database parallelism, we developed our analytic query engine **DCODE** on the following foundation: parallel processing of columnar data. Our original objective was to develop an efficient parallel processing engine for analytic workloads. Along the way, we investigated novel techniques, all implemented and verified in experiments. The major challenges and our responses can be outlined as follows: (i) Given column data distributed across multiple servers, the query processing engine has to be aware of the partitioning scheme so that it can dispatch tasks in a query plan to the proper servers for parallel processing. (ii) If a query contains a join operator over columns that differ in their partitioning keys or a group-by operator over non-partitioning keys, it is impossible to complete the execution without re-distributing or re-shuffling the original data. We address this issue by allocating a pair of exchange operators in the distributed query plan whenever re-shuffling is a must. Furthermore, as the dispatched query plans are running in parallel asynchronously, a light-weight scheduler is employed so that data dependencies between distributed operators are always guaranteed. (iii) Materialization strategy in a distributed column database engine has gone beyond the meaning of a non-distributed version [8]. Here we studied not only when the column data needs to be stitched together into rows, but also when a particular column requiring a re-shuffling operation has to have its value vectors re-shuffled during query execution. (iv) Finally, we investigated optimization opportunities such as remote query compilation, operator push-down, and optimal table selection for partitioned, multithreaded processing, which affect processing efficiency significantly in many types of analytic queries based on our complementary empirical investigations.

The rest of this paper is organized as follows. Section 2 describes major technique components and optimizations in the DCODE system. Section 3 briefly presents implementation details and evaluation results of the DCODE system. Our conclusions are presented in Sect. 4.

2   System Overview

2.1   Computing Architecture

The DCODE system consists of multiple shared-nothing commodity server nodes interconnected by high bandwidth Ethernet as shown in Fig. 1. Each server node is running an independent, full-fledged engine instance, so that users can submit queries to any node in the system for distributed processing. The server node accepting user query will be in charge of coordinating all servers involved in query processing progress. After query processing is completed, it will also be in charge of aggregating partial results from all servers and presenting final results to users.

Each server node employs a query parser module which is capable of parsing query text into a query plan where each operator is an atomic sequence of low-level operations over columnar data. A scheduler module decomposes the query plan into multiple sub-plan tasks and assigns those tasks to corresponding servers that possess the column data. It also arranges the execution order of all tasks to ensure that data dependencies are always satisfied across multiple tasks. An access engine executes the operations over the column storage and generates results. Many optimization techniques are used in an optimizer for further improving DCODE's processing efficiency.

2.2   Parallel Query Execution

Horizontal Partitioning. The DCODE system is capable of analytic query processing over a distributed column storage. For the purpose of parallel query execution, it partitions large tables across multiple server nodes horizontally according to either a range-based or a hash-based partition key values from the *partitioning* column or attribute. All other columns of the same table are co-partitioned horizontally with the same partitioning column. Small tables whose sizes are below a certain threshold are simply duplicated across all server nodes for saving the cost of potential data transmission over network.

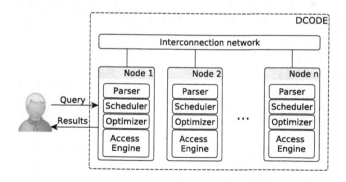

Fig. 1. Architecture of DCODE

The partitioning column can be selected either manually or in a principled manner based on a query workload model to minimize data transmission cost. For example, choosing two columns of different tables that appear in an equi-join query condition as partitioning columns will increase data affinity and eliminate re-shuffling transmission cost. However, an optimal horizontal partitioning scheme of a database containing multiple tables will vary for different query workloads and data distributions. Thus, it is hard to achieve [18].

Exchange Operator Allocation. One key issue towards parallel query execution in DCODE is to deal with incompatible keys. In a distributed query plan, the input values of an operator might be partitioned in a different way than needed by the operator. For example, when there is a join operator over two columns differing in their partition keys, no matter whether these keys are from the partitioning columns or not, they cannot be joined directly. Instead, the values from one joining key have to be re-distributed using the same manner as the other, such as re-hashing based on a hash function. A similar situation happens when we have a group-by operator over a non-partitioning column. We abstract this re-distributing or re-shuffling process in an *exchange* operator in a distributed query plan, adopting notion similar to the Volcano model [12] for parallel query processing.

In principle, a pair of exchange operators, i.e., `exchange_p` (producer) and `exchange_c` (consumer) will be allocated in a distributed query plan where data re-shuffling is a must. Operator `exchange_p` obtains intermediate results from the previous operator and stores them in a local memory pool, which are then re-shuffled and consumed by a remote `exchange_c` operator based on a new partitioning criterion required by the next operator. Note that we employ two exchange operators instead of one due to the fact that a consumer operator might absorb output results from multiple remote producer operators and they might be running in different operating system processes on different server nodes. An example of allocating exchange operators is shown in Fig. 2, where the original plan is to join two tables T1 and T2 on keys T1.a and T2.b (in Fig. 2a). Assuming these two keys are incompatibly partitioned, they cannot be locally joined. A pair of exchange operators are allocated in a distributed query plan for data re-shuffling (shaded in Fig. 2b) to make the join possible. When there are multiple

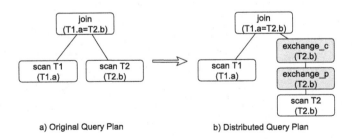

a) Original Query Plan   b) Distributed Query Plan

Fig. 2. Exchange operator allocation

places needing re-shuffling in a query plan, multiple pairs of exchange operators have to be allocated and data will be re-shuffled several times.

Operator Scheduling. As discussed above, a pair of exchange operators might be running on different sever nodes, and a consumer operator has to collect results from all working producer operators. A consumer operator has to wait if some of the producer operators have not yet finished their portion of assigned tasks. In order to coordinate all operators involved in such distributed computing tasks, a light-weight scheduler is deployed for synchronization of tasks, so that an operator will not be executed unless all input it requires has already been prepared. Before the intermediate results are collected by a consumer operator, they are temporarily stored in a local memory pool for better utilization of distributed memory storage. The scheduler module is duplicated across all servers, so that any one of the servers can be in charge of coordinating tasks. However, as for individual queries, DCODE activates only the scheduler on the server node accepting the query.

An example of operator scheduling in parallel query execution of a simple group-by query is shown in Fig. 3. We assume the group-by query is on a non-partitioning column. The scheduler module will then be activated on the server node accepting the query, i.e., Node 3 in Fig. 3. The sequence of function calls as well as data transferring flow are labeled as (1)–(9) in Fig. 3. In (1), the scheduler on Node 3 will first send an execution request (as a remote function call) to the producer operators `exchange_p` on all available server nodes that possess the column data, i.e., Node 1 and 2 in Fig. 3. In (2), each corresponding producer operator obtains the data through an access engine of column storage (as a local function call). This data will be stored in a local memory pool in (3). The producer operator will then notify the scheduler that the request has

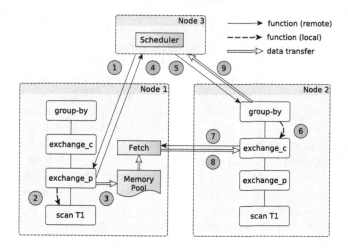

Fig. 3. Operator scheduling in DCODE

been completed in (4). The scheduler will wait till all execution requests are completed to begin next operation. In (5), another execution request is sent to the group-by operator on each server which starts the consumer operators exchange_c in (6). The consumer operator will call a remote *Fetch* function to obtain data from the memory pool in (7). The data will then be re-shuffled and sent back to a corresponding remote consumer operator in (8). In the end, after all nodes finish the group-by operator, the results will be transferred back to Node 3 in (9). Note that instead of collecting data directly from the consumer operator and doing all aggregation on Node 3, we apply the group-by operator to the intermediate results on each server node for better utilization of distributed computing resources.

2.3   Materialization Strategy

In a column database engine, although the intermediate computation could be based on column formatted data, the final results still need to be delivered as row formatted tuples. The operation that transforms columns into rows is called *materialization*. (1) An *early materialization* (EM) strategy [13] will start forming row formatted tuples as soon as query processing begins. (2) A *late materialization* (LM) strategy [8], on the contrary, will not start forming tuples until part of the query plan has been processed. The advantage of EM is that it reduces disk I/O cost for data access. As columns are added to tuples immediately when they are encountered, the column values are accessed only once during query processing. The advantage of LM is that it is more CPU efficient as it requires fewer tuples to be transformed from column formatted data into row formatted data during query processing. It also allows query operators to use high performance vectorized operations over the compressed value list of offset positions.

In a distributed column database engine, besides the aforementioned CPU and disk I/O cost, data re-shuffling incurs additional network transmission cost in the total cost of a query plan. We investigated three different strategies: an early materialization strategy, a late materialization strategy, and a *mixed materialization* strategy [11]. In an early materialization strategy, column values are stitched into row formatted tuples as soon as a column is encountered. After column values are added into intermediate results, they will be re-shuffled together with the re-shuffling column. The consequence of early materialization is that although CPU and disk I/O costs are reduced, network transmission cost is increased for re-shuffling more data. In a late materialization strategy, the offset positions are used in both processing intermediate results and re-shuffling. Although CPU and disk I/O costs increase, network transmission cost reduce. Since there exists a trade-off between early and late materialization, we further proposed a mixed materialization strategy to take advantage of both. When there are multiple operators accessing different columns in a distributed query plan, for columns whose early materialization would have higher network latency during re-shuffling steps than re-access latencies, it is better to delay their materialization; while for others, the conclusion will be the reverse.

2.4   Optimizations in Query Processing

Beyond the core techniques discussed above, we have identified some subtle or system-dependent optimization opportunities in query parsing, query execution, and multithreaded processing during the implementation of DCODE system.

Remote Compilation. During query processing, the input query text has to be first transformed into a query plan as an operator tree, and then transformed into a sequence of lower-level instructions accessing and operating column data. Such a process is called query compilation. Instead of compiling an entire query on a single server node and then sending generated code fragments to corresponding servers, it is more efficient to have all servers compile the same query simultaneously. Such remote compilation has two benefits: 1. No code transmission is needed. 2. The code generated locally can be optimized for execution based on different data characteristics and computing resources that are actually available, such as the number of CPU cores and the size of memory.

Operator Push-down. Push-down optimization is also supported for a number of operators such as group-by, order-by, and top-N. And it is not only for reducing the intermediate result size but also for reducing the network transmission cost in distributed query processing. However, these operators cannot be directly moved down in an operator tree of a distributed query plan. Instead, an equivalent query plan has to be derived by keeping additional information for these operators. For example, if a group-by operator has to be moved down through a pair of exchange operators, the additional information kept will depend on the type of aggregation function, such as SUM() and AVG().

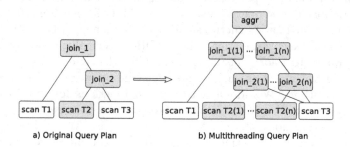

a) Original Query Plan   b) Multithreading Query Plan

Fig. 4. Partitioning table selection for optimizing multithreading processing

Optimization for Multithreaded Processing. In modern DBMSs with multiple CPU cores, each thread is in charge of subtasks of computation with partial data. One key issue for gaining better performance using multithreading is load balancing. In the base open-source engine system of DCODE, a simple heuristic is employed to always partition the largest base table in a query plan, presumably dividing the largest computation task. However, as the size of intermediate results also depends on the previous operations and the selectivity of corresponding operators, a larger base table does not guarantee larger intermediate results.

We adopt a cost-based optimizer for finding the best partitioning table to improve multithreaded processing efficiency [15]. The optimizer searches a space of all possible tables for partitioning, and ranks those partitioning tables based on a scoring function that captures multithreading efficiency. Once the optimal table for partitioning has been discovered, it generates a multithreaded execution plan. A concrete example of multithreaded processing is shown in Fig. 4. Assume there are three tables T1, T2, and T3 in the query. T2 first joins with T3, and then joins with T1 (Fig. 4a). If the cost-based optimizer determines that partitioning T2 will lead to the most efficient multithreading performance, it will split T2 into n parts with each part assigned to a separate thread (CPU core) for parallel processing. As shown in shaded region of Fig. 4b, each thread computes a partial join of T2 with T3 and then a partial join with T1 separately. The final result is obtained by aggregating results from all threads.

3   Implementation and Evaluation

3.1   Implementation

We developed the DCODE system based on MonetDB [10], a state-of-the-art open-source column-oriented database engine optimized for analytic query processing over large data sets. MonetDB revolutionized almost all layers of a database management system. Its innovative contributions include a vertical partitioning storage model, a hardware conscious query execution architecture, vectorized execution, jut-in-time light-weight compression, adaptive indexing, and database cracking. The good performance of the DCODE system is largely based on the outstanding query execution engine built inside MonetDB.

To achieve distributed query processing capability for a column database, we have added additional data structures and optimization algorithms in many core components of the execution engine of MonetDB. Specifically, we added functions for parsing query text for generating a distributed query execution plan. We defined new query operators such as an exchange operator and corresponding evaluation algorithms. We added optimization functions for improving query processing efficiency. We added new statements for function generation and new low-level instructions for query execution. In total, we have developed over 10K lines of code inside the MonetDB kernel, and over 20K line of debugging code for testing and verification.

3.2   Evaluation

We deployed both a physical Linux server cluster and a virtual Linux container (LXC) cluster in our lab environment. Each physical server node in our cluster is running an Ubuntu Linux 3.5.0-17-generic x86_64 operating system on 2x Intel(R) Xeon(R) E5-2680@2.70 GHz processors each with 16 effective threads and 20,480 KB cache. Each server node has 188 GB of RAM.

We used the standard TPC-H benchmark [5] to evaluate the performance of the DCODE system for analytic queries. We modified the DBGen program to generate distributed data by hash partitioning over a particular key column. The partitioning profile is stored locally so that each server node can access column data properly based on the distribution information. As discussed previously, because an optimal partitioning scheme is hard to achieve for distributed query processing, we simply partitioned the largest table in the TPC-H benchmark such as LINEITEM and ORDERS table in experiments although DCODE can handle arbitrary horizontal partitioning.

We evaluated parallel query performance of the DCODE system by comparison with other cutting-edge analytic query processing systems such as Impala v1.1.1 [3], Hive 0.10 [2] (in CDH 4.3.1), and Spark v1.0 [6]. Note that, these versions were the most up-to-date available when we completed our development, test and benchmarking work. For fairness, all systems are set up and evaluated in the same environment. For Impala and Spark, all tables were stored using its column format defined by Parquet [7].

In Fig. 5, a selection of parallel execution experiment results are shown for TPC-H queries Q1, Q3, Q4, Q6, Q8, Q14 and Q16 of scale factor *SF1000* on 16 server nodes. Missing results for a particular system means the query was not supported. From these and other results we concluded that the DCODE system has better coverage for TPC-H queries. As Fig. 5 shows, when using query latency as the yardstick, DCODE always outperforms the other systems. With Q1, Impala and Hive achieved similar performance results to DCODE. Both were orders of magnitude slower in executing the remaining queries. Hive also suffered from the overhead of its MapReduce framework. Spark 1.0 did not achieve comparable performance because the project was still in an early stage especially for query processing supports. We expect all these systems to have made improvements since we completed our study.

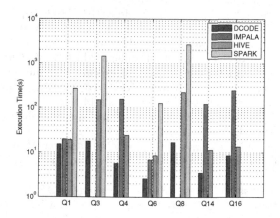

Fig. 5. Evaluation on TPC-H queries

4 Conclusion

In this paper, a novel distributed column-oriented database engine (DCODE) is proposed. The framework uses multiple techniques, e.g. data horizontal partitioning, exchange operator allocation, operator scheduling, materialization strategy selection, and some other optimizations for query processing, the details of which are introduced respectively. We measured the performance of our DCODE system using the TPC-H benchmark. We examined system effectiveness. Our system can automatic process queries in SQL which made comparison with existing advanced systems, such as HIVE, IMPALA and SPARK quite possible. Our results demonstrate that column orientation is ideal for analytic processing. We also demonstrate that with the right architecture and judicious selection of implementations, we can assemble just the right technology to enable parallel distributed query processing in an existing open-source database.

References

1. http://incubator.apache.org/drill/
2. https://archive.apache.org/dist/hive/hive-0.10.0/
3. https://impala.io/
4. http://prestodb.io/
5. http://www.tpc.org/tpch/
6. https://spark.apache.org/releases/spark-release-1-0-0.html/
7. http://parquet.incubator.apache.org/
8. Abadi, D.J., Myers, D.S., DeWitt, D.J., Madden, S.: Materialization strategies in a column-oriented DBMS. In: Proceedings of the 23rd International Conference on Data Engineering, Istanbul, Turkey, 15–20 April 2007, pp. 466–475 (2007)
9. Abouzeid, A., Bajda, K., Abadi, D., Silberschatz, A., Rasin, A.: Hadoopdb: an architectural hybrid of mapreduce and DBMS technologies for analytical workloads. Proc. VLDB Endow. 2(1), 922–933 (2009)
10. Boncz, P.A., Zukowski, M., Nes, N.J.: MonetDB/X100: hyper-pipelining query execution. In: Proceedings of International Conference on Verly Large Data Bases (VLDB) 2005. Very Large Data Base Endowment (2005)
11. Ku, C., Liu, Y., Mortazavi, M., Cao, F., Chen, M., Shi, G.: Optimization strategies for column materialization in parallel execution of queries. In: Decker, H., Lhotská, L., Link, S., Spies, M., Wagner, R.R. (eds.) DEXA 2014, Part II. LNCS, vol. 8645, pp. 191–198. Springer, Heidelberg (2014)
12. Graefe, G.: Volcano - an extensible and parallel query evaluation system. IEEE Trans. Knowl. Data Eng. 6(1), 120–135 (1994)
13. Lamb, A., Fuller, M., Varadarajan, R., Tran, N., Vandiver, B., Doshi, L., Bear, C.: The vertica analytic database: C-store 7 years later. Proc. VLDB Endow. 5(12), 1790–1801 (2012)
14. Lee, R., Luo, T., Huai, Y., Wang, F., He, Y., Zhang, X.: Ysmart: yet another sql-to-mapreduce translator. In: Proceedings of the 2011 31st International Conference on Distributed Computing Systems, Washington, DC, USA, pp. 25–36 (2011)
15. Liu, Y., Mortazavi, M., Cao, F., Chen, M., Shi, G.: Cost-based data-partitioning for intra-query parallelism. In: Proceedings of International Baltic Conference on DB and IS (2014)

16. Melnik, S., Gubarev, A., Long, J.J., Romer, G., Shivakumar, S., Tolton, M., Vassilakis, T.: Dremel: Interactive analysis of web-scale datasets. Proc. VLDB Endow. **3**(1–2), 330–339 (2010)
17. Stonebraker, M., Abadi, D.J., Batkin, A., Chen, X., Cherniack, M., Ferreira, M., Lau, E., Lin, A., Madden, S., O'Neil, E., O'Neil, P., Rasin, A., Tran, N., Zdonik, S.: C-store: a column-oriented DBMS. In: Proceedings of the 31st International Conference on Very Large Data Bases, VLDB 2005, pp. 553–564 (2005)
18. Zhou, J., Bruno, N., Lin, W.: Advanced partitioning techniques for massively distributed computation. In: Proceedings of the 2012 ACM SIGMOD International Conference on Management of Data, New York, NY, USA, pp. 13–24 (2012)

Incorporating Big Data Analytics
into Enterprise Information Systems

Zhaohao Sun[1(✉)], Francisca Pambel[1], and Fangwei Wang[2]

[1] Department of Business Studies, PNG University of Technology,
Lae, Morobe 411, Papua New Guinea
{zsun, fpambel}@dbs.unitech.ac.pg, zhaohao.sun@gmail.com
[2] School of Information Technology,
Hebei Normal University, Shijiazhuang 050032, China
fw_wang@mail.hebtu.edu.cn

Abstract. Big data analytics has received widespread attention for enterprise development and enterprise information systems (EIS). However, how can it enhance the development of EIS? How can it be incorporated into EIS? Both are still big issues. This paper addresses these two issues by proposing an ontology of a big data analytics. This paper also examines incorporation of big data analytics into EIS through proposing BABES: a model for incorporating big data analytics services into EIS. The proposed approach in this paper might facilitate the research and development of EIS, business analytics, big data analytics, and business intelligence as well as intelligent agents.

Keywords: Big data · Big data analytics · Enterprise information systems · Business intelligence · Intelligent agents

1 Introduction

Big data has become a big gold mine of the 21st century because of the miraculous success for big data companies such as Facebook, Google and QQ in the recent years. Big data and its emerging technologies including big data analytics have been making not only big changes in the way the business operates but also traditional data analytics and business analytics become new big opportunities for academicians and enterprise CEOs [1]. Big data analytics is an emerging big data science, and has become a mainstream market adopted broadly across industries, organizations, and geographic regions and among individuals to facilitate data-driven decision making [2, 3]. According to a study of Gartner, worldwide BI (business intelligence) and analytics software, consisting of BI platforms, analytic applications and advanced analytics, totalled $14.4 billion in 2013, an 8 % increase from 2012 revenue [4]. This fact enhances unprecedented interest and adoption of big data analytics. According to the annual survey results of 850 CEOs and other C-level executives of global organizations, McKinsey [5] concludes that 45 % of executives put "big data and advanced analytics" as the first three strategic priorities in both strategy and spending in three years' time and more than one thirds of executives will now spend or in three years' time in this area. IDC (International Data Corporation) predicts that the business

I. Khalil et al. (Eds.): ICT-EurAsia 2015 and CONFENIS 2015, LNCS 9357, pp. 300–309, 2015.
DOI: 10.1007/978-3-319-24315-3_31

analytics software market will grow at a 9.7 % compound annual growth rate over the next five years from 2012 to 2017 [3].

Enterprise information systems (EIS) have been implemented or adopted in many firms in general and Fortune 500 companies in particular, and achieved performance excellence and enhanced decision making over the past few decades [6, p. 381]. EIS are based on organization-wide data and big data beyond the enterprise including that from the Web [7]. How to use big data and big data analytics for improving EIS has become a big challenge for enterprises and the development of EIS recently [1, 7].

The above brief literature review and discussion implies that the following important issues have not drawn significant attention in the scholarly peer-reviewed literature:

- What is the relationship between big data analytics and EIS?
- How can big data analytics be incorporated into EIS?

This paper will address these two issues through reviewing and extending our early research on analytics service oriented architecture for EIS [1]. More specifically, we first propose an ontology of big data analytics in Sect. 2 through overviewing our early work on business analytics and big data analytics [1]. To address the first issue, this paper looks at EIS and its relationship with big data analytics in Sect. 3. To address the second issue, this paper proposes BABES: a model for incorporating big data analytics into EIS. The final sections discuss the related work and end this paper with some concluding remarks and future work.

2   An Ontology of Big Data Analytics

This section proposes an ontology of big data analytics and looks at the interrelationship between big data analytics and data analytics. To begin with, this section first examines big data analytics.

Big data analytics is an integrated form of data analytics and web analytics for big data [1]. According to Beal [8] and Gandomi and Haider [9], big data analytics can be defined as a process of collecting, organizing and analyzing big data to discover patterns, knowledge, and intelligence as well as other information within the big data. Based on this definition, big data analytics can be considered a combination of big data management and big data mining, because the process of collecting and organizing big data belongs to big data management while the process of 'analyzing big data to discover patterns, knowledge, and intelligence as well as other information within the big data' is the main task of big data mining, where big data mining is a modern form of traditional data mining in the age of big data.

More generally, big data analytics is an emerging science and technology involving the multidisciplinary state-of-art information and communication technology (ICT), mathematics, operations research (OR), machine learning, and decision science for big data [1, 10]. The main components of big data analytics include big data descriptive analytics, big data predictive analytics, and big data prescriptive analytics [11].

- Big data descriptive analytics is descriptive analytics for big data [12]. It is used to discover and explain the characteristics of entities and relationships among entities within the existing big data [13, p. 611]. Big data descriptive analytics addresses what happened, and when, as well as what is happening through analyzing the existing big data using analytical techniques and tools.
- Big data predicative analytics is predicative analytics for big data, which focuses on forecasting trends by addressing the problems such as what will happen, what is likely to happen and why it will happen [12, 14]. Big data predicative analytics is used to create models to predict future outcomes or events based on the existing big data [13, p. 611].
- Big data prescriptive analytics is prescriptive analytics for big data, which addresses the problems such as what we should do, why we should do it and what should happen with the best outcome under uncertainty through analyzing the existing big data using analytical techniques and tools [11, p. 5].

An ontology is a formal naming and definition of a number of concepts and their interrelationships that really or fundamentally exist for a particular domain of discourse [15]. Then, an ontology of big data analytics is a network consisting of a number of concepts and their interrelationships for big data analytics.

Based on the above discussion, we propose an ontology of big data analytics, as illustrated in Fig. 1. In this ontology, big data analytics is at the top while big data and data analytics are at the bottom. Big data descriptive analytics, big data predictive analytics, and big data prescriptive analytics are at the middle level as the core parts of any big data analytics.

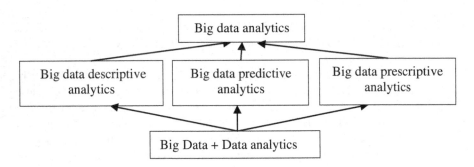

Fig. 1. An ontology of big data analytics

In Fig. 1, data analytics refers to as a method or technique that uses data, information, and knowledge to learn, describe and predict something [14, p. 341]. Data analytics is a science and technology about examining, summarizing, and drawing conclusions from data to learn, describe and predict something. In brief, data analytics can be then considered as data-driven discoveries of knowledge and intelligence and communications [12].

The fundamentals of big data analytics consists of mathematics, statistics, engineering, human interface, computer science and information technology [1, 10].

The techniques for big data analytics encompass a wide range of mathematical, statistical, and modeling techniques [13, p. 590]. Big data analytics always involves historical or current data and visualization [16]. This requires big data analytics to use data mining (DM) to discover knowledge from a data warehouse (DW) or a big dataset in order to aid decision making, in particular in the text of big business and management [14, p. 344]. DM employs advanced statistical tools to analyze the big data available through DW and other sources to identify possible relationships, patterns and anomalies and discover information or knowledge for rational decision making [13, p. 590]. DW extracts or obtains its data from operational databases as well as from external open sources, providing a more comprehensive data pool including historical or current data [13, p. 590]. Big data analytics is also required to use statistical modelling (SM) to learn something that can aid decision making [1]. Visualization techniques as an important part of big data analytics make any knowledge patterns and information for decision making in a form of figure or table or multimedia. In summary, big data analytics can facilitate business decision making and realization of business objectives through analyzing current problems and future trends, creating predictive models to forecast future threats and opportunities, and optimizing business processes based on involved historical or current big data to enhance organizational performance [12]. Therefore, big data analytics can be represented below.

$$\text{Big data analytics} = \text{Big data} + \text{data analytic} + \text{DW} + \text{DM} + \text{SM} + \text{Visualization} + \text{optimization} \tag{1}$$

This representation reveals the fundamental relationship between big data, data analytics and big data analytics, that is, big data analytics is based on big data and data analytics. It also shows that computer science and information technology play a dominant role in the development of big data analytics through providing sophisticated techniques and tools of DM, DW, machine learning and visualization [1]. SM and optimization still play a fundamental role in the development of big data analytics, in particular in big data prescriptive analytics [11].

3   Enterprise Information Systems and Big Data Analytics

This section examines enterprise information systems (EIS) and its relationships with big data analytics.

EIS has drawn increasing attention in academia, organizations and enterprises over the past decades. EIS is also called enterprise systems [14]. There are many different definitions on EIS. For example, EIS refers to as

1. Systems that help managers and companies to improve their performance by enabling them to seamlessly share data and information among departments and with external business partners [14, p. 287]. These systems integrate the functional systems such as accounting, finance and marketing as well as operations.
2. Enterprise software that are based on a suite of integrated software modules and a common central database [6, p. 363].

3. Information systems that support activities in multiple departments of an enterprise [17, p. 605].

The first definition is self-contained for an EIS and emphasizes sharing data and information. The second stresses enterprise software with a common central database. The third one is a general definition. By integrating these three definitions, we can define an EIS as an information system that has a common central database and support activities in multiple departments of the enterprise through integrating the functional information systems (IS) such as accounting, finance, marketing and other operations' IS, and accessing the data resources available in the enterprise and on the Web. The support activities included will help managers and the enterprise to improve their business performance and decision making by enabling them to seamlessly share data and information among departments and with external business partners [1].

EIS mainly consist of ERP (enterprise resource planning) systems, SCM (supply chain management) systems, CRM (Customer relationship management) systems and KM (knowledge management) systems [6, 14]. The ERP system is an EIS that processes the information of multiple departments such as human resources management, finance and accounting management, sales and marketing management, manufacturing and production management of an enterprise in a unified way [6, pp. 81-2]. The SCM system is used to manage the relationships with the suppliers. The CRM system is used to manage the relationships with the customers of the enterprise. The KM system is used to manage the processes for capturing and applying knowledge and expertise of enterprise.

Based on the previous subsection's discussion, big data analytics can facilitate the development of EIS, because it can support business decision making in the age of big data [1]. Big data analytics also allows enterprises to enhance business performance, efficiencies and guides decision processes [18]. Both EIS and big data analytics are common in emphasizing the big data as a strategic resource for the development of enterprises, in particular for global enterprises. EIS involves interactive visualization for data exploration and discovery [19], which can be considered as a part of big data analytics, as mentioned in Eq. 1 of Sect. 2. EIS include analytical tools for using big data to evaluate the business and marketing performance [1]. The analytical tools are a fundamental part of any big data analytics systems. This implies that EIS and big data analytics share some common tools to support business decision making and improve the business performance of enterprises.

Based on the research of IDC [20], Australian organizations expect big data and advanced analytics projects to deliver outcomes that will improve competitive advantage, enhance customer service and support, and aid with customer acquisition and retention. However, big data and big data analytics technology in the Australian industry demonstrate considerable variation in progress with some quite advanced with sophisticated and deeply embedded deployments within core business processes, whilst others are just beginning the journey [21].

EIS are important information systems for improving business performance and business decision making of CEOs and enterprises. Big data analytics is a pivotal part for developing EIS [1]. From a technological viewpoint, big data analytics is data-driven business oriented technique and facilitates business decision making, and improves EIS as a system component. From a data viewpoint, big data analytics relies on big data and data analytics; and big data have become a strategic resource for any organization and enterprise, in particular for multinational organisations as well as any EIS. Discovering useful patterns, information and knowledge from big data has become the central topic both for business operations and marketing and for EIS. This is just the task of big data analytics.

4 BABES: A Model for Incorporating Big Data Analytics into EIS

This section addresses how big data analytics can be incorporated into EIS through presenting a model for big data analytics-based EIS, for short, BABES.

Standalone enterprise systems have become a thing of the past [22, p. 382]. BABES incorporates big data analytics services into an EIS that consists of main functions of SCM systems, CRM systems and KM systems, as shown in Fig. 2. In what follows, we will examine this model in some detail.

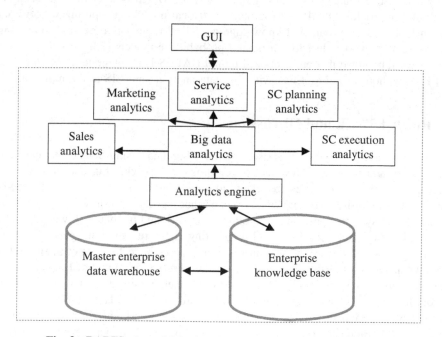

Fig. 2. BABES: A model for incorperating big data analytics into EIS

SCM systems are classified as either SC (supply chain) planning systems or SC execution systems [6, p. 370]. Then SC planning and SC execution are main functions of SCM systems. CRM systems mainly consist of sales, marketing and services [6, p. 379]. A KM system mainly is used to create, capture, refine, store, manage, disseminate, and share knowledge [23]. Therefore, BABES includes SC planning analytics, SC execution analytics, marketing analytics, sales analytics, service analytics and big data analytics.

Master enterprise data warehouse (MEDW) mainly consists of data related to sales, marketing, services, customers, SC planning, and SC execution flowing from departments of marketing, human resources, and other data related to departments. All these can be considered as structured data. Enterprise knowledge base (EKB), a part of the KM system, consists of information and knowledge from the Web, call centers, direct mails, emails, retail stores, and clients and partners [6]. All these data of EKB are mainly semi-structured or unstructured data and information. EKB will play a more important role in EIS with incorporating big data analytics, because unstructured data constitutes about 95 % of big data [9].

Big data analytics is based on MEDW and EKB, and provides related information and techniques for sales analytics, marketing analytics, service analytics, SC planning analytics and SC execution analytics, each of them can be considered as an intelligent agent [24].

Analytics engine is a mechanism, as an intelligent agent, for managing and producing SC planning analytics, SC planning analytics, marketing analytics, service analytics, customer analytics, and big data analytics. Based on the foregoing Eq. (1), Analytics engine has OLAP, data mining, statistical modelling, optimization, visualisation tools and other data and knowledge analytical tools including soft computing, fuzzy neural networks, decision trees, and probabilistic models [10].

It should be noted that our proposed model BABES is to integrate SCM and CRM and KM, without including ERP, with big data analysis into EIS at the moment.

5 Related Work and Discussion

The authors have searched "enterprise systems" "big data" using ScienceDirect (on 18 May 2015), and there are a few real development of applying big data in enterprise systems. In which, two articles are related to our research. One is the Special Issue on "Intelligent Enterprise Systems" which means that big data has drawn attention from the intelligent systems community. Another is on ERP and big data [7], which focuses on aligning big data with ERP and suggesting a future research agenda to bring together big data and ERP whereas our research focuses on techniques of incorporating big data analytics into EIS. We share the similar observation to that of Elragal [7] that there are only a few research reports on how to integrate big data analytics into EIS although there are a significant number of researches on big data analytics. Furthermore, a basic search in Scopus and Google scholar (i.e. article title and key words) reveals that the number of papers published on "big data analytics enterprise system" (in the title of papers) in journals and proceedings is small excepted our earlier work (retrieved on 8 April 2015). Therefore, how to integrate big data analytics with EIS is still a big issue for research communities. This motivates us to examine techniques for how to incorporate big data analytics into EIS.

We have mentioned a number of scholarly researches on data analytics, big data analytics, and EIS. In what follows, we will focus on related work and discussion on ontology of big data analytics, and the work of SAP as well as incorporation of big data analytics into EIS.

Ontology has been important in computer science and artificial intelligence [1]. A basic search in Google scholar (i.e. article title and key words) reveals that there are a few publications entitled "ontology of big data analytics". We then explored it and put it as a part of this research through updating our early work on data analytics, business analytics and big data analytics [1]. We try to explore the interrelationship among big data analytics, big data descriptive analytics, big data predictive analytics, and big data prescriptive analytics using the proposed ontology. The result reported in this paper on ontology of big data analytics and big data analytics equation, which is an updated form of our early work, is only a beginning for providing a relatively comprehensive ontology of big data analytics. In this direction, we will investigate more academic reviewed sources as a future work to develop an ontology of big data analytics with three levels of knowledge concepts for each related analytics, that is, for each analytics in the ontology of big data analytics, we will examine its concepts, fundamentals, methodologies, tools and applications. Such an investigation would become an important guide for the research and development of big data analytics, and EIS.

SAP, one of the leading vendors of ERP [7], has introduced its enterprise service-oriented architecture [6, p. 383]. SAP's architecture specifies general services to enterprise services whereas our BABES model specifies general services to big data analytics as a service. Big data analytics services should be a part of enterprise services, and then our BABES can be considered as a concrete application for the enterprise service-oriented architecture of SAP. However, SAP's enterprise system focuses on enterprise services in finance, logistics, procurement and human resources management as a part of its ERP system [6]. We conceive that our DBABES will be incorporated into the next generation EIS integrating SCM, CRM, and KM systems, in particular the cloud-based version of EIS.

6 Conclusion

The paper presented a timely critical investigation of an emerging area of big data analytics and its relationships to existing fields of IS research in general and EIS in specific. The two main contributions of this paper are an ontology of big data analytics and BABES: a model for incorporating big data analytics into EIS. The ontology of big data analytics is used to address what is the constitution of big data analytics and how its components are networked. The BABES reveals how to incorporate big data analytics into EIS. The discussion of the related work of SAP implies that the proposed DABES is useful for the development of EIS. The proposed approach in this paper might facilitate research and development of business analytics, big data analytics, EIS, and BI.

Besides mentioning in the previous section, in our future work, we will explore enterprise acceptability of DABES for EIS. We will also explore how to design and implement DABES. More specifically, we will address the main functions of EIS that should be based on DABES, and how DABES can be developed in order to incorporate big data analytics into EIS using intelligent agents technology [24].

Acknowledgments. We gratefully thank the four anonymous reviewers for their erudite comments which make us improve the quality of this paper.

References

1. Sun, Z., Strang, K., Yearwood, J.: Analytics service oriented architecture for enterprise information systems. In: Proceedings of iiWAS2014, CONFENIS 2014, 4–6 December 14, Hanoi (2014)
2. Sun, Z., Firmin, S., Yearwood, J.: Integrating online social networking with e-commerce based on CBR. In: The 23rd ACIS 2012 Proceedings, 3–5 December, Geelong (2012)
3. Vesset, D., McDonough, B., Schubmehl, D., Wardley, M.: Worldwide Business Analytics Software 2013–2017 Forecast and 2012 Vendor Shares (Doc # 241689), 6 2013. http://www.idc.com/getdoc.jsp?containerId=241689. Accessed 28 June 2014
4. van der Meulen, R., Rivera, J.: Gartner Says Worldwide Business Intelligence and Analytics Software Market Grew 8 Percent in 2013, 29 April 2014. http://www.gartner.com/newsroom/id/2723717. Accessed 28 June 2014
5. McKinsey, The digital tipping point: McKinsey Global Survey results, June 2014. http://www.mckinsey.com/insights/business_technology/the_digital_tipping_point_mckinsey_global_survey_results. Accessed 1 July 2014
6. Laudon, K.G., Laudon, K.C.: Management Information Systems: Managing the Digital Firm, 12th edn. Pearson, Harlow (2012)
7. Elragal, A.: ERP and Big Data: The Inept Couple. Procedia Technology **16**, 242–249 (2014)
8. Beal, V.: Big data analytics. http://www.webopedia.com/TERM/B/big_data_analytics.html. Accessed 20 August 2014
9. Gandomi, A., Haider, M.: Beyond the hype: big data concepts, methods, and analytics. Int. J. Inf. Manage. **35**, 137–144 (2015)
10. Chen, C.P., Zhang, C.-Y.: Data-intensive applications, challenges, techniques and technologies: a survey on Big Data. Inf. Sci. **275**, 314–347 (2014)
11. Minelli, M., Chambers, M., Dhiraj, A.: Big Data, Big Analytics: Emerging Business Intelligence and Analytic Trends for Today's Businesses, Wiley & Sons (Chinese Edition 2014) (2013)
12. Delena, D., Demirkanb, H.: Data, information and analytics as services. Decis. Support Syst. **55**(1), 359–363 (2013)
13. Coronel, C., Morris, S., Rob, P.: Database Systems: Design, Implementation, and Management, 11th edn. Course Technology, Cengage Learning, Boston (2015)
14. Turban, E., Volonino, L.: Information Technology for Management: Improving Strategic and Operational Performance, 8th edn. Wiley, Danvers (2011)
15. Gruber, T.: Toward principles for the design of ontologies used for knowledge sharing. Int. J. Hum Comput. Stud. **43**(5–6), 907–928 (1995)
16. Sun, Z., Yearwood, J.: A theoretical foundation of demand-driven web services. In: Demand-Driven Web Services: Theory, Technologies, and Applications, IGI-Global, pp. 1–25 (2014)
17. Kroenke, D., Bunker, D., Wilson, D.: Exerperiencing MIS, 3rd edn. Pearson, Australia (2014)
18. Kambatla, K., Kollias, G., Kumar, V., Grama, A.: Trends in big data analytics. J. Parallel Distrib. Comput. **74**(7), 2561–2573 (2014)
19. Brust, A.: Gartner releases 2013 BI Magic Quadrant (2013). http://www.zdnet.com/gartner-releases-2013-bi-magic-quadrant-7000011264/. Accessed 14 February 2014

20. Parker, S., Hira, A.T.: Australia Reaches a Tipping Point for Big Data Adoption, Says IDC Australia, 23 June 2015. http://www.idc.com/getdoc.jsp?containerId=prAU25707715
21. Ditton, E., Parker, S.: Big Data and Analytics in the Australia Industry April 2014. http://www.idc.com/getdoc.jsp?containerId=AU245426
22. Laudon, K., Laudon, J.: Management Information Systems-Managing the Dgital Firm. Pearson, Boston (2012)
23. Sun, Z., Finnie, G.: Experience Management in Knowledge Management. In: Khosla, R., Howlett, R.J., Jain, L.C. (eds.) KES 2005. LNCS (LNAI), vol. 3681, pp. 979–986. Springer, Heidelberg (2005)
24. Sun, Z., Finnie, G.: Intelligent Techniques in E-Commerce: A Case-based Reasoning Perspective. Springer, Heidelberg (2004). (2010)

Analytical Platform Based on Jbowl Library Providing Text-Mining Services in Distributed Environment

Martin Sarnovský[✉], Peter Butka, Peter Bednár, František Babič, and Ján Paralič

Faculty of Electrical Engineering and Informatics,
Department of Cybernetics and Artificial Intelligence,
Technical University of Košice, Letná 9/B, 042 00 Košice, Slovakia
{martin.sarnovsky,peter.butka,peter.bednar,
frantisek.babic,jan.paralic}@tuke.sk

Abstract. The paper presents the Jbowl, Java software library for data and text analysis, and various research activities performed and implemented on top of the library. The paper describes the various analytical services for text and data mining implemented in Jbowl as well as numerous extensions aimed to address the evolving trends in data and text analysis and its usage in various tasks reflecting the areas such as big data analysis, distributed computing and parallelization. We also present the complex analytical platform built on top of the library, integrating the distributed computing analytical methods with the graphical user interface, visualization methods and resource management capabilities.

Keywords: Text and data mining · Software library in java · Data preprocessing · Web portal

1 Introduction

Question of integrated analytical solutions has become interesting in recent years to improve the end-users orientation in wide range of available services, methods, algorithms or tools. The aim was to bring these services closer to the non-expert users and provide the possibilities to use them without deep knowledge about their implementation details or internal modes of operation.

The work presented in this paper represents our activities in building of the coherent and complex system for text mining experimental purposes built upon the distributed computing infrastructure. Such infrastructure can offer computational effectiveness and data storage facilities for proposed on-line analytical tool that comprises of various services for knowledge discovery in texts and provides specific data and computing capacity. Our main motivation is to provide coherent system leveraging of distributed computing concepts and providing simple user interface for users as well as administration and monitoring interface.

Text mining [1] aims at discovery of hidden patterns in textual data. For this topic, there is available a textbook [2], which we wrote in Slovak for our students. It describes

© IFIP International Federation for Information Processing 2015
I. Khalil et al. (Eds.): ICT-EurAsia 2015 and CONFENIS 2015, LNCS 9357, pp. 310–319, 2015.
DOI: 10.1007/978-3-319-24315-3_32

the whole process of knowledge discovery from textual collections. We describe in details all preprocessing steps (such as tokenization, segmentation, lemmatization, morphologic analysis, stop-words elimination), we discuss various models for representation of text documents and focus on three main text mining tasks: (1) text categorization [3, 4]; (2) clustering of textual documents [5, 6]; (3) information extraction from texts [7, 8].

Finally, we describe service-oriented view on text mining and present also selected distributed algorithms for text mining. Second part of the textbook [2] is devoted to description of our Jbowl (Java bag of words library) presenting its architecture, selected applications and a couple of practical examples, which help our students easier start for practical work with Jbowl on their own text mining problems. In this paper we want to present the latest advancements in Jbowl library, which makes it usable also for big data text mining applications and invite broader audience of the World Computer Congress to use this library in various text mining applications.

2 Concept of Analytical Library

2.1 Jbowl

Jbowl[1] is a Java library that was designed to support different phases of the whole text mining process and offers a wide range of relevant classification and clustering algorithms. Its architecture integrates several external components, such as JSR 173 – API for XML parsing or Apache Lucene[2] for indexing and searching.

This library was proposed as an outcome of the detailed analysis of existing free software tools in the relevant domain [9]. The motivation behind the design of this library was existence of many fragmented implementations of different algorithms for processing, analyses and mining in text documents within our research team on one hand side and lack of equivalent integrated open source tool on the other hand side. The main aim at that time was not to provide simple graphical user interface with possibility to launch selected procedures but to offer set of services necessary to create the own text mining stream customized to concrete conditions and specified objectives. The initial Jbowl version included:

- Services for management and manipulation with large sets of text documents.
- Services for indexing, complex statistical text analyses and preprocessing tasks.
- Interface for knowledge structures as ontologies, controlled vocabularies or lexical WordNet database.
- Support for different formats as plain text, HTML or XML and various languages.

These core functionalities have been continuously extended and improved based on new requirements or expectations expressed by researchers and students of our department. Detailed information can be found in [10] or [11].

---

[1] Basic Jbowl package - http://sourceforge.net/projects/jbowl/.

[2] https://lucene.apache.org/.

The second main update of the library offers possibility to run the text mining tasks in a distributed environment within task-based execution engine. This engine provides middleware-like transparent layer (mostly for programmers wishing to re-use functionality of the Jbowl package) for running of different tasks in a distributed environment [12]. In the next step, new services for aspect-based sentiment analysis or Formal Concept Analysis – FCA (cf. [13]) were added [14] to extend application potential of the library in line with current trends. In case of FCA subpart related to processing of matrices from Jbowl BLAS (Basic Linear Algebra Subprograms) implementation was used and extended in order to work with FCA models known as generalized one-sided concept lattices [15] and use it for other purposes like design and implementation of FCA-based conceptual information retrieval system [16]. There is also extension of services related to processing of sequences within the data sets and processing of graph-based data, which is partially based on Jbowl API and its models.

2.2 Services for Distributed Data Analysis

Our main motivation was to use the problem decomposition method and apply it in data-intensive analytical tasks. Distributed computing infrastructure such as grid or cloud enables to utilize the computational resources for such kind of tasks by leveraging the parallel and distributed computing concepts. There are also several existing frameworks available offering different methods of parallel/distributed processing using the principle such as mapreduce, in-memory, etc. In order to support computation-intensive tasks and improve scalability of Jbowl library, we have decided to use GridGain[3] platform for distributed computing.

Jbowl API was used as a basis for particular data processing and analytical tasks. We decided to design and implement distributed versions of classification and clustering algorithms implemented in Jbowl. Currently implemented algorithms are summarized in Table 1.

Table 1. Overview of currently implemented supervised and unsupervised models in Jbowl.

	Sequential	Distributed
Decision tree classifier	✓	✓
K-nearest neighbor classifier	✓	✓
Rule-based classifier	✓	
Support Vector Machine classifier	✓	
Boosting compound classifier	✓	✓
K-means clustering	✓	✓
GHSOM clustering	✓	✓

In general, the process of the text mining model (classification or clustering) creation is split into the sub-processes. As depicted in Fig. 1, one of the nodes in

---

[3] http://www.gridgain.com.

distributed computing infrastructure (master node) performs the decomposition of particular task (data or model-driven) and then assigns particular sub-tasks onto available resources in the infrastructure (worker nodes). Worker nodes produce partial outputs which correspond to partial models (on partial datasets). Those partial models are collected and merged into the final model on the master at the end. The concrete implementation of sub-tasks distribution is different in particular model types, we will further introduce the most important ones.

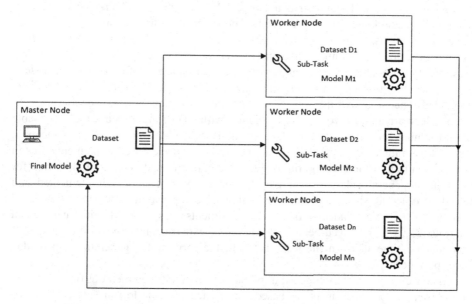

Fig. 1. General schema of the sub-task distribution across the platform

For induction of decision trees, Jbowl library implements generic algorithm where it is possible to configure various criteria for splitting data on decision nodes and various pruning methods for post-processing of the induced tree. Distributed version of the classifier [17] considers the multi-label classification problem, when the document may be classified into one or more predefined categories. In that case, each class is considered as a separate binary classification problem and resulting model consists of a set of binary classifiers. In this case, particular binary classifiers represent the sub-tasks computed in distributed fashion.

Our distributed k-nearest neighbor (k-NN) classification algorithm was inspired by [18]. In this solution we used the Jbowl k-NN implementation as a basis and modified it into the distributed version that split the input data into the chunks and calculates the local k-NN models on the partitions.

Another set of Jbowl algorithms modified into the distributed versions were clustering ones. Distributed implementation of GHSOM (Growing Hierarchical Self-Organizing Maps) [19] implementation uses MapReduce (GridGain implementation) paradigm and is based on parallel calculation of subtasks, which in this case represents the creation of hierarchically ordered maps of Growing SOM models [20]. Main idea is parallel execution of these clustering processes on worker nodes. Distributed version of K-Means clustering algorithm is based on methods presented in [21, 22]. Our approach separates the process of creation of k clusters among the available computing resources so the particular clusters are being built locally on the assigned data.

The FCA algorithms are in general computationally very expensive when used on large datasets. This issue was solved by decomposition of the problem. Starting set of documents were decomposed to smaller sets of similar documents with the use of clustering algorithm. Then particular concept lattices were built upon every cluster using FCA method and these FCA-based models were combined to simple hierarchy of concept lattices using agglomerative clustering algorithm. This approach was implemented in distributed manner using the GridGain, where computing of local models was distributed between worker nodes and then combined together on master node.

Further, we have implemented specialized FCA-based algorithms of generalized one-sided concept lattices using the Jbowl API for sparse matrices and operations with them, which are able to work more efficiently with sparse input data usually available in text-mining and information retrieval tasks. Here we have provided experiments in order to test ratios for computation time reduction of sparse-based implementations in comparison to the standard algorithms [23]. Then, distributed version of algorithm for creation of generalized one-sided concept lattices was designed, implemented and tested in order to show additional reduction of computation times for FCA-based models [24]. The extended version of experiments was realized with real textual datasets [25], which proved behavior of previous experimental results on reduction of computation time using mentioned distributed algorithm for generalized one-sided concept lattices.

Also, we have currently finished implementation of selected methods (classification and clustering) provided in portal-based way which are able to run tasks for experiments defined by user in BOINC-based infrastructure. BOINC[4] is well-known open-source platform for volunteer distributed scientific computing. In this case Jbowl package is in the core of the system and is used for running of text mining experiments defined by user setup. These experiments are decomposed to BOINC jobs, pushed to BOINC clients and result of their distributed computations is returned back to server and provided to user [26].

The vision of the whole system is to re-use computational capacities of computers within university laboratories for volunteer-based computation. Our system has potential to support researchers to start their experiments and use additional cloud-like features of distributed computing using BOINC-based infrastructure. Currently, we have implemented also a graphical user interface which hides complexity behind creation of BOINC jobs for clients using dynamic forms and automation scripts for creation of jobs and analysis and presentation of the results provided to the user.

---

[4] BOINC - https://boinc.berkeley.edu/.

2.3   Services for Optimization

In some cases, the analytical processes can be complex, so our plan for the future development is to extend the system with the recommendations for less experienced users to improve their orientation in computing environment. These recommendations will be generated based on the observed patterns how other users are using the system and generating the results. For this purpose we will use our analytical framework designed and developed within KP-Lab project[5]. The core of this framework includes services for event logging, logs storage, manipulation with logs, extraction of common patterns and visualization of event/pattern sequences [27].

Patterns can be understood as a collection (usually a sequence) of fragments, each describing a generalization of some activity performed by users within virtual environment, e.g. sequence of concrete operations leading to the successful realization of clustering analysis. The success of this method for generating recommendations based on actual user behavior in virtual computing environment strongly depends on the quality of collected logs. Extracted and visualized information and patterns can be used not only for recommendations generation, but also for evaluation of user behavior during the solving of the data analytical tasks.

Another kind of optimization methods were implemented on the resource usage level. As mentioned in previous sections, several models are deployed on and use the distributed computing infrastructure. Main objective of these optimization methods is to improve the resource utilization within the platform based on type of performed analytical task as well as on the dataset processed. Several methods were designed for that purpose.

In general, system collects the dataset characteristics, including the information about its size and structure [28]. Another kind of data is collected from the infrastructure itself. This information describes the actual state of the distributed environment, actual state of the particular nodes as well as their performance and capacity. Depending on the type of analytical task, such information can be used to guide the sub-task creation and distribution. Sub-tasks are then created in order to maintain particular sub-task complexity on the same level and distributed across the platform according to the actual node usage and available performance and capacity.

2.4   Infrastructure Services

An important condition for the proper functioning and efficient of the presented services is a technical infrastructure providing necessary computing power and data capacity. We continuously build our own computing environment in which we can not only deploy and test our services, but we're able to offer them as a SaaS (Software as a Service). Simplified illustration of the used infrastructure is shown in Fig. 2.

Basic level contains several Synology network attached storages (NAS) with WD hard drives providing customized data storage capacity for various purposes; i.e. it is possible to use SQL or NoSQL databases or some types of semantic repositories. The

---

[5] http://web.tuke.sk/fei-cit/kplab.html.

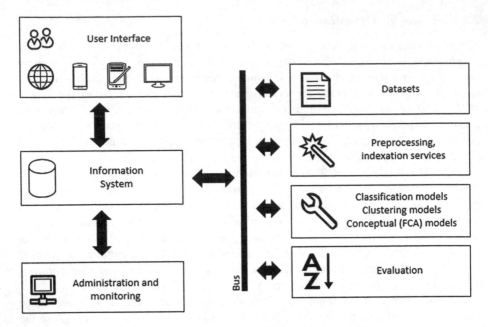

Fig. 2. Architecture of text mining analytical system

second level is represented by high-performance IBM application servers that are used for execution and data manipulation. This part of the infrastructure is separated and inaccessible to external users.

Graphical user interface with offered services and user functionalities is provided by web server and available for different end-user devices as traditional PC, laptops or tablets. Specific part of the deployed analytical system is the administration and monitoring module. Several modules are deployed on distributed computing infrastructure and interface to manage the platform itself is necessary. Such administration interface is implemented as a web application and enables to monitor the current state of the environment, including the operational nodes, their actual state, load, capacity as well as running tasks. If necessary, it is possible to disconnect the node from the platform, or add a new node, check their state and perform several actions to interact with them (stop halted tasks, free memory/space, check the network latency and restore the default configuration). Data collected using this module is also utilized in task distribution, as briefly described in Sect. 2.3.

On the other hand, people interested in our analytical and data processing services can download them, customize services based on their own preferences or requirements and finally deploy the customized platform on their own infrastructure.

Also, as it was written in Sect. 2.2, we have created some BOINC infrastructure from computers in our laboratories for students, which is able to provide additional computing capacity for BOINC-based applications. This paradigm is known as virtual campus supercomputing center and BOINC is widely used by several universities in the world in order to get some more computational capacities from their computers within campuses. After completion of testing phase we would like to provide graphical user interface for more researchers to run Jbowl experimental tasks, for which particular models are computed on BOINC clients and returned to user. In the future it can be interesting to find interoperable connection in usage of cloud-based infrastructure defined above and volunteer-based BOINC infrastructure under one common platform, e.g., where capacities of both parts are managed together in order to achieve more efficient analytical services.

3 Conclusion

The need for software libraries for support of text mining purposes is not new, but their importance is increasing because of new requirements arising in the era of big data. An important factor is the ability of the existing products to respond to the changes in the areas as IT infrastructure, new capacity opportunities for parallel computing, running the traditional text and data mining algorithms on the new infrastructures, development of the new algorithms for data processing and analysis using new computational possibilities and finally the design and implementation of simple understandable and easy to use user environment.

Basically, presented work seeks to respond to all of these challenges and address them in the practical output of the relevant research and implementation activities. The presented library does not try to compete with the other available text mining platforms, but rather represents the output of our continuous work. The developed system presents an ideal platform for our ongoing research as well as for the education. Presented tools are used by the students and teachers in teaching tasks; serve as the platform for numerous master theses and regularly being used in data analytical and research activities.

Acknowledgment. The work presented in this paper was partially supported by the Slovak Grant Agency of Ministry of Education and Academy of Science of the Slovak Republic under grant No. 1/1147/12 (40 %); partially by the Slovak Cultural and Educational Grant Agency of the Ministry of Education, Science, Research and Sport of the Slovak Republic under grant No. 025TUKE-4/2015 (20 %) and it is also the result of the Project implementation: University Science Park TECHNICOM for Innovation Applications Supported by Knowledge Technology, ITMS: 26220220182, supported by the Research & Development Operational Programme funded by the ERDF (40 %).

References

1. Feldman, R., Sanger, J.: The Text Mining Handbook: Advanced Approaches in Analyzing Unstructured Data. Cambridge University Press (2007)
2. Paralič, J., Furdík, K., Tutoky, G., Bednár, P., Sarnovský, M., Butka, P., Babič, F.: Text Mining (in Slovak: Dolovanie znalostí z textov). Equilibria, Košice, p. 184 (2010)
3. Sebastiani, F.: Machine learning in automated text categorization. J. ACM Comput. Surv. (CSUR) **34**(1), 1–47 (2002)
4. Machová, K., Bednár, P., Mach, M.: Various approaches to web information processing. Comput. Inf. **26**(3), 301–327 (2007)

5. Sarnovský, M., Butka, P., Paralič, J.: Grid-based support for different text mining tasks. Acta Polytechnica Hungarica 6(4), 5–27 (2009)
6. Rauber, A., Pampalk, E., Paralič, J.: Empirical Evaluation of Clustering Algorithms. J. Inf. Organ. Sci. 24(2), 195–209 (2000)
7. Sarawagi, S.: Information extraction. J. Found. Trends Databases 1(3), 261–377 (2007)
8. Machová, K., Maták, V., Bednár, P.: Information extraction from the web pages using machine learning methods. In: Information and Intelligent Systems, pp. 407–414, Faculty of Organization and Informatics Varaždin (2005)
9. Bednár, P., Butka, P., Paralič, J.: Java Library for Support of Text Mining and Retrieval. In: Proceedings of Znalosti 2005, pp. 162–169, VŠB TU Ostrava (2005)
10. Butka, P., Bednár, P., Babič, F., Furdík, K., Paralič, J.: Distributed task-based execution engine for support of text-mining processes. In: 7th International Symposium on Applied Machine Intelligence and Informatics, SAMI 2009, 30–31 January 2009, Herľany, Slovakia, pp. 29-34. IEEE (2009)
11. Furdík, K., Paralič, J., Babič, F., Butka, P., Bednár, P.: Design and evaluation of a web system supporting various text mining tasks for the purposes of education and research. Acta Electrotechnica et Informatica 10(1), 51–58 (2010)
12. Butka, P., Sarnovský, M., Bednár, P.: One Approach to Combination of FCA-based Local Conceptual Models for Text Analysis - Grid-based Approach. In: Proceedings of the 6th International Symposium on Applied Machine Intelligence, pp. 31–135. IEEE (2008)
13. Ganter, B., Wille, R.: Formal Concept Analysis: Mathematical Foundations. Springer, Heidelberg (1999)
14. Butka, P., Pócsová, J., Pócs, J.: Design and implementation of incremental algorithm for creation of generalized one-sided concept lattices. In: 12th IEEE International Symposium on Computational Intelligence and Informatics, CINTI 2011, pp. 373–378. IEEE, (2011)
15. Butka, P., Pócs, J.: Generalization of one-sided concept lattices. Comput. Inform. 32(2), 355–370 (2013)
16. Butka, P., Pócsová, J., Pócs, J.: A proposal of the information retrieval system based on the generalized one-sided concept lattices. In: Precup, R.-E., Kovács, S., Preitl, S., Petriu, E.M. (eds.) Applied Computational Intelligence in Engineering. TIEI, vol. 1, pp. 59–70. Springer, Heidelberg (2012)
17. Sarnovský, M., Kacur, T.: Cloud-based classification of text documents using the Gridgain platform. In: 7th IEEE International Symposium on Applied Computational Intelligence and Informatics, SACI 2012, pp. 241–245 (2012)
18. Zhang, C., Li, F., Jestes, J.: Efficient parallel kNN joins for large data in MapReduce. In: Proceedings of the 15th International Conference on Extending Database Technology (EDBT 2012), pp. 38–49. ACM, New York (2012)
19. Ditttenbach, M., Rauber, A., Merkl, D.: The Growing Hierarchical Self-Organizing Map, In: Proceedings of International Joint Conference on Neural Networks, Como (2000)
20. Sarnovský, M., Ulbrik, Z.: Cloud-based clustering of text documents using the GHSOM algorithm on the GridGain platform. In: IEEE 8th International Symposium on Applied Computational Intelligence and Informatics, SACI 2013, pp. 309–313 (2013)
21. Joshi, M.N.: Parallel K-means Algorithm on Distributed Memory Multiprocessors, Project Report, Computer Science Department, University of Minnesota, Twin Cities (2003)
22. Srinath, N. K.: MapReduce Design of K-Means Clustering Algorithm. In: proceedings of International Conference on Information Science and Applications, (ICISA) 2013, pp. 1-5 (2013)
23. Butka, P., Pócsová, J., Pócs, J.: Comparison of Standard and Sparse-based Implementation of GOSCL Algorithm. In: 13th IEEE International Symposium on Computational Intelligence and Informatics, CINTI 2012, Budapest, pp. 67–71 (2012)

24. Butka, P., Pócs, J., Pócsová, J.: Distributed Version of Algorithm for Generalized One-Sided Concept Lattices. In: Zavoral, F., Jung, J.J., Badica, C. (eds.) IDC 2013. SCI, vol. 511, pp. 119–129. Springer, Heidelberg (2013)
25. Butka, P., Pócs, J., Pócsová, J.: Distributed Computation of Generalized One-Sided Concept Lattices on Sparse Data Tables. In: Computing and Informatics, vol. 34, no. 1 (2015) (to appear)
26. Butka, P., Náhori, P.: Using BOINC software to support implementation of research and project text mining tasks (in Slovak: Využitie softvéru BOINC pre podporu realizácie výskumných a projektových úloh dolovania v textoch). In: Proceeding of the 9th Workshop on Intelligent and Knowledge oriented Technologies, WIKT 2014, Smolenice, Slovakia, pp. 22–26 (2014)
27. Paralič, J., Richter, Ch., Babič, F., Wagner, J., Raček, M.: Mirroring of knowledge practices based on user-defined patterns. J. Univ. Comput. Sci. 17(10), 1474–1491 (2011)
28. Sarnovský, M., Butka, P.: Cloud computing as a platform for distributed data analysis. In: 7th Workshop on Intelligent and Knowledge Oriented Technologies WIKT 2012, November 2012, Smolenice, pp. 177–180 (2012)

Social Impact of EIS and Visualization

Corporate Social Responsibility in Social Media Environment

Antonín Pavlíček and Petr Doucek[(⊠)]

University of Economics, Prague,
W. Churchill sq, 130 67 Prague, Czech Republic
{antonin.pavlicek,doucek}@vse.cz

Abstract. The paper describes corporate social responsibility (CSR) communication on Facebook and Twitter – how the companies use the social media for accomplishing their CSR communication goals. On the sample of ten global companies with the best CSR reputation research tracks down their social media activity, as well as posts, likes and comments of their customers. Observed companies on average dedicate about 1/10 of their social media communication bandwidth to CSR topics, mainly on Facebook. CSR topics do not seem to be of much interest to the readers (CSR posts are mostly ignored), but at least user sentiment related to CSR messages has been proven to be mostly positive. CSR on social networks is well established, leading CSR companies use this communication channel extensively.

Keywords: Corporate social responsibility · CSR · Facebook · Twitter · Good practice · Social media

1 Introduction

The article deals with corporate social responsibility (from now on "CSR") activities published on Facebook and Twitter. We have analyzed ten multinational companies that ranked in the world's 100 most CSR reputable companies in Forbes [1].

1.1 Corporate Social Responsibility

Corporate social responsibility is capturing an idea of responsible companies respecting the concept of people, planet, and profit[1]. First debates about CSR published in 1930's Harward Law Review. Professors Adolf A. Berle [2] and Merrick Dodd [3] asked: Do the managers have responsibility only for their firm or do they have a wider range of responsibilities?

Today world has started to care about global and local issues with social and environmental aspects "Corporate Social Responsibility is a way of doing business that matches or exceeds ethical, legal, commercial and social expectations." [4] Sometimes CSR is called sustainable, responsible business, corporate citizenship, etc. CRS is

---

[1] People, planet, profit are also called three pillars of sustainability or triple bottom line.

© IFIP International Federation for Information Processing 2015
I. Khalil et al. (Eds.): ICT-EurAsia 2015 and CONFENIS 2015, LNCS 9357, pp. 323–332, 2015.
DOI: 10.1007/978-3-319-24315-3_33

may be still perceived as something like a charity or donation pleading, but donations and similar activities are only a part of it. CSR cover topic like transparency and responsible attitude in everyday work and decision-making. Current trends in CSR are water and energy wasting, carbon printing, transparency, traceability, human rights, and labor standards.

We can divide the motivation for CSR into four main areas of benefits. First – business benefits. They are connected with gaining money, power, market share, etc. Next benefits are about individual/personal values. The company is trying to be seen in a better light. It's connected with branding since the reputation of the company is getting more and more important in business relationships. A third group of benefits is about complying with industry's social and legislative expectations. And of course we can't forget stakeholders – the company has to fulfill their expectations as well. These expectations can be diverse since stakeholders are varied. For example, the expectations of employees are reliability, future development, sustainability, the transparent benefits system, HR care, outplacement, etc. Crucial stakeholders became business partners, especially European companies require trading with companies proving they're caring about environment and society. To identify benefits, which company wants to gain is paramount for further setting CRS activities.

From theoretical concept, CSR has evolved to a sophisticated managing tool used not only to build company's reputation, but also to enlarge its competitive advantage.

Until recently, CSR in the company was mainly about overtimes and sexual harassment, shortly it was about keeping the company out of the trouble. Now the companies are implementing CSR in more far-reaching ways. There are four recognized stages of CSR in enterprise – see Fig. 1.

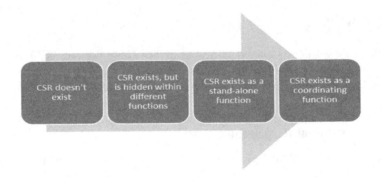

Fig. 1. Four stages of CSR in enterprise

Just a few companies are in the stage one. A lot of activities, companies are actually doing, even unknowingly, are CSR. For example benefits for employees or HR policies. The goal for every CSR oriented company is to reach enterprise CSR maturity. It includes changes in company values and business thinking, as well as official standards. Employees should share CSR values too. Without integrating employees into the process, CRS strategy fails.

1.2   CSR in the Czech Republic

After 1990 companies usually focused just on one goal – the maximization of financial profit. Later some firms realized that it is quite important to look towards the further future and consider public gains as well. CRS has very deep roots in the Czech Republic – the first businessman involved in CSR activities was Tomáš Baťa (founder of Bata shoemaking company). Long time before official term CSR was used he realized, that if he wanted to make high-quality shoes, he has to have satisfied employees. The logical conclusion of dissatisfied and stressed employees are mistakes and non-functional plant. Tomáš Baťa became a role model for other businessmen not only in his days. [5] Czech Republic understands corporate social responsibility the same way as EU does. The European Commission defined CSR as "the responsibility of enterprises for their impacts on society".

CSR activities are also closely related to another important topic – quality. Czech Ministry of Industry and Trade adopted programs that should help companies improve quality and also cultivate market environment. The government nominated The Council of Quality as an advisory authority on CSR. One of the programs adopted by Council of Quality is "National Quality Policy of the Czech Republic for CSR activities". The primary aim of this program is to make CSR activities popular and award the most social responsible companies.

2   Social Media

There are many definitions of social media – it is possible to define social media from the user, content, business or technological perspective [7]. Figure 2 shows such triangle of content, technological and sociological aspect of social media. Andreas Kaplan and Michael Haenlein in their paper define social media as "a group of internet-based applications that build on the ideological and technological foundations of Web 2.0, and allow the creation and exchange of user-generated content." [8] In other words, Kaplan and Haenlein build their definition on technological aspect.

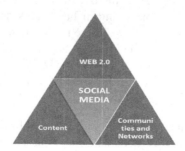

Fig. 2. Three key elements of social media [9]

We can also break the term social media into two words – social and media in order to describe and understand meaning of the whole. Social can be described as a group of people with relations between them while media can be described as an instrument with the purpose to provide communication. By putting these two words together, we get, that social media is an instrument of on-line communication between people (users of social media). These people can create information, share and exchange them with other users in specific places such as networks or in general virtual communities. Social media affects our everyday personal or business life in both positive and negative way.

Negative Effects of Social Media. The most discussed issue with social media is a trustworthiness and reliability of information that they provide. Social media websites or posts in social networks are, in general, easy to create, and can contain (knowingly or accidentally) a lot of false statements and information that can confuse other users.

People can even become "addicted" to social media by spending a too much time online and lose their personal life. Loss of privacy is another critical issue of social media [10, 11].

There is also possible thread on user's computer security. Many social media can be intoxicated with security risks (viruses such malware of spyware etc.) or bugs that allow criminals to access victims' computer or even bank accounts and steal (or delete) information or finances.

Positive Effects of Social Media. The existence of social media allows the democratization of the internet. Users can share what they want, express their feelings and opinions on topics or for example vote in online polls. Information flows have been relaxed and enriched by them.

As the biggest advantage of social media is considered the fact, that people can stay in touch with friends, families and also connect with other users and make new friends or form relationships. Social media is also used for learning and gaining new skills and knowledge. By using social media, people can reach a wider audience in comparison with traditional media and they can also, individually or in collaboration, create new content and manage it. Social media can be used in education too. Knowledge bases like Wikipedia contain a lot of information and can help users to understand what they are looking for or help solve problems.

Social media is very powerful tool in business too. It helps to expand the markets, or promote a brand to a wide audience or improve the relationship with customers among many other things. These days, marketing in business is one of the most important things for a company to stay competitive. There is no better place where to make good marketing strategies than social media [9, 12].

3 Research Questions

Our goal is to understand how the successful and worldwide famous companies are using social media for their CSR activities promotion and communication with customers and the general public. We have formulated following research questions:

- How do successful companies use the social media to spread CSR news?
- How do users of social networks respond CSR news? Does a reaction to CSR messages differ in comparison with other non-CSR messages?

We will closely look at the interaction of the general public and the companies – by analyzing the posts structure/Commercials, HR News, CSR/and focusing on the interaction with the audience.

4 Research Methodology

We decided to research corporate social responsibility activities on the two prominent social sites – Facebook and Twitter. The period of observation was three months (September – November 2014), during which we recorded all the posts of the selected companies.

The selection of the companies was based on Forbes' article The Companies with the Best CSR Reputations. [1] It covers 50.000 consumers' opinions about the list of 100 most reputable companies. We have focused on the top 10 of the list: Volkswagen, Sony, Colgate-Palmolive, Lego Group, BMW, Mercedes-Benz (Daimler), Apple, Google Inc., Microsoft Corporation and Walt Disney. All the companies have the official Facebook and Twitter profile except Apple. Therefore, we had to replace Apple by another major ICT company – SAP Corporation.

Our main goal was to track CSR activity of each company across the social media. We observed and analyzed all and every post of selected companies both on Facebook and Twitter. Then, based on meaning of the posts, we categorized these social media posts into following categories:

– non-CSR messages (advertisements/commercials, staff hiring, new technology announcements)
– CSR activity.

We noted the number of "likes" each post received and also positive and negative feedback in the comments.

5 Results

The results may be affected by the time-constraints since we only tracked social media activity for three months. Nevertheless, we have collected and analyzed in total:

- 466 posts of the observed companies (in the structure of 375 advertisements, 26 new technologies announcements, 4 HR announcements and 60 CSR announcements)
- 1,407,108 likes of above-mentioned posts
- 139,421 shares of above-mentioned posts
- 13,816 feedbacks (both positive and negative) to above-mentioned posts.

General result is, that CSR activity on social media highly varies among all observed companies. Fewer CSR messages are published on Twitter (just 26 %, as opposed to almost 44 % of advertisements). For CSR messages, companies like to use advantages of Facebook with its billion + users. To show some examples of typical CSR Facebook activity, there are some typical Facebook CSR posts:

- *Man with Down syndrome empowers others using technology (14/11/2014) - Microsoft*
- *Introducing Microsoft Health (30/10/2014) - Microsoft*
- *From 1st till 10th August the Think Blue (2/8/2014) - Volkswagen*
- *ALS Ice Bucket Challenge (27/8/2014) - Colgate-Palmolive*
- *Fight Ebola (10/11/2014) - Google*
- *Hyper build (14/9/2014) - Lego*
- *The Autism Society Philippines (20/11/2014) – SAP*
- *Event: St. Moritz Art Masters 2014 – Mercedes-Benz (Daimler)*

From the collected data is quite clear, that companies primarily (80.47 %) advertise their goods and products – 375 out of 466 posts were categorized as Advertisements. CSR messages, on the other hand, accounted for 12.88 % of posts, which makes them the second biggest category (Table 1).

Table 1. Structure of the social media posts (authors)

	Total number of posts	Advertisements	New Technologies	Staff Hiring	CSR messages
Colgate	**5**	2	0	0	3
Lego	**18**	12	1	0	5
SAP	**44**	15	4	1	24
Sony	**45**	41	2	0	2
Volkswagen	**47**	39	5	0	2
Google	**48**	43	1	0	4
Walt Disney	**50**	50	0	0	0
Microsoft	**56**	43	8	0	5
BMW	**63**	62	1	0	0
Daimler	**90**	68	4	3	15
Total	**466**	**375**	**26**	**4**	**60**
	100 %	*80.47 %*	*5.58 %*	*0.86 %*	*12.88 %*
Facebook	268 (58 %)	208 (56 %)	15 (58 %)	1 (25 %)	44 (74 %)
Twitter	198 (42 %)	167 (44 %)	11 (42 %)	3 (75 %)	16 (26 %)

As for feedback, it can be measured in three different ways. The first and most obvious one is the number of "likes", which are awarded by readers to all posts. Table with the numbers of received likes by the companies in different categories follows (Table 2).

The second way how to measure feedback is number of "shares"[2] – i.e. how many times the users "pass on" the recommendation for posts. Again, here are the numbers (Table 3):

---

[2] There is a difference between "like" and "share" on Facebook. "Like" just means that user finds something interesting, "Share" actually distributes the message to other users.

Table 2. Total number of "likes" for different categories of posts (authors)

	Fans	Advertisements "likes"	New Technologies "likes"	Staff Hiring "likes"	CSR messages "likes"
Colgate	2,800,000	2,599	N/A	N/A	593
Lego	10,200,000	122,076	N/A	N/A	2,789
SAP	590,000	777	109	48	284
Sony	6,800,000	127,354	10,426	N/A	10,867
Volkswagen	1,600,000	45,201	8,391	N/A	1,450
Google	18,400,000	21,641	135	N/A	1625
Walt Disney	860,000	59,468	N/A	N/A	N/A
Microsoft	6,500,000	83,388	1,976	N/A	3,003
BMW	18,300,000	416,586	N/A	N/A	N/A
Daimler	18,250,000	477,186	134	68	8,934
Total	**84,300,000**	**1,356,276**	**21,171**	**116**	**29,545**

Table 3. Total number of "shares" for different categories of posts (authors)

	Advertisements "shares"	New Technologies "shares"	Staff Hiring "shares"	CSR messages "shares"
Colgate	119	N/A	N/A	85
Lego	11,351	N/A	N/A	274
SAP	68	8	1	32
Sony	4,812	437	N/A	620
Volkswagen	2,318	871	N/A	134
Google	12,551	169	N/A	379
Walt Disney	21,163		N/A	N/A
Microsoft	20,880	541	N/A	590
BMW	21,001	N/A	N/A	N/A
Daimler	39,806	78	46	1,087
Total	**134,069**	**2,104**	**47**	**3,201**

Lastly, we have also measured the feedback, provided by the users. After careful individual analysis of the content of their comments, we have divided the reactions to positive and negative feedback – both for CSR and non-CSR posts. The results are following (Table 4):

6 Findings and Interpretation

Observed companies had in total almost 85 million strong audience on Facebook and 27.5 million followers on Twitter. It is really large amount of potential customers that companies definitively can't ignore. Over 80 % of the Facebook and Twitter posts were advertisements directly targeted to drive costumers' attention to new advertised goods

Table 4. Positive and negative feedback for CSR and non-CSR posts (authors)

	Non-CSR posts			CSR posts		
	Positive feedback	Negative feedback	Positive / Negative ratio	Positive feedback	Negative feedback	Positive / Negative ratio
Colgate	28	35	0.8	5	3	1.67
Lego	600	221	2.71	16	5	3.2
SAP	9	2	4.5	0	0	
Sony	479	119	4.03	86	2	43
Volkswagen	357	190	1.88	16	4	4
Google	6,439	1024	6.29	50	1	50
Walt Disney	364	177	2.06	0	0	
Microsoft	967	827	1.17	215	6	35.83
BMW	235	57	4.12	1	1	1
Daimler	1,256	10	125.6	10	1	10
Total	**10,734**	**2,662**	**4.03**	**399**	**23**	**17.35**

or services. However, the second most frequent (almost 13 %) type of communication were CSR messages.

The prevalence of CSR messages was different on Facebook and Twitter. Companies have shared ¾ of all CSR communication on Facebook, leaving just ¼ for Twitter channel, although general ratio of Facebook /Twitter communication in the observed period was almost half to half. It means that companies prefer Facebook as their main channel for CSR announcements. There were no exemptions from this rule observed during our study.

As for audience appreciation (measured by Facebook likes) – it turns out, that CSR messages are surprisingly "unpopular". Although the CSR messages accounted for 13 % of the traffic, they generated only slightly over 2 % of total "likes". The average number of likes per commercial post was 3064, the average number of likes per CSR-related post was 903. Worse "underperformer" was only category of HR related messages, which was ignored by users almost completely. The relation of re-tweeting of CSR message was also significantly lower than expected, as opposed to Technological news category tweets, which – on the other hand – were re-distributed enthusiastically through Twitter environment.

The same picture is seen when we analyze the content "shared"[3] on Facebook. Again, the majority of shared content – almost 98 % - was related to products, services or new technologies, leaving CSR messages with just 2.3 % share.

The only good results scored by CSR communication was positive "sentiment" of the feedback. When analyzed on positive/negative scale, the user comments related to CSR activities were four times more positive than the rest. Positive/Negative ratio of the Non-CSR post was in average 4.03 – which means four positive comments to each

---

[3] There is a difference between "like" and "share" on Facebook. "Like" means that user finds something interesting, "Share" actually distributes the message to other designated users.

negative one; CSR-related posts achieved on average over 17 positive remarks to one negative.

Our findings prove that advertisements (commercial news) are way ahead of CSR activity on Social Networks. Almost all companies have more commercial focused Facebook and Twitter posts then CSR related posts. For example, Google has 43 commercial posts and only 4 about CSR. It is a similar situation with Volkswagen. They have 39 commercial posts yet only 2 dedicated to CSR. The only exception is company SAP, which has twice as much CSR posts in comparison with commercials.

Based on our research, we found out that most of the observed companies include CRS in their communication strategy. Almost all of observed companies use social media to advertise new product or strategies (Fig. 3).

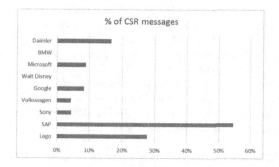

Fig. 3. Comparison of companies by the percentage of CSR posts (out of all posts)

Companies SAP and Lego belong to the most active from the perspective of CSR posts, on the other hand, The Walt Disney Company and BMW do not publish their CSR activity on social networks at all.

7   Conclusions

Our study showed that worldwide leaders in the field of CSR do not underestimate their CSR activity on social networks, and they actively promote there. The rate of CSR-related communication varies, but in average amounts to 13 % and CSR is the second most frequent subject on social media.

Slightly worse is the reaction of the audience to CSR-related posts and tweets. CSR-related communications received on average only one-third of "likes" compared with other posts, and people do not tend to pass on the message– "viral effect" of CSR is just 2 %. Still, when the CSR-related messages do get some response, then the comments are exceptionally positive.

The conclusion is clear – CSR on social networks is well established, leading CSR companies use this communication channel extensively. A similar trend can be expected in the future also from other firms, which CSR do not follow yet.

Acknowledgments. The research for this paper was conducted with help of students from the course 4SA526 New Media at University of Economics, Prague.

References

1. Dill, K.: The Companies With The Best CSR Reputations, Forbes, New York (2014)
2. Berle, A.A.: Corporate powers as powers in trust. Harward Law Rev. **44**, 1049–1074 (1931)
3. Dodd, E.M.: For whom are corporate managers trustees. Harward Law Rev. **44**, 1145–1163 (1932)
4. Sigmund, T.: Ethics in the cyberspace. In: Doucek, P. (ed.) IDIMT-2013 Information Technology Human Values, Innovation and Economy, vol. 42, pp. 269–279. Trauner Verlag, Linz (2013). ISBN 978-3-99033-083-8
5. Briš, P., Svoboda, J., Brišová, H.: The growing importance of the practical application of corporate social responsibility in the management of companies in the Czech Republic. J. Competitiveness. **5**(2), 124–138 (2013). doi:10.7441/joc.2013.02.09
6. Hykš O., Plášková A.: The Czech National CSR Award Model. In: VIII International Science Conference, pp. 1636–1638. WASET, Zurich (2014)
7. Skrabalek, J., Kunc, P., Nguyen, F., Pitner, T.: Towards effective social network system implementation. In: Pechenizkiy, M., Wojciechowski, M. (eds.) Marek Advances in Intelligent Systems and Computing. New Trends in Databases and Information Systems, vol. 185, pp. 327–336. Springer, Heidelberg (2013). doi:10.1007/978-3-642-32518-2_31
8. Doucek, P., Pavlicek, A., Nedomova, L.: Information management in web 2.0 technology context. In: Strategic Management and Its Support by Information Systems. Čeladná, VŠB TU Ostrava, Ostrava, pp. 34–45. 05–07 Sept 2011. ISBN 978-80-248-2444-4
9. Ahlqvist, T.: Social media roadmaps: exploring the futures triggered by social media, VTT (2008)
10. Boehmova, L., Malinova, L.: Facebook user's privacy in recruitment process. In: Doucek, P. (ed.) IDIMT-2013 Information Technology Human Values, Innovation and Economy, vol. 42, pp. 159–166. Trauner Verlag, Linz (2013). ISBN 978-3-99033-083-8
11. Sigmund, T.: Privacy in the information society: how to deal with its ambiguity? In: Doucek, P., Gerhard, C., Vacklav, O. (eds.) IDIMT-2014 Networking Societies – Cooperation and Conflict, vol. 43, pp. 191–204. Trauner Verlag, Linz (2014). ISBN 978-3-99033-340-2
12. Smutny, Z., Reznicek, V., Pavlicek, A.: Measuring the effects of using social media. In: Doucek, P. (ed.) IDIMT-2013 Information Technology Human Values, Innovation and Economy, vol. 42, pp. 175–178. Trauner Verlag, Linz (2013). ISBN 978-3-99033-083-8

Usage of Finance Information Systems in Developing Countries: Identifying Factors During Implementation that Impact Use

David Kiwana, Björn Johansson$^{(\boxtimes)}$, and Sven Carlsson

Department of Informatics, School of Economics and Management,
Lund University, Ole Römers väg 6, SE-223 63 Lund, Sweden
{david.kiwana,bjorn.johansson,
sven.carlsson}@ics.lu.se

Abstract. An explorative study of factors affecting implementation and use of finance information systems (FISs) in developing countries is presented. The result is based on a field study investigating implementation of a finance information system at Makerere University, Uganda. Current literature suggests that how to implement information Systems (ISs) successfully is challenging, especially in developing countries. The research question addressed is: What factors during implementation impact use of FISs in developing countries? Empirical data was gathered through face-to-face interviews with involved stakeholders in the implementation project. Analysis was done as a within-case analysis and supports the findings of nine factors that are of specific importance in developing countries. The findings can help decision-makers in guiding implementation processes of large enterprise systems especially in the accounting and finance management disciplines in developing countries.

Keywords: ERP · Financial information systems · Implementation · Use · Success and failure factors · Developing countries

1 Introduction

Finance information systems (FISs) take financial data and process it into specialized financial reports, saving time and effort in dealing with business accounting [1], it also provide decision-makers with information to perform managerial functions [2].

While FISs have many benefits, it should be noted that putting them in place can be costly and in most cases requires a lot of training and commitment by people involved [1]. As a result many organizations find difficulties to attain the desired success during their implementations, and many critical success factors for IS implementation have been suggested, however actual evidence to devise solutions for failed projects has not been clearly established [3].

In this paper we present research that was conducted to explore factors that shape implementation and later on use of FISs in the context of developing countries. According to Mulira [3] emerging public organizational networks in developing countries work with unpredictable environments and resource scarcity that have led to higher failure rates of Information Systems (IS) implementation projects. This research

© IFIP International Federation for Information Processing 2015
I. Khalil et al. (Eds.): ICT-EurAsia 2015 and CONFENIS 2015, LNCS 9357, pp. 333–342, 2015.
DOI: 10.1007/978-3-319-24315-3_34

builds on a retrospective field study describing implementation of a FIS at Makerere University (Mak) in Uganda. The FIS whose implementation was studied is a component of an integrated enterprise system called Integrated Tertiary Software (ITS), a South African software product that was installed at the University to manage finances/accounting, students' records and human resource functions.

Before proceeding to the sections that follow, it is important to clarify that finance information systems (FISs) many times are implemented as part of ERPs ([4, 5]). This means that implementation issues that are pertinent to ERPs are largely pertinent also to implementation of FSIs. This research therefore is premised on the ideology that what is said about ERPs in terms of implementation is largely applicable to FSIs implementations as well.

The next two sections present problematic issues in IS implementation and what is known about ERP/FIS implementation. Section 4 presents the research method. This is followed by a presentation of research findings. Section 6 presents and discusses the nine factors that emerged during the analysis.

2 Problematic Issues in IS Implementation

Research findings have reported that failure of large information systems implementations like ERPs are not caused by the software itself, but rather by a high degree of complexity from the massive changes that the systems cause in the organisations ([6, 7, 8]). According to Helo, et al. [7], the major problems of ERP implementations are not technologically related issues such as technological complexity, compatibility, standardisation etc., but mostly about organisational and human related issues like resistance to change, organisational culture, incompatible business processes, project mismanagement and lack of top management commitment. Furthermore, Huang and Palvia [9] has identified other issues like inadequate IT infrastructure, government policies, lack of IT/ERP experience and low IT maturity to seriously affect the adoption decision of ERPs in developing countries. What is not clear therefore is whether all such factors are exhaustively known and if so, how they (the factors) impact on eventual use of the systems considering the fact that the failure rate is still high. The failure rate of major information systems appears to be around 70 % [5, 10]. Chakraborty and Sharma [11] state that 90 % of all initiated ERP projects can be considered failures in terms of project management. Ptak and Schragenheim [12] claim that the failure rates of ERP implementations are in the range of 60-90 %. Helo, et al. [13] make the statement that in the worst scenarios, many companies have been reported to have abandoned ERP implementations. From this discussion it can be said that in FIS implementation, as a case of ERP implementation, the issues of concern are either technologically related or contextually related. Technologically related issues are not reported as problematic since they are probably more or less the same in different contexts. This means that the contextually related issues may be more problematic and interesting to address. Contextual factors have mainly been researched in developed country contexts, the challenge is researching these issues in a developing country context. This supports the need for studying: What factors during implementation impact use of FISs in developing countries?

3   What is Known About ERP/FIS Implementation?

FISs implementation is an emblematic of complex project that constantly evolves and as it is the case with design and implementation of any complex system the aspects of leadership, collaboration and innovation are of importance in the implementation process [14]. A successful completion of a FIS implementation depends on external factors as well and the adverse effects of country-specific political economy issues and political environment [14].

Pollock and Cornford [15] argue that the need for implementation of FISs in high education sectors is a response to both internal and external factors requiring more efficient management processes due to increasing growth of the numbers of students, changes in the nature of academic work, increasing competition between institutions, increasing government pressure to improve operational efficiency, and growing diversity of expectations amongst all stakeholders [16].

3.1   Causes of Failure of ERP/FISs Implementation

Senn and Gibson [17] point to user resistance as symptomatic of system failure as users may aggressively attack the system, rendering it unusable or ineffective, or simply avoid using it. Ginzberg [18] found that possible causes of implementation failure being user dissatisfaction with scope, user dissatisfaction with system goals, and user dissatisfaction with the general approach to the problem that the system is meant to address. In other words, system implementations are more likely to fail when they are introduced with unrealistic expectations.

As presented by Calogero [19], excessive focus on technologies rather than business user needs is one of the determinations of ERP implementations failures. Projects initiated due to technology are more likely to be unsuccessful than the business-initiated projects due to the fact that technology-initiated projects are most frequently driven by such goals as replacement of an old system with a new one which is a complicated task [20].

Lack of proper user education and practical training is another cause of a failure of IS implementation projects. According to Nicolaou [20] conducting user training upfront could cause unsuccessful ERP implementation due to limited scope of training possibilities before implementation. Kronbichler, et al. [21] say that unclear concept of nature and use of an ERP system from the users' perspective due to poor quality of training and insufficient education delivered by top management and project team also leads to failure. In developing countries where there are more challenges due to unstable infrastructure, funding and unstable social/economic organizational environment the quality of training becomes even poorer which leads to more failures of ERP implementations compared to developing countries [3].

3.2   Specific Issues for ERP/FIS Implementation in Developing Countries

Heidenhof and Kianpour [22] claim that many African countries struggle with public financial management reforms whereby institutions, systems, and processes that deal with various aspects of public finance are weak, non-transparent, and often incapable of developing adequate budgets and providing reliable data for economic modeling.

IS implementation failures keep developing countries on the wrong side of the digital divide, turning ICTs into a technology of global inequality. IS implementation failures are therefore practical problems for developing countries that need to be addressed [23]. The information, technology, processes, objectives and values, staffing and skills, management systems (ITPOSMO) checklist adapted from Malling [23] shows that the technological infrastructure is more limited in developing countries; the work processes are more contingent in developing countries because of the more politicized and inconstant environment; developing countries have a more limited local base in the range of skills like systems analysis and design, implementation of IS initiatives, planning, and operation-related skills including computer literacy and familiarity. When it comes to management and structures organizations in developing country are more hierarchical and more centralized, and in addition the cost of ICTs is higher than in developed countries whereas the cost of labor is lower [24]. This supports that an explorative study of: What factors during implementation impact use of FISs in developing countries, are of interest.

4 Research Method

This research was carried out at Makerere University (Mak) through a retrospective field study, investigating aspects of implementation of the ITS (Integrated Tertiary Software) finance subsystem. Empirical data was collected by face-to-face interviews guided by semi-structured questions. Mak was selected because it has an enrolment of about 40,000 students and therefore has a potential to provide a good ground for a wide range of issues pertinent to the study.

A total of ten people were interviewed and these included the head of the finance department, the head of the IT unit, the person who was responsible for the user team, the coordinator of NORAD (Norwegian Funding Agency) in the University's Planning Unit who funded the implementation costs and six accountants from the Finance Department. The respondents were chosen based on their relevance to the research question and closeness to the subject matter rather than their representativeness. The interviewer (one of the researchers) has a position at Mak and was to some extent involved in the implementation process of the system. The interviewer's position at Mak at that time was in the IT unit of Mak as Systems Manager with the role of assisting various units in the university in acquisition and implementation of central software resources.

Questions asked during interviews were mainly in four areas: general information about the organisation and the system, information on how the implementation was done, and information on how the system was being run and used. Analysis of the data was done using within-case analysis whereby the general patterns and themes were identified. The analysis aimed at identification of factors that were presented as influential in the implementation process by the respondents. The next section presents briefly the case and then the identified factors are presented and discussed.

5 Presentation of Research Findings

Makerere University is a public university in Uganda with an enrolment of approximately 40,000 students and 5,000 staff members. The university procured an integrated enterprise system called Integrated Tertiary Software (ITS) to be used in finance management, students' administration and human resource management. In this study we focussed on the finance subsystem. Next we present why the FIS was bought and why; how and when was the time for the implementation decided; how was the actual implementation done.

5.1 What was the Origin of the Idea to Buy the FIS and why?

In regard to issues for why the system was implemented, one thing that was mentioned by almost all interviewees was a ***problem of lack of efficiency in managing fees payments of students due to very large numbers of students***. The Head of the Finance Department said: "*the problem was the number of students and the most risky area was revenue. As a finance manager that was my main focus. The rest we could afford to handle manually. For example, with the expenditure the vouchers are with you, but with revenue you would not know who has paid and from what faculty*". The Senior Assistant Bursar and the person who headed the implementation team said: "*The privatisation scheme that was introduced in the nineties brought an increase in student population. Mak could no longer accurately tell how much money was being received and reports could no longer be given in a timely manner*". The Head of the IT unit said: "*The main motivating factor for the implementation was the big number of students and lack of efficiency that subsequently followed*".

In addition donor influence and best practice also played big roles in influencing the decision to procure the system. The Head of the IT unit said: "*Donors were looking at institutions within the country to create efficiencies, and automation was being seen as the best practice that was being proposed elsewhere. Mak had started looking ahead towards automation but already there was a move by development partners requiring public institutions to improve performance. So Mak's big numbers coincided with the push by the development partners to automate systems and being the highest institution of learning in the country, Mak was a prime choice for donors to fund*". The Head of the IT unit continued to say that automation was not decided by the players like the head of the finance and head of academic records. "*What they presented was just increasing challenges to support top management in their bid to solicit funding from the donors for the automation.*" In other words, according to the Head of the IT unit, the push for implementation was a top-down approach motivated by a position that institutions in developing countries needed to comply with donor requirements. The Head of IT summarised by saying that "*things actually happened in parallel. Donors came in to look for efficiency and they found Mak already grappling around to see how to solve the problems of inefficiency*".

Another influencing factor had to do with best practice. The Head of Finance said: "*When I joined the university everything was manual and the thinking at the time was how to make Mak ICT enabled. That urged us to look into that area and we wanted to catch up with other universities so we said that we would look for funders because government wouldn't"*. The Head of the IT unit head also said *"the adoption of systems in many institutions of higher learning, and automation of functions whether administrative or academic is not a reinventing the wheel, most institutions follow best practice. What is important is that you have a champion to introduce the automation; you need to have the funding and the team players. Then at the end you need to have a change management team that can influence and affect the changes. So it is essentially adopting best practice and that is what Mak did."*

5.2   When and how was the Time to Start the Implementation Decided?

According to Tusubira [25] it was during a conference for all heads of departments that was organised by the Vice Chancellor in 2000 to discuss a question of ICT development in the university. A resolution was made to develop an ICT policy and master plan that was aimed at defining a strategy that the university would take in its bid to develop the use of ICT in its management systems. The master plan comprised of all the planned ICT activities for the university for a period of five years (2001 to 2004) and the implementation mandate was given to DICTS. Among the activities was the implementation of the university information systems that included the finance system.

In summary the factors found motivating the implementation were:

- The need by the university top management to give development partners satisfaction that Mak had the necessary capacity to manage finance information efficiently.
- A need from the finance department to find a way of managing increasing student fees records in time as a result of increasing student numbers following issuance of a policy by Mak to start admitting privately sponsored students in the 1990's.
- Influence from best practice that pointed to automation of systems as a must way to go during that time as seen by top management and DICTS.
- Need by Mak under the stewardship of the Directorate for ICT Support to execute the activity of implementing information systems that included the FIS as had been prescribed in the University ICT master plan for 2001–2004.
- Funds provided by a developing partner, NORAD under stewardship of the Mak Planning Unit, which had to be utilised within a specific period, 2001–2004, being available.

5.3   How the Actual Implementation was Done

After the system was procured, several activities related to the actual implementation took place. These are shortly described below in chronical order: (1) installation and customising the system, (2) formation of the implementation teams, (3) training, about 30 people were trained over a period of about two months, and (4) user acceptance and commissioning: by the end of 2006 all the modules were found to be functional although only three were being used at that time (i.e., student debtors, cash book and electronic banking) and the system was commissioned in February 2007.

6 Identified Implementation Factors Impacting FIS Use

A large part of the interviewees (more than 60 %) said that the system and especially the interface for capturing data was not easy to use and this seemed to have discouraged many people from using the system. One accountant specifically said: "*the system is not user friendly, for example, for a transaction to be completed you have to go through several steps, and in case you forgot a step you have to repeat*". We label this as a: **Factor of System Usability**.

There were too many bank accounts as each unit in the university had its own bank accounts and supervision of staff was not adequate. It was therefore very hard to have all the cashbooks across the university up-to-date to enable a complete set of reports to be generated in a timely manner. The head of implementation said "*the cash books were too many as a result of the big number of bank accounts which were almost over 200. The people working on them and who were scattered in many different units could not all update them in a timely manner to have any meaningful reports generated in a timely manner*". We suggest categorising this as a **Factor Evaluation of Staff Performance.**

The study showed that there was a lack of a clear plan for how persons should stop using the older systems. When one accountant was asked why the modules to do with the expenditure failed to be operationalized whereas the revenue module for student debtors was a great success he said "the *form of record keeping at that time was in decentralized manner, so supervising people was not easy and secondly the people were allowed to continue with the older systems. Student debtors succeeded only because there was no alternative*". Talking about the same, the Head of the Finance department said: "*In the beginning the problem was the number of students, and the most risky area was revenue. So there was much focus on revenue. The rest you could afford to handle manually. For example, with the expenditure the vouchers are with you, but with revenue you do not know who has paid and from what faculty*" We suggest categorising this as a **Factor of Change Management Program.**

It was found that a lot more was acquired in terms of modules than required to solve the actual problem that was prevailing. This was found to be due to the fact that the push to implement was from the top to the bottom because the funds (which were being provided by development partners) were readily available.

When the Head of the IT unit was asked whether the story would have been different if Mak was to finance the project from its own internal budget instead of donor funds she said: "*If there were budget constraints whereby Mak would have to look for donors then Mak would think a lot more about how that money would be spent, and if Mak was using their own money they would have asked the finance department from inception more, because they would have said that we do not have money tell us only those critical modules that have to be funded within a constrained budget*". The Head of the IT unit added:" *but we have a top down approach supported by challenges from below that already has funding coming from some source aside so we do not have to involve them too much because they have already given us their challenges to support our case and we got the money. And once we put up a bid and the best system came up it was adopted in its entirety*". In conclusion the Head of the IT unit said:" *budgeting constraints would have forced a more concise scheme and more involvement of the user department. But this was not the case. They were there to support the cause by only challenges as the money had been got from somewhere else".* We suggest categorising this as *a Factor of Project Management.*

According to the Head of the IT unit, the human resource structure had not been fully designed to be compliant with the new automation aspect. She said *"The human resource had been used to using a manual system and now they had to take on a new system, and with too many modules, and the structural adjustments started being done after the system was installed".* She added: *"It was much later after evaluating the system when a decision was made to strike off some particular modules. If this had been done at the beginning, the people would have easily mastered the system and the university would have saved money."* We suggest categorising this as *a Factor of Change Management Program.*

It was found that support was always never timely causing frustrations to many people. One accountant commented: *"Support was always not timely and this rendered people to fall back to their original work practices in order to meet targets.* We suggest to categories this as *Factor of Technical support and Effective IT unit* Another accountant said: *"Nobody took initiative to operationalise the entire system".* We suggest categorising this as *Factor of Top Management Support.*

It was observed that some people did not know and did not believe that adequate searching for a suitable system was done before the system was procured. One accountant commented that *"the university should have taken time to do more research and come up with a system that would perform better. ITS was only at Mak with no any comparisons within Uganda".* It was discovered the belief of the accountant was not correct because it was established from other sources that before the decision to procure was made Mak sent a team of people in a foreign university where a similar system was being used to find more about it. This means that there was lack of information with some people and we therefore suggest categorising this as *a factor of Effective Communication.*

It was found that all the trainees (about 30) were pulled together in one big group and it turned out to be very difficult for each individual to get direct contact with the trainers. Secondly after training the trainers immediately went back to South Africa (where they had come from) keeping very far away from users who were just maturing. The head of the user team said: *"the whole department was trained together as one group for two months, but in addition the trainers should have also done individualised training, and they should have remained in close proximity".*

And when asked to comment on the fact that during training people were taken through the entire system but that the situation on ground did not reflect that, the Head of the Finance department said that that was the case because they were doing an implementation of this kind for the first time. He added that" *People went for training only once, so after time they forgot and the problem was that there was a lack of people to guide Mak. The consulting firm reached a point when they would want to charge whenever they would be called and so financial implications came in. They could help on the system but they could not help on the functionalities."* We suggest categorising this *as a factor of Education and Training.*

It was found that due to some omissions or/and deficiencies that existed in the Requirements Specifications Document, some functionalities could not adequately run. For example, when an accountant was asked whether the organisation took time to review all the relevant organisation policies to ensure that they were all adequately accommodated in the automated environment, he said: *"Some were done like the registration of students but at a later time. Some were not done, for instance, the system could not handle multicurrency features for fees"*. In some instances the consultants would accept to quickly do the necessary rectifications and in some instances they would not, which would cause problems. We suggest categorising this as *a factor of Flexible Consultants*.

7 Conclusions and Future Research

The aim of this study was to answer the research question: What factors during implementation impact use of FISs in developing countries? Previous studies on FIS implementation show that the design and implementation of FIS solutions is challenging and requires development of country specific solutions to meet the associated functional and technical requirements. Previous studies also show that as a result of increased challenges in developing countries due to unstable infrastructure and unstable social economic organisational environment, the quality of training gets poorer which leads to increased implementation failures compared to the situation in developed countries. The starting point for identification of factors was system usability. From that we identify nine factors that shaped the implementation and use of the FISs. These are: Project management, evaluation of staff performance, effective communication, instituting of change management programs, provision of technical support by consultants, effective IT unit, providing education and training, top management support, and flexible consultants. These factors are related to different activities in the implementation and they all influence the results of the implementation expressed as systems usability in positive or negative directions. Future research will focus on to what extent the different factors influences use of implemented systems in developing countries.

References

1. Morgan, R.: "What are the benefits of financial information systems," (2014) http://www.ehow.com/info_7893940_benefits-financial-information-systems.html
2. Hendriks, C.J.: Integrated financial management information systems: guidelines for effective implementation by the public sector of South Africa: original research. S. Afr. J. Inf. Manage. **15**, 1–9 (2013)
3. Mulira, N.K.: Implementing inter-organisational service systems: an approach for emerging networks in volatile contexts: TU Delft, Delft University of Technology (2007)
4. Bancroft, H., Seip, H., Sprengel, A.: Implementing SAP R/3: how to introduce a large system into a large organization (1997)
5. Davenport, T.H.: Putting the enterprise into the enterprise system. Harvard Bus. Rev. **76**, 121–131 (1998)

6. Scott, J.E., Vessey, I.: Implementing enterprise resource planning systems: the role of learning from failure. Inf. Syst. Frontiers **2**, 213–232 (2000)
7. Helo, P., Anussornnitisarn, P., Phusavat, K.: Expectation and reality in ERP implementation: consultant and solution provider perspective. Ind. Manage. Data Syst. **108**, 1045–1059 (2008)
8. Maditinos, D., Chatzoudes, D., Tsairidis, C.: Factors affecting ERP system implementation effectiveness. J. Enterprise Inf. Manage. **25**, 60–78 (2011)
9. Huang, Z., Palvia, P.: ERP implementation issues in advanced and developing countries. Bus. Process Manage. J. **7**, 276–284 (2001)
10. Drummond, H.: What we never have, we never miss? Decision error and the risks of premature termination. J. Inf. Technol. **20**, 170–176 (2005)
11. Chakraborty, S., Sharma, S.K.: Enterprise resource planning: an integrated strategic framework. Int. J. Manage. Enterp. Dev. **4**, 533–551 (2007)
12. Ptak, C.A., Schragenheim, E.: ERP: Tools, Techniques, and Applications for Integrating the Supply Chain. CRC Press (2003)
13. Helo, P., Anussornnitisarn, P., Phusavat, K.: Expectation and reality in ERP implementation: consultant and solution provider perspective. Ind. Manage. Data Syst. **108**, 1045–1059 (2008)
14. Dener, C., Watkins, J., Dorotinsky, W.L.: Financial Management Information Systems: 25 Years of World Bank Experience on What Works and What Doesn't. World Bank Publications, Washington, DC (2011)
15. Pollock, N., Cornford, J.: ERP systems and the university as a "unique" organisation. Inf. Technol. People **17**, 31–52 (2004)
16. Allen, D., Kern, T.: Enterprise resource planning implementation: stories of power, politics, and resistance. In: Russo, N.L., Fitzgerald, B., DeGross, J.I. (eds.) Realigning Research and Practice in Information Systems Development, pp. 149–162. Springer, US (2001)
17. Senn, J.A., Gibson, V.R.: Risks of investment in microcomputers for small business management. J. Small Bus. Manage. **19**, 24–32 (1981)
18. Ginzberg, M.J.: Early diagnosis of MIS implementation failure: promising results and unanswered questions. Manage. Sci. **27**, 459–478 (1981)
19. Calogero, B.: Who is to blame for ERP failure?. Sun Server Magazine (2000)
20. Nicolaou, A.I.: ERP systems implementation: drivers of post-implementation success. In: International Conference Decision Support in an Uncertain and Complex World: The IFIP TC8/WG8.3, pp. 589–597 (2004)
21. Kronbichler, S.A., Ostermann, H., Staudinger, R.: A comparison of ERP-success measurement approaches. JISTEM-J. Inf. Syst. Technol. Manage. **7**, 281–310 (2010)
22. Heidenhof, G., Kianpour, P.: Design and Implementation of Finanicial Management Systems: An African Perspective (2002)
23. Malling, P.: "Information Systems and Human Activity in Nepal," Information Technology in Context: Implementing in the Developing World. Ashgate Publishing, Aldershot (2000)
24. Heeks, R.: Information systems and developing countries: failure, success, and local improvisations. Inf. Soc. **18**, 101–112 (2002)
25. Tusubira, F.F.: Supporting University ICT (Information and Communication Technology) Developments: The Makerere University Experience. Africa Dev. **30**(1–2), 86–97 (2005)

Software Model Creation
with Multidimensional UML

Lukáš Gregorovič[1], Ivan Polasek[1(✉)], and Branislav Sobota[2]

[1] Faculty of Informatics and Information Technologies Institute of Informatics
and Software Engineering, Slovak University of Technology in Bratislava,
Bratislava, Slovakia
{xgregorovic, ivan.polasek}@stuba.sk
[2] Faculty of Electrical Engineering and Informatics,
Department of Computers and Informatics,
Technical University of Košice, Košice, Slovakia
branislav.sobota@tuke.sk

Abstract. The aim of the paper is to present the advantages of the Use Cases transformation to the object layers and their visualization in 3D space to reduce complexity. Our work moves selected UML diagram from two-dimensional to multidimensional space for better visualization and readability of the structure or behaviour.

Our general scope is to exploit layers for particular components or modules, time and author versions, particular object types (GUI, Business services, DB services, abstract domain classes, role and scenario classes), patterns and anti-patterns in the structure, aspects in the particular layers for solving cross-cutting concerns and anti-patterns, alternative and parallel scenarios, pessimistic, optimistic and daily use scenarios.

We successfully apply force directed algorithm to create more convenient automated class diagrams layout. In addition to this algorithm, we introduced semantics by adding weight factor in force calculation process.

Keywords: 3D UML · Analysis and design · Sequence diagram · Class diagram · Fruchterman-Reingold

1 Introduction

Increasing requirements and the complexity of designed systems need improvements in visualization for better understanding of created models, for better collaboration of designers and their teams in various departments and divisions, countries and time zones in their cooperation creating models and whole applications together.

In software development, Unified Modeling Language (UML) is standardized and widely used for creation of software models describing architecture and functionality of created system [4].

There are many tools that allow creation of UML diagrams in 2D space. Moving UML diagrams from two-dimensional to three-dimensional space reduces complexity and allows visualization of the large diagrams in modern three-dimensional

© IFIP International Federation for Information Processing 2015
I. Khalil et al. (Eds.): ICT-EurAsia 2015 and CONFENIS 2015, LNCS 9357, pp. 343–352, 2015.
DOI: 10.1007/978-3-319-24315-3_35

graphics to utilize benefits of the third dimension and achieves more readable schemas of complex models to decompose structure to particular components, type layers, time and author versions.

We need to decompose behaviour and functionality to particular scenarios of the system, alternative and parallel flows, pessimistic, optimistic and daily use scenarios.

2 Related Work for 3D UML

There are some existing alternatives how to visualize UML diagrams in 3D space. Paul McIntosh studied benefits of the 3D solution compared to traditional approaches in UML diagrams visualization. Because of using combination of X3D (eXtensible 3D) standard and UML diagrams, he named his solution X3D-UML [9]. X3D-UML displays state diagrams in movable hierarchical layers [3].

GEF3D [5] is a 3D framework based on Eclipse GEF (Graphical editing framework) developed as Eclipse plugin. Using this framework, existing GEF-based 2D editors can be easily embedded into 3D editors. GEF3D applications are often called multi-editor. Main approach of this framework is to use third dimension for visualization connections between two-dimensional diagrams.

Another concept in field of 3D UML visualization is on virtual boxes [8]. Authors placed diagrams onto sides of box allowing them to arrange inter-model connections which are easily understandable by the other people. GEF3D does not allow users to make modifications in displayed models. Due to fact that UML diagrams can be complex and difficult to understand, geon diagrams [7] use different geometric primitives (geons) for elements and relationships for better understanding [11].

3 Our Approach

Our method visualizes use case scenarios using UML sequence diagrams in separate layers all at once in 3D space, transforms them to the object diagrams (again in separate layers) and automatically create class diagram from these multiple object structures with real associations between classes to complete structure of designed software application.

Sequence diagrams in 3D space of our prototype allow to analyse and study process and complexity of the behaviour simultaneously and compare alternative or parallel Use Case flows.

Identical elements in object diagrams have fixed positions for easy visual projection to the automatically created class diagrams with classes derived from these objects. Their relationships (associations) are inferred from the interactions in the sequence diagrams and class methods are extracted from the required operation in the interactions of these sequence diagrams.

3.1 Our Prototype

We have created our prototype as a standalone system in C++ language with Open Source 3D Graphics Engine (OGRE) or OpenSceneGraph as an open source 3D graphics application programming interface and high performance 3D graphics toolkit for visual simulation, virtual reality, scientific visualization, and modeling.

For integrated development environment (IDE) we can use Eclipse or Microsoft Visual Studio and build standalone system with import/export possibilities using XMI format (XML Metadata Interchange) or plugin module to IBM Rational Software Architect or Enterprise Architect.

Our prototype allows to distribute diagrams in separate layers arranged in 3D space [10]. In this tool is possible to create UML class diagram, sequence diagram and activity diagram in multidimensional space with 3D fragments [6].

Layers can be interconnected and diagrams can be distributed to the parts in these separate layers to study interconnections and for better readability.

3.2   Diagram Transformation

In software analysis and development is good practise to start with describing and capturing system behaviour. For this purpose of behavioural modeling we can use sequence diagrams.

```
classReferences = {};

foreach layer in layers do
    foreach lifeline in lifelines do
        sourceClassName ← getClassName(lifeline);

        if sourceClassName not in classReferences then
            append Class(sourceClassName);
        end
        foreach message in lifeline do
            source ← sourceLifeline(message);
            target ← targetLifeline(message);

            targetClassName ← getClassName(target);
            if targetClassName not in classReferences then
                append Class(targetClassName);
            end

            appendMethod(targetClass, message);
            createAssociation(sourceClass, targetClass);
        end
    end
end
```

Algorithm 1. Class diagram creation algorithm

Creating sequence diagrams we automatically identify essential objects and their methods that are necessary for functionality of the system. Thanks to element similarities between sequence diagram and object diagram in the UML metamodel definition, it is possible to use same shared data representation. Object diagram can be rendered from sequence diagram. Modifications are made in drawing algorithms. Instead of drawing full timeline graphic, lifelines are ignored and only upper part with object names is drawn. Messages between lifelines are moved from original position to directly connect appropriate objects. Transformation can be visible in Figs. 1 and 2.

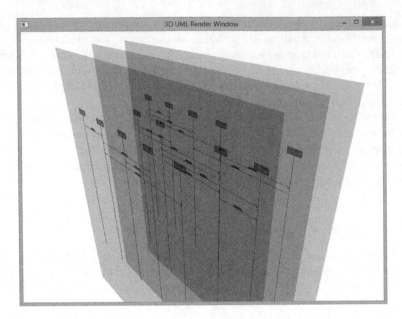

Fig. 1. Example of sequence diagrams in 3D UML.

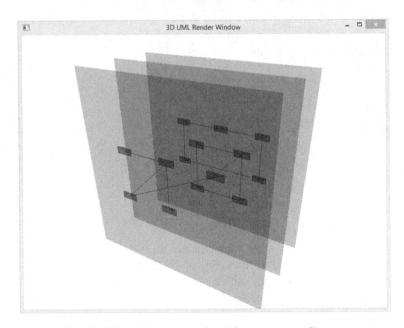

Fig. 2. Object diagrams rendered from sequence diagram.

For development in early phases of testing the concept we used layout algorithm that can be seen in Algorithm 1. Each unique element was placed on next available cell in imaginary grid. Advanced layout creation with force-directed algorithms is described in the next section of this paper.

Class diagram is gradually created. Instead of multiple passes through sequential diagrams to create the classes and append methods to these classes in the next iteration, algorithm for class diagram creation was optimised with buffering and memorisation. Each time when unknown class type is found for lifeline, new class instance in class diagram is created and reference is stored under unique identifier matching class name. Class types are then complemented with method names.

4 Class Diagram Layout

In transformation process we use some basic grid algorithms to arrange the objects in the matrix. With the growing number of the objects also grows the complexity of the diagram and relations between vertices, so it is crucial to create layout that is clear and readable.

4.1 Force-Directed Algorithms

One way how to accomplish better layout is to use force-directed algorithms, so the diagram will be evenly spread on the layer and elements with real relations are closer to each other as to the other elements. We have tested Fruchterman-Reingold and FM3 algorithms.

Fruchterman-Reingold. Fruchterman-Reingold (FR) is simple force-directed algorithm. Each vertex is repelled from the other vertices. Edges between vertices acts as springs and pulls vertices to each other, counteracting repulsive forces.

Algorithm iterates through the graph many times and each time decreases the magnitude of changes in positions, this effect is called cooling down. It could settle in some configuration to ensure the layout instead of oscillating in some other cases. Speed of layout generating is $O(n^3)$, where n is number of vertices [1].

Fm3. FM3 algorithm is more complex approach. Basic idea of the forces is the same, but FM3 uses principle of multiple levels of layout. Main difference is in the step, where provided graph is reduced into smaller subgraphs by packing multiple vertices into one. Analogy of this principle is based on finding so-called *solar systems*, where one vertex is identified as the sun and the other edges that are related to the sun are marked as the *planets* and the *moons*.

Reduction of the graph is recursively called on subgraphs until simple graph is reached, then the subgraphs are arranged and unfold, so it is returned to its higher graphs (see Figs. 3 and 4). These steps are repeated until we reach original graph. Last step arranges the final graph.

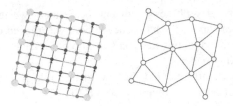

Fig. 3. FM3 - solar systems collapsed into subgraph [2]

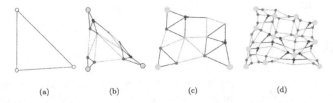

(a)   (b)   (c)   (d)

Fig. 4. FM3 - unfolding sub-graphs and layout creation [2]

This solution is significant quicker than Fruchterman-Reingold algorithm. It is possible to reach speed $O(|V|\log|V|+|E|)$ [2].

4.2 Problems of Force-Directed Algorithms

Unfortunately the outputs of these algorithms were not good enough for proposed use. More appropriate applications are the visualisation of large graph with tree structures.

Both these algorithms have a tendency to create uniform distribution of elements in diagram. Users have a tendency to arrange elements into groups, order elements by priority, hierarchy and so on. They are looking for patterns, relations, semantics and other hidden aspects of model. This is important factor for conservation the readability and understandability of the modelled diagrams. Deficiency of this features in force directed algorithms make them not ideal to create class diagram layout.

Our focus in this phase was on the creation of the algorithm that is more appropriate. Starting point and proof of concept was considering simple semantics in diagram layout creation. Assuming that in class diagram the most important relation between two elements from semantic view is generalisation, then aggregation and finally association, it is possible to modify output of layout algorithm by adding weight factor in attractive force calculation process.

Analysing mainly two mentioned force-directed algorithms (but also the others) was created some methods how to accomplish the task of incorporation the semantic into the selected algorithms.

In case of Fruchterman-Reingold it is possible to introduce weight to vertices or edges. By adding weight, it is possible to modify the original behaviour of algorithm.

Modifying process of solar systems selection in FM3 could allow to create subgraphs, where semantically relevant objects are merged into one vertex. This ensures the separation of less relevant parts of diagram in space and then the layout is enriched by adding more elements in relevant places by reversing graph into its higher sub-graphs.

Our decision was to utilise Fruchterman-Reingold algorithm. Time complexity of the algorithm in comparison with FM3 does not become evident according to the scale in which we use these algorithms: class diagram with size of 10-100 classes, layout calculation is fast. Implementation of the algorithm is simple and it is possible to make modifications more easily than in FM3. Implementation using FM3 can be realized in the future if it.

4.3   Weighted Fruchterman-Reingold

Simple modification of FR algorithm in the form of adding weight to edges in calculation of attractive forces make desired layout improvement. Weight of edge is taken into account in process of calculating attractive forces of edge connecting two vertices.

Calculated force is multiplied by weight of corresponding type of edge. It is necessary to identify current type of the edge while calculating attractive forces. Implementation of the system distinguishes different relations as instances of different classes and therefore it is easy to use appropriate weight.

While prototyping phase, weights of relations-edges were experimentally set as follows:

- generalisation $\to$ 200
- aggregation $\to$ 100
- association $\to$ 10

Application of the selected weights affected the outputs of the algorithm in desired manner. To escalate effects of attraction, reflecting the semantics of the diagram, vertices are repelling each other with equivalent force, but magnified by factor of 10 according to original force calculated by algorithm. This tends to push vertices more apart, so the difference in distances between related and unrelated vertices is greater. This allows to make semantics patterns of class diagram more visible.

5   Results and Evaluation

New weighted Fruchtermant-Reingold algorithm was tested against Fruchterman-Reingold algorithm. Empirical comparison of generated layouts on multiple class diagram examples indicates, that our new algorithm provides more appropriate layout.

First example in Figs. 5 and 6 shows one of tested class diagrams: Sequence diagram metamodel. Differences between both layouts are clearly visible. Figure 6 shows layout generated by Fruchterman-Reingold algorithm. This layout is evenly distributed across available space and it has symmetrical character.

Distribution of the classes is not optimal and orientation in such diagrams is still not easy and natural. Random scattering of connected classes is not very useful in case of readability and understanding of created class diagram.

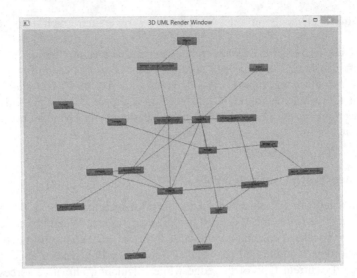

Fig. 5. Sample (Sequence diagram metamodel) - layout generated with Fruchterman-Reingold algorithm

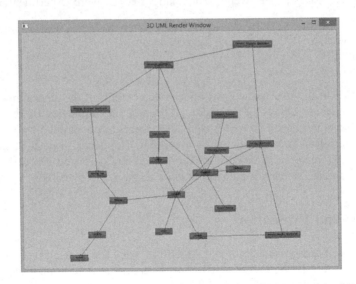

Fig. 6. Sample (Sequence diagram metamodel) - layout generated with Weighted Fruchterman-Reingold

Using weighted Fruchterman-Reingold algorithm on the same class diagram example achieves significantly better layout. Main difference is that layout put relevant classes more together and creates smaller chunks of classes instead of one big mass as it was in the previous case. This means better readability, understanding and modifying designed diagrams.

Algorithm still creates some unwanted artefacts. For example, by pushing on some classes creates unnecessary edge crossings. These problems may be addressed in the future.

Nevertheless algorithm is able to create decent layout for the class diagram. Output is not perfect, but it is an initial layout, which could be corrected by the user: weighted Fruchterman-Reingold algorithm is suitable for this purpose.

6 Conclusion

We applied force directed algorithm successfully in the second phase of transformation from object diagrams (derived from use case scenarios in sequence diagrams) to class diagram representing static structure of the modeled software system.

In addition we introduced semantics by adding weight factor in force calculation process in the layout algorithm. Type of relation between vertices influence weight applied on the attractive forces. This creates more useful layout organisation, as elements are grouped by semantics that is more readable.

Research started with software development monitoring [13] and software visualization [12] and now, we are preparing interfaces and libraries for leap motion, 3D Mouse, and Kinect to allow gestures and finger language for alternative way of creating and management of the particular models.

Acknowledgement. This work was supported by the KEGA grant no. 083TUKE-4/2015 "Virtual-reality technologies in the process of handicapped persons education" and by the Scientific Grant Agency of Slovak Republic (VEGA) under the grant No. VG 1/1221/12.

This contribution is also a partial result of the Research & Development Operational Programme for the project Research of Methods for Acquisition, Analysis and Personalized Conveying of Information and Knowledge, ITMS 26240220039, co-funded by the ERDF.

References

1. Fruchterman, T.M., Reingold, E.M.: Graph drawing by force-directed placement. Softw. Pract. Experience **21**(11), 1129–1164 (1991)
2. Hachul, S., Jünger, M.: Large-graph layout with the fast multipole multilevel method. Online verfügbar unter http://www.zaik.uni-koeln.de/~paper/preprints.html (2005)
3. McIntosh, P., Hamilton, M., van Schyndel, R.: X3d-uml: Enabling advanced uml visualisation through x3d. In: Proceedings of the Tenth International Conference on 3D Web Technology, Web3D 2005, pp. 135–142, New York, NY, USA, 2005. ACM
4. OMG. OMG Unified Modeling Language (OMG UML), Infrastructure, Version 2.4.1, August 2011
5. Pilgrim, J., Duske, K.: Gef3d: a framework for two-, two-and-a-half-, and three-dimensional graphical editors. In: Proceedings of the 4th ACM Symposium on Software Visualization, SoftVis 2008, pp. 95–104, New York, NY, USA, 2008. ACM
6. Škoda, M.: Three-dimensional visualization of uml diagrams. Diploma project, Slovak University of Technology Bratislava, Faculty of informatics and information technologies, May 2014

7. Casey, K., Exton, Ch.: A Java 3D implementation of a geon based visualisation tool for UML. In: Proceedings of the 2nd international conference on Principles and practice of programming in Java, Kilkenny City, Ireland, 16–18 June (2003)
8. Duske, K.: A Graphical Editor for the GMF Mapping Model (2010). http://gef3d.blogspot.sk/2010/01/graphical-editor-for-gmf-mapping-model.html
9. McIntosh, P.: X3D-UML: user-centred design. implementation and evaluation of 3D UML using X3D. Ph.D. thesis, RMIT University (2009)
10. Polášek, I.: 3D model for object structure design (In Slovak). Systémová integrace **11**(2), 82–89 (2004). ISSN 1210–9479
11. Ullman, S.: Aligning pictorial descriptions: an approach to object recognition. Cognition **32**, 193–254 (1989)
12. Polášek, I., Uhlár, M.: Extracting, identifying and visualisation of the content, users and authors in software projects. In: Gavrilova, M.L., Tan, C., Abraham, A. (eds.) Transactions on Computational Science XXI. LNCS, vol. 8160, pp. 269–295. Springer, Heidelberg (2013)
13. Bieliková, M., Polášek, I., Barla, M., Kuric, E., Rástočný, K., Tvarožek, J., Lacko, P.: Platform independent software development monitoring: design of an architecture. In: Geffert, V., Preneel, B., Rovan, B., Štuller, J., Tjoa, A.M. (eds.) SOFSEM 2014. LNCS, vol. 8327, pp. 126–137. Springer, Heidelberg (2014)

Author Index

Printed in the United States
By Bookmasters